God's Mountain

God's Mountain

The Temple Mount in Time, Place, and Memory

Yaron Z. Eliav

The Johns Hopkins University Press
Baltimore

The Johns Hopkins University Press
2715 North Charles Street
Baltimore, Maryland 21218-4363
www.press.jhu.edu

Library of Congress Cataloging-in-Publication Data
Eliav, Yaron Z.
    God's mountain : the Temple Mount in time, space, and memory /
Yaron Z. Eliav.
        p. cm.
    Includes bibliographical references and index.
    ISBN 0-8018-8213-3 (hardcover : alk. paper)
    1. Temple Mount (Jerusalem)—History—To 1500.   2. Temple of
Jerusalem (Jerusalem)—History.   3. Temple Mount (Jerusalem) in
rabbinical literature.   4. Rabbinical literature—History and criticism.
5. Jerusalem—Antiquities.   I. Title.
    DS109.28.E45 2005
    296.4′82—dc22
                                                            2004030322

A catalog record for this book is available from the British Library.

לע"נ אסתר גולדה (גולדי) כהנא
תנצב"ה

Stones do not lie . . .
Men lie about the past because the past is not dead,
because they are still struggling with it.
ARNALDO MOMIGLIANO,
Journal of Renaissance Studies 53 (1963): 107

Contents

Illustrations

Preface

I first encountered the Temple Mount when I was four years old. Together with my Orthodox Jewish family, I joined the streaming crowds of hundreds of thousands who visited the Western ("Wailing") Wall in the Old City of Jerusalem soon after it came under Israeli control in the Six Day War of 1967. Only years later I would learn that this renowned structure was no more than one of the outer retaining walls of the compound built by King Herod at the site of the Second Jewish Temple. At the time of my first visit, an air of mystery and sanctity pervaded the site. Worshipers packed the narrow open area in front of the Wall. I remember old, bearded men in black, and the sour-sweet smell of sweat. Everyone clung to the Wall's huge, bare stones, stuffing the cracks and fissures with scraps of paper on which they had written appeals to the King of Kings. Above them, in what was then and still remains an Islamic sanctuary, domes of gold and silver glittered against the sky.

My cousin, Shimon Markowitz, had driven us there in his police car. He was a Holocaust survivor, a former yeshiva student who in the 1948 war was taken prisoner by the Jordanians in the battle of Gush Etzion. There, in a POW camp, he had lost his faith, shaved off his beard, and upon his return enlisted in the police force and become a high-ranking officer in Jerusalem. In retrospect, although my own life has been very different than my cousin's, I can see a certain parallel between us. I also left, or perhaps reshaped, most of the elements in my past—putting aside my religiosity, abandoning the political orientation that guided my youth, and reformulating my cultural textures. In a strange way, style sheets and philological rules took in my world the place of halakhic (Jewish legal) regulations, and I exchanged religious practice for the joys of creative innovation in research—an intellectual climax that, once experienced, you can never again live without.

When I completed this journey, I found myself at the starting point—back at the Temple Mount. I chose to write my Ph.D. dissertation at the Hebrew University on the physical and cultural history of the sacred compound in Jerusalem. The subject attracted me because it promised to combine my areas of specialization—Talmud, ancient Jewish history, archaeology, classical studies, and the early Christian works known as patristic literature. To acquire the knowledge and skills necessary for this kind of investigation, I had wandered far afield—from Jerusalem to Princeton to Oxford, and, later, to New York. My research required visits to numerous libraries; in Jerusalem I worked at the National and University Library at Givat Ram, the École Biblique, the Rockefeller Museum, and the library of the Hebrew University's Institute of Archaeology. At Oxford I used the Ashmolean, Bodleian, and Oriental Institute libraries; at Princeton I worked in the Firestone and Speer, and in New York City I frequented the Public Library, the Jewish Theological Seminary Library, and its sister across the street at Union Theological Seminary. But throughout those long years of research, and especially during innumerable visits to the enclosure of the Temple Mount both above and below the walls that surround it, I never lost sight of the irony that I had returned to the precincts of my childhood. But I had come back with something new and different: travel chronicles by Christian pilgrims; excavation reports, decades, and sometimes more than a century old, written by archaeologists of at least six nationalities; and most of all texts—scores and scores of ancient words, in Hebrew, Aramaic, Greek, Latin, and Syriac, about the mountain, writings that molded its image and that waited for a reader to decipher them. The myth of the Temple Mount had remained essentially the same since my first visit to the Wailing Wall (although it had become much broader and infinitely more complicated). But this time instead of internalizing it, I endeavored to dissect and understand it. The result lies before you.

Like every scholarly project, the current one was not accomplished alone. During the twelve years that I studied and wrote about the Temple Mount I received assistance and advice from numerous people and organizations. It gives me the greatest pleasure to be able to fervently thank them. As already noted, the current volume emanates from my Ph.D. dissertation at the Hebrew University of Jerusalem. I had two advisers, one at the Department of Jewish History, Moshe-David Herr, and one at the Institute of Archaeology, Yoram Tsafrir. While Professor Tsafrir disagreed with many of my arguments, especially those that appear in chapter 4, he graciously invested many hours in guiding me down the path I chose. I admire him for that and am deeply grateful. At Princeton, John Gager was both a teacher and a friend. He showered me with his knowledge of early Christianity and ancient Judaism and forced me to reevaluate the nature of the dichotomy we impose on them.

Researching the dissertation was only the first round of work I did for this book. When I completed my Ph.D. project, I decided that instead of trying to get the dissertation published as it was, I would rewrite and reorganize it into a book addressed to a broad and varied audience. In addition to changing the language from Hebrew to English, I also reformulated my arguments and consequently reshaped the narrative that had been built upon them. Beyond that, during the course of my later work I amended many of my dissertation's models, to the point that often this book offers entirely different conclusions than appear in the earlier work. My editor at the Johns Hopkins University Press, Henry Tom, stood by me during this last round with patience and affability and helped me identify the stumbling blocks and challenges in such writing. Many other people—teachers, colleagues, and friends—read chapters, commented, criticized, polished, pointed out errors, and most importantly contributed their time and judgment, two of the most valued commodities in the world of scholarship. It is difficult to put into words the debt that I owe them. Here they are, in alphabetical order (and my apologies if I missed someone): Gideon Bohak, Glen Bowersock, Yossi David, Leah Di Segni, Werner Eck, Paula Fredriksen, Joseph Geiger, Benjamin Isaac, Richard Kalmin, Jodi Magness, David Rokeah, Jeffrey Rubinstein, Daniel Statman.

Some people merit special recognition. My friend Nimrod Luz, a geographer and scholar of Arab cultures, took me on my first tour through the Temple Mount compound and taught me the nuances necessary to pick my way through the overgrown political and cultural thicket that burdens the site in our day. Martha Himmelfarb of Princeton read my entire first draft. The imprint of her wisdom and of her sharp editorial eye is evident in more places than I can list. My student Aaron Brunell meticulously assisted me with preparing the bibliography. In the transition from Hebrew to English, I was frequently aided by the translating talents of Haim Watzman. Peg Lourie of the University of Michigan Kelsey Museum read the entire manuscript and rooted out the many verbal weeds that tend to grow in the work of one who writes in an adopted language. Lorene Sterner, also of the Kelsey, produced with great talent and an artistic hand the maps and drawings included in the book.

Over the years I have lectured about various aspects of my research in a number of venues. It would be impossible to catalog the multitude of useful comments I have received from those who responded to my arguments on these occasions. The best and most productive listeners were always the students in my research seminars, first at New York University and then at the University of Michigan. During a long Ann Arbor winter in 2003–4, the members of my Holy Sites seminar painstakingly read every word of my final manuscript and gave me no quarter as I attempted to convince them—not always with success—of the correctness of my claims. My thanks to all of them.

Prior to the completion of this book, I published pieces of the work in a variety of academic settings. I did this especially when I felt unsure of my thesis and wanted to test the waters, or when my arguments were too elaborate and technical to include in the kind of book I have sought to produce here. For a full list of these articles the reader can consult the bibliography of this book. I am grateful to the editors of those publications for allowing me to profit from the feedback of their readership and then incorporate my work in the current format.

During my years of research I benefited from the financial assistance of a number of funds and institutions: the Rotenstreich Fellowship of the Israeli Council for Higher Education, the Francis Günter Fellowship for Jerusalem Studies, the Gutwirth Fellowship, and the Bernard M. Bloomfield Prize for Outstanding Doctorate Dissertation in the Humanities, all from the Hebrew University; a Fulbright Fellowship for a year of study and research at Princeton University; a multiyear Research Fellowship from the Jewish Memorial Foundation; and a Dorot Post-Doctorate Fellowship at NYU.

In the fall of 2000, my family and I moved to Ann Arbor, Michigan, where I was offered the Samuel and Jean Frankel Chair for Rabbinic Literature and Ancient Jewish History at the University of Michigan. I profited from this celebrated center of scholarship and haven of collegiality and friendship in more ways than I can express. Numerous university units supported my work with grants and fellowships: the Office of the Vice President for Research; the Rackham School for Graduate Studies; the College for Literature, Science, and Arts; and most of all my two academic homes—the Department of Near Eastern Studies and the Frankel Center for Judaic Studies. Behind this long list of organizational names stand dear people who believed in me and my work, and I thank them all deeply and hope this book will fulfill their expectations.

Finally, when I returned to Israel in 2004–5 for a year of research at the Hebrew University's Institute for Advanced Studies in Jerusalem, a number of friends helped me obtain illustrations and the permissions necessary to use them in the book: Gideon Avni and the staff of the Mandatory Archive of the Israeli Antiquity Authority, Leah Di Segni, Elḥanan Reiner, and Dror Wahrman. None of this would have been of much use, however, without the technical assistance of Ofer Arbeli in scanning the pictures and configuring their electronic format.

Last and most important, my family. My wife, Milka, made me promise not to dedicate the book to her, and I will respect her wishes. Only she and I are aware of the many sacrifices—large and small—she made along the way in order for this volume to be published. My daughter, Avishag, often distracted me from my work with the charm that only a seven-year-old is capable of. I cherish the light she has brought into my world, without which all else would be worthless. My parents, Yaʿacov and Esther, have been and remain my most faithful fans, and I will always love them for that. My father-in-law, Dov Kahanah, a *talmid ḥakhamim* (Torah scholar) and erudite man of learning, has stood by me always. It is deeply unfortunate that his wife, Esther-Golda (known to all of us as Goldie), whom I grew to dearly love, did not live to see the completion of this project. Cancer took her from us before her time during the Sukkot holiday of 1998. I dedicate this book to her blessed memory.

A Note on Translation and Transliteration

The book includes references and quotations from hundreds of ancient sources in most of the spoken languages of the Roman Mediterranean. I translated all passages into English. In doing so, I consulted modern translations (where those were available), but often abandoned them and provided my own more literal (and thus, I think, more accurate) rendition of the original. The bibliography provides a full list of the primary texts, and available critical editions and translations used in this volume, as well as the various abbreviations that I employed when referring to the texts in the notes (the latter appear in square brackets after the name of the text).

Occasionally, I felt it necessary to include a word or phrase from an original text in the discussion; at those times I adopted, with slight changes, the common transliteration method of *The SBL Handbook of Style: For Ancient Near Eastern, Biblical, and Early Christian Studies,* edited by Patrick H. Alexander, et al. (Peabody, Mass.: Hendrickson, 1999), page 28 (which I used for Hebrew and also for Aramaic and Syriac) and page 29 (for Greek). In such cases, I strove to simplify the identification of these foreign (from the point of view of most English readers) ancient words but not to exhaust their grammatical nuances (which would have required a much more elaborate and crowded system of signs). Thus, I distinguish, for example, between *ḥet* (*ḥ*) and *he* (*h*), or between *ʿayin* (ʿ) and *ʾaleph* (ʾ), but do not go into the differences between tav and tet (both represented with *t*). The vocal sheva appears as an *e*, and the dagesh forte is shown by doubling the consonant. However, when a certain convention for a word or a name was already in existence in English, I preferred it over my own transliteration. For those interested in the original sources and wording, my detailed reference system in the notes, combined with the bibliographic list at the end of the book, should allow tracing those texts with relative ease.

Introduction

Space constitutes a fundamental dimension of human experience: nations inhabit countries; tribes dwell in territories; families inherit estates; and individuals constantly engage the ubiquitous, endless corners that fuse into one's life—the bridge under which one first kissed, the stream by which she contemplated her options, the tree where they engraved their names, the tower, the intersections of roads, and so on. As always, social dynamics provide the interaction between people and places with substance—elevating some localities, denouncing others, and producing in the process the textures, both physical (architecture) and nonphysical (literature, folklore, heritage) that shape the way a certain space registers in our minds. Religion furnished the discourse on space with the incandescent language and imagery of holiness. Religion has always been inseparable from sacred sites.[1]

One of the most famous among the sacred spaces is a flat, trapezoidal, walled compound located on the eastern edge of Jerusalem's Old City (see map 1, fig. 1). Commonly translated in English as "the Temple Mount," the literal translation of the original Hebrew *har ha-bayit* would be the "Mount of the House." The designation Temple Mount refers both to the topographical elevation, the hilly figure of the place (although by no means the tallest or most imposing in the area), and to the architectonic structure in the shape of a huge precinct that sits on its top. Ancient Near Eastern monotheistic religions, Judaism and Islam in particular (but also Christianity), still revere the site as holy, and the faithful are careful to observe special religious strictures and practices there. The Temple Mount's importance, however, has long gone beyond its specifically religious significance. Over the years, it has been transformed into a national, cultural, and political symbol, deeply entrenched in the foundations of both the Jewish-Zionist and Arab-Muslim-Palestinian ethos. Poets have elegized it; writers have extolled it in essays and stories. The Mount has inspired spiritual leaders and generated countless images for artists from many varied schools and traditions. At the same time, it has cost political leaders many a sleepless night.

This book seeks to describe the way this highly valued site began and developed as a physical entity as well as a religious concept and a cultural image. This

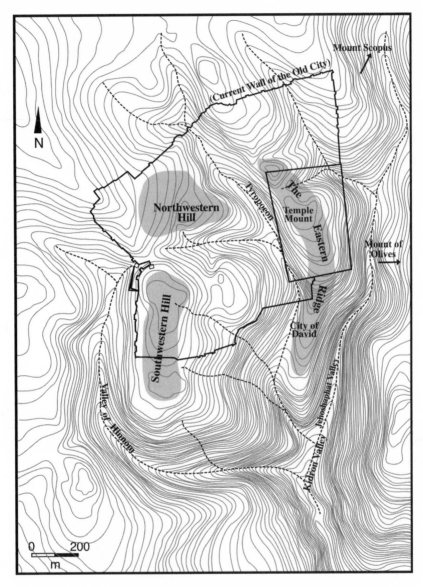

Map 1. Jerusalem's topography

chapter in the history of the ancient Mediterranean is often distorted and obscured by contemporary political events. How and why did the Temple Mount come to be one of the most renowned sacred spaces of the Middle East and, to many, a notorious emblem of its ruptured civilizations? To answer this question we need to leave modern politics behind and travel back in time to what many consider to be the cradle of Western civilization, the Roman Near East.

To reconstruct the early story of the Temple Mount, this book explores the various notions and images that people weaved around this space, and its role in their lives. It endeavors to trace the Temple Mount's origins and to sketch the formative stages of its unique status. At the same time, the book also investigates the history of the Temple Mount as an architectonic unit from its establishment through its several incarnations, with the aim of explicating the circumstances in which it was created and the factors that subsequently shaped it both physically and conceptually.

The period under discussion reaches from the destruction of the Second Jewish Temple in the year 70 CE until the Arab conquest in the seventh century, a period of some six hundred years. This chronological framework, however, is by no means hard and fast. For reasons that will become apparent in chapter 1, I devote a significant amount of attention to the preceding eras, to the First Temple period (ending in 586 BCE) as well as the Second Temple, and in particular to the reign of King Herod (37–4 BCE) and the following decades leading up to the demolition of the Temple by the Romans in 70 CE.

The choice of the destruction of the Second Temple as terminus a quo in the periodization of Roman Palestine (at least in everything regarding its Jewish areas) has been accepted as a cornerstone of scholarship, challenged by only a few.[2] While my original intention was to conform to the contours of this "classic" time division, my investigations showed it to be only partially adequate. Even though the destruction catalyzed various processes tied to the Temple Mount and was indeed a significant turning point in the creation of a "Mount without a Temple," processes that shaped both the physical and conceptual substance of this entity, two other moments, one prior to 70 CE and one subsequent, also contributed a great deal to the story. The first was Herod's building project; the second, the aftermath of the Bar Kokhba rebellion (132–35 CE) and the urban and social changes that took shape in Jerusalem in its wake. This seemingly confused timeline is clarified in chapters 1 and 3, which address the question of how the "Mount" came into being.

Ending this study in the mid-seventh century with the Arab conquest is eas-

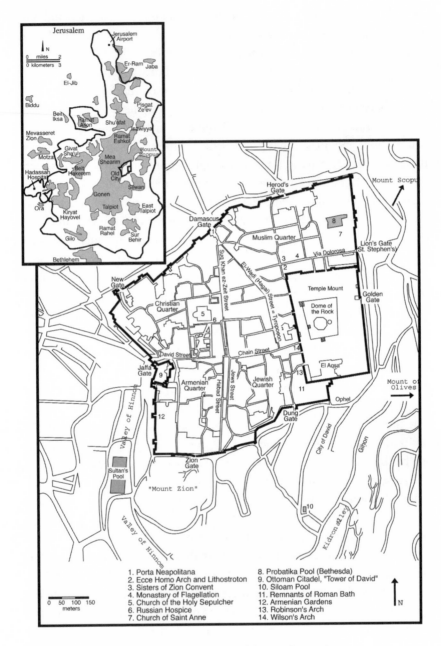

Map 2. Contemporary Old City of Jerusalem

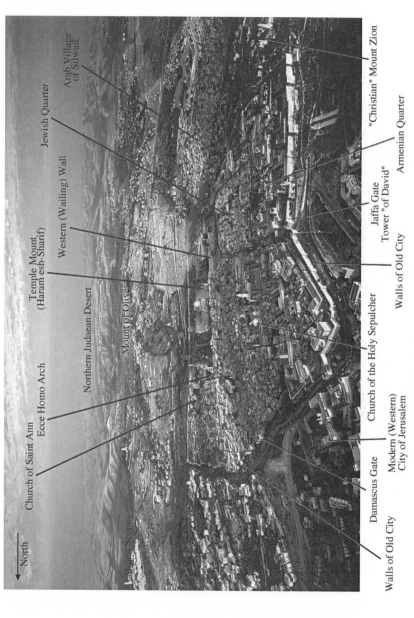

North

Walls of Old City

Church of Saint Ann
Ecce Homo Arch

Northern Judaean Desert

Mount of Olives

Mount Scopus

Temple Mount
(Haram esh-Sharif)

Western (Wailing) Wall

Jewish Quarter

Arab Village
of Silwan

Damascus Gate

Modern (Western)
City of Jerusalem

Church of the Holy Sepulcher

Walls of Old City

Jaffa Gate
Tower "of David"

Armenian Quarter

"Christian" Mount Zion

Fig. 1. General overview of the Old City of Jerusalem looking east. From Duby Tal and Moni Haramati, *Kav ha-Ofek* (Jerusalem: Ministry of Defence Pub. House, 1993). With permission from Albatross.

ier to justify. The arrival of Islam transformed the political, religious, and cultural landscapes of Jerusalem in many ways. The Temple Mount had a central role in that process. But these developments represent a totally new story, told through a fresh set of sources and languages. Although many of its roots can be traced to earlier periods, this saga would entail a separate study.

In terms of content, the boundaries of this study are more clear-cut. It addresses neither the Jewish temples that stood on the Mount (map 3: A) for over a thousand years nor their absence. Nor does it take up corollary issues related to that institution, such as the priesthood or the sacrificial system, and certainly not the city of Jerusalem as a whole. All these subjects have been written about extensively elsewhere and are referred to here only when they shed light on the Temple Mount. The close epistemological and physical relation between the Temple, Jerusalem, and the Temple Mount has led many scholars to conflate these three elements and, at times, even to use them interchangeably. However, unlike the city and the Temple, which have been the subjects of numerous detailed studies, there is not a single book or article among the hundreds, even thousands, that have been written on Christianity and Judaism and their ties to Jerusalem during the period here examined whose subject is the Temple Mount itself. The exceptions are the many archaeological studies devoted to the compound atop the Mount and halakhic (traditional Jewish law) studies proposing the boundaries of the mountain and the exact site of the destroyed Temple.[3] This imbalance demonstrates a serious lacuna in the scholarship on the Temple Mount. On the one hand, the Mount is a hugely impressive architectural structure that justifies large numbers of archaeological studies; on the other hand, insufficient attention has been given to the way the Mount has functioned in and influenced history, to its conceptualization, and to the place it has occupied in the consciousness of those involved with it. This study fills that gap.

From Terminology to Conceptuality in the Study of Sacred Space

Sifre Deuteronomy, a rabbinic text from the early first centuries CE, contains the following account:

> Another time they [a group of sages] were going up to Jerusalem. [When they] arrived at [Mount] Scopus, they rent their garments. [When they arrived] at the

Temple Mount and saw a fox emerge out of the [ruined] building of the Holy of Holies, they began to weep, while R. ʿAkiva laughed. They said to him: "ʿAkiva, you never cease to astonish us—we are weeping, yet you laugh!" He replied: "And you, why are you weeping?" They said to him: "Should we not weep when a fox emerges from a place of which it is written 'And the stranger [non-priest] who comes near shall be put to death [Numbers 1:51]'; indeed the following [verse] has been fulfilled concerning us 'For this our heart is faint . . . for Mount Zion which lies desolate, the foxes walk upon it' [Lamentations 5:18–19]." He said to them: "This is exactly why I laughed, for it is said 'And I will take unto me faithful witnesses to record, Uriah the priest and Zekhariah the son of Jeberekhiah [Isaiah 8:2].' Now what is the connection between Uriah and Zekhariah? What did Uriah say? 'Zion shall be plowed as a field, and Jerusalem shall become heaps and the Temple Mount [literally: the Mountain of the House] as a wooded height [Jeremiah 26:18 = Micah 3:12].' What did Zekhariah say? 'For thus says the Lord of hosts—there shall yet old men and old women sit in the streets of Jerusalem [Zechariah 8:4].' Said God: 'these are my two witnesses. If the words of Uriah are fulfilled, so will the words of Zekhariah; if the words of Uriah are not fulfilled, neither will the words of Zekhariah.' I [R. ʿAkiva] rejoiced therefore that finally the words of Uriah have been fulfilled, because this means that the words of Zekhariah will be fulfilled too." They [the rest of the sages] replied to him with the following words "ʿAkiva, you have comforted us."[4]

This well-known rabbinic story, whose language and form have been assimilated into a number of rabbinic compositions (cited in n. 4), has preserved a portrait of Jerusalem as it was absorbed in the minds of the authors. For our purposes, neither the date of the segment nor the historicity of the account—that is, whether it conveys an actual event—are as important as its realistic texture. Mount Scopus, Jerusalem, Temple Mount, and the Holy of Holies delineate a graphical organization of the area, almost a map, and inscribe a palpable landscape in the mind of the audience. True, the narrator parallels the different elements of the narrative with the biblical verses that its speakers quote. Accordingly, just as the fox conforms to the verse from Lamentations, "foxes prowl over it," the Temple Mount coincides with the verse from Micah, "and the mountain of the house as a wooded height." On the path laid out by the various landmarks, the Temple Mount is given as a familiar designation that demands no explanation. The author portrays it as a real place that is known by everyone. Indeed, anyone acquainted with rabbinic literature, even if not in depth, can identify the term "Temple Mount" and place it in the scenery that serves as the backdrop to this story. Who does not know where the Temple Mount is? Consequently no one wonders why the story mentions not the Temple but rather the Temple Mount and the Holy of Holies, the latter being only one room in the building of the Temple. After all, the Temple Mount and the Temple are interwoven in many rabbinic passages (discussed in depth in chapter 6). So it is only natural that when one was destroyed, as is the case in the quoted portion from the *Sifre*, the other remained.

But the issue is much more complicated than it seems at first glance. Consider, for instance, terminology. Browsing through hundreds of years worth of Israelite and Jewish texts points toward the prophet Micah as the first to combine the two words "Temple Mount" into a specific phrase, incorporating it into his famous admonitory prophecy, also cited in the foregoing rabbinic passage, "Therefore shall Zion for your sake be plowed as a field, and Jerusalem shall become heaps, and the mountain of the house [*har ha-bayit* = Temple Mount] as a wooded [thicket] height" (Micah 3:12). Yet it is extremely doubtful that Micah here preserved a concrete name that was part of the active lexicon of his contemporaries. A close reading of the passage from Micah shows that the phrase "Mountain of the House" is merely a literary variation of a longer term, the "mountain of the House of the Lord" (three words in Hebrew—*har beyt 'adonay*), which appears in the next verse (4:1):

> (3:12) Therefore because of you Zion shall be plowed as a field, and Jerusalem shall become heaps and the Mountain of the House a wooded height. (4:1) It shall come to pass in the latter days that the mountain of the house of the Lord shall be established as the highest of the mountains, and shall be raised up above the hills, and people shall flow to it. (4:2) And many nations shall come and say: "Come let us go up to the mountain of the Lord, to the house of the God of Jacob, that he may teach us his ways and we may walk in his paths."

The writer places the complete, three-word phrase—mountain of the house of the Lord (*har beyt 'adonay*)—in the middle and "plays" with its constituent parts (both pieces come out to two words in Hebrew) in the previous and subsequent verses (3:12; 4:2).[5] Just as in the third instance the prophet deletes the term "House" and uses the name "Mount of Lord" (*har 'adonay*), so in the first instance the name God is deleted, leaving the term "Mount of the House" (*har ha-bayit*), or Temple Mount.

These variations are characteristic of the common literary diction used by the prophets, suggesting a literary stimulus for the device of the appellation Temple Mount by Micah, rather than a term taken from the vocabulary and experiences of daily life, although admittedly it could have been both.[6] Further support for the former, that the term Temple Mount did not originate in the spoken, everyday lexicon of First Temple Judeans or Second Temple Jews, derives from the fact that nearly a thousand years will pass from the time of Micah until the specific name Temple Mount reappears in the Mishnah. In the interim, the precise designation Temple Mount is not used in even one of the existing hundreds of sources, except in a few works quoting and using the entire phrase from Micah. It seems therefore that the name Temple Mount—*har habayit*—was not used in earlier periods, even though the image of a mountain as a place for a temple was both known and probably, at least to some degree, widespread. (This subject is discussed in detail in chapter 1, which also contains a discussion of other biblical terms linked to Jerusalem, such as "Mountain of God" and "My Holy Mountain.")

A two-pronged question about the designation Temple Mount thus accompanies the discussion throughout this book. First, if indeed this name came into regular usage only at a particular point in time, what were the reasons for its sudden appearance? Second, and more significant than the terminology itself, is the matter of perception—was the site of the Temple always registered in people's consciousness as the Temple Mount? Or did a "new" term, Temple Mount, enter the public lexicon, suggesting a change in that generation's worldview and in the ways they grasped and engaged the landscape of Jerusalem? If there was this kind of shift in the way the place was imprinted in their minds, then its nature and boundaries must be determined. When and why did this occur, and what is the significance of this change?

The Sequential Development Model and Its Alternative

One convention in the study of Jerusalem of the Roman-Byzantine period, as in the study of Judaism and Christianity of those days, is that the Temple Mount, both the spatial entity and the idea, has occupied Jewish consciousness from the earliest times (that is, at least from the First Temple period onward). In fact, innumerable studies apply the term Temple Mount to the Temple site in discussions of events as far back as the time of ancient Israel of the first Temple and throughout the Second Temple period.[7] The prevalent view, whether implicit or explicit, has applied to the Temple Mount and its status a model that can be named "sequential development," a popular research paradigm in the academic circles of religion studies. To put it briefly, this view posits that the Mount in Jerusalem possessed special qualities, designating it as a unique sacred space, from the earliest days of Israelite-Jewish history and that this structure (or topographical elevation) has retained this eminence ever since. This stature, thus goes the common wisdom, began in the First Temple environment, with texts lending an aura of holiness to the site, such as Isaiah's pronouncement that "the mountain of the house of the Lord shall be established on the highest of the mountains" (2:2, and Micah 4:1), or similar pronouncements in Psalms:—"Who shall ascend the mountain of the Lord? And who shall stand in his holy place?" (24:2), and "Extol the Lord our God, and worship at his holy Mountain" (99:9). A direct line stretches, according to this approach, from the First to the Second Temple period, and later, after the destruction of the Second Temple, the holy mountain remained as it was, its sanctity unchallenged. The subsequent stations in the mountain's story, according to this accepted approach, are, first, the attempt (or at least the aspiration) during the Bar Kokhba revolt (132–35 CE) to restore the Mount, to rebuild the Temple, and to reestablish its ritual; and, second, when the Romans established a colony—Aelia Capitolina—on the ruins of Jerusalem, the emperor Hadrian ordered a Capitoline temple to be erected at the precise location of the Jewish Temple. The next stage was the retention of the area in its destroyed state, perhaps serving as the city garbage dump, during the Byzantine period (with a short break in the 360s during the emperor Julian's reign). According to the sequential development view, these two reactions, the pagan and the Christian, represent two sides of the same coin, and the site's sanctity is evident also in the acts of those who tried to deny it. The circle closes with the Arab capture of the Temple compound, when it again became the city's holy site (the Ḥaram). The sequential development model thus presents a kind of chain consisting of six interlocking links: First Temple, Second Temple, Bar Kokhba rebellion, Aelia Capitolina, the Byzantine city, and the Muslim city. The thread that runs through them is the holiness ascribed to the Mount, while they differ only in whether the ruling powers implemented this sanctity positively or negatively.

The conclusions this study reaches refute this convention or, at the very least, complicate and reshape it. The notions and images associated with the "Temple Mount," as the initial chapters of this book attempt to prove, were crystallized in a tortuous process only during the first century CE. Although the roots of this entity lay in the lexicon and conceptual environment of the First Temple period, it was only toward the close of the Second Temple era that the Temple Mount emerged as an independent constituent of Jewish consciousness and experience.

This new chronology provides the framework for a fresh consideration and consequently a new reconstruction of the literary, religious, and social dynamics that shaped the image of the Temple Mount as a sacred space for both Jews and Christians of antiquity. The various chapters of the book follow the developments in the conceptuality of the Mount over several centuries. It begins with the distinctive category reserved for this entity in the lives of first-century Jewish groups (chapters 1 and 2) and concludes by tracing its status in more articulated works of church writers and Jewish rabbis spanning the second to seventh centuries (chapters 5 and 6). All these chapters explore how various groups perceived the mounts against the background of the great changes that took place in the city, whether in the days of Herod, after the destruction of the Second Temple, or in the time of Constantine and thereafter. Here, too, the picture differs from the standard one. It turns out that different groups endowed the Mount with diverse, at times opposing, qualities while integrating it into their way of life. Reading the sources produced by these groups in chorus offers a rare glimpse into the convoluted cultural mechanisms that were at work in Palestine during the Roman and Byzantine eras, enabling a reevaluation of the traditional scholarly understanding of the relationships between Jews and Christians in general and in regard to the Temple Mount's status in particular.

The other part of this study (chapters 3 and 4) deals with the physical evidence. The designation Temple Mount obviously signifies a material reality; it points to topographical and architectural units that existed, and still exist, in Jerusalem. The people who heard or used this pair of words knew what it referred to. The investigation of such an entity must thus move between clarifying the physical texture behind this name and illuminating the conceptual content that was channeled into it. The precinct called the Temple Mount is the most architecturally prominent element in the city of Jerusalem (see map 2). It overshadows every other component of the city, especially if we restrict our attention to the limits of today's Old City—which reflects, more or less, the size of the Roman and Byzantine city. The compound's dominance implanted it in the minds of both the public at large and the scholarly community as an organic limb of the ancient city. Today it would be difficult to conceive of and portray ancient Jerusalem without the gigantic rectangular (or, to be more precise, trapezoidal) platform of the Temple Mount. But was that always the case?

As hinted already, my claim is that in addition to the destruction of the Temple in 70 CE the two most important defining moments that affected the mountain's physical appearance were King Herod's construction project (discussed in chapter 1) and the period of the emperor Hadrian (to which I devote chapter 3). Herod completely overturned the physical reality of the city and, for all practical purposes, created the topographical unit called the Temple Mount. The 570 years between the destruction of the Second Temple and the arrival of Islam, however, represent an exceptional time in the history of the Temple Mount. During this period the area of the Mount lost its important place in the geographical-urban fabric—what I later call the spatial organization[8]—of the city. For the first (and last!) time in Jerusalem's recorded history, the grounds that constitute the Temple Mount were not a religious center. Moreover, I propose that, at least for the first few centuries of this period, the Mount was not part of the city at all.

Such statements, of course, require evidence (which I hope to provide in chapters 3 and 4) and raise questions: What was there before Herod's time? What happened after the destruction? Did the Mount go back to being a mountain like all other mountains? What was, in fact, the nature of the Capitoline temple, which prevailing scholarly opinion has placed on the Temple Mount from the time of Hadrian onward? And, most important, what impact did these urban transformations have on the conceptuality of the site? The central argument that threads this book holds that its two parts—the physical and the conceptual—are closely related. The Mount's material permutations significantly affected a wide range of factors, from the spatial organization of the city's urban landscape to its daily life, from the varied literary representations produced by those connected with the Mount, Jews and Christians, to the symbolism and imagery they were conversant with.

Some Theoretical Considerations

Through the ages, material reality and human consciousness have been entangled in an endless reciprocal dance that cannot be definitively grasped. Scholars have devoted much attention to this intricate association, striving to decipher its combination in any given period. Yet no consensus has been achieved. Many have reasoned that we should not look for a crystal-clear connection between the world of ideas of a given era, as recorded in the written works of that time, and the physical realm, which is generally buried under clods of earth (although at times also reflected in writings of various sorts). One of the auxiliary goals of this study is to reassess this relationship. Is such a separation really possible? The working assumption here suggests that the two cannot be divorced entirely, that people's perceptions, especially those that are pervasive and conventional, are associated with what they see in their physical surroundings. Consequently, such an encounter marks the beginning of the convoluted and mutually dependent journey from thought to actuality and vice versa.

This theoretical framework holds direct implications for the study of sacred space. The history-of-religions approach, usually associated with the work of Mircea Eliade, portrays the creation of holy places in an almost metaphysical manner—the so-called Eliadian rapture—speaking of "divine intervention" in the making of space and famously asserting that sacred place is not chosen but rather chooses. This approach has long come under fire.[9] More recent scholarship tends to examine holy sites as multifaceted phenomena, with archaeology closely linked to other disciplines such as anthropology or literary and cultural criticisms.[10] The current study follows these methodological principles and examines the evolution of a particular sacred space in Jerusalem through manifold dimensions, ranging from urban geography to memory and including hermeneutics, etiology, and semiotics.

One rudimentary manifestation of the interaction between people and their physical surroundings can be discerned in the terms they apply to what they see. Assigning names to the constituents of landscape has been a habitual human activity from earliest times, and it is no coincidence that the biblical story of creation, to mention one example, begins in precisely this way. One of the most explicit reflections of a person's mental capacity resonates in the words that make up her or his lexicon. Many of the ancients acknowledged this practice and devoted much effort to decipher its nature (such as Plato in *Cratylus*). In modern scholarship, the process of "naming" has been studied within the fields of philosophy of language, linguistics, and semantics, and some of its aspects have also been explored in anthropology. It was the Swiss linguist Ferdinand de Saussure, at the end of the nineteenth century, who applied the categories "signifier" and "signified," the first representing the word and the second what lies behind it (that is, the consciousness, or the way in which an article is perceived, and not, as some believe, the physical object to which the word refers). Jacques Derrida and Saul Kripke have continued this inquiry into what Kripke called the act of naming, both seeking to clarify the linguistic, sociohistoric, and epistemological aspects of this phenomenon.[11]

Such theoretical works induce the historian who wants to learn about the ways in which a people of the past perceived their world to examine terminology. Human vocabulary amounts to a kind of middle ground between reality and consciousness. "Sudden" changes in the lexicon of a given society often signal a shift in the conceptual realm as well. The question is what role the real, the actual, had in the concept's inception. Are concepts created ex nihilo? Or are they dependent on some novelty in the physical world? In one frequently quoted passage, Derrida writes: "The writer writes *in* a language and *in* a logic whose proper system, laws, and life his discourse by definition cannot dominate absolutely. . . . And the reading must always aim at a certain relationship, unperceived by the writer, between what he commands and what he does not command of the patterns of the language that he uses."[12] Tangible, man-made elements of the environment and their interaction with written traditions constitute precisely one of these unperceived relationships, and therefore uncovering such a connection stands at the center of the current book.

The "Temple Mount" represents a type of term, a "rigid designator" in Kripke's language, marking a very specific object that inhabited the landscape of Jews and Christians in the first centuries of the common era.[13] Elucidation of how the people who used the term understood it can tell us how they perceived the reality it signified. Furthermore, if it can be proved, as I intend to do in chapter 1, that the appellation Temple Mount did not always exist, this would illuminate the processes that brought it about. What changed in the physical realm that required a new set of tags to label it? What changed in the conceptual realm that made possible or occasioned the labeling?

The work of Claude Lévi-Strauss (and many others subsequently) honed the principle that a change in one stratum of reality instigates changes in other parallel dimensions.[14] An altered municipal landscape, for example, would thus lead to modifications in terminology and consciousness by "compelling" people to match their conceptual outlook to the novelty ("necessity," in Kripke's language). From the historian's point of view, new urban designations often tell us that there has been some radical change in the architectural texture of the environment. Such a dynamic involves an intricate process of reciprocal relationships featuring numerous variables and should not be reduced to a single-factor formula. Although the present work focuses on one pair in this paradigm (physical landscape–ideas), it does not ignore other elements that contributed as well, whether literary, hermeneutic, polemic, or social.

This theoretical model is put to work at the two chronological foci of the book. Chapter 1 presents the claim that the new urban landscape that came into being as a result of Herod's construction enterprise in Jerusalem stimulated the formation of a new (though borrowed from ancient sources) term, "Temple Mount." Along the same lines, chapters 5 and 6 examine the effects that the new spatial organization of the Roman colony of Aelia Capitolina and the innovations of the time of Constantine and thereafter had on the evolving imagery of the Temple Mount in both rabbinic and patristic literature.

How can such a connection be established? There is certainly no empirical proof here, nor even literary confirmation, since we do not have, and should not expect to have, a text that declares something like "from the day Herod built the compound we began to call it the Temple Mount" (and even if we had such a text its credibility would be rather questionable). Support for these claims must thus be based on the collation of the physical reality with literature and consciousness.

Before arriving at this model, I rejected two alternatives. My first working hypothesis corresponded to the common scholarly notion that the term Temple Mount and the consciousness on which it is founded had existed from the earliest documented days of Israelite-Jewish civilization. I held, like many others, that a direct line tied the mountain's status in the Bible with the appearance of the term and the ideas associated with it in rabbinic literature. This assumption had to be discarded as a result of the unambiguous conclusions of chapter 1, which demonstrate that the mountain and/or the area surrounding the Temple lacked any substantial independent role in Jewish experience during most of the Second Temple period. An alternative premise, an ostensibly obvious one, suggests that the entity of the Temple Mount crystallized as a result of the destruction of the Temple. This causal equation too must be rejected, at least in its clear-cut formulation, since incipient forms of both vocabulary and consciousness appear prior to 70 CE (as argued in chapters 1 and 2), implying that at some time during this interval, between the greater part of the Second Temple period and the destruction, a new constituent began taking shape in people's minds. The theoretical model laid out here impels us to search for the causes of conceptual innovations in the realm of physical reality. Hence chapter 1 argues that Herod's project, which altered Jerusalem's landscape beyond recognition, stood behind the rise of the "Temple Mount." By no means do I mean to claim that the destruction of the Temple did not contribute to the evolution of the Temple Mount conceptuality. It obviously did; the disappearance of the sanctuary never to return fueled much of the process in ensuing generations, but it was not the sole factor, and the story is more complex.

Sources and Methodology

This kind of study looks to two major types of sources. When it comes to physical landscape, archaeology must play a leading role. In the present case, the Temple Mount's special religious status prevents archaeologists from systematically digging within the wall of the compound. Nevertheless, excavations carried out around the precinct often shed light on what transpired on the platform itself. Extensive archaeological research took place to the Mount's north, in the area of the Lion's Gate and the Probatika (Sheep's Pool; map 2: 8, fig. 11). To the south and southwest, the large-scale excavations directed by Benjamin Mazar provide useful findings; sporadic digs have been conducted here and there west of the compound as well. Similarly, findings unearthed at a greater distance, throughout the city and along its walls, can also contribute to an understanding of the situation on the Mount (see chapters 3 and 4).

Yet without written sources our knowledge of what evolved on the Temple Mount in antiquity would be tenuous at best. Historiographic writings, descriptions by pilgrims and travelers, and even theological compositions frequently speak of this area, and they should be used to supplement the archaeological data. The problem is that in many cases reality and idea have blended, and the literary evidence has concocted from the archaeological data pictures that are quite far from actuality.

Seeking to examine notions, ideology, and consciousness in a given period, scholars have almost nothing but what the members of that generation laid down in their writings (or, when available, in their art). Fortunately, the situation here is far better than with the archaeological data. The period under discussion produced a notably rich literature—Second Temple compositions in all their forms, writings that were eventually brought together in the New Testament, the rabbinic corpus, and Christian texts from the second century onward. It is hardly surprising that Jerusalem and its associated sites were referred to fairly often in these compositions, and from this point of view they offer a fertile ground for research.

Investigating this wide array of sources, the current study benefits from a cluster of fresh views and methodological precautions that have been voiced by scholars in recent decades. Foremost among these is the awareness of the non-historical nature of rabbinic material, best articulated in the sharp criticism of the traditional school of Jewish history by Jacob Neusner as early as the 1970s and 1980s. Although many, including this author, reject Neusner's extreme skepticism as well as the alternative convictions he tried to promote (mainly the ultimate focus on the final compositions of the rabbinic material), the core of his assertions maintains its validity and remains an important guideline.[15]

Second, for far too many years the study of Jewish history in the Roman-Byzantine period, as well as the study of Christianity at that time, has suffered from the notion of "a nation that dwells apart" (*'Am levadad yishkon;* known as Jewish exceptionalism). Even though many modern scholars acknowledged that the Jews were integral to the cultural setting of the eastern Roman Empire, they continued to study them as if they were an isolated group, describing the Jewish world as distinct from this milieu and indeed hostile to it. Recent studies have undermined this artificial dichotomy. Many scholars no longer see the early generations in the story of what came to be Christianity as distinct from Judaism—thus the term "Jesus movement," which consciously omits the notion of Christianity from these early phases. The same holds true for the study of rabbinic sources. The traditional paradigm considers "Judaism" and "Christianity" in antiquity to have been two distinct entities, each having gone its own way as soon as Christianity had split from Judaism, with not much in common except their intense hostility to each other. By contrast, this study joins the work of a group of scholars from various fields who have recently rejected this outlook. The alternative position, in the words of Daniel Boyarin, claims that there were "shared and crisscrossing lines of history and religious development" and that therefore "one could travel, metaphorically, from rabbinic Jew to Christian along a continuum where one would hardly know where one stopped and the other began."[16] Along these lines, the current study strives to reconstruct a discourse shared by the various groups that populated Palestine (and the Roman East in general) in antiquity around a palpable entity in their life—a sacred site in Jerusalem now called the Temple Mount.

Finally, two major tendencies in modern scholarship have informed my analysis of both textual and archaeological findings. On the general conceptual level, my study follows the lines laid down by deconstructionism, less out of identification with its principles or ideology and more out of the way its advocates have applied it to the study of the ancient world in general and in particular to the examination of New Testament material.[17] I use deconstruction more as an approach than a method. It provided me a view of the world that, in its application to the discipline of history, sets out to look at the past from the point of view of the periphery. The scholar executing this approach seeks the key to understanding reality in the margins, in figures or factors that were not in the center of the map even in their own day. Much of the present work turns its gaze to these sidelines. This is the case in my discussion of the tomb of James Brother of Jesus (chapter 2). It is also true of the chapters that address the Mount's position in the municipal layout of the Roman colony Aelia Capitolina (chapter 3), and even more so in the Christian city that developed from the fourth century onward, in which the compound was pushed to the fringes of the urban framework—one might even say "diminished" (chapter 4). Even in the Second Temple period, when the compound that housed the Temple stood proud and has been appropriately called "the inner heart of the city of Jerusalem," it was paradoxically "canceled out" in the consciousness of its contemporaries by the elements that dominated their reality, Jerusalem and the Temple (see chapter 1).

On the level of detail, this work aspires, by engaging approaches from the school known as New Historicism, to achieve new readings of mostly familiar texts. In presenting this trend in scholarship, Aram Veeser states: "New Historicists have evolved a method of describing culture in action. . . . they seize upon an event or anecdote . . . and re-read it in such a way as to reveal through the analysis of tiny particulars the behavioral codes, logics, and motive forces controlling a whole society."[18] In the wake of revolutionary archaeological and textual discoveries, where available information has been in fact radically altered, such strategies become even more decisive. I need only mention in this context the discoveries during the past two generations, at Qumran and Nag Hammadi, discussed in the various chapters of this book. Often, even when the scholarly world has acquired such new information, the understanding of existing texts—those that have been and remain the "classical" corpus of sources for the era—has hardly changed at all. The interpretation of the information adjusts, but the fundamental understanding of the text has, in many cases, remained the same. New Historicism defies this situation. This work sets as its goal the reexamination of the sources themselves, in an attempt to evaluate whether well-known sources say what they seemed to have said (or what scholars thought they were saying) in the past.

All in all, my approach combines new and traditional tools. Although my general sympathies lean toward deconstruction and New Historicism, for accurate reading of ancient sources there is no substitute for the still-vigorous "traditional" methods of study from the philological-historical school, without which, in my opinion, it is difficult to understand an ancient text. In addition, because most of the written sources from antiquity are in fact literature of one sort or another, their investigation should benefit from the tools developed in the field of literary criticism, in particular in the analysis of structure and form.[19] From this point of view the present work may be seen as an attempt to re-present the historical image of the Temple Mount with the help of an interdisciplinary investigation that uses tools and methods from archaeology, literature, and history. This attempt has produced a collection of new readings of familiar texts as well as some new understandings of archaeological data. Together they tell a rather different story of the Temple Mount from the one commonly told.

God's Mountain

CHAPTER ONE

Transmuting Realities

From David to Herod, From Micah to Josephus

Sometime around the mid-third century BCE, a majestic convoy of Egyptian delegates, representatives of King Ptolemy II (285–245 BCE), arrived in the small yet significant city of Jerusalem. Momentous matters were on the table, among them the release of a hundred thousand Jewish deportees and their compensation from the royal treasury, and the translation of the Bible into Greek. Admittedly, our report of the events in a letter attributed to one of the ambassadors, an Egyptian named Aristeas, to his brother Philocrates is rather shaky. But whoever produced this document (a matter of debate, although scholars tend to agree about his Jewishness) incorporated a revealing passage about how he viewed the city of Jerusalem: "When we approached near the site we saw the city built in the midst of the whole land of the Jews, upon a hill which extended to a great height. On the top of the hill the Temple had been constructed, towering above all."[1] If we shut our eyes and try to recreate the picture that the writer envisaged, the result should be familiar. It is safe to say that centuries of public imagination have etched an image of Jerusalem soaring high at the center of the earth, with a temple on a lofty mountain reaching for the skies. A glimpse at the numerous artistic representations of the city throughout the generations should suffice to demonstrate that this is one of the commonest images of Jerusalem and its temple—a city on a mount.

The sequential development model of the history of the Temple Mount (detailed in the introduction), which places its story on a long continuum stretching to the earliest days of Israelite history, rests on such texts as the *Letter of Aristeas*. From such a perspective, this excerpt manifests the idea of the Temple Mount, which, with slight variations, has persisted to this very day.

Less known is the gap between this image and the actual physical-topographical situation in the city.[2] "Jerusalem, mountains surrounding it," goes the famous line from the Psalmist poem (125:2), but the city and the Temple are actually located on one of the more unassuming ridges in the area (see map 1, fig. 1), which by no stretch of the imagination can be seen as a lofty mountain. Such a disparity signals the convoluted process through which the mountain image was carved and its concept shaped. The current chapter tries to go beyond the image—to investigate where the mountain figure came from, and who crafted the notions embodied in the Temple Mount and in what circumstances.

First Temple Roots and Their Uncertainties

The "House" in the original Hebrew designation behind the English "Temple Mount"—*har ha-bayit,* the Mount of the House, always with the definite article preceding the word "House"—refers to either of the temples that successively stood in Jerusalem during ancient times. This was no ordinary house but rather "The House of God." According to the biblical narrative, King Solomon built the First Temple. Scholars who accept this information as historically accurate (many today contest it) date this event to the beginning of the tenth century BCE. The Second Temple is easier to date. Judean expatriates from Babylon/Persia erected this sanctuary after their return from exile in the second half of the sixth century BCE. Six hundred fifty years later, in 70 CE, the Romans destroyed it at the culmination of the Jewish rebellion known as the Great Revolt. The very nature of the Temple Mount rests on these two temples and its stature stems from their reverence. As reflected by its name, people consider the Temple Mount today and have considered it in the past as the hallowed ground on which the temples stood.

The story, however, is more complicated. As told in the books of Samuel and Kings, David conquered Jerusalem (or Jebus, as it had previously been known) and established it as his kingdom's new capital, renaming it the City of David. He then contemplated building within the city a permanent sanctuary for the God of Israel, a plan that his son Solomon carried out. The authors of these two books, the earliest existing documents that relate the history of the Davidic dynasty,[3] do not indicate that the location the kings chose for the Temple had any special prior status. The writers use no particular name for this area, nor do they associate it with any illustrious tradition. All that can be inferred from these accounts is that the Temple site lay above the City of David, as on more than one occasion texts mention the need to ascend to it (for example, 1 Kings 8:1). Archaeological finds confirm this topographical portrayal of ancient Jerusalem. They show that the Jebusite city and its successor, the City of David, were situated on the lower part of the mountain ridge (see map 1, fig. 2), whose summit would later become the Temple Mount. The city fastened on the Giḥon spring (known today as the Siloam; see map 2), which in those days embodied Jerusalem's lifeblood, given the lack of technology for bringing water from remote locations. Solomon's Temple sprawled on the nearby peak, north of the City of David.

The terminology people applied to the space on which the Temple stood reflects the same complexity. The books of Samuel, for example, never mention Mount Zion, a celebrated appellation of the Temple Mount in future generations. In the books of Kings it appears only on one occasion, in the form of a quotation from the prophet Isaiah, but only as a synonym for the city of Jerusalem as a whole and without any reference to the location of the Temple.[4] Another alias used by later generations to refer to the site of David's and Solomon's Temple, lending it a special aura, was "Ornan's threshing floor." This designation never appears in the book of Kings. It originated in the second book of Samuel: David, heeding the instructions of the prophet Gad, purchases a plot of land from Ornan at the going rate to build an altar for God in the aftermath of a deadly pestilence.[5] The biblical author describes the threshing floor as located above the city and as the place in which God's angel stood when the disease came to a halt. Otherwise, however, the text lends absolutely no indication that this site overlaps with what later came to be Solomon's Temple. Moreover, scattered references imply that Ornan's property acquired no independent value in the eyes of these authors (beyond being uninfected by the disease because it was outside the city and therefore suitable for an altar): the Ark of the Covenant and the venues at which the Israelite offered sacrifices to the God of Israel remained inside the City of David, both before his purchase of the threshing floor and afterward, during Solomon's time. A later source mentions that the place was being used to process wheat, just like any other threshing floor.[6]

Fig. 2. The eastern ridge of Jerusalem looking north. With Mount Scopus in the background and the Jehoshaphat Valley to the right, at the center of the photo one can see the southern walls of the Temple Mount enclosure (now the Ḥaram esh-Sharif with the Dome of the Rock at its center); below the southern walls on the slopes of the ridge is the location of the biblical "City of David" (now topped by the houses of the Arab village of Siloam). From Duby Tal and Moni Haramati, *Kav ha-Ofek.* (Jerusalem: Ministry of Defence Pub. House, 1993). With permission from Albatross.

The significance of these observations becomes clearer if placed within the wider ideological context of First Temple Israel and seen against the role sacred space played in this ancient framework. Jerusalem's political centrality and the cult of the Israelite God whose rituals were performed in the city's Temple both played a pivotal role in the Davidic dynasty's ambitions to become the "eternal" and sole ruler of the tribes of Israel. The books of Samuel and Kings clearly articulate these notions, whether or not they accurately recount the early history of the kingdoms. Even if they were merely created by the later Davidic kings in order to anchor their heritage in firm ground, they still accurately reflect the dynasty's aspirations.[7] According to the biblical ethos, David abandoned Hebron, the traditional capital of his tribe of Judah, and relocated his center north, to Jebus, a non-Israelite town on the border between the tribes of Judah and Benjamin. This move manifests a calculated decision. Jebus's geographical position on the central mountain spine of the land, at the time the heartland of the "Israelite Nation," accommodated the political objectives of the new king. The three tribes that descended from the matriarch Rachel— Benjamin, Ephraim, and Menashe—shared the northern part of the central hill, whereas the southern part belonged to Judah, the major tribe that descended from the other matriarch, Leah. Conflicting political ambitions fueled the strife between these two groups. Separate capitals partitioned them: Hebron was Judah's while Givʿat (the Hill of) Benjamin and later Samaria were the centers of the northern tribes. The rivalry sometimes deteriorated into violent conflict: the tussle between David from the tribe of Judah and Saul the Benjamite, and later the division of Solomon's kingdom by Jeroboam son of Nebat of the tribe of Ephraim. By establishing a new capital in Jebus, a city unrelated to any of the old, tribal centers, David strove to create a new, unifying element for the tribes of Israel—the House of David—and hence its name, the City of David (fig. 2).[8]

The books of Kings and Samuel (and Deuteronomy, which is closely related to their outlook) place enormous significance on the establishment of Jerusalem as the Israelite nation's sole ritual center. These tracts delegitimize sacrifice in any other location, even if intended for the God of Israel, thus coinciding with the House of David's desire to perpetuate the political hegemony of both its capital and dynasty. Expressing this conception, for example, Solomon's prayer at the dedication of the Temple ties together the city, the Temple, and the House of David. The words of God, which Solomon claims to cite, clearly link these three elements: "Since the day that I brought forth my people

Israel out of Egypt, I chose no city out of all the tribes of Israel to build a house, that my name might be therein; but I chose David to be over my people Israel."[9] The author of the first book of Kings ascribes an identical position to the leaders of the ten northern tribes, the Davidic kingdom's major rivals, who emphatically denounced Davidic hegemony. Divulging the rationale behind Jeroboam's decision to found two alternative sanctuaries, at Dan and Beth-el, the biblical sequence runs as follows: "And Jeroboam said in his heart, Now shall the kingdom return to the house of David: If this people go up to do sacrifice in the house of the Lord at Jerusalem, then shall the heart of this people turn again unto their lord even unto Rehoboam king of Judah, and they shall kill me, and go again to Rehoboam king of Judah."[10] These passages reflect a clear religious-political ideology, espousing one city, one temple, and one kingdom (and, we might add, one god).

In such a conceptualization of space, the mountain on which the Temple stood falls short of any genuine substance. As noted, the Temple's placement in Jerusalem is highly significant, in fact essential, to the Davidic ideology. Its location on this hill or that, however, seems inconsequential. The significance of Solomon's Temple as the ritual center for the God of Israel, in the kingdom of Judah, is similarly beyond doubt. It is quite possible that some of the kingdom's governing institutions, such as the "House of the King," the "House of the People," and the "House of the Forest of Lebanon," stood close to the Temple, on the grounds presently referred to as the Temple Mount.[11] From the point of view of those generations (or whoever wrote about them), however, these buildings were there not because of the importance of the mountain but by dint of their proximity to the Temple.

The literary image of the Temple's place as a holy mountain first emerges only in Psalms and in the so-called books of the prophets. Names and descriptives woven repeatedly into these works render the idea that the Temple is located on a "mountain" possessing special qualities. A good example may be found in the famous prophecy of peace at the end of days, in the books of both Isaiah and Micah. The prophecy depicts the "mountain of the Lord's house" as "established in the top of the mountains and exalted above the hills." The Gentiles who stream to the place proclaim, "Let us go up to the mountain of God . . . and he will teach us of his ways and we will walk in his paths."[12] These verses encapsulate the visual impressions that engaged the consciousness of the authors and their audience.

Along these same lines, the works of the prophets frequently introduce the place of the Temple in a series of appellations that all share a mountain image: "holy mountain," "mountain of God," and, combining both, "My holy mountain."[13] Israelite poets as well as authors of eschatological and apocalyptic visions employed such a language. The prophets' longing for a better future lent political connotations to the Temple's mountain. The Psalmist provides one example of such formulations: "Yet have I set my king upon Zion my holy hill."[14] Similarly, the mountain relates to acts of worship, as found in Isaiah's vision: "Even [the Gentiles] will I bring to my holy mountain, and make them joyful in my house of prayer: their burnt offerings and their sacrifices shall be accepted upon mine altar" (56:7). Furthermore, these passages from the prophets and Psalms are the first to assign the name Mount Zion to the space on which the Temple stood. In Samuel and Kings, Zion signified only the City of David, and the image of the mountain is not found at all in reference to Zion.[15]

The tendency to exalt the Temple's grounds and represent them as a special mountain may also be found, somewhat later, when the place obtained the name Mount Moriah. This epithet first appears in the book of Chronicles' retrospective description of Solomon's Temple project: "Then Solomon began to build the house of the Lord at Jerusalem in Mount Moriah, where the Lord reappeared unto David his father, in the place that David had prepared in the threshing-floor of Ornan the Jebusite."[16] In what appears to be a brilliant intertextual maneuver, the author extracts the name Moriah from the only other passage where it appears in the Bible—the narrative about the binding of Isaac (Genesis 22:2)—and by doing so links that event with the Temple.

This attempt by the author of Chronicles to tie Moriah to the site of the Temple and Ornan's threshing floor embodies a hidden, interpretive trend. According to this writer, the Temple rests on the same grounds as the binding of Isaac, which also matches the site of Ornan's threshing floor mentioned in the story of King David in the book of Samuel. Underlying all three is a cultic concept of sacrifice as the ultimate manifestation of the encounter between God and his people. The construal (some would call this midrash) of the author of Chronicles presents the binding of Isaac as the primordial prefiguration of this ritual model.[17] Notably, however, the binding of Isaac story itself in the book of Genesis makes no mention of a specific mountain. It refers only to a region known as the "land of Moriah," and God commands Abraham to sacrifice his son on "one of the mountains" in that district.[18] The sacrifice story, or for that matter any other of the early traditions in the books of Samuel and Kings, provide no indication that this site corresponds in any way to the territory on which the future Temple would be erected.

A similar vagueness characterizes the first appearance of the precise pair of words "Temple Mount" in the writings of the prophet Micah: "Therefore shall Zion for your sake be plowed as a field, and Jerusalem shall become heaps, and the Temple Mount as a wooded height" (3:12). As noted in the introduction, this appellation lacks a factual basis in the lexicon of the time; I show it to be a product of the prophet's literary virtuosity rather than a concrete name for the Temple's location. Furthermore, even with this verse, it remains the sole occurrence of the exact appellation "Temple Mount" in the literary traditions of the First Temple.[19]

Tracing the roots of mountain imagery as the proper location for temples leads to the ancient Semitic idea of the cosmic mountain: a lofty place where the heavens and the earth converge and where the "divine" blazons itself in the terrestrial universe.[20] Indeed, verses such as "Jerusalem [has] mountains [all] round her" (Psalms 125:2) also express a topographic truth. But geography alone does not imbue these or any other peaks with holiness. The concept of the cosmic mountain, widespread in different forms throughout the ancient East, molded the religious landscape of many local cultures, from Mesopotamia and Ugaritic civilizations to Egypt and Greece. One of its central aspects involved the congruence between "mountain" and "temple."[21]

It seems reasonable to assume that such a cultural environment inspired the beliefs and values that fashioned the texture of the holy mountain as it appears in the prophetic books and the Psalms (and also as will be discussed shortly, in a variety of other texts from the early Second Temple period). Widely used appellations, such as "mountain of God" and "holy mountain," as well as the characteristics that seep into various descriptions of Mount Sinai and Mount Zion, weave nicely into the conceptualization of Near Eastern space. The holiness granted to the Temple's mountain in the symbolism of the prophets, as well as its representation as God's residence or as belonging to God, should be seen as vivid expressions of such a framework. But beyond these literary usages, widespread as they might be, it remains at best uncertain whether the mountain also constituted a definite category in the worldview of the First Temple era or whether it functioned as a palpable factor in the ritual framework of those days. The silence of Samuel and Kings in this regard seems rather revealing.

The City and God's Sanctuary in the Second Temple Period

The special status of Jerusalem and the Temple during the First Temple period takes on redoubled significance in the days of the Second Temple (516 BCE–70 CE) (map 3; fig. 3). No one now seems to embrace the views articulated by Wilhelm Bousset, prevalent in the early twentieth century, that the Temple had lost its importance among the Jews toward the end of that period.[22] As Shaye Cohen put it, "As the focal point of the religion, the Temple was the central communal institution not just for the Jews of the land of Israel but also for those of the Diaspora."[23]

Even though the city and the Temple shed the associations they had under the House of David, they were equally revered in the world of Second Temple Jewry. Jerusalem and the Temple took on as many shades of meaning as there

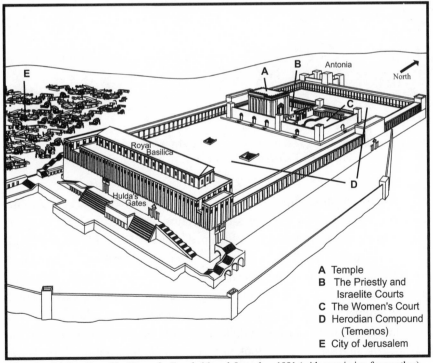

A Temple
B The Priestly and
   Israelite Courts
C The Women's Court
D Herodian Compound
   (Temenos)
E City of Jerusalem

Based on M. Ben-Dov, *The Dig at the Temple Mound,* Jerusalem 1981 (with permission from author)

Map 3. Second Temple compound

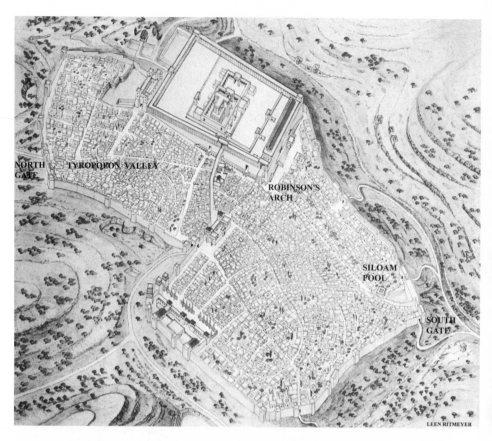

Fig. 3. A reconstruction of Second Temple Jerusalem (reflecting its layout in the middle of the first century CE). Courtesy of Ritmeyer Archaeological Design.

were groups and subgroups of Palestine and Diaspora Jews at the time. A wide conceptual gap, for example, separates Josephus, who cherished the Temple's corporeal nature, from Philo, who "stripped" the building and its constituent elements—such as the priesthood and the animal sacrifices—of their tangible form and fashioned them into allegoric motifs in his representation of the logos.[24] Despite their diverse views, both writers share a strong sense of affection for the Temple, and they care deeply about its sacrificial procedures. Likewise, the admiration for the city, the Temple, and the priests expressed by the authors of the *Letter of Aristeas* or the Book of Sirach is a far cry from the critical attitude taken in the writings of the Judean Desert group or later in the rebukes of Jesus and his disciples.[25] Overall, the common denominator of these varied and conflicting attitudes is the eminence of Jerusalem and the Temple in Jewish experience of this period.

Along these lines, with only a few isolated exceptions, Jerusalem and the Temple function as primary focal points throughout the varied writings of the period. In a detailed study Martha Himmelfarb demonstrated that early Jewish apocalypses of the Second Temple period patterned the image of Paradise on the Temple. From another angle, Otto Böcher pointed out what he calls the "Zionsschema," which served as a central axis in the development of apocalyptic writings of this time.[26] Even works written in the far reaches of the Hellenistic Diaspora often place Jerusalem at their core. The Hellenistic Jewish writer known as Philo the epic poet (to distinguish him from the famous Jewish philosopher), for example, whose fragments were preserved by Eusebius, named one of his works *About Jerusalem.*[27] Similarly, Jason of Cyrene, the writer whose abbreviated book we now call 2 Maccabees, voiced a prevalent disposition among Diasporean Jews when he described the Temple as "renowned throughout the entire world."[28] As shown in chapter 2, early traditions in the circles of Jesus espoused similar tendencies.

The uniqueness of the city and Temple, however, extended far beyond their literary stature. Many scholars have noted that Jerusalem and the Temple were significant factors in the major political and social developments, as well as the fundamental theological formulations, of the Second Temple period. Jerusalem served during that epoch as the unchallenged capital of the Jewish people, as well as the region's political and economic nerve center, both in times of independence (the Hasmonean era) and during the rule of the great empires (Persian, Greek, and finally Roman).[29] The Temple rounded out Jerusalem's supremacy by providing it a "religious" dimension. It was the primary ritual center for Jews in the land of Israel and throughout the world, the so-called Jewish Diaspora, as well as the spiritual focus of their worldview. As such, according to a common ideological formulation of the time, the heavens and earth met at the city and its Temple. Consequently contemporary Jews conceived it as the most appropriate of all places for people to worship their God. The "half shekel," a levy that many Jews of the ancient world collected and sent to the high priesthood in Jerusalem, is one expression of the centrality of the Temple. The large number of pilgrims who flocked to Jerusalem and the Temple for the three major festivals from throughout the Roman and Persian empires further indicates this same inclination. The city and the Temple occupied, along with other fundamental elements of Jewish thought and symbolism such as the House of David and the messianic idea, a leading position in the cluster of similes that shaped the historical heritage of Jews of all sects in the Second Temple period, as well as their hopes for the future.

The Fading Mount

And what of the Temple's mountain during the Second Temple period? From a geographical point of view, the sanctuary building certainly maintained its original position, resting on the same summit, on the ridge that divided the two eastern tributaries of the Kidron Valley—the Jehoshaphat Valley to the east and what is known as the Tyropoeon Valley to the west (see map 1). But how was this mountain crest registered, if at all, in the public consciousness? Are there Second Temple sources that point to a prevalent mind-set regarding this site? If so, what kind of perceptions do they communicate? As noted, from a terminological standpoint it was Micah, presumably a First Temple author-prophet who coined the term Temple Mount. But what was the history of this appellation thereafter? Was it in use during the Second Temple period? How was it related to other, popular names that represented the Temple and its constituents in that era's lexicon? From a more functional angle, what kind of status did the grounds surrounding the Temple attain at that time?

Much of the writing of the Second Temple period followed the contours marked out by the literature of the First Temple and ensuing Babylonian exile epochs.[30] Those Second Temple authors acquainted with the texts that later came to be the core of the Hebrew Bible (the books of Samuel, Kings, the early portions of Isaiah, and the other prophets, as well as the early Psalms) and writing under their influence could hardly conceive Jerusalem in any but mountain imagery—especially since the actual topography in Jerusalem, with which many of these writers were familiar, supports such a precipitous picture. Anyone climbing from the bottom of the hill—the area known as the City of David or in Josephus as the Lower City (see map 1, fig. 2)—to the peak where the Temple jutted out knew by the weariness of their feet that this was a hill. It is no wonder, then, that mountain scenery permeates many of the texts that deal with Jerusalem. The author of Judith, writing sometime in the late second or early first century BCE, for example, describes the entire Jerusalem settlement of the returning Babylonian expatriates as located "in the [region of the] hill."[31] From a narrower angle, the work called *Fourth Baruch* (or *Paraleipomena Jeremiou*), places "Agrippa's Garden/farm" outside of Jerusalem "by the mountain road."[32] The undulating setting of Jerusalem and the areas north of the city serve as the backdrop for the Qumranic composition now called *Joseph's Prayer*, as well as for Josephus, whose many descriptions of events in Jerusalem are repeatedly set on a hilly stage.[33]

Terms extracted from the "mountain lexicon" of the First Temple period, either borrowed directly from the ancient texts or originating in the Second Temple period, continue to appear in the literary works of that era in relation to Jerusalem and the location of the Temple. For example, in the apocalyptic chapters of the book of Daniel, usually dated to the first half of the second century BCE, the phrase "Thy Holy Mountain" is synonymous with Jerusalem.[34] The author of the text known as the Apocryphal Psalm borrowed the expression "the mountain of the height of Israel" from the book of Ezekiel, where it occurs several times. Similarly, the idiom "Thy Holy Mountain," found in the Wisdom of Solomon and 1 Maccabees (without the genitive), refers to the location of the Temple, and in the book of *Jubilees* the term "Mountain of God" signifies both Jerusalem and Mount Sinai.[35] Other authors routinely applied the designation Mount Zion throughout the entire period, from books written at the height of the era, such as *Jubilees* and 1 Maccabees, in which it functioned as the usual toponym for the Temple's site, to books written after the destruction, such as *Syriac Baruch* and *Fourth Ezra*.[36] Some new vocabulary, absent from First Temple literature but found here and there in the writings of the period, belongs to the same semantic field. Examples are the ambiguous phrase "summit [*koryphē*] of Zion" in Judith and the term "crest" (*lophos*) in Josephus s references to Jerusalem and the Temple.[37]

The reliance of Second Temple period authors on ancient, mainly First Temple or exilic texts goes beyond terminology. Many of these writers adopted and elaborated ideas that were originally conceived during the First Temple era or in the intermediate, and highly productive, period of the Babylonian Exile. The identification of the site of Isaac's binding, Moriah, with Mount Zion provides a prime example of this propensity. As mentioned earlier, this notion first appeared in the book of Chronicles (and in the editorial note to the text in Genesis), but it was widely espoused by the authors of the Second Temple period and expanded even further.[38]

Similarly, texts from early in the Second Temple period sporadically allude to the ancient idea of the cosmic mountain. The clearest example surfaces in the passage from the *Letter of Aristeas*. Two different conceptual paradigms are at work in this segment. The first enunciates the Greco-Hellenistic notion of the Omphalos, the "navel of the earth," whose foundation rests on a horizontal configuration of space, with the emphasis on its center. The second proclaims the Near Eastern archetype of "the high mountain," a vertically oriented concept that corresponds to the cosmic mountain of the First Temple prophets.[39]

An analogous worldview underlies the statement in the Qumranic text *Joseph's Prayer,* which observed of the Samaritans that "they make for themselves an altar on a high mountain," and contrasted this with "The mountain of my God [they made into a] wooded height." Something of this outlook also seeped into the book of *Jubilees,* where the author considers the Garden of Eden, Mount Sinai, Mount Zion, and an unidentified mountain as the four holy places. He also dubs Mount Zion the "navel of the earth" and envisages God as "king on Mount Zion."[40] The same set of spatial perceptions outlines the narrative in the *Book of the Watchers,* the first in an anthology of writings that make up the composition now known as *1 Enoch.* After visiting the Garden of Eden, Enoch continues his journey to the navel of the earth, where he encounters a high, holy mountain. Although, for whatever reason, the author of this passage declines to mention Jerusalem by name, various scholars, despite their disagreement about the nature and sources of the segment, all agree that its topographic layout corresponds to the city and its environs.[41]

All in all, it seems clear that the imagery of "the high and holy mountain," the roots of which trace back to the days of the First Temple period, did, in fact, penetrate Second Temple writings. This interconnection should hardly be surprising, since texts from the first millennium BCE, whether before or after the destruction of the First Judean Temple, partake in the same cultural, ancient Near Eastern milieu. But the question remains whether this "rise" on which the Temple stood acquired any substantial status, be it political, ritual, or cultural, in the consciousness of Second Temple Jews and in their experience. Given all that has been presented to this point, the answer appears to be affirmative, but actually it is not, or at least it is not as simple as it might seem at first. This conclusion emanates from the inherent differences between literature and historical reality, or between poetic imagery and day-to-day experiences. The very existence of an idea in old, well-regarded texts (considered, whether truly or not, to represent the heritage of the First Temple), even one that receives some attention in Jewish writings of the Second Temple period, does not necessarily imply that it was fully adopted by the people of that time or that it functioned in any noteworthy way in their world.

To elucidate this claim, it may be useful to examine how the discourse of a certain period expresses the importance of an inanimate element, whether political, ritual, or cultural. Analyzing two examples intimately related to the present discussion—the cases of Jerusalem and the Temple—might help clarify this matter. To determine the impact the city of Jerusalem or the structure called the Temple had on Second Temple Jews, one must examine how people felt about these entities and the effect they had on their lives. Sources indicating how Jews spoke and thought of the Temple, laws they passed regulating it as an institution and molding activities related to it, accomplishments they associated with it, the way they acted on its behalf, and the way they criticized it—all these illustrate the role of the Temple in their lives. The same holds true regarding the city of Jerusalem.

Second Temple religious experience—sacrifices, festivals, laws of purity, and the like—hinges almost entirely on Jerusalem's Temple and thus affirms its ritual status. The plethora of governmental institutions and events related to them that intersects with the Temple's function clearly indicates its political centrality as well. The abundant literary material surveyed thus far, which allocates so much attention to the city and the Temple, testifies to their prime position in the cultural milieu of this time. Not by mistake do we name this period after the Temple.

Were there, however, similar notions and emotions regarding the mountain on which the Temple stood? My answer is no. The fact that sporadic echoes of expressions and literary phrases with a mountainous ring reverberate in Second Temple texts, or that the ancient, Near Eastern notion of the cosmic mountain occasionally surfaces in those writings, does not prove that the mountain itself acquired any political, ritual, or cultural status in the eyes of Second Temple Jews. The life-span of vocabulary and terminology often exceeds the consciousness embedded in them; lifeless words lacking meaningful substance or functioning only as literary ornamentations are the products of such dynamics. Moreover, in this case hilly scenery constituted an integral part of the Jerusalemite experience, and as part of that environment the Temple occupied one of the city's hills. A clear distinction must be made, however, between topographical landscape that is essentially neutral and the ideological function that may be granted to any particular component of that reality.

This claim that the mountain itself fell short of significance in Second Temple experience relies primarily on a careful examination of all references to Jerusalem and its related sites in the texts from that time. Jewish writing during this period tends to be prolific and extremely varied. Due to their diversity, these sources could be taken as demonstrating the common features of Jewish consciousness of the era. Within this framework two major factors stand out from the start: the city of Jerusalem and its Temple, which appear in these texts hundreds, if not thousands, of times. The mountain on which the Temple stood, however, was devoid of any significant stature. Numerous cases may be brought to substantiate this argument.

Lexically, the precise name Temple Mount turns up but once throughout the multitude of available sources—in 1 Maccabees.[42] Even there, as I will show in detail later in this chapter, it operates only as a literary construction, inspired by the verse in Micah. This is a decisive finding, which proves that the term Temple Mount was not an integral part of Second Temple vocabulary.

Furthermore, not only does the period's literature lack any terminology granting the Temple Mount a special role in Jewish civilization and culture, but it contains no significant expression of a widespread public awareness that defined the Temple's location as a mountain. Although the rich array of mountain imagery was obviously well known to the Jews of the period, who were well versed in the books of what later became the Hebrew Bible (and for others the Old Testament), in practice, in their day-to-day routines and discourse or in the political and ritual dialect of Second Temple Judaism, mountain images embodying a certain evaluative flavor decrease appreciably. Thus, whereas the name Mount Zion frequently occurs in these writings (see n. 36), the more es-teemed "my holy mountain," a very common signifier of the Temple grounds for both First Temple prophets and the author(s) of Psalms as well as later in post–Second Temple Jewish and Christian contexts, seldom surfaces in writ-ings from the Second Temple period. I am aware of only three occurrences: a poetic literary passage without any realistic reference in the Wisdom of Solomon; a relatively ancient mythological segment about the cosmic moun-tain in the *Book of the Watchers,* which clearly builds on Ezekiel (see n. 41); and 1 Maccabees. Whatever weight might be ascribed to these sources, they defi-nitely do not amount to a ubiquitous phenomenon.[43] Another prevalent First Temple phrase, "the Mount of God," debuts in Second Temple texts in the book of *Jubilees* (see n. 40), then vanishes with no trace. These few mountain allu-sions stand in sharp contrast to the tens and perhaps hundreds of times that Jerusalem and the Temple are mentioned in Second Temple sources.

The waning references to ideas and imagery associated with the sacred mountain reflect analogous tendencies. The ancient Near Eastern myth about the "cosmic mountain" infiltrated the early writings of the Second Temple period, such as the *Letter to Aristeas* and the book of *Jubilees,* but gradually faded during the course of the period until it disappeared almost completely. By contrast, the Hellenistic notion of the Omphalos continued to appear for a long time, but with no relation to a mountain. Examples of this process from the latter years of the Second Temple period and the period immediately following the destruction of the Temple include Philo, Josephus, and the fifth book of the Sibylline Oracles. All three voice the concept of the Omphalos in reference to Jerusalem but make no mention of a holy mountain.[44] Even in texts entirely devoted to the holy aspects of the Temple and its surroundings, such as the *Temple Scroll* from Qumran, the mountain, the rise on which the sanctuary stood, does not appear even once. Apparently, during the last two hundred years of the Second Temple, the theme of the holy mountain almost completely evaporates.

A Mountless Second Temple

Literary works from the heart of the Second Temple period further suggest an absence of holy mountain consciousness. In fictional compositions such as the book of Tobit, which scholars tend to see as a product of the Diaspora, or the book of Judith, more likely composed by a Palestinian Jew,[45] the writers reveal the texture of Jerusalem as registered in their minds. When speaking of his protagonist Tobit and introducing his religious world, the author of the book of Tobit, for example, clearly delineates his own worldview. Although situated far from the city, the narrative stresses the hero's loyalty to Jerusalem and its Temple, contrasting it with the inclination prevalent among the Ten Tribes. Its setting in the Land of Israel is dominated by Jerusalem—considered the place chosen by God to which Jews go on pilgrimages, bringing their firstfruits and tithes. The Temple represents the major element in Jerusalem. Beyond these two, however, the author fails to allude to any other element within this framework.[46]

The absence of the rise on which the Temple stood becomes even more blatant later in the story, in Tobit's prayer in chapter 13. The detailed visual depiction of Jerusalem in this passage allows the reader to grasp the image of Jerusalem through the author's eyes. All other parts of the city seem to be present—houses, streets, gates, city walls, and towers—and, above all (in importance, not height), the Temple.[47] Only the Temple site is missing. If the various commentators are correct in their claim that the author bases his city plan on the biblical consolation prophecies, particularly that in Isaiah, our expectation of finding a mountain, to which Isaiah repeatedly refers, would become even greater.[48] Apparently, for the author of Tobit, Jerusalem did not include any significant "mountain." Palestine, Jerusalem, and the House of God feature prominently in this text, but no other element.

The author of the book of Judith, to mention another example, sets the story away from Jerusalem, but nevertheless binds the narrative very tightly to the city and the Temple. He perceives the advent of the Assyrians, the hostile element in the book, as a direct threat to Jerusalem and to "the Temple of the Lord their God." Judith, the protagonist, acts with the intention of protecting the city and the sanctuary. Thus the heroine's townspeople formulate her goal as "to glorify Israel and exalt Jerusalem," and her prayer expresses her prospectus with similar rubrics.[49] As is usual for Jews in the Second Temple period, the writer portrays Jerusalem as the center of Jewish experience—headed by a high priest, who also serves as the nation's leader, and containing only one inanimate element of value, namely, the Temple, which actually overshadows the city itself. But aside from various epithets that the author ascribes to the Temple, the only objects he mentions in connection with this institution are the altar and the sacred vessels.[50] No other element intrudes between the Temple and the city of Jerusalem. The hilly terrain of the region, well known to the author, peeks here and there from his descriptions (see n. 37), but it is not accorded any particular value.

A third example of this literary "omission" or neglect of the Temple Mount comes from the composition known as *4 Baruch*. The importance of this text for the present discussion lies in its relatively late date: references to King Agrippa and the destruction of the Temple (although unspecified as the event of 70 CE) have allowed scholars to establish the date of this document somewhere between mid-first century CE and 135 (the conclusion of the Bar Kokhba revolt).[51] The legendary plot, relating the departure from Jerusalem of Jeremiah and Baruch, the son of Neriah, just before the destruction of the First Temple and the concealment of the Temple vessels, is narrated against the backdrop of the city's landscape. It thus captures a picture of Jerusalem, whether realistic or imaginative, as perceived by a native author during the final decades of the Second Temple or thereafter (in a way, similar to that of Josephus Flavius who lived and wrote during the same time). The text offers not even the slightest hint that the Temple Mount functioned in any way in the worldview of the writer. He portrays the city of Jerusalem, with its hilly environs, city walls, markets, and gardens, in vivid colors, even though the gloom of the destruction of the Temple clouds them. The author does not omit the Temple, to be sure, elaborating on the inner sanctuary, the heikhal, as well as the innermost one, the Holy of Holies (the two rooms that comprise the structure of map 3: A), but pays no attention to the Temple Mount.[52] The only rise protruding from this text rests next to Agrippa's garden.

Non-Jewish sources dealing with Jerusalem further support this conclusion about the absence of the Temple Mount from the milieu of the Second Temple. A typical pagan visitor, shaped by Greco-Roman civilization, could certainly have grasped a conception that granted special value to a certain geographical feature, in this case a mountain. Although the idea of a "holy mountain" probably originated in the Orient, the Greeks and Romans embraced many mountains, such as Mount Olympus, widely known in ancient Greek mythology as "the home of the gods," as well as the Acropolis in Athens and *Capitolinus mons* in Rome.[53] The reputation of mountains in this realm would have made the notion of a "holy mountain" serving as a sacred foundation for a Jewish temple easy to detect. Yet the descriptions of Second Temple Jerusalem by non-Jews, whether in Greek or Latin, make no mention of such a mountain in Jerusalem. The same holds true for non-Jewish official documents concerning Jerusalem, such as the bill of rights granted to the Jews by Antiochus III. At the core of this certificate lies a recognition of the holiness of Jerusalem and the Temple, anchoring it in the laws of the Seleucid monarchy. But no indication of any mountain appears there. The "precinct of the Temple" that the document alludes to acquires its status from that of the Temple at its center.[54] Pagan literature renders a picture of Jerusalem very similar to the one preserved by Jewish texts—a holy city and a holy Temple, with no intervening element.

The one weakness of this argument about the lack of status of the Mount in Second Temple eyes is its reliance on the absence of evidence (the notorious *argumentum e silentio*). But two comparative arguments rectify this impediment. First, the nonexistence of the Temple Mount in Second Temple compositions stands out even more given that Jerusalem and the Temple receive immense exposure in those same sources. Second, its absence is sharpened by the frequent appearance of the Temple Mount in post–70 CE rabbinic literature. Were the

Temple Mount a significant factor in the eyes of Second Temple Jews, it might be expected to turn up as often as Jerusalem and the Temple and as frequently as the Mount itself in later periods. The comparative argument, then, especially when based on such a large and diverse corpus of sources as Second Temple literature, offsets the weakness of the argument from silence.

The Compound around the Temple

To complete the pattern of evidence on whether the Temple Mount constituted a particular category in Second Temple Jewish consciousness, one must examine the issue from another angel—the architectural viewpoint. How did Jews perceive the Temple's enclosure (map 3: D) in this era?

The Temple structure never stood alone. From its earliest days it included adjacent walled courtyards and buildings of many kinds (chambers, halls, meeting room, etc.).[55] Various authors applied different names to signify this multicomponent compound. Some labeled it according to the biblical term for "courtyard," whether in Hebrew (*ḥaṣer*) or in Greek (*aulē*); the Mishnah generally used the appellation *ʿazarah;* yet other writers drew on Greco-Hellenistic terminology, referring to the area by sundry designations common in temple vocabulary of the period *peribolos, temenos,* and sometimes, especially toward the end of the period, simply *hieron.*[56] In many cases, writers showed no consistency but rather interchanged these terms as they pleased. Josephus provides an extreme example of such a practice, applying all the terms alternately; a similar penchant may be found in other writers as well.

The enclosure around the Temple was bustling with diverse and vibrant activity. Some of this action naturally related to the Temple, such as the sale of sacrificial animals and the exchange of currency for the half-shekel levy. The site also attracted other activities that were not directly linked to the Temple. Sources such as Josephus or stories about Jesus and his disciples that were preserved in the Gospels and the book of Acts portray an array of colorful events, among them preachers giving sermons and individuals and groups decrying the regime. Some gathered there to study the Torah, while others came to close business deals. The legal system operated in the Temple precinct or nearby. The *Temple Scroll* from Qumran renders an elaborate literary description of the courtyards and expanses that surrounded the Temple, even if idealized and removed from reality.

But how did Jews view this architectural landscape surrounding the Temple; what role did it play in their consciousness, and how did it rank, if at all, in their worldview? Parallels from other places in the Roman world further enhance these questions. Greeks and Romans considered temples to be "the house of God," with entry forbidden to the populace. Laypeople gathered around the building, conducting rituals and ceremonies in front of it, where temple authorities usually placed the altar. This performance of religious activities in the area outside the Temple naturally raised the significance of this space—the *temenos,* as it was called in Greek—so that at times people assigned it holiness independent of that of the Temple itself.[57]

The Caesareum in the North African city of Cyrene offers a salient example of this phenomenon. Erected by Julius Caesar in 48–47 BCE, it comprised a rectangular precinct surrounded by colonnades and delimited on one side by a row of chambers, which later evolved into an impressive apsidal basilica, and by a notable entrance structure with a magnificent gate. The Cyreneian Caesareum preserved ancient traditions of holiness rooted in the Hellenistic period, but, more important for our purposes, it continuously functioned without any temple building at all until the second century CE, that is, for about 150 to 200 years.[58] Some striking similarities between the sacred compound in Cyrene and the enclosure around the Temple in Jerusalem as shaped by king Herod come to mind. Both precincts feature similar architectural elements— an encircling colonnade and a grand basilica along one side. Likewise, people associated both structures with ancient traditions (Mount Moriah, Ornan's threshing floor, in the case of the Jerusalem compound). It is therefore appropriate to ask whether the space around the Temple in Jerusalem had also become a separate entity, acquiring an independent category in people's minds, similar to some *temenē* in the Greco-Roman world.

Throughout most of the period, the compound enveloping the Jerusalem Temple did not attain any independent identity and was simply considered an integral part of the Temple itself. From a semantic standpoint, the various names given to this precinct—*ḥaṣer* (courtyard) in Hebrew or the Greek *peribolos* and *temenos*—describe a space that surrounds another architectural element. Grammatically, these designations are generally used in the construct state, that is, "the courtyard or *peribolos* of [a certain temple]," adjacent to and serving the central feature, the Temple. In such a formulation, then, the Temple functions as an architectural complex containing different components. Just as the altar, for example, operated as part of the Temple structure, so did the surrounding elements, the courtyards and galleries. This is not to suggest that all these parts shared an equal status or degree of holiness. A definite, hierarchical system calibrated them: the outer enclosure was not on a par with the inner court, and the inner court was not equivalent to the Holy of Holies. They were all, however, considered parts of a whole, which together formed the Temple.

It goes without saying that these spaces would be thought holy in one way or other. The author of 2 Maccabees calls them "hallowed precincts," and the *Temple Scroll* develops this sacredness to its fullest extent, designating the compound "holy courtyards" and elaborating on the halakhot (legal procedures) involving them.[59] Given that the expression "holy courtyards" had already appeared in the book of Isaiah (62:9), this comes as no surprise. It seems only natural that structures considered by the common view as part of the Temple should partake of its holiness. Indeed, many Second Temple texts configure this surrounding space as a sort of shield for the Temple. Thus, for example, the codes of purity that were (or at least were supposed to be) strictly enforced in these courts were meant to prevent any defilement from penetrating into the inner sanctuary. This is a far cry, however, from an independent status for the compound.

A case that further illustrates these claims comes from the Qumranic *Temple Scroll*.[60] Delineating his ideal Temple, the author of the scroll introduces an elaborate system of courtyards surrounding the Temple. Names and dimensions of these quads, as well as the halakhot involving them, take up a considerable portion of the scroll's text and therefore also of the attention of the scholars studying it. The obvious resemblance between certain statutes in the scroll involving the courtyards and rabbinic halakhot relating to the Temple Mount (see chapter 6) tempted scholars to conflate these two entities—the Temple courtyard in the scroll and the Temple Mount in rabbinic literature—and present them as practically identical. Based on these comparisons, some scholars went so far as to date the origin of the rabbinic Temple Mount laws in the pre-Herodian era (the days of the scroll).[61]

But it seems to me that, in the commotion surrounding the finding of the scroll and its initial study, some fundamental distinctions between the rabbinic Temple Mount and the scroll's courtyard went unnoticed. For one thing, from a terminological viewpoint, the *Temple Scroll*, although written in Hebrew just like the rabbinic material, never uses the appellation Temple Mount. This is not a mere detail, even though previous research has ignored it. If, as many scholars believe, the notion about the Temple Mount had indeed been created in an earlier time and the scroll actually voices it, then why is it not mentioned by name? And if the idea existed but under a different name, then the burden of proof is on those scholars who believe it is the same concept; they must explain what led to the change in name from "courtyards" in the *Temple Scroll* to Temple Mount in rabbinic literature. One must conclude that the author of the *Temple Scroll* was not familiar with the name Temple Mount.

Second, from a conceptual perspective (as many scholars noted), the scroll bases its description of the Temple as encompassing a schematic, symmetrical system of surrounding courtyards on the imaginary picture of the Temple in the visions of the book of Ezekiel. In fact, the roots of such a layout actually go back to the Pentateuch's arrangements of the camps of the tribes of Israel surrounding the Tabernacle in the Sinai Desert.[62] All this points toward the auxiliary nature of the scroll's courtyards in their relation to the Temple. Indeed, as mentioned earlier, both the semantics of the designation "courtyard" and its characteristics in such areas as ritual purification and temple worship, as formulated by the author of the scroll, indicate that he designed this space to serve the Temple at its center. The writer of this document channeled his efforts to safeguard the Temple's holiness into a schematic plan of symmetrical courtyards that protect the sacred. As scholars have shown, the substance of holiness, according to the scroll, spreads outward from the center and then transfers to Jerusalem as a whole.[63] That process also applies to all the areas around the Temple, including the courtyards. It is fair to conclude, therefore, that from the standpoint of the scroll the courtyards function as an integral part of the Temple complex, with no separate existence. The Temple Mount in rabbinic and early Christian literature, on the other hand, acquired an independent identity that ultimately stood without the Temple (see chapters 5 and 6).

All in all, we must not be misled by the similar squarish plan of the courtyards in the *Temple Scroll* and the later dimensions of the Temple Mount in the Mishnah; on every level these structures represent different entities. Just the same, despite the architectural similarity between the Herodian compound and Greco-Roman *temenē* such as the Caesareum in Cyrene, the structure in Jerusalem figured quite differently in the Jewish conception of space. For Jews the Temple was not subordinate to the areas surrounding it and did not derive its holiness from theirs. The opposite is true: the space surrounding the Temple was considered part of the Temple, and its status emanated entirely from that of the Temple.

A Mount in the Making

Two major events, set about 150 years apart during the Second Temple period, contributed to the creation of the physical structure we now call the Temple Mount. The first befell the Temple site sometime during the nine-year reign of the third Hasmonaean ruler Simeon (143–134 BCE). In what historians consider one of the great achievements of the relatively young independent Hasmonaean state, Simeon led the rebel Judean army in trouncing the Seleucid garrison that was stationed in Jerusalem in the mighty fortress known as the Acra. Situated in a strategic point, which made it practically invincible and, even more important, allowed the battalion deployed there to control the Temple site, this post posed a constant threat to Jerusalem and the Hasmonaean regime. According to Josephus, writing some two hundred years after the event, Simeon did not stop with the conquest of the citadel but strove to obliterate this military position entirely. Josephus goes on to describe how Simeon mustered the people to the task, which required three years of laborious exertion, day and night, until they entirely razed the ridge on which the Acra had stood and turned it into a plain. Closing his narrative, Josephus remarks on the significance of this act—elevating the Temple to preside over and above the city.[64]

Other sources also tell us that the Acra neighbored the Temple, allowing anyone who ruled it to dominate the Temple itself.[65] Without delving into the scholarly debate regarding the historical accuracy of Josephus's account, we glean from his report the great impression made by the conquest of the Acra and the traditions that developed in its wake—so illustrious that the people commemorated it in an official holiday, as recorded in the document known as the *Scroll of Fasting* (*Megillat taʿanit*).[66] In a similar vein, 1 Maccabees, although failing to mention the enterprise of flattening the hill, juxtaposes the conquest of the Acra to the fortification of the Temple as if they were two sides of one coin.[67]

Another three generations would pass before the Temple Mount precinct would acquire its final shape. One man, King Herod (37–4 BCE), more than anyone else contributed to the present form of the compound.[68] Herod embarked on a large-scale project meant not only to beautify and glorify Jerusalem's Temple but mainly to enlarge its size, so it would accommodate the multitudes of pilgrims who were streaming to Jerusalem in those days. In this endeavor, which extended beyond his lifetime, Herod expanded (and actually rebuilt) both the Temple building and the area around it, doubling the measurements of the enclosure and converting it into the largest temple complex in the eastern part of the Roman Empire at the time (see map 3).

Since the nineteenth century archaeologists have been toiling to document the remnants of Herod's architectural venture. Some of them, mainly in the nineteenth century, managed to breach the tight Muslim security that enveloped these hallowed grounds, whether with or without permission, and have contributed significantly to our understanding of the site. These pioneers were followed by present-day archaeologists who performed systematic excavations all along the external face of the walls—the French in the north and the Israelis in the west and the south.

Based on this century and a half of archaeological effort, scholars now agree that Herod's construction project in the Temple and its surroundings radically altered the physical reality encountered by residents of and visitors to Jerusalem. Three considerations substantiate this claim. First, from a comparative point of view, the premises of the Herodian compound considerably exceeded both what preceded it in Jerusalem and other contemporary temple precincts throughout the Roman Empire. The nearly thirty-six acres of this precinct rank it as the largest temple enclosure of its time (matching the size of about twenty-seven football fields). Scholars tend to compare it with the huge temple complexes in the Orient—the temple enclosure of Bel at Palmyra and the Jupiter compound in Damascus—or those in the Athenian Acropolis and in Olympia. But Herod's compound was the largest of all.[69]

Second, from a topographical perspective, in order to arrive at such immense proportions, Herod's architects and builders had to remold the contours of the terrain, thus dramatically transforming the surrounding landscape. North of the hill on which the Temple stood, they filled in the creek that had run into the Kidron Valley to the east (see map 1). They also diverted the ravine of the so-called Tyropoeon Valley, which marked the western edge of the Temple's hill, and whose channel flowed from northwest to southeast. To the north and south, they extended the mountain's limits by hundreds of feet, leaving only the eastern wall untouched, probably because of the Kidron Valley's steepness, which made any expansion on this side impossible. The colossal retaining walls that stand to this day, silent remnants of that astounding project, delimited the added territory. Inside, Herod's engineers designed a network of branched arches—traces of which may also be seen today on the southeast corner of the compound (known as Solomon's Stables; fig. 4)—and filled some of

Fig. 4. The so-called Solomon's Stables (here in a late nineteenth-century photograph) are actually subterranean halls and water reservoirs at the southeast corner of the Temple Mount precinct. They represent some of the best-preserved remnants of Herod's construction project that was meant to extend the enclosure around the Temple. Note the typically Herodian ashlars with the carefully smoothed surfaces and drafted margins that support the vaulted ceiling. These arches allowed the flattening of the surface above them with huge stone slabs, which then created the grounds of the Temple compound. From the Library of Congress, Prints & Photographs Division, G. Eric and Edith Matson Photograph Collection, online catalog, reproduction number LC-M36-384.

the empty spaces with soil. In this way, they leveled the compound and paved its surface. A huge flat platform was created. When done, Herod project established an artificial topographic entity in the shape of a trapezoid, of an area and size never before seen in Jerusalem (map 3).

Finally, from an architectural standpoint, Herod's project not only strengthened and glamorized the edifice of the Temple but also reshaped it altogether. Both Josephus and some rabbinic traditions provide a lengthy description— congruent in many ways, incompatible in others—of this structure, which later the Romans entirely obliterated in 70 CE.[70] It has been justly remarked by modern scholars that these depictions show Herod to be rebuilding a completely new structure.

Observers passing by repeatedly admired the majesty of the building. Indeed, Josephus's poetic description in book 5 of *The Jewish War* conjures up a breathtaking sight: the rays of the sun breaking against the gold leaf plating on the front of the Temple and blending with the alabaster whiteness of the stones to resemble a snowy mountain. Rumors about the Temple's beauty and prestige interspersed far beyond the boundaries of Palestine—its splendor acknowledged even by pagan writers of those days, such as Tacitus, in the famous fragment preserved in the Chronicles of Sulpicius Severus. Although a hostile writer embracing the Temple's magnificence to further his own ends, Tacitus still described the building as "more remarkable than any other human work."[71] On the other end of the ideological spectrum, a Talmudic statement reflects the same admiration: "Anyone who did not see Herod's building never saw a beautiful building in his life."[72]

Even more significantly in terms of the public's perception, the scheme carried out by Herod also transformed the entire surrounding area. With the completion of the project, colonnades ornamented the huge open courts that encircled the Temple, and two massive buildings sheltered the sanctuary: to the south, Herod's royal basilica, which Josephus considered the most spectacular building on the face of the earth; and to the north, the Antonia, a combination of fortress and palace, which held the entire area in thrall (see map 3).[73] Archaeological excavations show that the area adjacent to the Temple compound also received a momentous facelift during Herod's project. The enormous walls of the precinct, made of mammoth stones, flattened and smoothed, and decorated with pilasters, conveyed an impression of homogeneous and sturdy texture. Outside, to the west of the enclosure a new urban multiplex came into being: avenues up to seventy-five feet wide were paved with large stones and bordered with curbstones; beneath the streets lay a drainage and sewage system, and above them piazzas, fabulous stairwells, and—a rare sight before Herod's time—an impressive interchange that sat atop arches, leading to the royal basilica.[74] Such an urban enterprise had no equal in the Roman Near East of those days.

This monumental architectural accomplishment was superimposed on the likewise newly created topography, and together—in a long and tortuous process over a few decades[75]—they altered the landscape of Jerusalem. Change was flung at a population unaccustomed to such enormous dimensions, radically transforming the physical reality in which they lived. It is only natural, then, to ask whether this grandiose creation left its mark on their innermost consciousness. The following discussion attempts to trace such changes of perception—to unveil the seeds of the Temple Mount conception.

Spinning Perceptions: Resuscitated Imagery and Innovative Conceptualization

1 Maccabees and Simeon's Fortifications

1 Maccabees constitutes an exception to the rule, that Second Temple sources remained generally oblivious of a physical and conceptual entity associated with the mountain of the Temple. Written at the height of the Hasmonaean dynasty in the second half of the second century BCE (or according to some scholars some decades later) and situated at the hub of Jewish experience, this text generally follows the standard representations of Jerusalem during this period. For the most part, the author accentuates the dual centrality and exclusivity of city and Temple. Thus, for example, chapter 1 presents these two elements as related to each other without any other mediating figure. In this context, the writer assigns the area around the Temple no independent status but simply calls it "[the space] encircling the sanctuary."[76] In the same vein, a poem the author incorporates into his narrative laments the occupation of Jerusalem and the sanctuary but fails to mention any additional structure. In other places where he refers to the site of the altar, the author alternates its location between Jerusalem and the Temple, as if no other space could intervene between them.[77] He designates the architectural elements flanking the Temple as *aulē*—(the Temple) courtyard—in accordance with the terminology of the Torah.[78]

But these descriptions do not present the whole picture of 1 Maccabees. In several instances the author introduces a new, third factor into Jerusalem's landscape. Occasionally, he calls this element by the traditional appellation Mount Zion, clearly to mark the venue of the Temple. For example, when Judas Maccabeus, after a string of victories over the Seleucid army, proposes going up (the Greek verb *anabainein*) and purifying the Temple, the narrative recounts the people climbing Mount Zion and concludes with the Temple coming into sight before them as they reach its top. Alluding to the same scenery, the story relates that Judas and his men, after cleansing the Temple, went on to fortify Mount Zion with a wall and towers, and a little later, when conveying this incident as told to Antiochus by a messenger, the narrator replaces "Mount Zion" with "the Temple."[79] Similarly, when Judas returns from his victorious journey to Transjordan, they all ascend to offer sacrifices on Mount Zion; on another occasion, Nicanor goes up to Mount Zion, where the priests come out to greet him from the Temple; further on, we read about a pact between the people and Simeon inscribed on a pillar on Mount Zion as a memorial, with the same place later being called the compound (*peribolos*) of the Temple.[80] All these passages demonstrate that in the author's mind Mount Zion registered as the broad open area on which the Temple stood.[81]

The highlight of this text, from the viewpoint of the present study, is the appearance of the Greek appellation *to oros tou oikou*—literally "the Mount of the House"—a precise translation of the Hebrew *har ha-bayit,* the Temple Mount. In a passage dealing with the ritual cleansing of the Temple by Judas Maccabeus and his followers, the text voices Judas's concern that the Temple should be purified, then embarks on a detailed report of how this was carried out. The account progresses from the painful shock the men felt upon discovering the devastation in the Temple to the measures they undertook to restore the place to its previous glory. One of their acts included tearing down the sacrificial altar that the Seleucids violated and burying its stones "until a prophet will come to tell us what to do with them." The place where they stored the stones is called Temple Mount.[82] This passage, then, features the one and only time in the entire Second Temple literature where the exact expression Temple Mount appears.

This appellation conforms to the conceptual framework reflected in other parts of 1 Maccabees, which, as noted, reserves a special category for the site of the Temple and presents this location in mountain imagery. Thus, terminologically and conceptually, 1 Maccabees strikes a different note from other Second Temple works discussed in this chapter. This phenomenon finds no parallel until the very end of the Second Temple period.

What is the significance of this trend in 1 Maccabees to the study of the Temple Mount? A close reading of the passage in question—the purification story in chapter 4—seems to suggest that the rubric "Temple Mount" does not fit well into this narrative. The story begins with the ascent to "Mount Zion" (4:37) and ends with the actual purification and fortification of Mount Zion (59). As in the rest of the book, the Temple in this schema stands on top of Mount Zion. The narrator describes the various elements associated with the Temple in great detail—from the inner sanctuary, through the chambers and courtyards, to the sacred vessels that were located within or around the sanctuary. It is not clear where the Temple Mount fits into this picture. Is it synonymous with Mount Zion? If so, why does the writer deviate from his normal habit to maintain one designation per location throughout an entire literary pericope? Moreover, the author refrains from enumerating the Temple Mount in the list of places that were defiled (38) or purified (48), which suggests that he did not consider this entity sacred and thus capable of defilement and purification. How then did this unusual term end up in the story?

Modern commentators on 1 Maccabees have noted that the author's style, vocabulary, and imagery rely a great deal on the books that later came to be the Hebrew Bible.[83] Goldstein has shown that the symbolism of destruction at the beginning of chapter 4 hinges on Psalms 74.[84] Yet he overlooks the single appearance of the term Temple Mount and therefore fails to trace its source. It seems to me that the author of 1 Maccabees borrowed this appellation from another biblical sequence, namely, Micah 3:12.[85]

The primary evidence for this claim stems from the use of the "thicket" motif in verse 38 as an image of ruin. This verse reads as a sort of short poem,[86] depicting the wreckage witnessed by Judas's men as follows: "And they saw the sanctuary desolate, the altar profaned, and the gates burned; and in the courts they saw bushes sprung up as a thicket, or as on one of the mountains; they also saw the chambers of the priests in ruins." I concur with Goldstein's brilliant suggestion that the author borrowed the image of "bushes" from Genesis 22:13—the binding of Isaac story—and that the same source also inspired the phrase "on one of the mountains." But what is the source of "thicket" as a metaphor for destruction? The image of a "thicket," the Greek *drymos* translating the Hebrew *yaʿar*, does emerge in Psalms 74:5, but not as a simile of ruin. On the contrary, it communicates the prosperity cut down by the axes of the enemy. In general, although forests, like other constituents of nature, appear in many literary representations of the Bible, only rarely do they symbolize ruin.[87]

Indeed, the only biblical passage I am familiar with in which the image of a thicket functions as a metaphor for destruction is Micah 3:12: "Therefore shall Zion for your sake be plowed as a field, and Jerusalem shall become heaps, and the mountain of the house as a wooded [thicket; the same word in Greek is used for both—*drymos*] height." Evidently, this verse stirred audiences and impressed other writers, who regularly incorporated its imagery and vocabulary into their own depictions of devastations. It is one of the few verses explicitly quoted by another First Temple text, in Jeremiah 26:18. Earlier in this chapter I discussed another source that invokes it—the Qumran scroll known as *Joseph's Prayer*. Yet another allusion to it occurs in the well-known rabbinic story about R. ʿAkiva's visit to the Temple Mount (discussed in the introduction).

It would thus seem that when the author of 1 Maccabees utilized the thicket as an image of wreckage, he also had Micah 3:12 in mind. And if so, the source for the uncommon (at the time) appellation Temple Mount almost suggests itself. After all, the only known biblical text where this particular term appears is Micah 3:12. According to this reconstruction, the author of 1 Maccabees, like many other writers in his time, depended on earlier "biblical" texts for his literary conventions, "browsing" through earlier portrayals of demolition and mining them for phrases and images for his prose. Having imported the figure of the "thicket" from Micah 3:12 to illustrate ruin and devastation, he also borrowed another term from the same place, namely the Temple Mount. But incorporating this phrase into his narrative left it estranged from other elements in the story.

Nevertheless, even if I am right that the author of 1 Maccabees imported the term Temple Mount from the book of Micah, there is no denying that he makes generous use throughout the book of mountain images to depict the Temple's location. Two factors need to be considered here. On the level of significance, clearly the author of 1 Maccabees does not ascribe any particular value to this site, even though he mentions it more than once. The preceding literary analysis demonstrates the site's lack of status in the spatial organization of chapter 4, and the same holds true for other references to the site throughout the book. In all these instances, the mountain simply signifies the site where the Temple stood in the geographical and physical sense. This marks an essential difference between the attitude toward the Mount expressed in 1 Maccabees and the one that developed at the end of the Second Temple period and thereafter, according to which the Temple Mount figures independently and prominently, at times even overshadowing the Temple.

On the level of consciousness, the rising awareness of the location of the Temple in 1 Maccabees and its representation as a mountain corresponds to the big changes that transpired at the site in the wake of Simeon's achievements in Jerusalem. The fact that 1 Maccabees concludes with John Hyrcanus's rise to power and the relative length of its description of Simeon's reign connotes that the author lived during the time of Simeon and produced the text shortly after his death, in the early days of John.[88] Two-thirds of the references in 1 Maccabees dealing with the topographical elevation on which the Temple stood, under various names, concern its fortification (six explicit and two implicit references to the fortification out of twelve occurrences of the Temple site).[89] Read together, these passages narrate the various phases of the site's "history" as they were registered in the mind of the author: Judas Maccabeus encircled the mountain with a wall and towers; these were shattered during the reign of Antiochus V; Jonathan refortified the mountain; finally, the story hits its high point in the days of Simeon, who not only strengthened the Mount 's defenses but also decimated the dominating citadel of the Acra.

Organizing the narrative in this way, the author renders a picture of the mountain as a fortified entity. This depiction echoes Simeon's deeds. His military achievements and subsequent actions radically transformed the topographical design of the area as viewed by residents of Jerusalem. When he and his forces obliterated the threatening Acra and extricated the Temple from its oppressive authority, they also carved a new landscape. Inevitably, a new reality was conceived. This transformation, I argue, impacted the writing of 1 Maccabees about the Temple site. The new physical texture induced the author's perception of the geographical setting and introduced the area's image—its strength and fortified status—into his worldview.

The choice of terminology to describe the place—as Mount Zion, maybe the Holy Mount (see n. 81), and once as the Temple Mount—is entirely understandable. When people encounter a reality bathed in unfamiliar glamour, they often turn to their foundation texts, those literary cornerstones that fuel their existence, in search of prescriptions and vocabulary that will define this new experience. In the present case it was the Bible (or rather the Scriptures that later became the Bible) from which the author of 1 Maccabees retrieved his formulae; this is how the "Mount" in 1 Maccabees was fashioned. From his current perspective, the author looked at his past and painted it in the colors appropriate to his period. In his mind, the physical entity crystallized by Simeon's fortifications had always existed.

But even if one does not accept these explanations for the terminology used in 1 Maccabees, it is still clear that this book represents the exception that proves the rule. The attention its author pays to the rise on which the Temple stood remains unparalleled until near the end of the Second Temple period. Apparently, the conceptual processes instigated by the deeds of Simeon, as reflected in this text, did not have a wide impact. 1 Maccabees itself does not attribute any value to the Mount, although it does recognize it as a mighty, physical entity. Indeed, for another two hundred years none of the surviving sources ascribed any substantial significance to the location of the Temple in and of itself, nor do they ever return to the appellation Temple Mount. 1 Maccabees provides a preview of the later story, a glimpse into the conceptual dynamics, embracing physical reality and the perceptions evolving around them, that in the long run configured the image of the Temple Mount.

Josephus and the Herodian Compound

The books of Josephus provide a rare opportunity to investigate the formation of the Temple Mount imagery and its fusion into the consciousness of the time. Writing in the decades subsequent to the destruction of the Temple in 70 CE and residing in Jerusalem for most of his life before that, Josephus represents a local voice from Jerusalem just before the curtain fell on the Second Temple. As a young priest, this author strolled the Herodian compound on a daily basis. As a contemporary, he was immersed in the experiences of his time, be they political, cultural, or religious. Can we, therefore, locate in Josephus any traces of the evolving conceptuality of the Temple Mount? Map 3 offers a visual sense of what is involved in this question.

Herod's building endeavor defined four distinctive spaces in Jerusalem:

1. The inner Temple structure (map 3: A). Generally called *heikhal* (shrine) in Hebrew or sometimes simply *bayit* (house), and in corresponding Greek terms *naos* or occasionally also *oikos* (house), it featured a rectangular edifice made of three rooms: the inner Holy of Holies, also labeled by the biblical designation *devir;* to its east the "Holy," frequently also called *heikhal;* and, east of these two, functioning as a palatial entrance, the *ʾulam* (hall).[90]

2. The broader Temple structure (3: B, C). It consisted of an amalgamation of courtyards, halls, and chambers around the inner Temple (3: A). The structure that people generally identified as "the Temple"— *miqdash* in Hebrew and *hieron* in Greek—composed three elements: the Temple, priestly and Israelite courts, and the women's court (3: A, B, C). A strong and towering wall enclosed this space, separating it from the outer areas and defining it as a discrete unit. Two architectural features further enhanced its aloofness. A rampart in the shape of a staircase climbed from the outer platform and encircled the exterior of the wall around the courtyards. On the outer face of the rampart a low stone fence bore multilingual inscriptions that banned the entrance of non-Jews into this area (see fig. 5). A long list of halakhot, mainly laws of ritual purity, further differentiated the Temple, that is, the shrine and its surrounding courts, from the larger areas surrounding them.[91]

3. The huge Herodian compound (3: D). Sprawling around the Temple, it separated the Temple from the city of Jerusalem. The Mishnah refers to this enclosure as "Temple Mount," which remains its name to this very day.

4. The city of Jerusalem (3: E) extended to the south, west, and north sides of the compound.

So the question runs as follows: Did the precinct built by Herod around the Temple occupy any substantial, independent category in Josephus's mind? The answer to this question is not clear-cut. On one hand, Josephus seems in many respects to maintain the conventional worldview of Second Temple Jews about Jerusalem and its Temple. His writings share the widely accepted spatial paradigms of his predecessors, which center on Jerusalem and the Temple and overlook other elements within the urban framework of the city. On the other hand, here and there Josephus deviates from the common ground of Second Temple texts, endorsing an unprecedented perception of the area around the Temple. Such references attest to the beginnings of a new conceptualization of space in Jerusalem.

Two major characteristics of the way Jews viewed Jerusalem and its Temple throughout the Second Temple period continue to resonate widely in the writings of Josephus as well. He displays an intimate acquaintance with both the hilly topography of Jerusalem's terrain and the architectural layout—courtyards, chambers, and the like—that enveloped the Temple. At the same time, for the most part, like all of his contemporaries, he does not attribute any particular value to the rise on which the Temple stood, nor does he grant the architectural structures around the Temple any independent status.

Josephus describes Jerusalem as "built on two hills separated by a central valley."[92] Accordingly, one of the hills, which emerges from time to time in his narrative, functions as the natural substructure of the Temple. Indeed, in a passage dealing with the Temple, Josephus alludes to this hill, located east of the city (see map 1), enumerating its physical features—slopes and rocky texture—and fixing the Temple on its peak. On another occasion, he adds another characteristic by detailing the invincibility of this hill.[93]

But is this enough to show that this topographical elevation acquired any special status in the writer's worldview? Definitely not. None of these references contains the least hint of anything beyond innocent communication of basic geographic inventory. As a resident of Jerusalem, Josephus was well aware of its hilly profile. Just as he knew (or thought he knew) to situate the Acra citadel, long gone by his time, on one of the city's hills or locate the northern neighborhoods of Jerusalem on the hill of Bezetha, or just as he recognized other peaks in the area, such as Mount of Olives and Givʿat Shaʾul,[94] so he also acknowledged that the Temple stood on a rise. But communicating such knowledge is a long way from attributing any conceptual significance to any of these hills or mountains.

Furthermore, Josephus passes over the site's biblical names, such as Mount Zion, which never appears in any of his writings. A comparison with 1 Maccabees further elucidates the significance of this detail. Its author repeatedly used the appellation Mount Zion, alongside his emphasis on the fortifications of the site. Yet Josephus's paraphrases of this material from 1 Maccabees systematically fail to include the term Mount Zion.[95] In the same vein, Josephus evidently did not attach the same importance as did the author of 1 Maccabees to the Hasmonaean fortifications of the site; he entirely omits the passage in 1 Maccabees that describes in great detail Simeon's project of fortifying Mount Zion. Similarly, when Josephus accounts for the fortifications of Mount Zion that 1 Maccabees assigns to Judas Maccabeus, he shifts them to the city of Jerusalem.[96]

Additional evidence for the insignificance of the mount on which the Temple stood in the eyes of Josephus comes from his references to the Samaritan temple and its comparison with the Temple in Jerusalem. Josephus consistently links the Samaritan sanctuary with the mountain on which it stood, Mount Gerizim. When he juxtaposes this temple with the Temple in Jerusalem, he cites Mount Gerizim as the location of the Samaritan temple and compares it with the city of Jerusalem as the place of the Jewish one.[97] The asymmetry in this equation—on one side a mountain, and on the other a city—suggests that from Josephus's point of view Jerusalem's landscape lacks a feature parallel to the one on which the Samaritan temple stood; unlike the Samaritan case no special mountain functioned in Jerusalem. This formula, in which Mount Gerizim counters the city of Jerusalem, is not unique to Josephus; it appears in 2 Maccabees as well as in the Gospel of John.[98] Apparently this paradigm reflects a prevalent mind-set of Second Temple Jews, in which the elevation on which the Temple in Jerusalem stood, in contrast to Mount Gerizim, attained no conceptual category.

Similar tendencies underline Josephus's attitude toward the architectural structures that surrounded the Temple. Here too his picture corresponds to the general view of Second Temple Jews, with one difference: Herod considerably enlarged the compound and added to it new architectural units. These structures regularly turn up in Josephus's writings. But essentially, however, he remains faithful to the common Second Temple perception of the area. Reminiscent of all the texts from that era, Josephus considers the complex around the Temple an integral part of the Temple itself. To be sure, he, like his predecessors, calibrates the various units in the complex in regard to their holiness or the ritual purity required to enter them, but he nevertheless presents them as parts of one whole.

The terminology Josephus applies to the Temple and the areas adjacent to it further supports this claim. Here too Josephus follows in the footsteps of other Second Temple authors, borrowing his Temple vocabulary from either the biblical or Hellenistic lexicons. For the most part he relies on the terms prevalent among his Greek-speaking audience, such as *naos* (shrine) or *hieron* (temple), but he also avails himself of biblical terms, such as *hagios* (sacred) or *aulē* (court), and occasionally also the Hellenistic designations for temple precincts, *peribolos* or *temenos* (both meaning compound).[99]

The view of some modern scholars, that the Greek *hieron* in Josephus (as well as in the New Testament) is tantamount to the Hebrew *har ha-bayit*—Temple Mount—remains untenable.[100] Not only did Josephus describe the *hieron* as "seated on a strong hill"[101] (an element on top of a mountain cannot be the mountain itself), but, as I shall now demonstrate, he considered *hieron* to be the Temple itself.

On the one hand, *hieron* for Josephus often denotes the huge platform and open courts that were appended to the Temple during the Herodian project (3: D);[102] but, on the other, further instances of this term indicate that Josephus actually considered it to signify the Temple itself (3: A, B, C). For example, on several occasions Josephus presents the *hieron* as a nucleus structure and notes that other areas—mainly open courts—encircle it.[103] Such an organization of the Temple space rules out the possibility that the *hieron* itself be identified as these contiguous areas.

The same orientation that identifies the *hieron* as the structure of the Temple reverberates in the famous inscription barring non-Jews from entering the Temple complex, copies of which (only one of them complete) were unearthed in Jerusalem (fig.5). The complete version, which was discovered in the nineteenth century and published by Clermont-Ganneau, forbids Gentiles (literally, those from another nation) from entering "to the inside of the divider that encircles the Temple [*hieron*] and to the [inner] courtyard."[104] This clause implies that a divider adjoined the *hieron* on its outer face. Such a divider corresponds to the description of the area in the Mishnah and in Josephus in which a stepped ascent known as the rampart separated the Temple (3: A, B, C) from the outer compound (3: D), and encircling the rampart was a small dividing wall displaying these inscriptions. Such arrangement of the area constitutes clear evidence that in the mind of the writer of the inscription, the *hieron* occupied the space inside the dividing wall and the rampart, which in turn establishes it as the Temple structure and not as the outer platform of the compound. Meant to direct the traffic in the Temple area, such inscriptions, like today's road signs and billboards, almost certainly reflect everyday language as well as common perceptions in Second Temple Jerusalem.

Other references in the books of Josephus also sustain the identification of *hieron* with the Temple structure. In one place it is presented as the destination to which people send priestly gifts and tithes, obviously intended for the Temple, and in another as the location for offering animal sacrifices.[105] Likewise, Josephus depicts the destruction of the Temple as the burning and demolition of the *hieron,* just as in many instances he also labels other temples by this very same term.[106]

It seems to me that a proper explanation for this seemingly inconsistent usage in Josephus—in which on different occasions both the Temple structure exclusively (map 3: A, B, C) and the compound around it (D) are named *hieron*—derives from the way physical reality was engraved in the common worldview of those days. In Josephus's mind, *hieron* signified the Temple, but he also considered the areas surrounding it, the Herodian compound, to be part of that Temple. The assorted architectural pieces of the Temple complex united in his consciousness into one ensemble, the Temple. Such a mind-set allowed him to alternate between them and call two different structures by the same name.

More proof for this proposition comes from a careful reading of the passages in which Josephus delineates the various spaces that compose the Temple and its surroundings. He employs the adverbs "inner" and "outer" to differentiate between them and, at other times, itemizes them as first, second, and third, showing that they register in his mind as one entity composed of several units.[107] Indeed, anyone who referred to the large plaza built by Herod as "the outer *hieron* [Temple]" could by the same token dub the inner shrine "the holy *hieron,*" as Josephus was indeed inclined to do.[108] The *hieron* in these literary

Fig. 5. A Greek inscription marking the line in the Temple compound beyond which non-Jews are prohibited to enter (the word *hieron* can be seen a bit after the beginning of the third line, and it clearly signifies the structure of the temple itself). From Israel Antiquities Authority Archives: British Mandate Record Files: File 89. Courtesy of Israel Antiquities Authority.

sequences stands for the whole, while all the other areas—the halls, the chambers, the courtyards, and even the shrine itself—are assembled as its parts.

All this evidence comes to show that *hieron* in the writings of Josephus stands not for the Temple Mount but for the Temple. The very fact that Josephus called the compound by the same name as the Temple testifies that to him this structure did not attain independent status. It was merely part of the Temple. Herod increased the size of the Temple greatly as well as amplifying its compound, but Josephus continues to consider them organic parts of one whole.

Thus, from both topographic and architectural perspectives, Josephus's spatial conceptualization of the Temple and its surroundings adheres to prevalent Second Temple notions. Just as prior to the days of Herod, two elements dominated people's consciousness—namely, Jerusalem and the Temple itself, with the Temple courtyards and the other adjacent elements viewed as merely parts of the Temple—so it was for Josephus. The wide, and at times convoluted, array of terms and epithets he uses to mark the various components of this architectural complex reflects the growth that resulted from Herod's construction project. But this expansion does not necessarily imply an immediate change in people's perception of it, which in fact remained largely the same as before. Apparently, conceptual processes take much longer than physical ones.

The Seeds of the Temple Mount

The conclusions drawn thus far, however, are only partially valid. A closer look at Josephus's narrative reveals the beginnings of a conceptual change. Here are two examples.

In his *Jewish War* Josephus devotes substantial effort to describe the atrocities committed in the civil turmoil that raged within the walls of Jerusalem during the Great Revolt (66–70 CE). Toward the end of this detailed account, the author includes a short quasi-prophetic passage whereby he views these events as foreshadowing the imminent catastrophe of the destruction: "For there was an ancient saying of inspired men that the city would be taken and the holiest of all [the Temple] burnt to the ground by right of war, if and when it should be visited by sedition and native hands should be the first to defile God's precinct [literally, *temenos* of God]."[109] The closing line of this prophecy anticipates the defilement of the area around the Temple, for which the author uses the Greek term *temenos* (precinct or compound), by some local residents. Two aspects of this passage set it apart from other presentations of the Temple precincts. First, Josephus calls the area by the unorthodox term "the *temenos* of God." Usual formulations referring to Jerusalem's Temple subordinate the *temenos* to the Temple, not to God. In Josephus's expression "*temenos* of God," however, the Temple itself loses its central role, and the compound is directly partnered with the source of holiness.

The second aspect concerns the mind-set reflected in this passage. The two parts of the prophecy together display three physical factors. One part features the city of Jerusalem and the "holiest of all," the Temple; the other exhibits the *temenos* (compound) of God. In Josephus's formulation, the terrible events defiled only the compound. One would think that any damage to the compound would have a direct impact on the Temple, but had this been the case, Josephus would have written something like "local hands defiled the Temple" or "defiled the compound of the Temple." Such phraseology would have corresponded to the common Second Temple outlook that focused on the Temple and perceived the compound as ancillary and individually insignificant. In the eyes of Josephus, however, spiritual and moral impairments to the compound bear their own negative weight and may at the end of the "prophetic ledger" bring tragedy upon the perpetrators as well as upon the Temple and the city as a whole. To the best of my knowledge, this marks the first time that a writer of the Second Temple period attributes independent value to the area surrounding the Temple, which plays a self-sufficient literary role. Consciousness and terminology thus go hand in hand. The appearance of a new attitude brought forth a new term—the phrase "*temenos* of God."

From where did Josephus retrieve this new expression? And, even harder to answer, how did the new mind-set reflected here come into being? Two sources of influence may be suggested for the terminology. Presumably, biblical glossary, known to be a major inspiration for Second Temple writers, was at work here too. Biblical expressions such as "the Lord's courtyards" or "God's courtyards" could have had an indirect impact on Josephus's choice of vocabulary even if they were never translated as *temenos* (indeed, *temenos* never appears in the Septuagint at all in reference to the Temple in Jerusalem).[110]

Another stimulus stemmed from the cultural environment of the Hellenistic-Roman world. Within the semantic field of pagan temples, the terms *temenos* and its Latin equivalent, *area sacra,* circulated widely and many writers frequently ascribed them to a particular god.[111] The idiom "compound of god," where god stands for a pagan deity, occurs in Greek literature from the earliest times; Aristophanes used it in one of his comedies as early as the fourth century BCE.[112] Several decades before Josephus, Diodorus of Sicily applied it to the sanctuary of Poseidon, and several decades after him, the Macedonian rhetorician Polyaenus included it in his speeches in regard to Artemis. The author of the fifth book of the *Sibylline Oracles,* a Jewish contemporary of Josephus, drew on the same locution in his discussion of the ideal future Temple of the Jewish God that would be erected in Egypt. The historian Cassius Dio, in the late second century, used the same phrase, whether intentionally or coincidentally, with reference to the Jewish Temple in Jerusalem.[113]

Arguably, Josephus was well acquainted with the contemporary Greco-Roman lexicon, as attested by the many *temenē* he mentions. Sometimes he subordinates the compound to the temple at its center, but on other occasions he presents the enclosure alone for example, when writing about the precinct of Peace in Rome.[114] Thus, clearly Josephus did not create the expression "compound of God" out of whole cloth. Nevertheless, this derivativeness does not lessen the novelty of his unprecedented decision to apply the phrase and the spatial paradigm that comes with it to the landscape in Jerusalem. The innovation becomes even greater if we consider the conceptual aspect as well, since Second Temple Jews perceived the physical layout of Jerusalem as modeled on two features, the city and the Temple. Josephus here deviates from this norm by adding a third element—the compound—without attaching it to the Temple at its center and even endowing it with its own name. It seems to me that these measures amount to the beginnings of a new conceptualization of space.

A second example emerges at the height of book 6 of *The Jewish War,* in a passage recounting the burning of the Temple, which in many ways serves as the climax of Josephus's entire literary enterprise.[115] Epic clues strewn throughout the narrative lead the plot toward this tragic end, and when it arrives, the story pauses for a moment. Following a common literary (rhetoric) pattern of his time, Josephus creates a moment of drama by cutting off the flow of the story, as if to freeze the sequence of events and allow the reader to appreciate the enormity of the catastrophe before being drawn into the dreadful swirl. To establish this suspension, he introduces two segments immediately after his report of the burning of the Temple; these do not continue the narrative but arrest it by refocusing on what has just happened. The two passages differ in nature and content. While the first (265–70) completely swerves from the battlefield and expresses Josephus's sentimental and historical reflections, the second (271–76) returns to the stormy scene created by the conflagration and presents a vivid, hair-raising depiction of those moments. This second pas-

sage is an awe-inspiring composition intended to eternalize a particular moment and etch it on the reader's soul. The vivid descriptions are designed to
arouse readers' emotions, to make them feel the wall of fire and hear the cacophony of sounds.

Analyzing this passage will help clarify the development of the Temple
Mount image and its conception. Here is the full text (with my subheads):

I. The dead

While the shrine blazed, the victors plundered everything that fell in their way
and slaughtered wholesale all who were caught. No pity was shown for age, no
reverence for rank; children and graybeards, laity and priests, alike were massa-
cred; every class was pursued and encompassed in the grasp of war, whether sup-
pliants for mercy or offering resistance.

II. The fire

The roar of the flames streaming far and wide mingled with the groans of the
falling victims; and, owing to the height of the hill and the mass of the burning
pile, one would have thought that the whole city was ablaze.

III. The outcry

And then the din—nothing more deafening or appalling could be conceived
than that. There were the war cries of the Roman legions sweeping onward in the
mass, the howls of the rebels encircled by fire and sword, the rush of the people,
who, cut off above, fled panic-stricken only to fall into the arms of the foe, and
their shrieks as they met their fate, while the cries on the hill were blended with
those of the multitude in the city below; and now many who were emaciated and
tongue-tied from starvation, when they beheld the shrine on fire, gathered
strength once more for lamentation and wailing. Peraea and the surrounding
mountains contributed their echoes, deepening the din.

IV. The dead

But yet more awful than the uproar were the sufferings. You would indeed have
thought that the hill of the temple was boiling over from its base, being every-
where one mass of flame, but yet that the stream of blood was more copious than
the flames and the slain more numerous than the slayers. For the ground was
nowhere visible through the corpses; and the soldiers had to clamber over heaps
of bodies in pursuit of fugitives.

This excerpt consists of four sections. Part I focuses on the people of Jerusalem,
commencing with their unfortunate fate as they were slaughtered by the Romans in the wake of the failed rebellion and then detailing the various dead.

Part II delivers a harsh portrayal of the conflagration. The third part orchestrates the cacophony of noise: the din opens this section and brings it to an end. This horrific chorus includes battle shouts of the legions blended with the hue and cry of the rebels, as well as the heartbroken sobbing of the crowd. In a circular fashion the concluding fourth section (IV) returns to the dead with whom the passage opened, providing a sickening glance at the hoards of corpses. The rounded sequence establishes a certain coherence, thus defining the passage as a literary whole.

The author ties the various units together through a network of linguistic and semantic associations. Thus he interweaves fire motifs a little at a time throughout the passage—in the opening half-line of the first section (the blazing shrine), in the opening and closing of the third section (rebels encircled by fire, the shrine on fire), and twice more in the opening of the fourth section (hill boiling over, a mass of flame). For the same reason he imbues the flame in the second section, devoted entirely to the fire, with an aural quality (roar of the flames) and links it with the groans of the fallen victims. This technique establishes a connection with both the first and fourth sections, which describe the dead, and with the third section, which is entirely devoted to the sounds. Such skillful literary nuances result in a powerful, dramatic, and carefully wrought composition.

In addition to the three motifs just listed—dead bodies, fire, and cries—Josephus uses another leitmotif to shape the passage, the hill of the Temple. It appears in three of the sections (II, III, IV). Whereas in the second section this hill attains only minor importance, with merely its height mentioned, in its two subsequent appearances it becomes the most prominent element among the dramatic figures of the passage. The cries in section III, even though they obviously belong to human beings, are presented in one place as emanating from the hill (the cries on the hill). Thus, Josephus bestows upon the hill of the Temple vocal ability, listing it among the sources of the tumult. Immediately afterward, the author goes even further, describing a sort of chorus, with the voices coming from this hill and the lower city on one side and the *Peraea* (the regions east of the Jordan) and the surrounding hills replying like an echo on the other. The background of the unnamed hills emphasizes the literary function of the particular hill of the Temple. In section IV the hill changes costumes, appearing as a burning element, a sort of gigantic bonfire.

Three elements provide the physical texture of this literary composition—the shrine, the city of Jerusalem, and the hill. But while the shrine and the city appear only twice each, the hill appears three times. Moreover, on two of these occasions the city appears as adjacent to the hill, as an image serving to highlight the hill—once as burning (in II) and again as the source of voices (in III). By coupling the two in this way, the author crafts a new pair, city-hill, which replaces the traditional duo of Second Temple landscape, city-Temple.

The terminology Josephus employs in this passage further emphasizes the novelty of its conceptualization. On one occasion toward the end of the account, the author refers to the hill as "the hill of the Temple." To the best of my knowledge, such an expression does not appear elsewhere in the literature from the Second Temple period. As discussed earlier, only one other source renders a similar expression—1 Maccabees. Clearly the Greek "hill of the Temple" and the Hebrew *har ha-bayit* (Temple Mount) share in linguistic structure, but even greater is the contextual and semantic resemblance; in both cases the hill is no longer subordinate to some other element but rather takes center stage.

All in all, the sequences from Josephus, and to some extent 1 Maccabees, are worthy of being considered the seeds of the conceptualization of the Temple Mount. These sources are not unambiguous. On the one hand, they share many traits with the "classic" city-temple paradigm found in other Second Temple writings; on the other, they indicate a change in perception. They endow the area around the Temple with uncommon, though not totally new, names, and no longer do they portray this space as solely dependent on the Temple that stands at its center. Through these articulations (or as reflected by them) the Mountain of the Temple and its compound acquire an independent category in the spatial organization of Jerusalem. To demarcate this entity, these authors used vocabulary that was far from new. Like many of their contemporaries, they were immersed in both biblical and Greco-Roman imagery, which served as a natural source for expressions and similes as well as for stimuli. But the common ground should not blur the innovation. For the first time, the Temple Mount begins to function as an independent element.

Messing with the Sequential Model

The beginnings of a sacred mountain conceptuality in Jerusalem and its association with the location of the Temple are shrouded in uncertainty. The limited and rather humble goal of the current chapter was to disturb and complicate the ostensibly neat story of Jerusalem's sacred space, in which orderly lines of continuation concatenate detached links and organize them on a sequential axis. The earliest documents that articulate the ideology of the Davidic dynasty do not allude to any revered rise. Afterward, in the later portion of the First Temple period and in the early centuries of the Second Temple era, an image of a holy mountain resonates in some of the texts. But, as far as one can tell, its function stays within the confines of a literary trope, sort of a poetic ornament modeled on the symbolism of the ancient Near Eastern cosmic mountain. As such it does not manifest itself in "real life," that is, within the conceptuality of the sacred—the cluster of notions, perceptions, and ideology that fueled people's day-to-day experiences and molded their consciousness.

The following fictional incident illuminates the role the space of the Temple Mount lacked in the realities of life. Imagine a Second Temple Jew walking toward the Temple in Jerusalem. On the way she meets an acquaintance who inquires about her destiny—"Where are you going"? Is it possible that her answer would be, "I am heading to the Temple Mount"? I argue throughout this chapter that such an answer was inconceivable for people living in the time of the Second Temple. The only answer our protagonist could have produced would have been "I am going to the Temple." In other words: the texture of their spatial organization did not include an entity called the Temple Mount, although in their inventory of images they could find a literary simile labeled "god's mountain." This seemingly paradoxical statement summarizes the essence of the current chapter.

The second phase of this chapter traces the intricate relationship between physical reality and conceptuality. At the foundation of my discussion lays the claim that changes in the former steered the process that eventually remolded the latter. According to the reconstruction presented here, Simeon's actions and, even more so, Herod's building project in Jerusalem yielded a new situation, which in turn altered the conceptual framework registered in the minds of the city's residents. This launched a gradual course that in the long run would reshape both their lexicon and their consciousness. Obviously, a third event that contributed to these developments was the destruction of the Second Temple, which by erasing the structures on top of the mount pushed it to the forefront of Jewish experience. 1 Maccabees and the writings of Josephus express the beginnings of these dynamics. In an attempt to decipher the cultural mechanism that prompted them, the following chapter examines these same developments through the lens of the early followers of Jesus.

CHAPTER TWO

Locus Memoriae

The Temple Mount and the Early Followers of Jesus and James

> La mémoire s'accroche à des lieux comme l'histoire à des événements
> (Memory fastens upon sites, whereas history fastens upon events).
>
> PIERRE NORA, *Les lieux de mémoire*, 1:xxix

In his monumental work *Les lieux de mémoire,* the French historian Pierre Nora establishes the leading role of physical places in the creation of collective memory. The English translation of Nora's work bears the title *Realms of Memory,* which fails, however, to catch the full sense of the French title. For although Nora assigns to the phrase "places of memory," the *loci memoriae,* a much broader significance than that of particular confined spaces, he nevertheless devotes much of his discussion to untangling the convoluted interaction between inanimate sites and conscious recollections of people and communities about their past. Physical features of landscape—whether monuments, architectural structures, or well-demarcated areas—serve as magnets that attract some abstract reminiscences and repel others, thus organizing, classifying, and calibrating those traditions; and those physical features become the spine or binding whereby disparate details are stitched together as cultural textures.[1]

Reading this model backward, one may use memorable places and the traditions woven around them as a kind of porthole that allows a glance at the dynamics that shaped groups and societies. Attempting such a reading, this chapter investigates the Temple Mount and its role among the various groups in the

Jesus movement. After establishing the centrality of Jerusalem and the Temple to these early, proto-Christian communities, I move in two separate but closely related directions. In the first part of the discussion, I offer a new understanding to the famous literary piece that was preserved in the synoptic Gospels, known as the stone-upon-stone prophecy. Unlike generations of scholars, both ancient and modern, who associated this excerpt with the Jewish Temple, I argue that in its ancient setting people read and grasped it differently as relating to the space that surrounded the Temple, namely the Herodian compound that came to be the Temple Mount (map 3: D). The second part of the chapter focuses on the groups associated with James, the so-called Brother of Jesus, and their engagement with the place of his martyrological tomb. The discussion follows the intricate developments in the site's image and traces its mutating (real or fictional) locations in order to claim that the early memories about the tomb of James centered on the Temple Mount. Finally, piecing together the various fragments of information from the two parts of my discussion, I reconstruct an unknown chapter in the story of the Temple Mount as a *locus memoriae* in the realm of early Christianity.

Jerusalem and the Temple in the World of Jesus and His Early Followers

Jerusalem and its sanctuary rank high in the writings that were eventually (some time in the second and third centuries) compiled as the New Testament. In fact, they play a conspicuous part in its narrative that is unmatched by any other city or holy place. According to those traditions—whether representing actual events or literary constructs is none of our concern here—salient milestones in Jesus's life came about at the Temple. It was there that Simon prophesied the newborn Jesus's eventual anointment, when the family came to fulfill the required birth sacrifices and ceremony celebrating the redemption of the firstborn. And it was there that the young Jesus rose to prominence among the Torah students. Some traditions similarly place his experience with Satan on the pinnacle of the Temple.[2] Most significantly of all, Jesus's last journey, the chain of events that concluded his life on earth—the last supper, trial, crucifixion, and resurrection—transpired entirely in Jerusalem. In the realm of ideas too, attitudes toward sacrifice, approaches to spirituality, and the question of what should be the focus of religious life—whether on a national or a wider basis—were all frequently linked to Jerusalem and the gamut of images associated with it.[3] It should come as no surprise that various traditions, later gathered in the New Testament, draw upon images of the Temple and Jerusalem, whether to articulate the notion of "Heavenly Jerusalem" or, on occasion, as a label for the actual community of the Jesus movement.[4] After the destruction of the Temple in 70 CE, the authors and editors-compilers of these texts took pains to work this traumatic event into their developing Christology as well.[5]

The literature not included in the Christian canon reaffirms the paramount standing of Jerusalem and the Temple. A clear example of this trend resonates in a widely read second-century text that is now known as the *Protoevangelium of James*, which relates the story of Mary's childhood against the backdrop of the Temple in Jerusalem. According to this account, when Mary, the future mother of Jesus, reached the age of three, her parents brought her to the Temple, where she grew up among the priests.[6] Other works from the same time also locate important events in Jesus's life in Jerusalem, thus confirming the city's eminence in the eyes of early Christian readers. For example, the landscape of an incident detailed by the *Oxyrhynchus Papyrus* 840, in which Jesus quarrels with a high priest, features the Temple, and the core of its argument concerns the various legal (halakhic) matters related to its attendance.[7] Similarly, the *Acts of Thomas*, an apocryphal Syriac text of the early third century, echoes a more elaborate tradition than the one found in Luke about the whereabouts of the child Jesus in the Temple, maintaining that the Savior even participated in the offering of sacrifices.[8]

Affinity for the Temple among the early followers of Jesus is also behind his priestly image in the Letter to the Hebrews.[9] Despite its criticism of the existing Temple system and its consequent emphasis on the heavenly Jerusalem, this source depicts Jesus as the high priest who enters the Holy of Holies, atones for the people, and defies the traditional priesthood. In the same vein, the *Letter of Abgar*, a Syriac work apparently from the third century—fragments of which were preserved by Eusebius—describes Jesus as a savior who "has appeared in the region of Jerusalem."[10] Dating from approximately the same time, the Gnostic *Apocalypse of Peter*, although generally ignorant of Palestine's landscape, uses the Temple as the backdrop for its visions.[11]

The prestige of Jerusalem and its Temple among Second Temple Jews, of which the disciples of Jesus and even Paul were certainly an integral part, provides the immediate context for all these notions. Corresponding approaches can be found in the conceptual frameworks of various other branches of Second Temple Judaism, including Qumran and the Hellenistic Diaspora as reflected in the writings of Philo (see chapter 1).

Modern scholars devoted lengthy studies to clarify the ideas that clustered around the city and Temple in these texts and to trace their origin. Some attempted to represent the Jesus movement's attitude toward these constituents as clear-cut, but this could hardly be the case.[12] On the one hand, followers of Jesus refer to Jerusalem as the "Holy City" and portray the Temple as the house of Jesus's father.[13] According to their narrative, even Jesus's most drastic actions in the sanctuary—chasing away the moneychangers and overturning their tables—were not directed against the Temple itself but were rather done on its behalf. Jesus aspired to restore the Temple to its original purpose as a house of worship, as attested by the verse from Isaiah (56:7) that early authors incorporated into this story.[14]

On the other hand, a widespread convention stages Jesus as demolisher of the Temple, and the sources also voice his explicit demand that his followers leave the city and abandon all that it represents.[15] Other segments in what came to be the New Testament that are usually associated with the stance of Paul and Luke articulate similar tendencies, but only to a certain degree. Although many scholars view the approaches of these two apostles—intended for Gentiles—as a product of anti-Temple sentiment, they are actually not as definite as they might seem. Scholars like William Davies, followed by John Townsend in a detailed article, have claimed that Paul's own attitude toward the Temple before the destruction was rather positive.[16] In their view, negative tones first appear in post-destruction texts attributed to Paul. A similarly mixed picture, if with different emphases, is found in the position of the early so-called Judeo-Christians toward the Temple, as seen in Luke and in the book of Acts.[17] Slowly but surely, scholarship tends to doubt the estimation of the Tübingen school, which argued that Christianity had been ideologically opposed to the Temple even in its nascent stages. Today, even texts that were considered undeniably antagonistic toward this institution are no longer taken as unambiguous.[18]

The haziness surrounding Jerusalem and its Temple has bewildered modern scholars, just as it did Christian writers in antiquity. While some scholars have attempted to reconcile the contradictory undertones toward Jerusalem, others have felt compelled to admit that these texts do not communicate a uniform approach to the city and the Temple. Some of the latter have explained this multifariousness as due to historical circumstances that led to diverse positions on this matter among early Christian groups, whereas others have emphasized the shifting religious challenges (especially the delay in the *parousia*, the "second coming" of Jesus) and the need to adapt ideology to reality; a third group of scholars reduced the problem to literary considerations that confronted the editors of the texts.[19] In the 1950s Hugh Nibley's programmatic essay clearly reflected the ambivalence around this issue when it labeled the early Christians' stance toward the Temple as "envy," a designation embracing both love and hatred.[20]

And What of the Temple Mount?

Do the traditions that emanated from the early followers of Jesus recognize the Temple Mount in any way, either as a physical component of their landscape or a conceptual entity in their worldview? At first glance the answer seems negative, and my conclusions regarding other Second Temple sources (in chapter 1) apply here as well. Texts preserved in the New Testament never allude to the word combination "Temple" and "Mount." The term "Mount Zion," absent from the works of Josephus, appears only rarely in the traditions of the Jesus movement as well; the Gospels do not mention it even once. The fact that mountains do turn up in these texts, some of them quite intrusively—Mount Sinai, Mount Gerizim, and the anonymous mountain that hosts the Sermon on the Mount—underscores the absence of the Temple Mount even further.[21] When it comes to Jerusalem, the city and the Temple monopolize the entire literary spectrum of writers from the Jesus movement, and even if they mention mountains from time to time, they relegate them to the margins.

The dialogue between Jesus and the Samaritan woman in the Gospel of John illustrates this conclusion.[22] In order to contrast the Samaritans' venue of worship with that of the Jews, the passage situates "this mountain" of the Samaritans on the one end against Jewish Jerusalem on the other as two competing figures. Such a literary arrangement almost requires contrasting one topographical elevation with another—mountain against mountain, as later Christian writers did (see chapter 5). But the actual formulation of this pericope corresponds to common Second Temple conceptions, as perceived by the writer. Indeed, such an equation, which considers Jerusalem to be the place—*locus/ topos*—in which Jews venerated their God, fits well with the notions found in Josephus and other Second Temple Jewish writers who discuss the same topic (see chapter 1). Jerusalem in this context functions as the exclusive location of God's worship. The Temple by all means embodies the city's essence, operating as the heart of the sacred body, but the mountain on which it stands lacks a task or a status within this religious framework.

A similar conclusion can be drawn when examining the Temple Mount not as a topographic feature—that is, a mountain—but as an architectonic unit that encompasses the huge enclosed precinct around the Temple. One may ask whether this space on its own holds any particular value in the traditions of the Jesus movement. Here too, as in the discussion about Josephus in chapter 1, the relevant term to consider is the Greek *hieron,* which the authors of these writings often apply to the Temple surroundings. Hugues Vincent correctly points out that, in contrast to Josephus, the authors of the Gospels and the book of Acts did not feel obliged to describe the Temple structure systematically. His subsequent assertion, however, that *naos* in the books of the New Testament means the Temple (map 3: A, B, C, and mainly the inner sanctuary A) and *hieron* stands for the whole complex, including the outer platform and the surrounding porticoes (map 3: D), fails to notice the gist of this designation.[23]

Various modern lexicons of New Testament Greek have already noted that the writers of these texts assign *hieron* with equivocal connotation. Because most of the activities of Jesus and his disciples occurred on the open-air platform of the Herodian complex surrounding the Temple, *hieron* often denotes these areas. This definition, however, extends the original purport of the term. In its basic meaning, still apparent in some early installments preserved in the New Testament (as well as other Second Temple writers such as Josephus), *hieron* signified only the structure of the Temple building and its immediate inner courts. For example, in the famous incident in which Jesus overturns the moneychangers' counters, he applies the biblical verse "*My house* shall be called a house of prayer for all nations" (Isaiah 56:7) to the *hieron.* Likewise, the author details the scene in which the parents of the infant Jesus present him as a firstborn son and offer the appropriate sacrifice as taking place in the *hieron.* Similarly, Paul propels the Nazirites to fulfill their vows and offer their sacrifice in the *hieron.* And, finally, the Letter to the Corinthians depicts the priestly vocation as happening in the *hieron.*[24]

These sources place the *hieron* within the semantic field of other Second Temple Jewish writings. In the vocabulary of that era, *hieron* simply denoted the Temple, which in its rudimentary definition included the central shrine (known as the *heikhal* or *naos;* map 3: A) and its inner courts (the Hebrew *ʿazarot;* map 3: B, C). The Hebrew equivalent of *hieron* was thus the *miqdash.* Because Second Temple Jews considered the compound around the Temple (map 3: D) to be part of the sanctuary, they extended the meaning of *hieron* and applied it to those areas as well. But this shows only that they regarded the enclosure as part of the Temple.

It is thus clear that for the most part the architectonic structures that encircled the Temple, like the elevation on which the sanctuary stood, had no particular value in and of themselves in the cluster of traditions that represent the Jesus movement. But this conclusion is only ostensibly true. In the following, I propose to demonstrate that various traditions incorporated into the New Testament and other early Christian compositions contain the seeds of the "Temple Mount" image and the concept it embodies. I also intend to show that this space, the surrounding precinct of the Temple (map 3: D), occupied a place in the consciousness of the early followers of Jesus before the destruction of the Temple and in the few generations thereafter, not merely as an adjunct, subordinate constituent of the Temple but as an independent entity. In dealing with the following extracts from the Gospels, one must remember that in their current form they are dated to the generations following the Temple's destruction, when these texts took on their final literary shape, but much of the material included in them originally belonged to the collection of traditions composed by the "school" of Jesus's disciples and followers during the decades that preceded the destruction. For our purposes, it does not matter whether a particular idea came from Jesus himself or was developed by those who followed him.

A Prophecy of Destruction and Its Spatial Organization

The synoptic Gospels hand down the famous saying attributed to Jesus about "stone upon a stone" in three similar versions. In Mark, who arguably presents the earliest available adaptation, it reads as follows:

1a.   And as he came out of the Temple [*hieron*]
1b.   one of his disciples said to him "Look, teacher, what wonderful stones and what wonderful buildings!"
2a.   And Jesus said to him "Do you see these great buildings?
2b.   There will not be left here a stone upon a stone that will not be thrown down."[25]

Adopting a prophetic tone, all three Gospels configure this anecdotal pericope as a harsh prediction of the future. Chronologically they locate it during Jesus's last journey to Jerusalem, after his austere denigration of the "scribes and Pharisees" and before the apocalyptic foretelling (known as the "Little Apocalypse") on the Mount of Olives. Scholars agree, however, that originally it was not an integral part of this literary sequence. They see this two-verse pericope as a homogeneous, independent segment, similar in style and shape to other stand-alone sayings and short tales that circulated among the followers of Jesus. Some of these traditions were later preserved in the *Gospel of Thomas* that was found in Nag Hammadi, or to the literary fragments customarily known as Q (even though this particular portion belongs to none of these collections), which the authors of the Gospels integrated only later into their books.[26]

What, then, is the essence of this literary unit? What is the issue it endeavors to communicate? Nineteenth-century scholarship shared the view that the stones and buildings that Jesus and his entourage encountered must be decoded against the background of Josephus's depiction of the marvelous gigantic stones of the Herodian Temple (*Antiquities* 15:392). Based on this view, the conventional interpretation since then, espoused in every commentary and study I have found, identifies the content of the excerpt as the destruction of the Temple.[27] Whether actually spoken by the historical Jesus (*ipsissima verba*) or not, scholars construe this anecdote to represent an approach (some say ideology) resistant in one way or another to the Temple, either anticipating its destruction or looking back in subsequent years to rationalize it. But is this really the case? The third-fourth century Palestinian scholar and bishop Eusebius, for example, similar to nineteenth-century scholars, presents the stone-upon-stone prophecy according to the "official" view of his time as indeed relating to the Temple and its destruction. At the same time he mentions "persons who interpret the passage differently."[28] In what follows I try to uncover this different interpretation and trace its roots back to the Jesus movement.

The three synoptic versions agree that Jesus uttered his prophetic response when the group departed from the Temple. All three accounts render the content, both diction and prose, in virtually identical wording. Yet careful analysis of the literary structure, language, and linguistic nuances of this piece, which allows for a more precise explication of its content, reveals some fundamental differences among the various versions, especially concerning its actual subject matter. The passage clearly divides into two parts. The first conveys the disciple's remark, while the second offers Jesus's response. The first part breaks down further into two sections: 1a sets the stage for the episode by establishing its exact location—as the group left the Temple, that is, at or near one of the gates; 1b quotes the disciple's exclamation, which arose from his encounter with the architectural surroundings—the spectacular stones and buildings. The correlation between these two sections (1a and 1b) registers clearly, and they are meant to provide both the course and rhythm on which the scene evolves. As they were leaving the Temple, Jesus and his disciples came across some structures that drew their attention and evoked the disciple's astonishment. This in turn instigated Jesus to react. His reply is also divided into two sections: 2a repeats the disciple's remark, this time from the mouth of the master Jesus, in order to focus and highlight the topic; 2b delivers the punch line of the anecdote in the form of a prediction or prophecy about the future destruction of the buildings.

All three synoptic versions of this portion share many traits. They draw on the same vocabulary—nouns, verbs, prepositions, and negations—and function within a similar broader literary context. The internal structure, in which a disciple voices a rhetorical fascination with the objects in front of him and Jesus responds,[29] is unvaried as well. But significant differences separate the versions. One major change involves the identification of the structures that serve as the target of the oracular wrath. At what stones and buildings does Jesus direct the prophecy? Whereas Mark's phrasing does not explicitly identify them, either in the disciple's avowal or in either section of Jesus's reply, in the other two synoptic accounts additional wording clearly pinpoints these elements. In Matthew the disciple's observations do not include any reference to the stones mentioned in Mark, but the buildings are labeled "of the Temple" (*tou hierou*). The author of Luke also offers supplementary clarification, but unlike Matthew, he mentions the stones in the disciples' statement (21:5) and introduces them as those "adorning" the Temple.

The absence of the Temple from the dialogue between Jesus and his disciple in Mark seems rather significant, especially in light of the other Gospels' insistence to include it. It suggests, to me, that according to Mark Jesus's prediction of destruction may not have been intended for the Temple. If the stones and buildings really belonged to the Temple, this fact would be the central point of the prophecy. However, unlike Matthew and Luke, whose authors clearly saw a need to tie the buildings and stones to the Temple, Mark strikingly remains silent about them.

Additional confirmation for such a reading of Mark derives from the spatial setting of this segment. The passage commences with the seemingly unimportant detail that the dialogue between Jesus and his disciples that led to the prophecy transpired as they were leaving the *hieron*. In such a short, scrupulously recounted anecdote, the meticulous form of which is evident from its tight structure, I take this detail as a pointer toward the scenery that unfolded before the group. When people depart from a place, they are facing the outside. In such a setting, the group exits the *hieron* and is faced by the magnificent buildings and structures of the surrounding compound. *Hieron* in such a context would befit its basic, primary meaning, namely, the structure of the Temple and its inner courts (map 3: A, B, C), the place of departure. Otherwise, if, for example, it were to refer to the whole compound (map 3: D), the appearance of huge stones and magnificent buildings as the group retired from the site would make no sense. According to my understanding, as the group exited the Temple (probably through the women's court), they were struck by the magnificent landscape of the Herodian compound, which indeed included monumental buildings and huge stones (see map 3, fig. 3). If the group had wished to face the Temple, they would have had to turn around and look back at it. A maneuver of that sort would leave the pericope detailing their departure from the Temple superfluous.

I propose that in this literary design the disciple's exclamation, "what wonderful stones and buildings!" targets not the sanctuary itself but rather the structures outside the Temple. Consequently, according to Mark, Jesus too aimed his prophecy at the compound surrounding the Temple and not at the Temple itself. Arguably, Mark's text preserves the earliest version of this segment.[30] If so, this defines the topic of the passage, the subject of Jesus's anger and prophetic forecast of destruction, as the space that came to be the Temple Mount. Only the authors of Matthew and Luke (or the creators of the installments that were preserved in these compositions), at a later stage in the evolution of the tradition, shifted the focus of Jesus's judgment to the Temple. Originally it had been directed at the compound around the Temple.

To be sure, this proposed reading of Mark does not completely refute other possible interpretations of the segment. For example, the fact that the text commences with the group's leaving the Temple does not necessarily require that the objects of Jesus's words stood outside this structure. One might argue, as scholars traditionally have, that Jesus was denouncing the place they had just left. But the preceding proposal appears preferable for three reasons. First, it takes into account the subtle changes in wording among the three synoptic versions, while the accepted interpretation does not ascribe any significance to the fact that the earliest version, that of Mark, does not identify the stones and buildings as belonging to the Temple. Second, my reading accounts for the exposition, the literary moment created by the opening half-verse that sets the episode at the point of departure, as the group was leaving the Temple. Finally, it anchors the passage in the physical layout of the site at the time it was formulated—that is, the landscape of the Herodian Temple complex. Previous scholarship did not pay sufficient attention to the physical setting of the text, and many failed to notice it at all.[31]

Explicit support that such an understanding of the stone-upon-stone tradition indeed prevailed in early Christian circles comes from the writings of Eusebius. In his fourth-century composition *Theophany* (Divine Manifestation), Eusebius vigorously confutes opposing views regarding the fulfillment of Jesus's previsions. Often, his deliberations remain the only surviving record of "nonauthoritative" positions that propagated among the early followers of Jesus. Chapter 19 in the fourth book of the *Theophany* centers on the destruction of the Temple. As expected, in his reading of the stone-upon-stone excerpt Eusebius endorses the interpretation that this segment foretells the destruction of the Temple. More revealing, however, are the opposing views he contests. Eusebius takes issue with "Persons who interpret the passage differently" who claim "that this was not said on all the buildings, except only on that place which the disciples, when expressing their wonder about it, pointed out to him." Previously in the same chapter, Eusebius makes clear that "Walking by the side of the Temple . . . the disciples [were] wondering at the building [structure] which surrounded it."[32] Here is a fourth-century source telling us that some "nonauthoritative" tradition explicated the stone-upon-stone segment as referring to the structures surrounding the Temple and not the Temple itself. The reading Eusebius denounces matches the reading of Mark that I suggested based on the close literary analysis of the section. This leads me to believe that in its early stages, various groups in the Jesus movement debated the meaning of the passage, and at least some saw it as dealing with the space around the Temple (map 3: D) and not the Temple itself (map 3: A, B, C).

The Literary History of the Stone-upon-Stone Prophecy

Almost every tradition, whether oral or written, embodies at least two separate histories. One precedes it and consists of the sum of events and circumstances that led to its creation. The other begins once the tradition is already formed and includes the story of its transmission. The current section deals with the latter, with the mutations and changes brought upon the stone-upon-stone excerpt by those who consumed it and passed it down the generations.

By adding the wording about the Temple, Matthew and Luke (or whoever it was before them) endowed the prophecy with new meaning. By doing so, these authors-editors diverted its focus from the compound around the Temple to the Temple itself. The book of Mark itself also shows signs of a later editor's intervention, particularly in the weaving of the literary unit within the broader arrangement of the text. In the portion preceding the prophecy anecdote (12:41–44), Jesus observes people who make monetary contributions to the Temple. Contrasting the large amounts given by the rich with the poor widow's mite, he expresses a clear preference for the lesser donation.[33] The editor of Mark binds the two units, especially by referring to Jesus in the opening of the stone-upon-stone pericope through the use of the personal pronoun "he," which sends the reader (or an audience listening) to the previous section.[34] Within this textual configuration, the stone-upon-stone prophecy receives its meaning from the context of the event described just before it, the widow's mite. The disciple's remark now challenges Jesus's preference in the previous section, as if he were saying, "Such small contributions will not enable the construction of such spectacular buildings." The narrative then climaxes with the Savior's riposte: "These spectacular buildings will not remain standing." This sequence in Mark, therefore, focuses not so much on the destruction of the various structures as on the immanent clash between the rich and the poor, the strong and the weak. Jesus's declaration addresses the strong as symbolized by the sumptuous buildings, asserting that "Might does not last forever."[35]

A third phase in the evolution of this anecdote occurs in Luke 19:44, in which the author directs the same prophecy at the entire city of Jerusalem. This segment conveys Jesus's lamentation upon his first sight of the city as he approached it from the east (apparently from the peak of the Mount of Olives). The two other synoptic Gospels and John also preserve this account, but only the version in Luke includes the verse, "And they will not leave a stone upon a stone in you," this time in reference to the entire city of Jerusalem.[36] Without delving into the scholarly debate about the relation between this extract and the other stone-upon-stone installments, it is fair to say that it imbues the prophecy with completely new meaning.[37]

In summary, if later alterations, such as those found in Matthew and Luke and to a certain extent even Mark (although his is the closest to the original version), are eliminated, what remains is a literary portion prophesizing about the complex surrounding the Temple and the magnificent buildings made of huge stones that populated that space. As Jesus and his disciples left the Temple structure, they encountered the mighty architecture of the Herodian compound. The students were greatly impressed, but their master condemned the area to destruction. Jesus was not directing his harsh predictions toward the Temple, as interpreted by the revised version that Matthew and Luke preserved. Instead, he aimed his condemning words at its surroundings. If I am correct in this reading, this excerpt offers one of the earliest significant references to the space that eventually constituted the Temple Mount. Such a conclusion has far-reaching implications for research on the New Testament, because the interpretation of the stone-upon-stone segment as relating to the destruction of the Temple has served as a cornerstone for the chronology of Mark as well as the study of the Jesus movement's attitude toward Temple issues. But what is important for the present study is that the passage demonstrates the presence of the area that came to be the Temple Mount in the mental framework of the author of Mark.

Evolving Perceptions of Space among the Early Followers of Jesus

Many questions still remain unanswered; the most pressing is, Why should a writer in the Jesus movement formulate such a harsh statement about the precinct that surrounded the Temple? To put it bluntly, What did he have against this space? The rest of this chapter is an attempt to resolve this question. First, in the current section, I contextualize the content of the stone-upon-stone segment. Then the discussion carries us into the admittedly vague and only partially traceable realm of early Christianity in its first century and a half, in an attempt to unravel the role the Temple Mount played for that movement.

An effort to contextualize the consciousness revealed here brings to mind two surprising parallels, from Josephus and the book of Revelation. As shown at length in the previous chapter, the famous prophecy of destruction in Josephus's fourth volume of *The Jewish War* (4:388) abandons the customary Second Temple model of Jewish sacred space, in which all components of the Temple complex are subordinated to the sanctuary at the center and labeled as such. In that segment, Josephus refers to the area between the city and the Temple with the rare formulation, "The *temenos* [compound or precinct] of God," which replaces the more common designation "*temenos* of the temple." Such a unique expression sheds some light on the formation of this area's spatial image. It is difficult to know, however, whether people of the Second Temple period employed such vocabulary or whether it belongs to the period immediately after its destruction, when Josephus wrote his *Jewish War*. Be that as it may, both the author of the pericope in Mark and Josephus present prophetic discourse of destruction directed at the area surrounding the Temple rather than at the Temple itself.

A three-way division similar to the one used by Josephus—city, Temple, and a third independent space between them—also occurs in a second parallel, in the book of Revelation, chapter 11. One segment in this apocalyptic sequence (11:1–2) deals with the Jerusalem Temple and its court. The author designed a scene in which an angel commands Jesus to measure the inner sanctuary—the Greek *naos*, equivalent of the Hebrew *heikhal* and usually standing for the actual building of the Temple (map 3: A)—the altar, and the worshipers of God in attendance. In contrast, he also instructs him not to measure the court, stating that it is doomed to be destroyed by the Gentiles, along with the Holy City.

To mark the Temple court, the author uses the Greek *aulē*, which usually matches the Hebrew *ḥaṣer*.[38] Drawn from the biblical lexicon, a popular source of terms and images for Second Temple writers, this pair-*aulē* and *ḥaṣer*-served as a common designation for the Temple compound. As I showed in chapter 1, Josephus too often applies the same designation in his accounts of the open platforms surrounding the Temple. But a closer look at the function of the court and the Temple in this literary piece, and especially at their mutual relations, reveals a new, largely unprecedented model. Unlike other Second Temple writers who fuse the Temple and its court into one inseparable unit, the apocalyptic setting of Revelation completely removes the two from each other. Fate separates them, with the angel foreseeing destruction for one and safety for the other.

Scholars have offered many interpretations for the detachment of these two usually merged elements. Wellhausen already suggested that this development might be connected with a concrete event during the Jewish revolt of 70 CE. He proposed reading this installment in relation to the internal clashes between Jewish parties, during which the group known as the Zealots entrenched themselves within the Temple structure and exchanged blows with other rebel factions.[39] According to his theory, the portion in Revelation resembles a fragment of a prophecy (oracle) from the rebel camps, like many other predictions of redemption and devastation that were prevalent in Jerusalem at that time. This particular pericope foretold salvation for those who were sheltered in the Temple and destruction for everyone else.

Wellhausen's conjecture cannot be supported by evidence. As to content, the prophecy contains no hint of groups fortifying themselves in the Temple or any sort of conflict between those inside and those outside. In fact it never mentions anyone outside the *naos*. Rather, the text confronts one well-defined category with another—the followers of God who are worshiping inside the sanctuary versus the Gentiles, destroyers of the city and the Temple court. Furthermore, recent research, which places the writing of Revelations in Asia Minor and fixes its date just before the destruction of the Temple, make Wellhausen's suggestion highly unlikely.[40]

Nevertheless, his analysis provides important insights into how the author of the section in the book of Revelations perceived the Temple landscape. In particular, the text does not coincide with customary Second Temple notions, which view the entire area as one entity and consider the outside space an integral part of the Temple. Instead, the author distinguishes the court from the Temple and provides the former with both a new life and a different future. Without confining this phenomenon to a particular historical moment, as in Wellhausen's interpretation, this excerpt marks the same new stage in the evolution of consciousness associated with the Temple area as the two other prophecies discussed previously. All three prophecies—Jesus's "no stone upon a stone," Josephus's prophecy about "God's *temenos*," and the segment in the book of Revelations—correlate in two significant ways. First, they are all directed at the area outside the Temple, which would later be called "the Temple Mount," even though this term does not appear in any of them. Second, they have a similar attitude toward this area, as all three predict that it will be destroyed.

These are the very beginnings of the consolidation of an independent identity for the space outside the Temple, similar to the one detected in the previous chapter in the writings of Josephus (and to a lesser degree in 1 Maccabees). In their current state, however, they are left as textual presentations that contextualize each other literally, but lack a broader anchor in life, be it historical, social, or religious. They are like dots missing the line that will bear out the picture they are meant to form. One may wonder how the Temple compound became such an autonomous structure that some members of the Jesus movement would wish for its destruction, and what circumstances contributed to this development. The following discussion offers a partial answer.

James, Jerusalem, and the Temple

Despite considerable scholarly effort, the figure of James Brother of Jesus remains largely obscure.[41] For more than 150 years, the nature of the group that formed around this character, and especially what emerged from it later on, have fueled a heated debate.[42] The major reason for the paucity of information about James's actions and beliefs is apparently that he eventually "lost the battle," and thus the extant writings—mainly those preserved in the Christian canon—reflect the views of his opponents.[43] The following discussion is therefore less about James himself than about the fragmentary traditions about him and the various aspects of his image cherished in the shared memory of his followers. I investigate how certain conventions about his death and burial functioned in the consciousness of those who followed James and absorbed what they considered to be his legacy into their teachings, as well as the manner in which these views materialized in the religious landscape this group carved for itself.

Various documents related to James and the community that formed around him share a common trait: they emphasize the centrality of Jerusalem and the Temple. These two elements figure prominently in the collective recollections of this early Jewish Christian community, to be known later as "the church of the circumcised in Jerusalem" or even "the mother of the churches." Before the destruction of the Temple, however, these people formed merely one group of Jews among many others.[44] The book of Acts, for example, features none other than Jesus himself as instructing his disciples not to flee Jerusalem. In sharp contrast to Peter, not to mention Paul, both of whom leave Jerusalem and operate in many other places, the few stories told about James and his followers in this text all occur in Jerusalem or in the Temple.[45] When it comes to James, almost no one seems to remember him outside Jerusalem for the twenty-two years or so between Jesus's crucifixion and his own execution.[46]

Preserved in the first Codex of Nag Hammadi (the Jung Codex), the work known as the *Apocryphon of James* provides a similar picture. According to that narrative, which differs somewhat from the book of Acts, Jesus's disciples dispersed in various directions, while James ascended to Jerusalem.[47] The two apocalypses associated with James, of which Coptic translations were also discovered at Nag Hammadi bound next to each other in Codex V, communicate analogous tendencies. In spite of his unfavorable opinion of Jerusalem, the writer of the *First Apocalypse of James,* dated to the second century CE, connects James in an almost "existential" way to the city.[48] The writer of the *Second Apocalypse of James* considers the Temple in Jerusalem to have been the only stage for James's performance; he taught on the Temple steps, foretold its destruction, and met his death immediately thereafter among its columns.[49] In the same vein is the tradition about James embodied in the Pseudo-Clementine literature, in a portion that many nowadays call (after Epiphanius) *The Ascent of James*. Here too, in spite of its animosity toward the Temple and what transpired there, the text considers the Temple, and in particular its "steps" (*gradus; darga'*), to be the natural setting for James's activities.[50]

But the tradition that most clearly affiliates James with the Temple is transmitted by the second-century writer Hegesippus in a well-known fragment preserved by the fourth-century church historian Eusebius.[51] The passage anchors James's very being in the Temple. While still in his mother's womb, he was considered "holy," which in the Judeo-Christian literary context of Hegesippus implies that he was intended for the Temple. He grew up as a Nazirite, refrained from wine and meat, and, reminiscent of an actual priest, spent long hours in the Temple in prayers and supplication for the atonement of his people. It takes no great imagination to recognize that the author molded James's figure on the prototype of the high priest entering the Holy of Holies on the Day of Atonement. This explains the repeated insistence that James entered the sanctuary alone (*monos*), just like the high priest on that day, and directed his measures toward expiation.[52] Unsurprisingly, the crescendo of this narrative—James's death as a martyr—occurred in the Temple as well, where he was also buried.

This story bears a striking resemblance to the *Second Apocalypse,* and other literary representations of James convey similar trends. For example, the tradition transmitted by the bishop and church writer Epiphanius, in the generation following Eusebius—the second half of the fourth century CE—depicts James as "priest in accordance with the ancient priesthood."[53] The bloody assault on James recounted in the Pseudo-Clementine literature, even though it does not culminate with James's death, also happened at the foot of the altar, a place allowed by Jewish law to priests alone.[54] Furthermore, Hegesippus establishes a clear causal relation between James's death and the fall of Jerusalem, claiming, in contrast to Josephus's dating of the event, that Vespasian laid siege to the city immediately after James died.[55] A similar link also appears in the so-called *First Apocalypse of James,* where Jesus prophesies that James's departure from Jerusalem will bring war upon the country.[56] Finally, another fragment from Josephus that is cited by Origen and Eusebius, although missing from all known versions of this historian and seemingly a Christian interpolation, contains identical details and thus makes for a Jewish-Christian parallel of the same views.[57]

Identifying the Tomb of James: A Critique

I do not intend to discuss the tangled history of the traditions about James's martyrdom, neither that of Josephus nor those formulated in various early Christian settings. Nor do I intend to deal with the ways in which these documents shaped the figure of James.[58] Rather I focus on the one aspect of his martyrdom related to the present study—namely, the question of James's burial place.

The account of James's martyrdom in the fragment from Hegesippus situates his killing in the *pterygion* of the Temple (map 4). The word *pterygion* is literally a diminutive of a noun meaning "wing," and its closest English translation in this architectural context embraces features such as "pinnacle" or "turret" of the Temple (*hieron*).[59] This detail was preserved almost verbatim in Coptic in the *Second Apocalypse of James*.[60] According to Hegesippus, the scribes and Pharisees coerced James into coming to this elevated spot and demanded that he address the crowds in the Temple area in an attempt to undermine their belief in Jesus. When they realized that he was doing the exact opposite, taking advantage of this opportunity to disseminate the faith that his brother was the Messiah, they conspired to kill him. Carrying out their plot, they tossed him off the *pterygion* and then completed the task by stoning him. One of them delivered the coup de grace crushing James's head with a wooden club. Finally, Hegesippus relates that James was then buried "on the spot by the shrine [*naos*]" and that this tomb, or at least the gravestone above it, still existed at his time.[61]

Two questions may be asked about this account: What was the *pterygion* of the Temple, and where was it located, if it existed at all? Where were the tomb and the monument, and what can this tell us about the community that established them and preserved their memory?

Much has been written about the first question, and in the past century scholars have proposed almost every possible spot in the Temple area as that place: from the roof of the Temple to the roof of the royal basilica on the south of the Temple Mount (see map 3), through the various entrance structures to the area, to locations on its walls, both those surrounding the Temple and its inner courts and those encircling the whole compound.[62] Scholars vigorously explored this issue not so much because of the story of James as because Matthew and Luke mention the *pterygion* as the place where the "temptation of Jesus" oc-

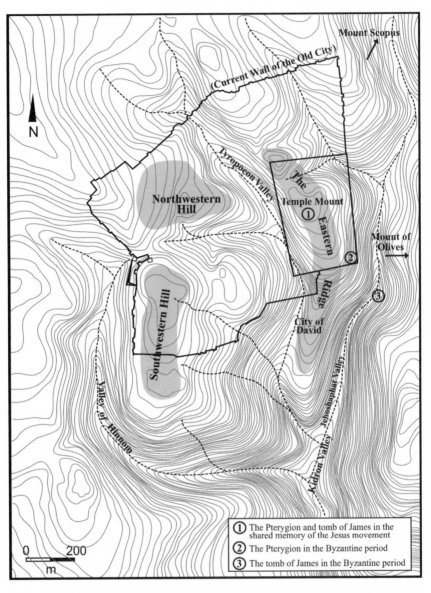

Map 4. Shifting locations of the *pterygion* and the tomb of James

curred.[63] Aside from the temptation excerpt in the Gospels, Hegesippus, and the *Second Apocalypse of James,* the *pterygion* of the Temple appears in two other sources from the first and second centuries. One version of Theodotion's translation of Daniel 9:27 rather opaquely interprets the prediction of destruction, "And upon the wing of abomination [shall come one who makes] desolate," as referring to the "ruined *pterygion.*"[64] A second text, the *Testament of Solomon,* a Jewish-Christian work whose early layers are generally dated to the first and second centuries CE, features a certain *pterygion* of the shrine (*naos,* not *hieron* as in most other sources) as an architectural component of Solomon's Temple.[65] Later, from the fourth century CE onward, a long-lived tradition, transmitted by pilgrims, monks, and others who visited Jerusalem, identified the *pterygion* with assorted spots around the city (see also chapter 4).[66]

The numerous propositions for the location of the *pterygion* all emanate from the lack of any detailed description of it in the various sources. Some scholars cling to one particular piece of information and insist that it is the ultimate clue for solving the mystery. Joachim Jeremias, for example, favored the *Testament of Solomon* as the most reliable source to mention the *pterygion,* thus deducing that it represented the lintel of the Temple gate and probably referred to the entrance of the so-called women's court (map 3: C).[67] Mainly because most sources contain no knowledge that could contribute to a concrete identification of the site, other scholars did not limit themselves to documents explicitly alluding to the *pterygion* but embarked on far-fetched attempts to link it with other structures in the Temple area. One widely endorsed inference adduces Josephus's sketch of the fearsome height of the royal basilica on the southern portion of the Temple compound (see map 3) to conclude that this is the most appropriate place for the *pterygion.*[68] Another suggestion associates the *pterygion* with the *'agof* (doorway) of the Temple Mount mentioned in the Palestinian Talmud.[69]

Clearly, these are speculative conjectures. It is hard to trust the *Testament of Solomon,* a magical text of the second century that makes purely literary use of a motif evidently well known to its readers. Likewise, it is unreasonable to attempt to identify the site solely on the basis of information that it was high enough that a fall from the *pterygion* would be deadly; this criterion could obviously tally with several other locations on the Temple Mount.[70] All in all, based on available sources, it seems impossible to determine the nature and precise location of the original *pterygion* of the Temple or to establish if there ever was one.

Rather than seeking the geographic identity of the site, a focus on the conceptual arrangement in which the *pterygion* operates is preferable. I claim not only that such a framework is traceable but that the (relatively) recent discovery of the *Second Apocalypse of James*, unavailable to previous generations of scholars toiling to identify the geographical location of the *pterygion*, permits us to delineate the formative stages that shaped the collective memories about this element. Even if we will never know exactly the geographic location of the *pterygion*, it is entirely within our reach to determine its "conceptual geography"—that is, the place it occupied in the consciousness of the people who used it. Thus the image of the *pterygion* and its cultural and religious contexts are the focus of the following discussion.

Conceptual Frameworks and Their Changing Landscapes

Importantly, all early traditions cited in the preceding section consider the *pterygion* an integral component of the Temple. This cannot be deduced simply from the literary definition of the word, which includes "wing," "top," "edge," "corner," "point," and "pinnacle," as well as sometimes a projection of a building and even a tower or turret. Indeed, in the Septuagint, for example, the word occasionally bears these meanings without any relation to the Temple.[71] On the other hand, in the verse from Daniel cited earlier, however obscure, *pterygion* undoubtedly denotes a particular element in the Temple, as can be inferred from the other objects that are named in the same context—namely, the altar and the sacrifices. The same holds true for the story relating the construction of the First Temple in the *Testament of Solomon*, in which the *pterygion* serves as part and parcel of the building.

The nature of the *pterygion* in Theodotion's translation of Daniel and the *Testament of Solomon*—as an organic constituent of the Temple—resembles its character in the traditions about James's death. Hegesippus explains that the *pterygion* was chosen as the venue for James's speech because it was "clearly visible on high" so the speaker's words would be "audible to all the people" who attended the Temple on the holiday of Passover.[72] The story thus implies that in its author's mind, the *pterygion* registers as directly linked with the Temple and situated within its confines. Relying on a similar spatial layout, Hegesippus located James's tomb "on the spot by the *naos* [inner shrine of the Temple]" (map 3: A).[73]

Scholars felt uneasy with such a positioning because it appears to contradict

Jewish law. Strict halakhic rules forbid any sort of impurity in the Temple area, making a grave at the site of the Temple highly unlikely; indeed, a human corpse is considered the most patent source of impurity. Yet proposals that would resolve these difficulties by relocating the tomb elsewhere—for instance, to the ravine east of the city known as the Valley of Jehoshaphat (see map 4: 3)[74]—are totally at odds with the picture drawn by the tradition. Hegesippus repeatedly underscores the close proximity of James's tomb to the Temple. Not only does he formulate the site's name as the "*pterygion* of the Temple," he also locates the burial site and monument, which according to him survived to his day, in the immediate vicinity of the Temple's shrine. Throughout his account, the narrator never hints, however subtly, at any difficulties this might have entailed. Furthermore, fixing the site of James's martyrdom, and therefore also his burial spot, within the grounds contiguous to the Temple derives from the inner logic of the tradition Hegesippus recounts. After all, that narrative portrays James as someone whose entire world was molded by the Temple. It accentuates the tragedy of this man, who devoted himself to atoning for the people through the Temple and eventually lost his life in that very place. In the view of whoever designed this well-crafted saga, its setting needed to include nothing other than the Temple and the area directly adjacent to it; that was the place where James was active, and it was there that he died and was laid to rest.

Other accounts of James's death, whether literarily dependent on Hegesippus or not (a matter that is heatedly debated among scholars; see n. 58), contain details that support this conclusion. The description of the events in the *Second Apocalypse of James* is practically identical. The only site mentioned in that narrative is the Temple; it is there that James was captured, and because the author does not state that he was taken away, he apparently believes that James was killed (and buried) in the same place.[75] Likewise, the Pseudo-Clementine tradition maintains that the attack on James took place next to the altar, and that in its course he was thrust down the Temple steps, left for dead, and eventually rescued by his supporters.[76] Comparable claims that James's death and entombment took place in the area of the Temple itself resonate in later adaptations of his martyrdom as well. Although these versions often owe a great deal to early sources (mainly Hegesippus and the Pseudo-Clementines), they attest to the ways the writers who retold the early stories comprehended them. For example, an Arabic translation of a Coptic text, which was discovered and published by Agnes Smith Lewis, reports that James was buried under the Temple walls, while a Latin manuscript, published by Richard Lipsius in the mid-nineteenth century, states that James "was buried next to the altar [of the Temple]."[77]

This assortment of diverse sources indicates the vital role of the Temple among the cluster of tropes that shaped the early Christian traditions about James's death. Established as the central location of the course of events that led to his martyrdom, the image of the Temple was channeled into the consciousness of the group and engraved in their shared memory. This obviously comports with the status of the Temple in other stories about James, as discussed earlier in this chapter. The same spatial organization structured the memories about his life and death.

The exact location of the tomb, if there ever was one, remains unknown. As a result of the marginality of James, one of the great losers among the protagonists of pre-Constantinian Christianity, traditions about the location of sites associated with him declined or perished. For more than two hundred years, from the days of Hegesippus and the other authors of the second-century CE texts discussed earlier down to the late fourth century, the sources remain silent about any special locus related to James within the emerging religious topography of Jerusalem. Pilgrims to Palestine from the fourth century CE onward were no longer aware of the traditions about James's martyrdom; the anonymous traveler from Bordeaux, for example, comes across the "corner of a highly elevated tower" in the ruined Temple compound but knows of it only as the locus of the temptation of Jesus.[78] Egeria, the Spanish noblewoman who visited Jerusalem later in that century, does not mention it at all.[79] Apparently, the first few centuries of the common era witnessed the distortion of not only characteristic traits of James's figure and the ideological principles advocated by his followers but of the sites associated with him as well.

Only in the second half of the fourth century—most likely in tandem with the revitalization of the Jerusalem Church and its intense political activity[80]— did the figure of James regain its place of honor. For the first time in almost three hundred years, legendary accounts surfaced, reporting the miraculous recovery of his tomb, but this time in the Jehoshaphat Valley (map 4: 3).[81] The spirit of the times dictated that such a "discovery" would lead to the erection of some sort of structure, and we do indeed hear of a chapel that was built there at some point. The chapel in the Jehoshaphat Valley grew into a small monastery commemorating the special days of James, now recognized as saint, and celebrating his feasts. As befits a saint, parts of his body and other relics associated with him circulated to other portions of the city, such as the Church of Holy Zion, and arrived in locations as far away as Constantinople. From then on, the illustrious figure of Saint James was forever enshrined in the shared consciousness of the Christian communities of early Byzantine and Arab Jerusalem.[82]

The colorfulness and diversity embodied in this new phase of Christian experience fit well with a report by Jerome that, in his day, some believed that James's tomb was to be found on the Mount of Olives, as well as with traditions current a century and a half later that located the "cornerstone" (discussed in the next section) on Mount Zion.[83] This proliferation of accounts about James and the popularity of his figure in the rising new Christian realm of Jerusalem can also explain the role granted to him in the early Jerusalem liturgy. The Armenian version of these rites reserves a special holiday in the Church of Holy Zion in memory of "St. James and [King] David."[84]

In this later period, in the generations following the establishment of Christian hegemony in Jerusalem, the location of the *pterygion* was disengaged from its original Temple context and shifted to the southeastern corner of the Temple Mount enclosure (map 4: 2). The establishment of the tomb in the Jehoshaphat Valley and its rapid growth made this a natural choice. From the vantage point of anyone standing at the foot of the mountain, on the banks of the Kidron, gazing up at the remnants of the mighty fortifications of the Temple compound, the top of that wall of the southeast corner appears as a springboard, from which one who leapt or was thrown would land on the spot of the new tomb. As evident, for example, from the famous lithograph of the tomb of the sons of Ḥezir (fig. 6; see also fig. 7), which later Christians claimed to be James's tomb, the southeast corner of the Temple Mount is the only topographical feature that dominates the panoramic view available from the tomb.[85] Indeed, Félix Abel voices the common trend in scholarship on the presumed location of the Tomb of James in the Jehoshaphat Valley when he maintains that the place where James was venerated (in the fourth century) remained "close to the actual location of his death."[86] In that same argument, he also identifies the *pterygion* as the southeast corner of the Temple compound.

But an enormous difference separates the location of the tomb suggested by the earliest sources, especially Hegesippus, from the location proposed by the Byzantine traditions (accepted at face value by modern scholars) whose goal was to reconcile ancient traditions (whether the stories about the *pterygion* in the New Testament or the accounts about James's martyrdom) with the remains of the Temple Mount still visible in the fourth century CE. The direc-

Fig. 6. A nineteenth-century drawing (by Witts) showing the outer walls of the Temple Mount from inside the Second Temple tomb of the sons of the priestly family Ḥezir. In the Middle Ages the tomb was identified as James's. Note the southeastern corner of the Temple Mount enclosure that dominates the scenery, which helps to explain why people who located James's tomb at this location shifted the *pterygion* to the outer corner of the compound. From George Williams, *The Holy City* (2d edition; London: Parker, 1849), following p. 196. Courtesy of Jacob Wharman.

tion of viewing was completely inverted. The Byzantines stood in the Kidron Valley and looked north, thus seeing the wall of the Temple precinct from the outside. But the viewpoint, both physical and spiritual, of the early community of James's followers was completely centered on the Temple itself. Standing inside the compound, they focused on the Temple and its immediate vicinity. As I have shown, the events and the various sites associated with James and his early cohorts—the *pterygion,* the tomb, and the gravestone (as well as the great stone to be discussed later)—were all attached, even if only in their minds, to the structure of the Temple itself and the space adjacent to it (map 4: 1). Scholars were prone to project the Byzantine perspective onto the early sources, and to read the Byzantine physical circumstances into the early texts. From here it is but a step to situate the *pterygion* in the southeast corner of the Temple Mount and the tomb of James in the Jehoshaphat Valley, and to regard these identifications as incontrovertible facts.[87]

Fig. 7. A view of the Tomb of Ḥezir from the outside in a 1922 photograph (by Ben-Dov) showing the members of the Israel Exploration Society (with the future second president of the state of Israel, Yitshak Ben-Zvi) visiting the site and listening to the explanations of the archaeologist Naftali Sloshets. Note that Sloshets's view focuses on the same southeastern corner of the Temple compound. Courtesy of Elchanan Reiner.

The problem with these reconstructions is that the earliest traditions about James, from the late first and early second centuries CE, lack even the slightest allusion to the southeast corner of the Temple platform as the location of the *pterygion*. Even more so, the early sources contain no hint that James's tomb was ever believed to be outside the Temple area. Quite to the contrary, the early traditions cited here indicate that the *pterygion* and the tomb of James were both located at the top of the mount, immediately next to the Temple ruins. In chapter 4 I show that even in the Byzantine period, after so much time had passed and various locations had been attributed to the tomb, many still located the *pterygion* at the heart of the compound, near the Temple ruins and not in the southeastern corner.

It is hard to determine what led the Byzantine establishers of the new location of the tomb of James to "turn their back" on the Temple Mount. Perhaps intentional ideological motives caused this shift; perhaps it occurred simply because the Mount was not an integral part of Jerusalem at that time (as I argue in chapter 4); or perhaps it was merely circumstantial. Our inability to discern the motives behind this act, however, should not blur its innovative aspects.

Finally, to close the historical circle, during the Crusader era, with the renewal of intense Christian activity on the Temple Mount, various spots associated with James began to be "identified" once more in the compound itself.[88] These identifications did not supplant the Byzantine location of the tomb in the Jehoshaphat Valley but rather existed side by side with it, creating a double system of locations. Once again James and the spatial layout associated with him returned to their original home.

Evolving Traditions about the *Pterygion*

Among the array of images and physical details incorporated into the sources that mention the "*pterygion* of the Temple," one that stands out and that had not been present from the start features "the great cornerstone." A later source illustrates this point. When the pilgrim from Bordeaux recounts his visit to the Temple ruins in the fourth decade of the fourth century CE, he reports two adjoining objects: an impressive corner of a tower and a "huge cornerstone." He recognizes the former as the site of the temptation of Jesus, which various New Testament authors identified as the *pterygion* of the Temple. To be sure, the term used by the traveler to indicate the turret of this towering structure—the Latin *pinna*—serves as the equivalent of the Greek *pterygion*. As for the latter feature, the great cornerstone, the traveler cites Psalms 118:22 as a proof text referring to this particular stone: "The stone which the builders rejected has become the head of the corner."[89]

Surprisingly, both the cornerstone and the *pterygion*, as well as the associated verse from the Psalm, also appear in the *Testament of Solomon*, a legendary tale written approximately 150 years earlier about the construction of the First Temple by King Solomon. According to that story, Solomon's building enterprise concluded with the hoisting of a huge cornerstone onto the "*pterygion* of the shrine." Beyond human capacity, this final task hindered the completion of the project until an Arab demon named Epiphas arrived to help. King Solomon in turn, in his great joy at the completion of the project, cited the previously mentioned verse from Psalms—"The stone which the builders rejected has become the head of the corner"—and applied it to this stone.[90]

Scholars did not pay much attention to this parallel. Yet, although the source for the cornerstone image in the writings of the Bordeaux pilgrim remains unknown, the very fact that both the pilgrim and the *Testament of Solomon* know of the cornerstone in the Temple and associate that stone with the same biblical verse cries out for interpretation. Although this verse from Psalms was very popular among early Christian writers, insofar as Jesus is recorded not only to have expounded on it but also to have likened himself to that rejected stone,[91] the association of the same formula with the same physical feature in two independent sources should not go unnoticed.

New light on this issue, which elucidates the stages in the formation of this cornerstone tradition, may be shed by the martyrdom passage in the *Second Apocalypse of James*. In his account of James's capture by his opponents, the author of the apocalypse enumerates two spots where James stood. The first, regardless of the uncertain meaning of the Coptic word, undoubtedly represents the author's attempt to render the Greek *pterygion*.[92] The second location is absolutely clear—the great cornerstone. Like others who have pondered this passage, I cannot resolve the question of how James could have been standing in two spots simultaneously, or explain the need for this dual positioning. Nor do I hold the key to the mystery of the great cornerstone; its origin and purpose remain uncertain. The author of the *Testament of Solomon*, for example, maintained that the stone provided the material used for the erection of the *pterygion*, but this seems to be a harmonistic explication for an existing tradition in which the two items are operating side by side.

Yet, despite all the unknowns, the traits common to these three disparate sources—the story of James's martyrdom as it appears in the *Second Apoca-lypse of James,* the legend about the building of the Temple in the *Testament of Solomon,* and the tradition featured by the traveler from Bordeaux—reflect the same conceptual setting. Their geographic backdrop centers on the Temple (note that both the traveler from Bordeaux and the *Testament of Solomon* pre-sent it as Solomon's Temple),[93] and within this landscape they highlight two adjacent constituents—the *pterygion* and the "great cornerstone." At some point, not in the *Second Apocalypse* but in the two other texts, the verse from Psalms was linked to the cornerstone and continued to serve as its proof text for centuries.[94]

What prompted the shared texture of these traditions? Due to the common mention of the *pterygion,* many scholars associated them with the New Testa-ment account of the temptation of Jesus, and identified this account as the source of inspiration for all the others.[95] In their story about the series of temp-tations with which Satan tested Jesus, both Matthew and Luke include an inci-dent that occurred in precisely the site under discussion here, the *pterygion* of the Temple.[96] The accepted explanation for the relation between the New Testament temptation passage and other *pterygion* traditions holds that the Gospel story, gradually rising to the status of Scripture, impelled other writers to draw upon its motifs. This type of interpretation, however, presupposes the superiority of the New Testament passage about the temptation in the world-view of those who produced the other traditions. Such a perspective focuses on the temptation of Jesus and, while taking its details for granted, seeks an ap-propriate way to construe its meaning. This situation, however, may not have been the case in the first few centuries of the common era—prior to the con-solidation of the New Testament into a homogeneous and prominent docu-ment—when the previously mentioned traditions, such as those found in the *Second Apocalypse of James,* were formulated.

A different set of challenges confronts those attempting to reconstruct the physical context and the ideological tendencies embodied in the passages in their formative stage and their function in the life of the communities that pro-duced them. In this setting, the nature of the *pterygion* assumes greater im-portance; did the author of the passage in Matthew and Luke *create* the name of the place out of whole cloth? If so, what was he trying to achieve? Readers who focus on the events that "transpired" there—Satan's attempt to entice the future Messiah—and their New Testament legacy are liable to impose the events on the geography and arrive at peculiar conclusions, like that of Hyldahl, who claimed that the *pterygion* was the official execution site of the Sanhedrin, the Jewish high court, in the Second Temple period.[97] If, however, one is not to assume the priority of the New Testament tradition about the *pterygion,* such maneuvers become superfluous.

Indeed, the tradition handed down by Matthew and Luke does not endow the *pterygion* with any real substance. This site is not mentioned anywhere else in the New Testament, nor is it involved in any other event. Such omissions indicate that the name of the place was already registered in the mind of the audience targeted by the authors who recorded the temptation story. Rather than making the first use of the *pterygion* image, the temptation passage in the Gospels seems to rely on its established reputation.

Comparing the pericope about the temptation of Jesus in Matthew and Luke with the account in Hegesippus about the martyrdom of James reveals striking similarities in both the name of the site, *pterygion,* and the events that unfolded there, namely a deadly fall. Furthermore, both narratives represent analogous, though opposing, tendencies in the world of the Jesus movement. Both contemplate the combination of death and the dissemination of the belief in Jesus the Messiah, but the passage about James articulates a rather positive view of such a "martyrdom," whereas the temptation story remains reserved about it (after all, Jesus turned down Satan's proposal). Within these contrasting narratives, the *pterygion* serves an identical function: it is high enough that a fall from it would be fatal; it is centrally located so it could be observed by the multitudes; and, most important, it is incorporated in the structure of the Temple, the heart of Jewish life at the time. This analysis suggests that the *pterygion,* or the image about such a place, held a certain significance for the authors and their readers. The prestige of the *pterygion* led them to associate it with major events of their shared ethos and formulate around it various traditions, until it was finally memorialized as a pilgrimage site for Byzantine Christians.

Over the years the figure of the *pterygion* and its imagery continued to change, and some of these developments may still be discerned. Whereas in the Gospel stories of Jesus and in Hegesippus's account about James only the *pterygion* appears, a second, closely related entity—the "great cornerstone"—surfaces along with it in other traditions, which therefore should probably be dated to a later stage. Two second-century sources—the *Testament of Solomon* and the *Second Apocalypse of James*—link the "great cornerstone" with the *pterygion,* and remnants of this coupling were preserved until the time of the Bordeaux pilgrim. Such an analysis reveals a two-stage process in the crystallization of the *pterygion* image. First came traditions in the lore of the early Christian communities about meaningful events, either historical or legendary, that took place at the *pterygion.* The sources expressing this phase include the passage about the temptation of Jesus in Matthew and Luke and the passage about James preserved by Hegesippus. In the second phase the tradition was enhanced by the addition of the "great cornerstone." This stage also features the development of folkloristic legends about the *pterygion,* such as the one in the *Testament of Solomon,* and the configuration of biblical proof texts as an allusion to the site. The two sources conveying the events about James's martyrdom—Hegesippus and the *Second Apocalypse of James*—delineate the axis along which the representation of the site matured: the great cornerstone does not appear in the former but does occur in the latter.

The literary proliferation of traditions involving the *pterygion* reached its zenith in the second stage. It was then followed by a third phase, in which the traditions faded. This third chapter in the story of the *pterygion* is clearly demonstrated by the writings of the Bordeaux pilgrim. While his itinerary still includes the *pterygion* and the great cornerstone and shows some knowledge of their associated lore, namely the story about the temptation of Jesus and the application of the Psalm verse to the cornerstone, other components of the site's legacy have already begun to dissolve. The figure of James and the sites associated with him, all dominant factors in the earlier portrayal of the *pterygion,* have been "eliminated" from the picture. It would not be long before the ancient depiction of this feature would be forgotten altogether.

But this does not mean that the cluster of images and details associated with James were doomed to vanish completely. Traditions tend to fluctuate, and when they no longer retain their old shape, they are reinvented in a new one. In the case under discussion, this reinvention occurred in the Byzantine era. Christian inhabitants of Jerusalem at that time were no longer familiar with the anonymous Jewish authors among the Jesus movement or within the community of James in the late first and second centuries. Undoubtedly they were also far removed from first-century moral, ideological, and religious views. Yet when they encountered the traditions preserved in writings such as the fragment from Hegesippus in Eusebius and the segments in the Pseudo-Clementines, they revived them, while shifting the geographical arena from the Temple to the bottom of the Kidron Valley.

The Temple Mount as a Sacred Cemetery

Hegesippus concludes the story of James's burial next to the Temple by adding that "his gravestone still remains by the shrine [of the Temple]."[98] Such a proclamation is neither an integral part of the narrative about James nor relevant to the content of the tradition reported there. The double ending of the story, of which this sentence is part, seems to mark the seam between the segment quoted by Hegesippus and the closing remark he attaches to it.[99] In other words, after conveying the tradition about James's martyrdom, Hegesippus brings the passage to a close with a personal observation about the site in his own days. This does not imply that he knew anything reliable about James's burial site; perhaps he did, perhaps he did not. It does, however, provide a glimpse at how the place was seen in those days. A statement by a local second-century CE writer that the burial place of James right next to the (ruined) shrine of the Temple had been preserved down to his time sheds considerable light on the status of that place in his period.

Tombs of publicly acclaimed figures do not just endure fortuitously for decades; someone has to retain the memory of the deceased and ensure at least some minimal maintenance of the grave. Written at around the same time as Hegesippus, the *Martyrdom of Polycarp* provides a glimpse into the activities that commemorated such places: "Thus we, at last, took up his bones, more precious than precious stones, and finer than gold, and put them where it was appropriate. There the Lord will permit us to come together according to our power in gladness and joy and celebrate the day of his martyrdom."[100] This phenomenon immediately brings to mind another tomb in Jerusalem whose memory seems to have been preserved by the early Christians—namely, that of Jesus himself.[101] Indeed, tombs of saints, especially those whose deaths attested to their faith and thus strengthened the faith of others, were regularly incorporated into the believers' shared memory and religious practice.[102] A colorful blend of traditions often blossomed around such localities. Legends about the person buried there and exaggerated tales associating the site with other important figures were two common factors that shaped the public's consciousness about such places. The tradition reported by Hegesippus typifies the first model: a touching and gripping story, comprising both tragic and heroic elements, about an important personage from the past, which also emphasizes the religious aspect of the protagonist's

"testimony" before his death. Most important, the details of the past are fun-
neled into a specific physical point—a tomb or monument existing in the
present. The palpable reality of the present and the literature from the past
interact in a reciprocal dance; the tradition predicates the site's special quality, while the site in turn sustains the tradition and anchors it in the present.[103]

The area of the ruined Jewish Temple functions as the stage, and later as the
pilgrimage site, for another renowned figure in early Christian legacy, namely
Zechariah, whose tale is retold many times in both Jewish and Christian settings. The sources about the martyrdom of this character were gathered carefully, and his persona, blending together more than one person, has been extensively studied, so that there is no need to repeat the details here.[104] Four
issues are significant for the present study. First, the presentation of Zechariah
as linked with the Temple, and sometimes even as an actual priest, parallels the
way James is configured by Hegesippus. Second, the positioning of Zechariah's
martyrdom adjacent to the altar—a location repeated, in one form or another,
in most early sources—corresponds to the tradition about James as rendered
by the Pseudo-Clementine literature. Josephus's remark (*Bellum Judaicum*
4:343) that Zechariah was slain in the middle of the Temple is also reminiscent
of the location of James's martyrdom in Hegesippus. Similar proclivities for
placing the martyrdom of early Christian figures in the Temple can be detected
in other traditions as well.[105] Third, some of the traditions about Zechariah include a new element—that his blood turned to stone—that recalls the stone
that appears in some of the traditions about James. Finally, and most important, the Temple Mount becomes a pilgrimage site associated with the death of
both James and Zechariah. In conjunction with Hegesippus's report about the
gravestone of James, as well as the convoluted tradition about the *pterygion* and
the cornerstone, Christian visitors to the ruined Temple site also identified the
spot of Zechariah's slaughter as "next to the altar" and enumerated a variety of
legends associated with this incident. A contemporary rabbinic text adds that
the sightless and the lame would heal there.[106]

Another tradition that fits well with the image of the Temple Mount as the
locus of sacred tombs lurks behind the myth about Adam's burial under the
foundation stone (the reports about this stone are discussed in chapter 6).
Only vague recollections of this notion are preserved here and there. Isaiah
Gafni, who collected and studied the material, convincingly argues that the

belief about Adam's interment at Golgotha echoes an early conviction that located the site at the Jewish Temple. As with many other pieces of Jewish lore, later Christian authors transferred this tradition to the Holy Sepulcher.[107] Elusive as it might be, the folkloristic stories surrounding Adam's tomb adds another facet to the representation of the Temple Mount as a sort of sacred cemetery. Unexpectedly, rabbinic sources corroborate the existence of such notions. For example, one tradition reports that human bones were found in one of the Temple's chambers; another legendary account claims that Temple attendants unearthed the skull of Araunah the Jebusite under the altar; finally, a well-known and admittedly peculiar rabbinic statement asserts that "one who is buried under the altar [is] as if he is buried under the glorious throne."[108]

Generally speaking, many studies demonstrate that tombs of important figures, mostly with roots in the biblical past, occupied the cultural landscape and daily experience of Second Temple Jews.[109] Criticized by many, even within the Jesus movement, this trend retained its vitality in the generations following the destruction of the Temple, as illustrated by works such as the *Life of the Prophets* (*Vitae Prophetarum*), which emphasizes the motif of the tomb as a cultural topos. In an apparent reflection of the religious environment of late Roman and Byzantine Palestine,[110] numerous graves reported in this text, whether factual or fictional, are said to house a person who ended his life as a martyr, having been killed by the authorities or the people. Such was the case for the prophets Isaiah, Jeremiah, Ezekiel, Micah, Amos, and Zechariah. The resemblance to James is clear.

The most significant analogy to the traditions about James's burial place on the Temple Mount pertains to the Holy Sepulcher, the site of Jesus's tomb at Golgotha. Even a superficial glance at the wide array of sources that attest to the emergence of this locality reveals patent similarities to the story of James. Both individuals, central figures in their circles, died in tragic circumstances, each struggling to defend the rightness of his chosen path. In both cases, the threat felt by others lest the teachings of this individual be disseminated served as the main incentive for killing him. Both were buried in the immediate vicinity of the place where they were killed, and their tombs acquired a sacred status. Seeing the situation this way and knowing (in hindsight) the whereabouts of Golgotha only strengthen the conclusion that the Temple Mount is indeed the appropriate place to locate James's tomb.

The Temple Mount in the Historical and Cultural Context of Early Christianity

When did the awareness of holy burial sites on the Temple Mount take shape, and what induced the authors among the disciples of Jesus and the followers of James to mold these geographical designations the way they did? It is hard to answer these questions. As mentioned at the beginning of this chapter, various sources hint that the Temple ranked high among some early proto-Christian groups (the so-called Jesus movement). For example, traditions that locate major events of Jesus's childhood in this institution, as well as the assertion that Mary too grew up in the Temple among the priests, tally with Hegesippus's portrayal of James. In the same vein, the Letter to the Hebrews, despite its criticism of the existing Temple system and its consequent emphasis on the heavenly Jerusalem, depicts Jesus as the high priest who enters the Holy of Holies, atones for the people, and defies the traditional priesthood.[111] This image completely overlaps with that of James in the segment of Hegesippus. Other Christian works, such as the final version of the *Testament of Levi*, also polemicize against the Temple priesthood.[112] Moreover, corresponding to the negative attitude toward the sacrificial cult in the Temple, as articulated, among other sources, in the Letter to the Hebrews, some Christian writers tend to position James as a great opponent of Temple rituals. Such an assessment surfaces in the writings of the fourth-century church father Epiphanius, who cites a tradition about James's critique of Temple offerings, attributing it to the Ebionites.[113] The passage in Hegesippus also utters a dual, rather conflicting stance on this issue. James is perceived as at once a priest and a competitor and substitute for the priesthood.[114] It is difficult to determine whether these presentations voice one or many streams of thought within the Jesus movement, and much of this material is still shrouded in mist.

Likewise, due to the paucity of sources, the actual events that led to and followed James's death remain unknown. For example, the passage in Josephus describes a more moderate version of the proceedings that set James's killing in motion, in which the Temple and the Temple Mount do not appear at all. Was James really buried on the Temple Mount? The numerous cavities underneath the platform could provide potential sites aplenty. One cannot know for sure, and for the purpose of the present study it does not really matter. Even though it appears implausible that Temple authorities in the Second Temple period would allow a corpse to be entombed there, someone no later than the mid-second century had patterned the tradition in Hegesippus according to that very mode. The landscape envisioned in that spatial organization interspersed in the popular imagination until different forms of it were embedded in the apocalyptic writings unearthed in Nag Hammadi and the legends retold in the *Testament of Solomon*. Reverberations of the same paradigm, however dim, could still be heard at the time of the Bordeaux pilgrim. The people who designed these configurations clearly considered the space *near* the Temple to be a place of religious value—not the Temple itself but rather, in the words of Hegesippus, the area "near the shrine." The fragmentary traditions pertaining to this line of thought display the seeds of a new spatial order and the consolidation of a new holy site: not the Temple itself but the area in which it was located. Likewise, the Temple worship with the laws of purity associated with it and the classical elements representing it—the altar and the Holy of Holies— were supplanted by other concerns and new objects: the *pterygion*, the great cornerstone, James's tomb, and the monument of his gravestone. All these represent a new facet of the Temple Mount history.

Finally, I argue that this is also the context for the stone-upon-stone passage discussed in the first part of this chapter. While it accords with the physical layout of traditions about James, with its core lying in the area immediately outside the Temple structure, Jesus's prophecy, nevertheless, voices an opposite stance about it. Whereas the stories about James and Zechariah along with the traditions about the tomb, the *pterygion,* and the cornerstone elevate that space to sacredness, the pericope in Mark denounces it with the prediction of destruction. To me these present two opposing poles in the discourse about sacred space that engaged the Jesus movement (similar to the two sides in the dispute about martyrdom reflected in the stories about the temptation of Jesus and the death of James, which I discussed earlier in the chapter). According to this line of thought, the stone-upon-stone prophecy was not directed against notions outside the Jesus movement (denouncing the holy structure of "other" Jewish groups), but rather polemicized toward the inside, against competing notions within its own community. In their struggle to define their identity, the followers of Jesus strove to configure their own sacred space; some in the movement adhered to the Temple Mount (not the Temple), shaping its image as a sacred cemetery, while others rejected it.

This reconstruction of the religious-cultural milieu of the Jesus movement revises some central elements in the story of the Temple Mount. There is no neat continuation here (as in the sequential model I discussed in the introduction), where the stature of the space around the Temple flows smoothly from the Temple itself. Instead, the image of the Temple Mount functions as a *locus memoriae,* emerging from a dialectical, tortuous process of carving new identities and molding the spatial organization that will support them. Chapter 6 will add another facet to this quarrelsome process, by showing that the rabbis too were concerned with very similar challenges of identity, and engaged the same space—the Temple Mount—although in very different, rather contrasting, ways.

CHAPTER THREE

Delusive Landscapes

From Jerusalem to Aelia

The destruction of the Second Temple by the Romans at the end of the Great Revolt in 70 CE opened a new chapter in the annals of Jerusalem. Little is known about the events that transpired within the ruins of the city in the sixty-year period between 70 and Emperor Hadrian's building project, launched in the beginning of the 130s CE (perhaps as late as 135). According to Josephus, when the fighting in 70 settled down, the Roman Tenth Legion bivouacked next to the three Herodian towers in the western part of the Upper City (the area known today as the Tower of David; map 2: 9).[1] Except for this note, no other written documents or archaeological discoveries provide any significant data that can shed even the slightest light on the city's texture or the whereabouts of its inhabitants.[2]

Reliable information about events in the city both before and during the Bar Kokhba revolt (132–35 CE) is similarly wanting. Undoubtedly, the lingering anger and grief over the devastation of Jerusalem and destruction of the Temple, and the longing for them both, were among the main factors that fomented the uprising. Still, fundamental questions are left without clear answers: did the rebels capture the city, and if so did they resume the rebuilding of the Temple or revive any of its rituals?[3] The dearth of evidence leaves this portion of Jerusalem's story in the dark.

By war's end, however, a new urban and cultural landscape had begun to take form in Jerusalem. The Romans established a colony, Aelia Capitolina, on the ruins (or perhaps adjacent to them) of the Second Temple city.[4] But the town developed very gradually, and for 150 years, until the close of the third century, it lacked even a fortification system—as was the case with many of the period's municipalities. Roman veterans, mainly from the long-encamped Tenth Legion, made up the nucleus of the new settlement in Aelia. An imperial order forbade Jews and Christians from residing in the city, fostering the growth of a foreign, noncircumcised Christian community.[5] Jerusalem's former Jewish identity increasingly grew so remote that Firmilian, the Roman governor in Caesarea at the beginning of the fourth century, seemed no longer to know the name "Jerusalem."[6] Indeed, in the eyes of the Roman administration Aelia did not measure up to Jerusalem's ancient magnitude, which prompted the transfer of the regional administrative center to a more natural location in the coastal city of Caesarea, elevating it to the province 's capital. Jerusalem's reduced stature and dilapidated appearance continued until the rise of Christianity in the fourth century.

One unresolved question about Jerusalem at this time concerns the compound known as the Temple Mount, built by Herod, which stood at the hub of the ancient, Second Temple city and housed its most renowned institution, the Temple. What happened on the Temple Mount when the Romans established the pagan *colonia*? This chapter explores various facets of this question. It first discusses the two major structures that, according to scholars, were located on the mount—a pagan shrine to Zeus/Jupiter and a couple of Roman statues. It then considers the broader urban layout of Roman Jerusalem and the role of the Temple Mount enclosure within it. In doing so, it delineates the procedures by which scholars of the present attempt to recreate a picture of the past, the details of which are mediated through ancient texts and inanimate physical artifacts. This investigative process reveals the vulnerability of our knowledge. It demonstrates how delusive ancient landscapes can be but, at the same time, makes a case for a specific methodology by which these obstacles may be surmounted.

The Temple to Zeus/Jupiter and the "Hand" of Xiphilinus[7]

One passage in the sixty-ninth book of *Roman History,* written in the early third century by the prominent Roman historian Cassius Dio, has functioned as a cornerstone in the discussion about what happened on the Temple Mount after the Bar Kokhba revolt. In this pericope Dio recounts Emperor Hadrian's deeds in Jerusalem some three generations earlier, at the beginning of the third decade of the second century.

> At Jerusalem he founded a city in place of the one which had been razed to the ground, naming it Aelia Capitolina, and on the site of the Temple of the god he raised a new temple to Zeus [Jupiter]. This brought on a war of no slight importance nor of brief duration, for the Jews deemed it intolerable that foreign races should be settled in their city and foreign religious rites implanted there.[8]

Based on this extract, a widely endorsed opinion, already apparent in the earliest studies on Jerusalem in the seventeenth and eighteenth centuries and common thereafter, maintains that, in accordance with Emperor Hadrian's instructions, the Romans erected a Capitoline shrine on the Temple Mount, probably dedicated to the head of the Capitoline triad—Jupiter—in his Eastern or Greek simulacrum as Zeus. In the nineteenth century most scholars believed, to quote one popular formulation, that, "no place was more suitable for the Roman temple than the rocky surface of the Moriah."[9] So vivid was such a temple in their minds that one scholar could visualize its "pure style and admirable shapes" and claimed "in these the Jupiter shrine excelled all three temples of God which were situated at the very same place."[10] Another study went even further, not only "placing" the pagan temple on the Temple Mount but also relating all known archaeological remains to that edifice (Robinson's arch, etc.).[11]

At the turn to the twentieth century two scholars, Germer-Durand and Emil Schürer, fused the fragmented pieces of information about Aelia Capitolina and the pagan temple on the Temple Mount into a systemized reconstruction of Roman Jerusalem.[12] Germer-Durand innovatively envisioned the urban layout of Aelia as a Roman town par excellence, basing it mainly on what he had gleaned from the city plan of Gerasa (today the town of Jerash in Jordan) and framing it around the contours of the Arab Old City of Jerusalem (depicted in map 2). Schürer accepted this configuration of Aelia and supplied a systematic discussion of the written sources. For both, the existence of a Zeus temple on the grounds of the Temple Mount was self-evident. In the first half of the twentieth century great scholars of ancient Jerusalem such as Hugues Vincent and Félix Abel, and later also Michael Avi-Yonah, espoused the Durand-Schürer approach almost without reservations.[13] Since then, nearly every treatment of this period has included the Capitoline temple on the Temple Mount as a fixed tenant of Roman Jerusalem: late antique atlases of the city locate it on the site of the Second Temple (e.g., map 5); scholarly studies on a variety of subjects take its existence for granted; it was only natural, then, for popular books, guides, and museums to follow suit and for this pagan temple to become a "reality" in the public mind. The list of publications and popular expressions that evince this belief in the Roman temple on the Temple Mount extends over two centuries and runs the gamut from magazine articles through museum exhibitions all the way to the statements of the Israeli Supreme Court.[14]

The few scholars who have voiced some doubts about the passage in Dio have tended to reject Dio's remarks in favor of a series of Christian sources (Origen, Eusebius, the traveler from Bordeaux, and Jerome). These writers, acquainted with Roman Jerusalem, mentioned other pagan sanctuaries that had been built in different parts of the city but never spoke of any such shrine on the Temple Mount.[15] Glenn Bowersock went even further to suggest that scholars have mistranslated Dio's clause about the Temple Mount and that it should in fact read not that the pagan Temple stood "in the place" of the ancient Jewish Temple but rather "instead of" that institution, and so not necessarily in the same location.[16]

My own studies have led me to confirm the rejection of Dio's testimony, but on different grounds. Based on detailed philological dissection, I have concluded that the passage describing Hadrian's actions on the Temple Mount bears the stamp of a Christian writer. This inference rests on (1) content gaps in the structural design of the segment, which point to another "hand" interfering with the sequence of the narrative; (2) its vocabulary, especially one compound verb (*antegeiro*, "to raise against") reflecting Christian phrasing that only came into wide use after the days of Dio, in the writings of the so-called church fathers; and (3) the religious tendencies of the passage, which present this segment of Jerusalem history as a theological confrontation between Hadrian and the Jewish God.[17]

Scholars generally consider Cassius Dio, who wrote his *History* at the outset of the third century, a most reliable historian. He indicates that it took him a decade to collect the material for his grand opus and another twelve years to study and produce it.[18] Dio's relative closeness to Hadrian's time and his position in the upper echelons of the imperial bureaucracy allowed him easy access to its documents, thus enhancing his credibility. Yet all of Dio's books after volume 61 have been lost. A few portions are preserved in medieval anthologies and Byzantine lexicons, but these, which quote Dio quite carefully, are exceedingly fragmented. Two abridged editions (*epitomai*) prepared by Byzantine monks—Xiphilinus in the eleventh century and Zonaras a century later—have also come down to us.[19] The paragraph under discussion here survived only in Xiphilinus's abridgment of books 36–80, which he produced for Emperor Michael VII during the 1060s. Scholars have been familiar with these facts all along but failed to consider seriously both their textual implications and historiographic significance.[20]

My conclusions extract the historical barb from the story of the pagan shrine on the Temple Mount and show it to have been implanted by a religiously motivated writer. Dio's original version has been lost, but we can attempt to reconstruct it through clues left in the text. The second part of the previously quoted paragraph from Dio's *Roman History* recounts the Jews' dissatisfaction with the foreign shrines that were placed in their city. It may be that in the first half of the passage Dio described the events that resulted in those shrines— that is, Hadrian's founding of a foreign city and endowing it with a pagan shrine (or shrines). In the course of paraphrasing this passage, a later writer reformulated the circumstances into a theological confrontation between Hadrian and the Jewish God. This writer resituated the pagan shrine, shifting it from the city in general to the Temple Mount. Moreover, he painted a neutral act customary in the establishment of a new colony in the harsh colors of a religious confrontation by sprinkling the passage with loaded vocabulary and religious terminology that were familiar to his Christian readers. All in all, the pagan shrine dedicated to Zeus on the Temple Mount seems to be an imaginary creation of Christian polemics rather than an actual, historically corroborated structure.

The Life of a Temple That Never Existed

Presupposing the validity of Cassius Dio's report about the Zeus temple on the Temple Mount, scholars have construed other texts as relating to the same sanctuary. These sources, however, do not mention such a temple explicitly.

Thus, rather than supporting the claim of the temple's existence, these texts should actually be seen as resulting from erroneous convictions about it. Once we deprive the account attributed to Dio of its credibility, these references to the alleged pagan shrine on the Temple Mount lose their very foundation.

The *Epistle of Barnabas* provides a typical example of the type of process that could result in scholars conceiving of a sanctuary that never existed. In a chapter marked by a strong anti-Temple sentiment, the writer of the *epistle* quotes (rather liberally) from a Greek version of Isaiah 49:16: "They who destroyed this shrine will themselves build it." He then goes on to explain that "This [is] happening now. For owing to the war it [the Jewish Temple] was destroyed by the enemy; at present even the servants of the enemy will build it up again."[21] Many scholars have attempted to decipher the historical circumstances that lurk behind this admittedly obscure statement by attributing the deeds mentioned in the Barnabas passage to specific events and time periods.[22] One of these explanations posits that the writer speaks of the Capitoline temple that Hadrian had supposedly planned to erect on the Temple Mount. According to this suggestion, Barnabas draws on this event as proof that "God does not desire a temple . . . and now its disappearance will be made irrevocable by the Jews' enemies . . . who will build another temple in its stead."[23]

Without delving into this line of reasoning, all would agree that Barnabas's account contains no evidence whatsoever that could tie it either to Hadrian's reign or to an attempt to establish a pagan shrine at that time. These details were imported—introduced into the Barnabas text from the writings of Cassius Dio. The scholars who offer this reading argue that Dio's account sheds light on Barnabas's remarks. But if Dio did not actually write what these scholars believe he did, and if, moreover, no one ever thought of building a Capitoline temple on the Temple Mount—at least according to the sources that have come down to us—then this interpretation should surely be abandoned. We ought to reject it not because it cannot explain the Barnabas text but because its supposed historical basis is apparently nonexistent.

Another item that scholars sometimes associate with the Roman temple that Hadrian supposedly established on the Temple Mount is a structure named *aedes* (a common Roman designation for a temple building), which appears in the travel accounts of the Bordeaux pilgrim. Touring the ruins of the Jewish Temple in the 330s, this Christian visitor provides a detailed narrative of the numerous "attractions" he came across—among them the site of Zechariah's murder, which he locates "in the sanctuary [*aedes*] itself, where the Temple which Solomon built stood."[24] Various scholars proposed that the *aedes* refers here to the Jupiter shrine built by Hadrian or to its remains.[25] This far-fetched proposal totally ignores the context of the term in the traveler's journal. His narrative provides no hint of any encounter with remnants of pagan worship. Moreover, as Vincent has shown, the *aedes* in the pilgrim's narrative serves to demonstrate the hierarchy of the various sites that operate in the entangled biblical traditions about the death of Zechariah. Especially relevant is the verse in the Gospel of Luke that situates the event "between the altar and the house" (Luke 11:51; obviously referring to the inner shrine of the Jewish Temple). Because the traveler used *templum* at the beginning of his passage to represent the compound as a whole, and alternatively for what he perceived as the Temple of Solomon (probably the ruins of the Jewish Temple), the narrative required a special designation for the particular area of Zechariah's murder. In a spatial organization that rests on traditions such as this one from Luke, the Zechariah site registered as a more elevated space in the sacred hierarchy than just a plain *templum;* it occupied the area of the inner shrine itself. Jewish traditions— which, as many scholars have noted, the traveler was quite familiar with— clearly distinguish between *miqdash* (the Temple as a whole) and *heikhal* (the inner shrine), corresponding to the Greek division between *hieron* and the *naos*. It seems that the term *aedes* operates in the *Itinerarium* of the Bordeaux pilgrim precisely to express this distinction, demarcating the line of sacredness between the mere (ruined) Temple site and its inner sanctum.[26]

Be that as it may, quite clearly it is only the presupposition about the existence of a pagan temple on the grounds of the ruined Herodian compound that allowed scholars to "find" it in the account of the Bordeaux pilgrim. Without the passage in Cassius Dio, the *aedes* would never have been interpreted as indicating such a temple. Now that the initial source pointing to the existence of such a temple has been discredited, the suggested interpretation of the expression used by the traveler from Bordeaux should be rejected as well.[27]

Finally, scholars also tend to link the supposed Jupiter sanctuary with a phrase from the seventh-century composition known as *Chronicon Paschale*. In a section recounting Hadrian's response to the insurgence of the Jews (evidently the Bar Kokhba revolt), the author dwells on the fate of three elements: the Jews themselves; the Temple, which he calls "the shrine [*naos*] of the Jews"; and the city of Jerusalem. While the Romans, he says, despoiled the first two— enslaving the Jews and shattering their Temple—they spared the third, the city of Jerusalem. Not only did Hadrian refrain from destroying the city, but he even furnished it with a ramified system of public buildings, reorganized its neighborhoods and administration, and finally bestowed upon it the name Aelia, modeled on his own *nomen gentilicium:* Aelius (Hadrian's *tria nomina* being Publius Aelius Hadrianus).[28] The Hadrian building inventory provided by the author of this text concludes with a structure he calls the *kodra* (the square; line 12). By the end of the nineteenth century scholars had matched this square with the compound of the ruined Jewish Temple. Ever since, many have believed that the *Chronicon Paschale* pericope provides sound evidence for the restoration of the Temple Mount precinct, either to house the pagan temple that stood at its center or, as some put it, as "a sacred open area" with statues at its midpoint. Shortly after this identification had first been suggested, Adolph Schlatter wrote authoritatively, "Where in Jerusalem the 'square' is, one does not need to say; it stands powerfully enough around the whole Temple Mount." A century later scholars' acceptance of the reliability of the *Chronicon Paschale* report and the accuracy of the suggested identification remains mostly unquestioned, as can be seen in a recent statement by Nicole Belayche, who claimed that the *kodra* "must be recognized as the open court of the [Jewish] Temple."[29]

But even if one accepts the authenticity of the *Chronicon Paschale* list (i.e., as a record of actual buildings in Aelia, a question that merits a discussion in itself),[30] the issue of whether the *kodra* denotes the site of the Jewish Temple is far from settled. The fact that an image of a huge trapezoid called "the Temple Mount" is deeply etched in modern consciousness, so that almost any use of the word "square" in relation to Jerusalem's landscape seems to be associated with it, says absolutely nothing about the way the ancients perceived this site. The word *kodra* in Greek transliteration is extremely rare; its Latin source, *quadra,* subsumes many denotations and can stand for a variety of architectonic elements. Indeed, as noted by Vincent (n. 29), citizens of Rome applied this term to the *Urbs quadrata,* the sacred square on the Palatine Hill from which the city was supposed to have sprung. But this can hardly prove that residents of Aelia Capitolina, or anyone else for that matter, used it to mark the site of the Jewish Temple. In fact, popular usage of *quadra* in Roman discourse encompassed the meaning of "podium," making it appropriate to denote the results of the leveling and raising operations that the builders of Aelia carried out in the center of the colony (today's Christian Quarter; map 2: 5), impressive remains of which have been uncovered in archaeological excavations. From the Romans' point of view—especially if we disregard Dio's testimony about a pagan temple on the Temple Mount—there would be no reason to use the term *kodra* for what must have been a ruined (and, as I shall argue, neglected) compound.

Legends from the Time of the Muslim Conquest

Two seventh-century documents, published in 1992 by Bernard Flusin, have entered the discussion of the Temple Mount at the time of Aelia Capitolina; one, originally written in Greek but surviving only in Georgian translation, has been known to scholars for some time, while the other, a Greek text, was made available for the first time in Flusin's study.[31] These works transmit two legendary tales, composed in a didactic form, about incidents occurring in Jerusalem soon after the Muslim capture of the city. The first recounts the story of John, an archdeacon and marble artisan who cooperated with the Arabs in the restoration of the Temple Mount and was severely castigated for his actions. The other tells of demons that lent a hand in the clearing of the site and, in the process, terrified the city's inhabitants. Both documents call the Jewish Temple site the "Capitol." Flusin, followed by Cyril Mango, saw this as crucial supporting evidence for the existence of a Capitoline temple on the Temple Mount, and thus as also confirming Cassius Dio's report.[32] But it seems to me that this conclusion falls short on various grounds.

The two sources demonstrate that in the second half of the seventh century, several decades after the Arab conquest, some of Jerusalem's residents applied the name "capitol" to the site of the Jewish Temple. But the conclusion reached by Flusin and Mango that this name circulated widely throughout the Byzantine period, and, even more so, that the Temple enclosure had acquired this label because a Capitoline temple had been built there six centuries earlier, stretches the sources well beyond their limit. Such a conclusion is not so much a logical deduction as an arbitrary choice among many possible explanations of these texts. An alternative hypothesis might be that only in the seventh century, when the new rulers of Jerusalem revived the Temple area after centuries of devastation, did the name "capitol" emerge. To explain why seventh-century people would "invent" a new image of the Temple Mount as a "capitol," one need only observe the intensity of image making during this period. Late antique Jerusalem afforded a brisk, if unsettled, cultural environment, in which symbols and tropes changed hands rapidly; they fluctuated among the various religions, and their geographical anchors constantly oscillated between distinct locations. Some traditions that were first fastened upon the Temple Mount

were later assigned to Golgotha; Christian writers established the glorified reputation of the Church of the Holy Sepulcher by comparing its attributes to
those that had previously been reserved for the Jewish Temple. Others ascribed
expressions and formulae to this church that for centuries had been reserved
for other sites in Jerusalem. Subsequently, the new Muslim rulers transferred
much of this lore once again to the sanctuary (*haram*) and mosques they established on the Temple Mount. It is therefore not at all surprising that a tradition about an old pagan Capitoline shrine, which for generations had dwelled
elsewhere (probably in the area of the city forum, today's Christian Quarter),
traveled in the early Islamic era to the compound of the ancient Jewish Temple.

What, then, propelled Flusin's and Mango's hypothesis? Apparently their
overreliance on Cassius Dio led them to link the seventh-century legends with
the alleged Capitoline temple. But if we had never had Dio's report, would it
ever have occurred to anyone to put forward Flusin's and Mango's proposal
so definitively? Obviously not. As Murphy-O'Connor has pointed out, if the
text we attribute to Dio was actually written in the eleventh century, we should
explain him in light of the two seventh-century texts rather than vice versa.[33]
According to this line of thought, the traditions about the "capitol" were attributed to the Temple site only after the Arab conquest of Palestine, and
Xiphilinus's rewriting of Dio's text was influenced by these traditions.

Roman Statuary on the Temple Mount

Two fourth-century sources—the anonymous pilgrim from Bordeaux and
the church scholar Jerome—attest to one or two statues that stood in the space
of the Temple Mount during the days of Aelia Capitolina and the early decades
of the Byzantine period. In a passage invoking the precinct of the ruined Jewish Temple and detailing the various elements he encountered there, the traveler from Bordeaux mentions two statues of Hadrian that stood in the area.[34]
His neatly organized narrative follows what seems to be a conventional Christian sightseeing route throughout the city. Within this framework, the writer
locates the statues after the place of the ruined Jewish shrine and altar and before the nearby pierced stone—namely, somewhere close to the center of the
Temple Mount enclosure. The pilgrim's use of the present tense seems to indicate a report of what he witnessed with his own eyes.

Jerome conveys similar information. In his commentary on the Gospel of

Matthew, written toward the end of the fourth century, he dwells on the expression "desolating sacrilege," first mentioned in the book of Daniel (9:27 and more) and then predicted to materialize in a famous Gospel passage known as "The Little Apocalypse" (Matthew 24:15, and parallels). Jerome lists a number of historical episodes that represent the fulfillment of this prophecy, one of which features an "equestrian statue of Hadrian that has been standing till this present day in the holy of holies itself."[35] Some ten years later, in his commentary on Isaiah, Jerome repeats this observation, with certain variations. He ties the biblical clause, "So man is humbled and men are brought low" (Isaiah 2:9), to a concrete situation in which "in the place that the Temple and worship of God used to be, a statue of Hadrian and an idol of Jupiter were set." Here too Jerome goes on to associate this scenario with the prophesying about the "desolating sacrilege," but this time with reference to its version in Mark (13:14).[36]

Despite some discrepancies among the three traditions—for example, in the number of statues (one according to the first account in Jerome; two on the word of the others) and in their identity (Hadrian, Jupiter)—scholars tend to accept them as capturing an authentic situation on the Temple Mount. This seems like a reasonable deduction. But most studies take this idea even further. Many link the statues to the existence of a temple to Jupiter, integrating the sculptural pieces into the alleged sanctuary or placing them in its vicinity.[37] Others, although more doubtful about the pagan shrine, nevertheless find the traditions about the statuary sufficient to allow the inclusion of the Temple Mount compound within the city limits.[38]

This second set of contentions remains baseless. As I have shown elsewhere, the statements by the Bordeaux pilgrim and Jerome partake in a long and convoluted Christian and Jewish discourse about Roman statuary at the site of the Jewish Temple.[39] Alongside the tradition that associated these artifacts with Hadrian, other Christian writers have allied them with Titus, Vespasian, and Trajan. Yet others have associated them with conflicts between the Roman and Jewish nations that date back to the days of the Second Temple. All these constructions rely on hermeneutical and apologetical principles devised around the prophecy in the book of Daniel that forecasts an appalling desecration of the house of God. It seems as if Christian writers deemed every low point in the relationship between the Jews and the Roman Empire as appropriate for the erection of a statue on the Temple Mount.

Roman sculpture may have been placed in the ruined compound of the Jewish Temple at some point in time—perhaps immediately after the destruction of the Temple in 70 CE or on some other occasion. The fact that the Tenth Legion long remained stationed in Jerusalem provided ample opportunity for the erection of statues. Indeed, archaeological and epigraphic findings clearly indicate that sculptural artifacts populated the city space, and written sources support this as well. It is not impossible that such a piece or pieces were also placed on the site of the ruined Jewish Temple. In the absence of an inscription or some other trustworthy record, there is no way of knowing, however, who placed the statuary or when. Conversely, it is entirely possible that a visitor to the Temple area in the fourth century might have seen one or more sculptured pieces there, but there is no way of tying this to Hadrian's founding of Aelia Capitolina. It is even less reasonable to infer from these possibilities any meaningful conclusion about the state of affairs on the Temple Mount or its function in the *colonia*.

The Urban Layout of Aelia: An Archaeological Perspective[40]

For more than a hundred years, scholars have been trying to reconstruct the Roman colony Aelia Capitolina and fathom its urban infrastructure.[41] In what follows, I do not discuss all aspects of Aelia's landscape or physical layout but only those that pertain to the role of the Temple Mount within this municipality and shed light on its relation to the city. Although this enclosure is mentioned in all modern accounts of post–Second Temple Jerusalem (henceforth "the Roman period," without the finer distinction between "Roman" and "Late Roman"), it has never, as far as I know, been the focus of any discussion in and of itself. The question at the heart of the following discussion is therefore geographical-historical in nature: what place did the Temple Mount occupy in the urban plan of Aelia Capitolina?

Paucity of sources, both inanimate finds and written information, creates the principal difficulty for scholars who have attempted to envision the city's structure in the Roman period. Although Jerusalem has been the subject of many archaeological excavations, which peaked in the extensive projects after the 1967 war and now continue at a slower pace, no substantial findings have surfaced that could be dated to the Roman period after the destruction of the Second Temple. There remains in Jerusalem almost no evidence of public buildings, entertainment structures, or other edifices such as civic basilicas, temples, theaters, stadiums, and hippodromes, nor much of the city walls and streets—all of which serve archaeologists as a foothold for the work of reconstruction and have been discovered often enough at other ancient sites. The digs have indeed yielded a multitude of smaller objects—pottery shreds (especially roof tile fragments imprinted with the stamp of the Tenth Legion), coins, inscriptions, and other items—but, except for a recently rediscovered bathhouse, they produced very little evidence of well-defined architectonic wholes.[42]

Sometimes the absence of a certain structure simply reflects the city's history. For example, no remnants of the fortification system were discovered because, as most scholars now agree, Aelia did not have any such walls during the first century and a half of its existence.[43] But apparently substantial findings are scarce mainly because Jerusalem has remained a "living city" that has occupied the same territory ever since the days of Aelia Capitolina, and thus its ongoing life has caused considerable damage to its earlier layers. What has nevertheless survived of the Roman colony?

Gates

The most complete architectural units include two arched entrance structures. In the north, under the Ottoman Damascus Gate, which is still in use, a series of excavations from the 1930s onward has revealed the *Porta Neopolitana* (map 2: 1; fig. 8), a massive three-bayed triumphal gate, embraced by two pentagonal towers, one on each side, and a paved plaza on the inside. Built on an east-west axis, this gate served people entering the city from the north. Although scholars disagree about the stages of its construction, and in particular about whether an earlier gate, from the Second Temple period, inhabited this site, they concur in dating this structure to the early days of Aelia Capitolina. Only after the Romans erected city walls in the late third century (see chapter 4) was the gate made a part of it. For the first century and a half the gate stood independently and was not incorporated into any system of fortifications.[44]

A second entrance structure stands at the eastern side of town. This well-known architectonic unit, resembling a triumphal arch and consisting of three openings, is situated along the route of the Via Dolorosa (map 2: 2; figs. 9, 10). By the time of the Crusader conquest in the eleventh century, Christians already identified this structure as the place of Pontius Pilate's exclamation at the sight of Jesus the prisoner, "Here is the man" (John 19:5)—in Latin *ecce homo*. Perpendicular in its axis to the Damascus Gate, this entrance served travelers walking in the east-west direction.

In the 1850s Alphonse Ratisbonne, an affluent French Jew who converted to

Fig. 8. The Ottoman Damascus Gate (on top) and beneath it the remnants of one entrance bay of the three-bay Porta Neapolitana, which marked the northern entrance to the Roman city. From Land of Bible Photo Archive. Courtesy of Zev Radovan.

Fig. 9. A nineteenth-century lithograph (by Werner) showing the Ecce Homo arch embedded in the buildings of the Old City of Jerusalem. From *Enduring Images: 19th Century Jerusalem through Lens and Brush* (Jerusalem: Bible Land Museum, 1992). Courtesy of Amos mar-Ḥaim.

Fig. 10. A picture from 1858 showing the bare Ecce Homo arch as it was exposed during the construction of the Sisters of Zion Convent. From Colin Osman, *Jerusalem Caught in Time* (London: Garnet, 1999). Courtesy of Garnet Publishing.

Christianity and relocated to Jerusalem, acquired the site for the Sisters of Zion Convent (map 2: 3). The construction project that followed revealed the northernmost of the unit's three arches, which was then swallowed by the building of the new monastery. The southern arch remained hidden, flanked by the houses on the side of the street, and at present passersby can see only part of the central arch, which tops the path of the Via Dolorosa. Over the years, scholars have devoted much attention to this structure, beginning with Pierotti, who, during the construction of the Sisters of Zion Convent, drew the first plans of the gate and prepared a lithograph of its remains.[45] Also notable for their efforts are the French scholar (and Dominican monk) Louis Hugues Vincent and his nun students, who conducted a series of excavations at the site in the 1930s as part of their endeavor to locate the Antonia fortress of the Second

Temple period. One of the students published the results as a detailed study of the arch and nearby elements.[46] The Franciscans carried out additional digs in the nearby Monastery of the Flagellation, east of the convent (map 2: 4).[47]

As in the case of the northern Damascus Gate, an area paved with large stones lay adjacent to the Ecce Homo arch as well, except that here it consumed the external side, east of the arch. Supported by subterranean vaults, part of this flagstone pavement covers a Second Temple open-air reservoir, known as the Struthion pool. The pavement owes its famous name—*lithostroton* ("pavement" in Greek)—to the aspiration of some scholars to identify it with the courtyard of the Second Temple Antonia fortress and therefore to see it as part of the Praetorium, the seat of the Roman procurators in Jerusalem and thus the location of Jesus's trial. Despite these tendencies, as Pierre Benoit concluded based on excavations by Coüasnon, the paved plaza was actually an organic part of the Ecce Homo complex and thus dates to the same time as the arch.[48]

As for the arch itself, at first archaeologists contested its date and proposed the Second Temple period (in order to link it with Jesus's trial), but they now agree that, with its striking stylistic similarities to the Roman Damascus Gate, it actually belongs to the time of Aelia Capitolina in the second century.[49] Scholars also differed about the function of the arch. Benoit, countering the identification of the pavement with the Antonian *lithostroton,* suggested that it was the "eastern forum" of Aelia and that the Ecce Homo was a sumptuous passage to this civic center. Although it was only an exploratory alternative, presented to refute Vincent's opposing view that linked the arch to the days of the Second Temple, many scholars accepted Benoit's proposal as pure fact, and the "eastern forum" found its way onto various maps and reviews of Aelia Capitolina as an integral constituent of the city (e.g., map 5).[50] Others, including myself, as I argue shortly, agree with Benoit's criticism of his predecessors but reject his reconstruction, instead viewing this site as the eastern entrance to Aelia Capitolina.[51]

Other Archaeological Remains; More Scholarly Debate

Aside from the two monumental entrance structures—the Damascus Gate in the north and the Ecce Homo arch in the east—other architectural elements that can be attributed to the time of Aelia remain extremely fragmentary, and in many instances their identification and date are either doubtful or controversial. Such are the two additional arches that surfaced in the city and its vicinity. Savignac, a French archaeologist, reconstructed one of them as a triumphal arch from the days of Hadrian and placed it nine hundred feet north of the Damascus Gate. He based this restoration on two dedicatory inscriptions, to the emperors Hadrian and Antoninus Pius, that were found in the area by Clermont-Ganneau in the early twentieth century. Even scholars, such as Vincent, who accepted his suggestion (and many did not) had to admit that the preserved remains are insufficient for determining the nature and purpose of the structure.[52]

A number of archaeologists identified another arch, now on the grounds of the Russian Hospice, east of the Church of the Holy Sepulcher, as the entrance to the central forum of Aelia (map 2: 6). Here too, however, much uncertainty prevails. The arch functioned as part of an immense building project, which today lies beneath the Church of the Holy Sepulcher complex. It included huge supporting walls that leveled the surface and created a podium. The excavators found it hard to determine whether this construction endeavor belongs to the days of Hadrian (perhaps the foundation of the sanctuary he built there) or to the later Constantinian building venture. Equally ambiguous is the case of the arch under discussion, with some scholars attributing it entirely to the time of Constantine in the fourth century.[53]

In addition, other segments of massive pavement that excavators unearthed throughout the current Old City of Jerusalem and nearby areas were also associated with the Roman colony and identified as portions of its ramified street alignment.[54] Completing the picture of the city's thoroughfares are the colonnaded streetside walkways—huge columns made of marble or local stone and topped with floral capitals that the Romans placed along the street to support covered porticos on its sides. In accord with the common architectural practice of those days, these colonnades lined the central traffic arteries. A small number of such pillars can still be found in situ marking the course of Aelia's streets; others were found in secondary use elsewhere. A full illustration of these post-lined streets appears in the Madaba mosaic map (see fig. 15), which, as most scholars agree, reflects the Roman street plan, even though it was drawn some time in the sixth century.[55]

Following the 1967 war, Benjamin Mazar conducted a series of excavations on the external side of the southwestern corner of the Temple Mount walls. For the period under consideration here, however, these digs are of limited value. Mazar uncovered some fragmentary structures, architectonic elements (broken columns, stone flooring, and hypocaust bricks from a bathhouse), art objects (various types of broken statues), several inscriptions in secondary use, and some small articles (such as coins and oil lamps) that belong to the Roman period.[56] Recent excavations in the same area clarified the structure of a large Roman bath occupying the southwestern corner outside of the Temple Mount (map 2: 11).[57] Here too, however, most of the findings are inadequate to determine the nature of the area beyond the existence of the bathhouse. To this, one may add the upper aqueduct descending from the so-called Solomon's Pools some six and a half miles south of the city, which apparently reached the area of the present-day Jaffa Gate; a number of inscriptions on its sections mention the soldiers of the Tenth Legion as its builders, or at least its restorers to active use.[58] All in all, archaeological material supports the claim that some sort of urban construction did indeed take place in Roman Aelia, but its nature and scope remain undetermined.

Some Written and Inscribed Snapshots of the City's Texture

In addition to the inanimate evidence, information about the city's landscape can also be extracted from literary sources. As noted, the seventh-century *Chronicon Paschale* includes a rather elaborate inventory of public buildings in Aelia. Yet the list's omission of any concrete information about the location and nature of these structures attenuates its usefulness. Some scholars, myself included, doubt its authenticity altogether (see n. 30). Other sources are more helpful. Eusebius in his *Chronicon* refers to a gate adorned by a sculptured pig, which leads to the road to Bethlehem.[59] The anonymous pilgrim from Bordeaux alludes to another gate in the southern part of the city.[60] Several centuries later, another visitor to Jerusalem, who is known today by the name Antoninus of Piacenza, probably attests to the same gate. He describes an arch located at the site of what he claims to be the ancient gate of the city (*antiqua porta fuit civitatis*) and situates it along the eastern *cardo* (following the route of the "Tyropoeon") in its southern portion, thus encountered by people strolling from the Temple area toward the Siloam pool (map 2: 10).[61] Fragments of a hefty dedicatory inscription mounting a lost gate that were found in this area and dated to the days of the emperor Septimius Severus (193–211) may very well belong to the same structure.[62] The city's coins offer some engraved representations of its temples, but only schematically, which makes it difficult to glean information about concrete details.[63] Aside from Cassius Dio, the church scholar and historian Eusebius contributes valuable information about the city's temples. He refers to a temple of Aphrodite (Venus) that the Romans built near the site of Jesus's tomb. He also reports leveling and raising operations as well as stone flooring that covered this part of town.[64] Another spot that should be included with the city's religious establishments is the site north of the Temple Mount, neighboring the later Church of Saint Anne (map 2: 7); various votive objects discovered there attest to cultic activity and probable connections with Asclepius, the god of healing.[65]

Nineteenth-Century Reconstructions and Their Modern Counterparts

The scantiness of well-defined, meaningful finds compelled scholars to use other sorts of "information," mainly the data embodied in the city's landscape as it was preserved through the centuries. First and foremost, they examined the blueprint of the present city—that is, the Old City of Jerusalem (map 2). By the nineteenth century, many already shared the assumption that the intricate disarray of the Ottoman city conceals underneath it the plan of the Roman colony. Therefore, if later additions were subtracted, the skeleton of the Roman colony would be laid bare. The orderly base of straight streets, nearly vertical to one another, that can be discerned through the present irregular layout supported this conjecture. The discovery of the Madaba map (fig. 15) with its exquisite portrayal of Jerusalem reinforces this view even further. The map displays a great similarity between the main arteries it depicts—especially the two routes crossing the city from north to south (the *cardines,* in the language of the Roman engineers)—and the two major thoroughfares in the present-day Old City, namely, the Suq khan ez-zeit–Ḥabad streets and the El-Wadi (Ḥagai) street east of it (see map 2).

Many years prior to the discovery of the map, in the late nineteenth century, Germer-Durand made the first systematic presentation of this theory, drawing a hypothetical map of Aelia based on the map of the Old City of Jerusalem (plus insights from Gerasa). Almost unanimously accepted thereafter, his proposal allowed scholars to define the outline of the Roman city as following the boundaries of the Ottoman Old City walls and to envision its street arrangement according to existing major routes (as depicted, for example, in map 5).[66] In a recent encyclopedia entry, Oleg Grabar encapsulated this trend of 150 years of research in a short line describing Aelia thus: "Walls surrounded a squarish space (more or less today's old city) that included the area of the Temple and the western hills."[67] The plainness of the statement demonstrates how deeply ingrained in our consciousness such a picture of Roman Jerusalem has become.

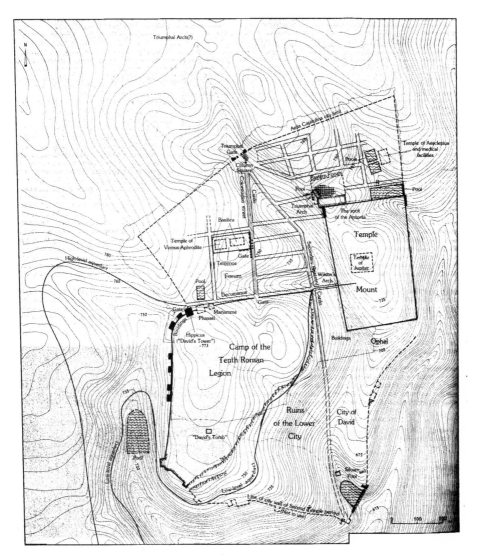

Map 5. A (more or less) common reconstruction of Aelia Capitolina (by Hillel Geva).
From *NEAEHL*. Courtesy of Hillel Geva and Israel Exploration Society.

Once Germer-Durand conceived this model, it became easier to fit the archaeological and literary pieces into a seemingly homogeneous picture. Scholars coupled the remains in the vicinity of the Church of the Holy Sepulcher with
the reports of Eusebius and Jerome about pagan temples, either to Aphrodite
or Jupiter or perhaps both, that were situated there, leading to a reconstruction

of the main forum of the city on the grounds of today's Christian Quarter ("the Muristan"). They reproduced the major civic center as a massive square, delimiting its eastern side with the Suq khan ez-zeit Street. The street itself was given the title *cardo maximus,* and, intersecting this line at a more or less right angle, the route of the David-Chain (Bab al-Silsila Road) streets was perceived as a *decumanus,* the classical transverse thoroughfare of a Roman city. Drawing on Benoit's proposition, various scholars characterized the *lithostroton* pavement and the Ecce Homo arch as a "secondary forum" in the eastern part of the city, positioning another temple to Asclepius adjacent to them to the east, in the area of the Probatika pool (map 2: 8). In this scheme, stone pavements throughout the city amounted to a well-defined street plan, and the ancient arched gate uncovered under the Damascus Gate corresponded to the structure appearing on the Madaba map as the central entrance in the north of the city. Details extracted from the literary sources were integrated into this reconstruction as well. A typical example is the attempts to arrange (or rather squeeze) the Aelia map, which became an identical twin to the map of the current Old City, according to the seven districts mentioned in the *Chronicon Paschale* and to locate the various public buildings that this document lists. In the same vein, the accepted view also included the Temple Mount in this layout, whether as the site of the Temple of Jupiter mentioned by Cassius Dio or as a plain and anonymous "place of worship." Illustrating this scholarly effort of nearly a century and a half are the numerous maps that strive to recreate the appearance of the Roman colony, which, in spite of their variations, all coincided, more or less, with the boundaries of the current Old City (see map 5).[68]

The major drawback of these reconstructions lies in the wide gap that separates the final result from the findings that presume to substantiate it. Two controversies that divide the scholarly world concerning Aelia can elucidate this claim. Did the main artery of Aelia—the *cardo maximus*—which stretched south from the area of the Damascus Gate, continue to the southern part of the colony as well, crossing the line of the David and Chain streets? The old maps drawn by the scholars who investigated the city in the nineteenth and early twentieth centuries—Germer-Durand, Wilson, and Vincent—naturally include such a route, which traverses the city along its entire north-south axis.[69] Yet the results of Avigad's excavations have shaken this assumption, if not proved it wrong altogether. Conducting a large-scale dig after the 1967 war in the so-called Jewish Quarter (map 2), Avigad and his team came across a magnificent colonnaded street in the southern part of the city, along the route of

Suq el-husur (the modern Jews and Ḥabad streets), and this thoroughfare indeed turned out to be a continuation (with a slight southwestern deviation) of the road emerging from the Damascus Gate in the northern part of the city. However, not only did the pottery that came from under the street date it to the Byzantine period—the sixth century—but no remains of any earlier Roman street were found there.[70] The question is how to construe this lack of finds and what its implications are for understanding the structure of the Roman colony. One group of scholars dealt with the problem by refuting the traditional assumption about an artery cutting across the city from north to south, claiming that in the days of Aelia the street ended at the northern edge of the southwestern hill (see map 1). In contrast, Yoram Tsafrir clung to the traditional view and offered various arguments to explain the absence of Roman material from Avigad's excavations. In his opinion, it would be incorrect to deny the possibility that the Roman road had indeed extended to the southern part of the city and that aggressive Byzantine development had caused it to "disappear."[71]

An even sharper debate surrounds the issue of the location of the Tenth Legion's camp. Since Wilson first proposed it in the late nineteenth century, nearly all scholars had acceded to what became the traditional stance, that this camp had been stationed at the southwestern hill (map 5). But some current views propose alternative sites for the camp all over Jerusalem: the Christian Quarter, the northern part of the Old City, even the Temple Mount itself.[72] In this case, too, archaeology had a hand in undermining the accepted opinion. Josephus reported a Roman camp set up in the wake of the Great Revolt near the three Herodian towers (in the site of what is today the Ottoman citadel or tower of David; map 2: 9), in the shadow of the wall encircling the city on the west.[73] Avigad's findings in the Jewish Quarter, however, as well as a series of smaller excavations in the enclosure of the Ottoman Citadel and the Armenian Gardens (map 2: 9, 12), brought Josephus's testimony into question. These digs, as in the case of the *cardo,* yielded no real remains of the military camp that supposedly populated the area. No streets were found, no typical structures were revealed, and, most important, there was no trace of the system of fortifications that would be expected in a camp of this sort.[74] Making sense of these results divided modern scholars once again into two groups. One maintains the traditional approach that the military nevertheless occupied the southwestern hill. Its advocates resolve the absence of any finds either by means of an archaeological interpretation that explains both how the material evidence "disappeared" and how it is still possible to find hints of such a military camp (Tsafrir) or through a new interpretation of the nature of the camp that justifies the lack of finds (Geva). The second group rejects the traditional location of the Tenth Legion camp and offers alternative sites (Isaac, Bar, and E. Mazar).

The common denominator underlying these two debates—about the southern portion of the *cardo* and the location of the Tenth Legion's camp—reveals the weak link in the research on Aelia Capitolina: the paucity of factual findings. Consequently, only a thin, often vague, line distinguishes the theory from the evidence that is supposed to support or refute it. The theory came first. Germer-Durand never doubted the shape he bestowed upon the colony and the manner in which he arranged its particular architectonic details. He did not, however, have much solid evidence to support his reconstruction, except, of course, for the silhouette of the nineteenth-century Ottoman city he saw in front of him. Attempts to draw an analogy from the circumference of the current city and the alignment of its streets to the pattern of the Roman city of the past are not totally implausible. Such a line of thought conforms to the principle of urban continuity and the construction processes that characterized many urban centers throughout the ages. But this remains no more than a working assumption that must be examined in the light of continuing research.[75] After all, no one would claim that some straight roads found among a disarray of winding streets in an Arab city must necessarily be a remnant from the Roman period. The Byzantines also knew how to build cities with perpendicular roads, as the Byzantine *cardo* uncovered by Avigad attests. If Justinian could execute such a plan of right-angled, crisscrossing streets in the sixth century, then surely Constantine, the founder and builder of Constantinople, could as well. Thus, although the lineal arteries spotted by Germer-Durand in maps of the City of Jerusalem could have originated during the time of the Roman colony, they could just as easily fit in a later period. And even if some of them—such as the northern part of the *cardo*, between Damascus Gate and David-Chain streets, whose dating to the days of Aelia no one doubts—do indeed belong to the Roman era, this is not enough to prove that *all* the streets come from the same period. Many scholars have rightly noted that Aelia developed sluggishly and that only the dramatic changes that Constantine introduced propelled the great momentum in building construction. Pace Germer-Durand, it is plausible that the Byzantine builders of Jerusalem, who had the task of planning and paving the roads, did this according to the orthogonal principle, which was still widely held in their day. All this argues against the sweeping acceptance of the nineteenth-century theories and points to the need to base any working assumption on better evidence.

A New Proposal for the Reconstruction of Aelia (map 6)

Any fresh consideration of Aelia Capitolina's physical layout ought to begin with the established facts about the city that have survived through the ages. Archaeology provides such solid information in the shape of the two splendid entrance complexes—the one found beneath the Damascus Gate and the Ecce Homo arch, which share similar architectonic traits and date to the second cen-

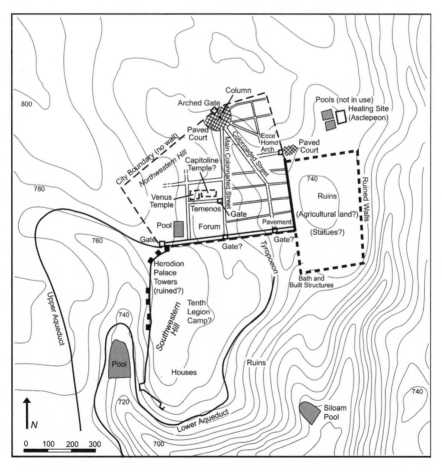

Map 6. New reconstruction of Aelia Capitolina

tury. The colony's lack of a fortification system for a century and a half, from the 130s to the late third century, seems verifiable as well. These two items are interrelated. Why would the builders of Aelia set up entrance complexes to a city without walls? Based on customary urban-planning procedures in the Roman world, the answer suggests itself: to mark its boundaries.[76]

Regarding these wall-less entrance structures, two other points come to mind. The city designers positioned the Damascus Gate in an ideal spot for an entrance arch—on the natural traffic route for people coming from the north, along the course of the central valley that traverses the town (known as the Tyropoeon). As for the Ecce Homo arch, they seem to locate it more or less on the same line with the Western Wall of the Temple Mount enclosure (see map 2: 2).[77] At present this fact goes very much unrecognized because the arch is submerged in the congested neighborhood around it. But that would not have been the case in the early days of the colony, when the territory north of the Temple Mount remained open and mostly unpopulated. As I see it, the placement of an arch along this line partakes in the same underlying planning principle just described, by which arches and gates demarcate the boundaries of wall-less municipalities. It manifests the wish of Aelia's founders to delimit the eastern environs of the colony by the Western Wall of the Temple Mount; they therefore placed an arch marking the eastern boundary on the continuation of the Western Wall of the Temple Mount, at its northern end.

Two additional finds coalesce with this restored logic of urban planning: the colonnaded street running south from Damascus Gate, along the route that is now represented by Suq khan ez-zeit and Ḥabad streets, and the massive construction that excavators uncovered on the northwestern hill, on the grounds of today's Russian Hospice and the Church of the Holy Sepulcher. As mentioned, most scholars have rightly associated the latter with the literary reports about pagan temples in this area, identifying the site as the forum of the Roman colony. In this case, the urban continuity implied by the massive building project at the same place during the time of Constantine supports the claim regarding the location of the Roman forum. It is more likely that Constantine would make use of the existing city center, endowing it with Christian character and consequently reshaping its appearance but at the same time maintaining its municipal nature, than that he would neglect and alter the urban texture altogether by shifting the core of the city somewhere else. The forum should be fixed (as indeed most scholars believe) on the northwestern hill, in the area where the Christian Quarter stands today.

Merging these pieces of information into one picture, or rather puzzle (whose parts do not produce a full map), allows a certain comprehension of the rationale behind the urban configuration of Aelia, which in turn provides the basis for a partial outline of the colony's plan. Most important, this examination shows that Aelia Capitolina, although situated adjacent to the old Jerusalem, the city of the Second Temple period, represents in many senses a new entity. The location of the Roman forum reflects a major transformation in the spatial organization of the city, shifting its core to the northwest. This change extends beyond a merely technical matter. It expresses the Roman builders' intention of abandoning the traditional municipal layout of ancient Jerusalem.

From the earliest days, the spring of the Gihon functioned as the city's source of life. Spouting at the bottom of the Kidron Valley, south of the Temple Mount, and flowing in a winding tunnel into the Siloam pool (map 2: 10), it provided Jerusalem with its most basic need: water. In addition, during the thousand or so years prior to the establishment of Aelia, a second municipal nucleus, the city's cultic center, took shape on the Temple Mount. These two foci laid the basis for Jerusalem's landscape, orienting its urban layout toward the southeast—whether on the Temple–City of David axis in the First Temple period or in the Temple–Lower City–Upper City triangle of the Second Temple period. Hadrian and his engineers did not return to this terrain, which at the time was undoubtedly strewn with ruins.[78] For the first time in Jerusalem's history, the hub of life relocated northward to the northwestern hill, an area that had always been far from the urban center, either outside the city entirely or at least on its periphery. Moreover, the foundation of both the forum and the Roman temples on that northwestern hill, now known as the Christian Quarter, created a new religious and economic center for a city used to associating these functions with either the Temple Mount or the markets on the southwestern hill ("the Upper City"). Finally, fixing the city's eastern edge on the line running from the Ecce Homo arch to the Western Wall of the Temple Mount left the compound of the old Temple, the Temple Mount, outside the boundaries of the Roman city (see map 6). Unlike the old southeast-oriented city, Aelia was now clustered around the northwestern hill.

The major arteries in Aelia also changed significantly. A totally new main street of the colony, which almost everyone agrees proceeded southward from the Damascus Gate along the path of the ottoman Suq khan ez-zeit,[79] replaced the traditional main road of the Second Temple city, which had run to the east of it, along the central valley (the Tyropoeon). This is an inevitable change, due to the northwestward shift of the city. The Romans also modified the eastward traffic arteries. During the Second Temple period, the Temple Mount precinct dominated the eastern part of the city, where all the roads from the Upper City and the Lower City converged. This is attested by the famous colossal arches in the Western Wall of the Temple Mount—named the Robinson and Wilson arches (map 2: 13, 14) after those who discovered them in the nineteenth century—and the huge staircases and perhaps even a bridge that they supported leading to the Temple grounds, as well as by the magnificent stairways allowing access to the Temple from the south. In ancient Jerusalem, all roads led to the Temple.

The planners of Aelia, in contrast, fashioned a completely new infrastructure. The Ecce Homo arch points to an east-west "detour" to the Temple Mount that bypassed the enclosure from the north. This change reflects the urban revolution that took place in the city. For the first time, so to speak, people walked eastward in Jerusalem without the primary intention of going to the Temple area.[80]

Within the framework of this reconstruction, the more obscure details concerning the Roman colony can find their place as well. The major unresolved problem remains whether the southwestern hill became an integral part of the colony. Due to insufficient evidence, the precise location of the Tenth Legion camp, for many years widely believed to be on the southwestern hill, cannot be established with certainty. Likewise, no decisive evidence has been offered to determine whether the streets descending from the north of the city continued into the southern part, beyond the David-Chain streets line. It seems preferable to leave such matters open. A looser conclusion may run as follows. The southern part of Jerusalem was definitely not totally abandoned at that time. Building fragments and remains of habitation, however small, surfaced in this part of town—at the Citadel, the Armenian Gardens, and other sites. Archaeologists have also unearthed traces of a paved street near the Chain Gate. The Mazar excavations at the southwestern corner of the Temple Mount have also revealed a well-defined Roman stratum with an impressive bathhouse (see n. 57). To be sure, city limits, especially when not rigidly fixed by walls, tend to be elastic, and, as the picture of Byzantine Jerusalem proves, the colony indeed grew beyond its own borders over the years. On the other hand, we do not know when this expansion occurred or at what rate. More important, even if the Romans settled in the southern area of the city at some stage, this does not refute my major claim that they shifted the center northward. The missing section of the puzzle does not detract from the general reconstruction.

The Area North of the Temple Mount

A major key in reassessing Aelia's layout and the place of the Temple Mount within the urban framework exists in the topographic unit north of the Temple Mount enclosure. Although most scholars include this area within the boundaries of Aelia (see map 5), they maintain a certain vagueness as to its substance. As mentioned, the commonly held view argues for the presence of a "second forum" in the paved square called *lithostroton*, east of the Ecce Homo arch (map 2: 3). It also claims that a few hundred feet to the east, neighboring the sheep pool (the Probatika; map 2: 8; fig. 11), stood a sanctuary to Asclepius.[81] What do the archaeological findings have to say about these assertions?

Benoit's meticulous criticism elucidated the speculative nature of the detailed reconstructions of the *lithostroton* plaza devised by Vincent and his students and, later on, by Bagatti. According to his sharp tongue, it is all but a "châteaux en Espagne." Neither the porticoes surrounding the square as some sort of a praetorian *peristyle*, nor the galleries, nor the stone benches, all central features in the common reconstructions of the site, can be supported with conclusive evidence.[82] At most the area consisted of some rooms, whose nature cannot be determined with certainty. Moreover, not all the findings at this location can be attributed to the same period. A bulky stone wall positioned west of the Ecce Homo arch, one of the more impressive remnants in the area, certainly dates to a later period, since it blocks the arch's path, making it impossible to use.[83] It is not even clear whether all the flagstones in the pavement belong to the same construction stage. The broad plan of the pavements shows a clear difference in typology between the large stones used to pave the rectangular plaza east of the Ecce Homo arch, which are oriented along a north-south axis, and the grooved stones that almost certainly belonged to an east-west transversal road that stretched from the arch eastward (known today as the Via Dolorosa). Archaeologists found no evidence to determine whether the plaza and the road were built during the same period. Like Hadrian, the Byzantines knew how to pave streets with grooved stones (or rather smooth stones that were grooved over the years), and it might very well be that the road east of the Ecce Homo arch belongs to their building efforts in the city.

Nothing therefore prevents us from seeing the *lithostroton* as an external pi-

Fig. 11. The huge water reservoirs of the Probatika pool after they were excavated and cleaned (in a 1914 picture from the American Colony Archive). From Library of Congress, Prints & Photographs Division, The American Colony Archive, online catalog, reproduction number LC-DIG-matpc-07493.

azza of the gate at the egress of the city, similar to the internal plaza at Damascus Gate. The placement of the pavement on the exterior of the arch should not be surprising; I believe it derived directly from its original purpose—to cover the open-air Struthion pool, which operated at this spot during the Second Temple period, and thus to create a leveled ground that would allow people to exit or enter the city through the Ecce Homo arch.[84] As Geva recently admitted, the term "forum" that early scholars applied to the site does not faithfully reflect its actual function, and even Benoit, who first used the term in this context, did not see it as anything more than a "small commercial plaza ornamenting the eastern exit of Aelia Capitolina."[85]

With regard to the Probatika pool, we are on firmer ground. French archaeologists have conducted extensive excavations in the area of Saint Anne's Church since Sultan Abd al-Magid handed the site over to the French after the Crimean War of 1856.[86] From the very start, the excavations at the site unearthed various votive objects. Already in 1866, workers had come across a broken marble foot with a dedication inscription by a woman named Pompeia Lucilia. Later they uncovered a broken marble statue of a recumbent nude woman; a clay statuette of a female figure taking off her clothes; stone models of small boats; and two relief fragments of a colonnaded building topped by a gable—one with a snake curled around it, and the other with the tip of a spike showing at its side, which is generally considered part of an offering tendered by the figure standing to the left of the structure (see reconstruction in fig. 12). Possibly related to these findings, coins minted in Aelia that date to the mid-third century show an image of Hygieia, the personification of "health" and the daughter of Asclepius, sitting on a stone and feeding a snake.[87]

Already in the 1920s, before the French launched their extensive excavations, Vincent had collected all the literary evidence about the Probatika, summarized the archaeological data that had been discovered thus far, and formulated a theory about a consecrated healing institution (not necessarily a temple) at the site. He brilliantly suggested tracing the origin of this setting back to the Second Temple pools, whose waters were known for their miraculous remedial powers, as reflected in John 5:2–4. Based on all this, he outlined the evolution of the site—first into a pagan establishment in the days of Aelia and then into the Byzantine churches that later populated the area (fig. 13).[88] The ensuing excavations at the site largely supported Vincent's views.

As mentioned previously, Vincent also proposed that the site might be related to Asclepius, the god of medicine. He based his case on the votive objects that were found in the area and the story about Jesus healing the paralyzed man (John 5:1–9), which supposedly took place at the pool of the Probatika. The excavations of the 1950s largely corroborate this hypothesis as well.[89] The area probably encompassed a healing complex relying on the miraculous qualities of the place and under the aegis of Asclepius. Structures of this sort were wide-

Fig. 12. A reconstruction of a relief fragment from the Probatika pool showing a colonnaded building toped by a gable, perhaps to be associated with the figure of Asclepius. Drawing by Leen Ritmeyer. Courtesy of Ritmeyer Archaeological Design.

spread in the Roman world. Aside from the famous large Asclepiea compounds—in Epidaurus, Pergamum, and the island of Cos—hundreds of smaller ones dotted the empire. Predominantly, these institutions provided medical services and sometimes hospitalization as well. In the cultural milieu of the ancient world, where medicine and religion intermingled indiscriminately, a system of ritual worship, including ceremonies, sacrifices, and offerings, probably operated at the site as well.[90] Recently, Avalos has demonstrated the close association between the ancient world's conceptions of medicine and

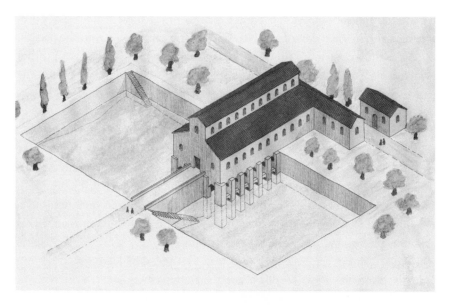

Fig. 13. A reconstruction of the Byzantine complex of the Probatika (Bethesda) pool and church. Drawing by Leen Ritmeyer. Courtesy of Ritmeyer Archaeological Design.

ritual worship, especially in the Orient, as well as the continuity between Near Eastern localities where healing was practiced and their counterparts in the Hellenistic and Roman periods.[91] Considering the evidence in John, it is not impossible that the Roman colony in Jerusalem retained a local custom that assigned special curative powers to the Probatika pool and erected a "healing center" at the site of the ruined pools from the Second Temple period.

If this area indeed functioned as a medical multiplex, it is unnecessary to include it within the municipal boundaries of Aelia Capitolina. Healing sites of this kind sprang up in many places with special "supernatural traits," in the vicinity of springs and caves or at the shores of seas and lakes. The exclusivity of such geographical locations, which endowed the medical facilities with their extraordinary status, was anchored in past traditions, not determined by city boundaries. The particularity of such sacred spaces and their association with "historical" records registered in the mind of people of antiquity as somewhat analogous to the scientific formula that makes modern medicine work. Therefore, where healing sites were built depended not on the borders of the city but rather on the special location that had been transmitted from one generation to the next. In the words of Ramsay MacMullen, "Holy places only by chance lay where cities grew."[92] Moreover, in the case of Asclepiea, people clearly preferred to situate such complexes outside the cities and away from the general public, mainly in order to prevent the spread of disease.[93] Therefore, if other evidence were to indicate that in Aelia this northeastern sector was part of the city, there might be reason to reconsider the matter, but it should not be annexed to the city just because of the Asclepieon on the site.

These conclusions may also shed new light on the nature of the *lithostroton* pavement and its function outside the city entrance structure of the Ecce Homo. As mentioned, a flagstone-paved square near a city gate is not an unusual phenomenon, especially in the particular circumstances that emerged in this part of town. A healing complex with special miraculous qualities only a few hundred feet outside the city limits probably attracted native inhabitants as well as visitors and no doubt acquired an aura of holiness over time. Visitors who walked out of the Ecce Homo arch to visit the sacred site would require animals to sacrifice or votive objects on which to have their names incised; on their way back they would probably want to buy some souvenirs. The gate through which they would leave and eventually return to the city would thus naturally become a bustling place that would draw peddlers, merchants, artisans, and, as accepted in Roman cities, especially a colony with a nearby military camp, prostitutes and other idlers as well. Such a reality, for example, reverberates in the book of Acts in the story about Paul and Barnabas's visit to Lystra in Asia Minor. There the city gates served as a gathering place for a pagan festival arranged by a priest at the Temple of Zeus, which stood outside the city.[94]

All in all, such an understanding of the Probatika site clarifies the socio-urban nature of the *lithostroton* plaza. In this (extra)urban context its existence seems natural and expected, and it fits in well with the texture of the area, as do the rooms (possibly shops?) that were built around it over time. The *lithostroton* should therefore be seen more as a commercial "piazza" just outside the city entrance than as a "city forum." The northeastern topographic unit as a whole should be left, according to my reconstruction, outside the limits of Aelia Capitolina.

The Temple Mount Area

How does the discussion thus far affect our understanding of the Temple Mount enclosure and its relation to the Roman colony? Reexamination of Dio's passage about the Capitoline Temple and of the archaeological material leads me to argue that the Romans left the area of the Jewish Temple, which had been in ruins since the destruction of the Second Temple in 70 CE, outside the city boundaries.[95] Without a pagan sanctuary, any real incentive to include the Temple Mount compound within the confines of the new colony evaporates. The huge enclosed platform built by Herod dominated the topography of Second Temple Jerusalem. If the builders of the Roman colony had desired to incorporate it in their new city, they could have embraced its remains, but it would entail significant human and financial resources. If the great terraced trapezoid had been cleared of rubble, it would have been an ideal location for many urban functions, such as temple compound, forum, or military camp. Yet the new spatial organization of Aelia's urban landscape, as analyzed here, reflects a certain detachment from the Temple Mount area. The northwestward shift of the municipal center and the creation of roads that detoured around the Temple Mount demonstrate this distancing. The placement of the entrance arch, which I argue signifies the eastern boundary of the city, on the line of the Western Wall of the Temple Mount further supports this conclusion. This structure excludes everything to the east of it, including the Temple Mount itself, from the city limits.

It is difficult to determine why the Roman engineers and architects who sketched the plan of the Roman colony abandoned the traditional layout of Jerusalem and left the Temple Mount precinct outside their city's boundary line. Did they have logistical concerns about an old city filled with ruins? Or was their stimulus more ideological? As noted, Christian writers tended to portray Hadrian's moves in Judea and Jerusalem as defiant toward Judaism and its people. Modern scholars have often adopted this position as fact without critically examining it. According to this view, the new colony is to be seen as motivated by anti-Jewish sentiment.[96] I tend, however, to agree with those scholars who find the attribution of such a position to Hadrian anachronistic, especially in regard to his actions prior to the Bar Kokhba revolt.[97] In the absence of evidence for any animus against Judaism, it seems more likely that practical considerations dictated the moves that ultimately left the enclosure of the ruined Temple outside the newly built colony. One such impetus may have been the difficulty of clearing the huge stacks of debris from the ruins of the Second Temple edifices. It had taken Herod and his successors, with all the manpower and means that were available to them, sixty-five years to build the place; imagine how long it would have taken the Romans to clear it.

To be sure, as already mentioned, for at least the first 150 years of its existence, Aelia Capitolina lacked a well-defined fortification system; walls did not encircle it. This does not, however, imply amorphous city boundaries in the eyes of either the planners or the local residents. Marking the inner territory of a city, aside from functioning as a religious rite in the Roman realm, was a basic municipal requirement. It is hard to imagine an urban community in the ancient world doing without it. One of the most rudimentary manifestations of such conceptualization of urban space required that not only officials but also city dwellers and visitors could easily distinguish between what remained inside and what was left outside the city. For this reason unwalled cities established other techniques for designating their borders, such as placing gates and monumental arches on the four edges of town. This, I claim, was the case in Jerusalem as well, and within this urban framework, the Romans renounced the territory of the Temple Mount.

Ruined Sacred Compounds and Roman Urbanism

Scholars only rarely offer parallels to the phenomenon presented here—namely for the Romans, when founding a new colony, to erect their new religious center on grounds that abut the ruins of an earlier local sanctuary but at the same time to relinquish the latter's actual site, or even leave it outside the new borders altogether. The widely held view, especially in its more romantic nineteenth- and early twentieth-century version, which directly associated "urbanism" and "Romanization," expected the Romans to incorporate a prestigious and ruined sanctuary into their new municipality.[98] Indeed, one does not have to think far to come up with very famous examples for such procedures. The celebrated Greek polis Corinth, destroyed by Lucius Mummius in 146 BCE and left more or less in ruins for 102 years, was rebuilt as a colony—Colonia Laus Iulia Corinthiensis—occupying similar grounds and resurrecting the sacred Greek compounds.[99] On the other side of the Mediterranean, almost identical measures were carried out in Carthage, captured and burned to the ground by Scipio Aemilianus Africanus in 146 BCE only to be refounded in 44 BCE "on the ruins [*in vestigiis*] of Great Carthage," to use the words of the Elder Pliny.[100] It is very likely, although admittedly not explicit, that a conceptual outlook of this kind induced modern scholars reconstructing Aelia Capitolina to include the Temple Mount within the Roman colony. It may have seemed to them inconceivable for the Romans to leave out such a structure.

Reality, however, yielded much more diversity. For one thing, some of the Roman colonies—whether Eburacum (modern York) in Britannia or Thamugadi (modern Timgad) in the North African province of Numidia, to name two well-known western instances—originated more or less from scratch, preceded only by either a legionary fortress, as at York, or practically nothing, as in Timgad. In such cases, the logistics and the economic quality of the spot ranked as the primary considerations for the new city's location, and there were no exalted ancient sanctuaries to be included.[101] In numerous other cases, colonies emerged within the framework of existing and established, even if not always the most prominent, settlements. At their inception, these urban ventures typically involved adding new settlers, usually military veterans, to the local population, restructuring the political systems, and upgrading the legal status of the old town (at times, especially from the second century on, it entailed only the legal change). Many of the colonies in both Anatolia and Gallia illustrate such measures.[102] In regions neighboring Aelia, such *coloniae* as Acco-Ptolemais, dating from the days of Claudius, and Caesarea Maritima, from the days of Vespasian, exhibit similar procedures.[103] Although certainly not always pleasant for the locals, the urban transformation in these cases unfolded relatively peacefully, involving neither destruction of existing temples nor reconstruction of ruined ones.

Most important, when rebuilding ruined towns that retained important local cult centers, it was not utterly predetermined that the Romans would return to the former site and restore the old sanctuary. More than a few cases, especially from the western part of the empire, each arising from different circumstances, demonstrate this claim. In Germania Inferior, for example, when the Romans burned down the major town and cultic hub of the Batavi—the *oppidum Batavorum*, as Tacitus calls it—during the upheaval known as the Batavian Rebellion (69–70 CE), they relocated the civic center a few miles west and rebuilt it as the new town of Noviomagus (under the heart of the modern city of Nijmegen in the Netherlands), later to be promoted to colonial status by Trajan.[104] In other towns in the same region, Roman authorities acted quite differently. In Xanten, for example, about seventy miles east of Noviomagus, when the nearby military camp at Vetera perished during the same uprising, the new fortress that the Romans established nearby carried on until the third century. So when Trajan, at the turn of the first century, sought a place for a new colony, he chose the grounds of an existing prosperous town, probably the center of the local tribe (Ciberni/Cugerni), for his new Colonia Ulpia Traiana.[105]

Clearly, a major difference distinguishes the two cases, because in Xanten there was no ruined local center to replace. Nevertheless, here are two urban endeavors, relatively close in both time and space, in which the Romans treated the indigenous hubs in distinct, if not opposing, ways; one swings away from the local center, whereas the other adheres to it. These divergent measures point to the lack of uniform paradigms for such actions, which is precisely my current argument.[106]

From the more immediate vicinity of Jerusalem, it is also worth considering the Roman temple dedicated to Zeus on Mount Gerizim, at that time part of the town of Neapolis (Shechem). The Romans founded the two pagan sanctuaries, in Aelia and Neapolis, during the first half of the second century.[107] Whether Hadrian himself commissioned its building, as attested by some written sources, or Antoninus Pius, as seems to be indicated by the numismatic evidence,[108] some interesting analogies tie the Zeus (Jupiter) shrine on Mount Gerizim and its contemporary twin in Aelia Capitolina. The two places share similar historical roots. Their prestige emanated from an ancient local tradition that grew up around a celebrated city with a sanctuary at its core. Similar to urban developments in Second Temple Jerusalem, a large city on Mount Gerizim, not just a holy precinct as scholars previously thought, has recently been uncovered, with the cultic Samaritan compound at its center.[109] The political events that led to the extinction of the two local temples and the construction of alternative pagan sanctuaries correlate to some degree as well. Both cities had been devastated in wartime and their temples demolished—the Jewish temple in Jerusalem by the Romans in 70 CE, and the Samaritan temple on Mount Gerizim about 180 years earlier by John Hyrcanus I. In both instances the obliteration of the shrine did not impair the veneration of the site among its people, and both places continued to function in the national and religious spotlight for many years.[110]

If I am correct in my claim throughout this chapter, the Roman planners in Jerusalem abandoned the old urban layout and, for practical reasons, shifted the city center about six hundred feet northwest. They acted similarly on Mount Gerizim, although the political circumstances and the chronological framework there were quite different. When Vespasian established the town Flavia Neapolis in 72/3 CE, the Romans did not revert to the old Samaritan city atop Mount Gerizim but chose a site about a mile north, at the base of the mountain. As with the practical considerations that dictated the relocation of Aelia, in Neapolis too the new site provided a more convenient topography, being on a main road and near the sources of water.[111] Admittedly, some major differences also set the two situations apart. In deciding the location of Neapolis, unlike Jerusalem, the Romans probably took into account a second settlement, the old city of Shechem, as well as a village by the name of Mabartha, both ensconced in the valley below Mount Gerizim.

Nonetheless, the status of Mount Gerizim within the new town deserves further attention. Apparently, the founders of Neapolis in the early 70s CE decided against including the Samaritan sacred mountain in the new municipal infrastructure. It took another two generations, until the days of Hadrian and/or Antoninus Pius, to erect a temple on its hilltop. Even more illuminating is the fact that, when they returned to the mountain, the Romans did not retrace the old enclosure, although the ruins of the ancient Samaritan sanctuary protruded in plain sight. Rather, they selected a new location for the Zeus temple, about half a mile north of the sacred Samaritan site, on a summit now called Tel er-Ras.[112]

The motives behind this move are far from obvious. We cannot say for sure whether they took this action because they wished to avoid Samaritan outrage. The possible result of such wrath was revealed three centuries later, when the construction of the Mary Theotokos (the mother of God) Church by the emperor Zeno (in 484) on top of the Samaritan sanctuary inflamed the region with fierce Samaritan riots. By the same token, however, there is no evidence to suggest, as some scholars do, the opposite: that this was an anti-Samaritan gesture that eventually led to a Samaritan rebellion. Likewise, the view that the new temple site manifested the Samaritans' religious syncretism—a desire to integrate their sacrosanct altar on one hilltop with a pagan temple built on another—is mere speculation.[113] It seems to me that, even if such factors played some role, we should not ignore the simpler aspect of urban planning—the need to merge the new temple and the existing town it now belonged to, Flavia Neapolis. A monumental staircase rising from the bottom of Mount Gerizim to its top amalgamated the municipality in the valley with the temple on the summit. The city's coins reflect this binding and feature its components—city, temple on a hill above it, and stairway climbing to that hill (see fig. 14). Archaeological excavations have uncovered portions of the steps, and various literary sources also mention the three-part complex as one civic unit.[114] According to this line of thought, the old Samaritan site was simply too far away, and placing the Roman temple there would have created a topographic gap between the city at the bottom of the hill and its sanctuary on one of the faraway summits.

Fig. 14. A bronze coin, struck in the local mint of Flavia Neapolis (Shechem), from the days of the emperor Elagabalus (218–22 CE), who is shown on the obverse. Depicted on the reverse is Mount Gerizim with a monumental staircase climbing to the sanctuary on its top. Courtesy of Israel Museum, Jerusalem.

In any case, the correspondence to the temple in Jerusalem is more than apparent. Just as the Romans neglected the old temple site of Jerusalem and shifted the new temple in Aelia Capitolina about fifteen hundred feet northwest of the Temple Mount, to the northwestern hill (see maps 1, 6), so too did they transfer the new temple on Mount Gerizim about twenty-one hundred feet north of the old site in order to link it with the new urban setting. This demonstrates the Romans' willingness to pass over traditional temple grounds when those obstruct other practical exigencies. New cities created new needs, and these led to the adoption of new sites.

There is no point in pressing these comparisons too far. As in any two cases, they are not totally identical. Striking disparities divide the two cities, such as the topographic situation (the difference in altitude between Neapolis and the top of Mount Gerizim greatly exceeds that in Jerusalem), the period when they were built, and the circumstances that led to their establishment. Aelia became a typical pagan city, while Flavia Neapolis sustained a mixed population and culture. Variations with respect to the temples reinforce these differences. Unlike at Jerusalem, the ancient Samaritan sanctuary continued to function in one way or another within the framework of the new pagan entity, as can be seen, for example, in the city's coins, which represent a hill crowned by a pagan temple adjacent to another hilltop with a (Samaritan?) altar.[115] Yet the uniqueness of any particular case does not preclude the possibility of isolating comparable features. After all, this is what comparative research is all about. In the present case, I use such analogies to argue that the Romans did not necessarily return to ancient temple sites when establishing a new city. Just as they did not revert to the old situation in Noviomagus or Flavia Neapolis, so it was not imperative for them do so in Jerusalem. All in all, no one can assure us that the question of what to do with a ruined local temple when refounding a city had an inexorable answer, and it seems very likely that it did not.

Aelia's Urban Landscape and the Story of the Temple Mount

In order to appraise the landscape of the Roman colony Aelia Capitolina and come to terms with its urban layout, we must detach ourselves from the traditional model of the city as it has been fixed in our consciousness by local traditions (both Jewish and Muslim) throughout the centuries and study it from the viewpoint of its Roman founders. The evidence analyzed in the present chapter indicates that for the most part the builders of Aelia forsook the boundaries of the old Second Temple city, which lay in ruins, much of its ground sprinkled with broken walls, fallen columns, and debris. They reconfigured the spatial organization and designed their colony in an innovative urban setting, with the municipal centers, traffic arteries, temples, and other architectonic elements joining together to form its new shape.

According to the reconstruction suggested here (map 6), Aelia started as a relatively small, unwalled colony with monumental, triumphal-style entrance structures marking its limits: the Damascus Gate to the north, the Ecce Homo arch to the east, most probably also a gate to the west near the site of the present-day Jaffa Gate, and perhaps a southern gate as well. Due to inconclusive information, the structure and extent of the city in its early stages, especially in the southern part, remain rather vague. But even without determining the southern portion precisely, we may safely conclude that the city's area stretched over approximately 75 to 125 acres. On the one hand, these seem relatively small measures compared with the large metropolis of Jerusalem during the late Second Temple period or with the city's later size in the Byzantine era. On the other hand, there have been times when Jerusalem's dimensions were even more modest.[116] In comparison with other cities and colonies that were founded at the same time in various parts of the Roman Empire, Aelia should be considered among such middle-sized settlements as Camulodunum in England (today's Colchester), which extended over approximately 110 acres; at the same time Aelia was larger than various cities in Asia Minor or Timgad in North Africa, which at the time of their inception covered only about 30 acres.[117]

Naturally, the official city limits in Jerusalem did not confine the settlement, and as the population grew, the territories too expanded outward. The therapeutic installation under the patronage of Asclepius operated northeast of the colony, and some sorts of buildings occupied the area south of the ruined Temple enclosure. Here too the landscape dynamics of Jerusalem follow the common pattern of urban growth, with parallels all over the Roman Empire. In Timgad, for example, the westward expansion of the city included the construction of an arch, an external square, a market structure (the market of Sertius), a temple, and a fountain, as well as a freestanding gate intended to mark the boundary of the amplified area, some nine hundred feet from the city wall. Another example closer to Jerusalem comes from the growth of Caesarea, on the Mediterranean coast of Palestine, beyond the walls of the Roman city. Its grounds extended so far that the Byzantine authorities found it necessary to build new city walls to enclose the area outside of the old walls.[118] As I demonstrate in chapter 4, a similar process occurred in Jerusalem, and over the years a larger territory, to be encircled by the Byzantine fortification system, swallowed Aelia's original space.

What happened to and on the Temple Mount in all this? The religious and economic center of the new city, the heart of the colony, became the northwestern hill, in the area of the present-day Christian Quarter. Naturally, and following the common practice in those days, the Romans situated there the forum of the city and its temples. The Temple Mount was not part of this newly shaped reality. The planners who designed the city's landscape apparently found no use for this enclosure, which at the time overflowed with rubble, and it remained desolate, outside the limits of the colony.

This conclusion calls for significant revisions to the commonly told story of the Temple Mount. At least on a certain level, we no longer need to see the post–Second Temple phase of Jerusalem's history as a narrative of oppressive and demeaning domination, in which the ruling powers confiscated the Jewish sacred site and tainted its holiness with a pagan shrine. In the following chapters I propose that it is rather the availability of the Temple Mount enclosure within the new spatial organization of Aelia that allowed, and perhaps attracted, Jews and early Christians to interact with it and formulate their manifold conceptualities about sacred space.

CHAPTER FOUR

A Lively Ruin

The Temple Mount in Byzantine Jerusalem

The Momentum of a New Era

In 313 CE, the Roman emperor Constantine declared Christianity a permitted religion. Eleven years later, when he became the sole ruler of the Roman realm, Constantine elevated Christianity even further, making it the official religion of the Roman Empire. These events opened a new era in Jerusalem's history. Constantine's deeds transformed—almost in an instant—the small, unknown colony situated on the periphery of the Roman world into a central metropolis whose Christian past endowed it with a lustrous aura. As in other periods, both political and religious considerations were at work. As befit a city consumed by momentous historical memories, Jerusalem played a major role in the Holy Land policy that Constantine launched as part of his efforts to repair growing rifts and instability in the ecclesiastical network of his time. With the assistance of his mother Helena, and in close cooperation with the local bishops, Constantine embarked on an ambitious building project in Jerusalem and other major sites in the region.[1] From that point on—throughout the entire Byzantine period—Jerusalem sparkled as an energetic and prosperous city. Rulers took an interest in its well-being and sought to provide for its needs; pilgrims of all walks of life and from the far-flung regions of the empire designated it the destination of their voyages; and monks settled within and around its limits.

While pre-Byzantine textual and archaeological records provide only an incomplete and discontinuous picture of Jerusalem as a Roman colony, from the beginning of the fourth century CE a profusion of accounts from a variety of sources paint a portrait of solid lines and hues. Historical compositions—the most important being those of Eusebius of Caesarea, an eyewitness to the changes that took place in the city at the beginning of the era—complement travelogues and guidebooks for pilgrims, biographies of monks, and other works. In addition, archaeologists have uncovered an abundance of Byzantine remains. This wealth of primary material has served as the basis for a proliferation of scholarly works on Byzantine Jerusalem, ranging from monographs devoted to specific parts of the city (Mount Zion, the Church of the Holy Sepulcher, the Probatika pools and their associated churches, and the Mount of Olives) to discussions of various theological issues. There are also authoritative reviews that synthesize this diverse material into a comprehensive portrait of the city.[2]

These studies allow us to trace the city's urban character and contours with considerable confidence. The new Christian authorities replaced the pagan temples, which originally flanked the municipal forum in what is now the Christian Quarter, with the aggregate of buildings and architectonic units customarily known as the Church of the Holy Sepulcher (see map 7: 3). This complex comprised a variety of structures, including the Martyrion Basilica, the Golgotha Atrium, and the Anastasis marking Jesus's tomb. It functioned as the religious and municipal center, from which the city expanded south and east. The Church of Holy Zion served as the principal focal point in the southern part of the city (map 7: 7). Later, apparently toward the middle of the fifth century, an additional impressive structure for a church was built to its southeast, next to the Siloam pool (map 7: 6). Development around these sacred buildings eventually led to the inclusion of the entire southern area within the city fortification line.

To the east, from the beginning of the Byzantine period, various churches also clustered on the Mount of Olives. As early as Constantine's reign, the Church of Eleona was erected over the cave where, tradition has it, Jesus taught his disciples. Later on, in the fourth century, the Church of the Ascension was raised nearby.

The municipal spaces created between these foci to the south and east of the Church of the Holy Sepulcher were gradually filled with additional structures.

At the foot of the Mount of Olives, on the slopes of the Kidron Valley, the Geth-semane compound developed (map 7: 2), and to its north another set of build-ings commemorated the site identified as Mary's tomb. In the fifth century, a church marking the home of Mary's parents was constructed west of this clus-ter, in the area north of the Temple Mount precinct, next to the Probatika pools (map 7: 1). In the sixth century, the emperor Justinian initiated the erection of

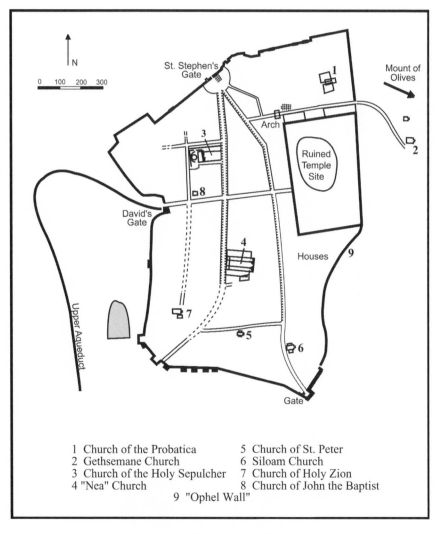

1 Church of the Probatica   5 Church of St. Peter
2 Gethsemane Church   6 Siloam Church
3 Church of the Holy Sepulcher   7 Church of Holy Zion
4 "Nea" Church   8 Church of John the Baptist
                 9 "Ophel Wall"

Map 7. Jerusalem at the end of the Byzantine period

a huge new church in the area between the Church of the Holy Sepulcher and Mount Zion (but slightly east of the midpoint between them). He named it Nea (New) Church, also consecrated to Mary, Mother of God (map 7: 4).

Roads crisscrossed the city, most of them stretching in a straight line, as was the accepted practice at the time, with only slight deviations caused by topography. A wall enclosed the city, although scholars disagree about its precise date (as discussed later in this chapter). At the height of this period, it climbed from the Siloam pool and circled Mount Zion, running north through David's Gate, turning east to the Damascus Gate (then called St. Stephen's date), and finally—supposedly—reaching the eastern wall of the Temple Mount (see map 7). Only the Mount of Olives and its slopes were left outside.

Written sources and archaeological excavations provide the information needed to complete this picture. Pilgrimage literature as well as ecclesiastic biographies allude to dozens of churches and monasteries. The Madaba map, a sixth-century mosaic that depicts the city quite realistically, although tainted with some religious bias, further testifies to the tightly packed nature of Jerusalem's landscape (fig. 15). Secular architecture also abounded. Even if our documentary evidence, which concentrates on Jerusalem's sacred ambience, records municipal buildings only in passing, such structures were undoubtedly the city's backbone, and many of them surface in archaeological excavations: homes, bathhouses, shops, markets, column-lined streets, and other such architectonic elements.

How did the compound that Herod built around the by-now long-gone Jewish Temple fit into the urban design of the Byzantine city? Did it become part of the city, and if so what municipal function did it serve? Modern scholars believe that the new Christian rulers integrated the Temple Mount within the walls and boundaries of the city but at the same time left it desolate, appending it to the city as an afterthought.[3] These scholars usually offer the Artemis temple precinct, located in Gerasa, Jordan, as another example of the Byzantine tendency to leave pagan temple enclosures desolate within the urban layout. The Temple of Artemis, Gerasa's pride and joy until the late Roman period, stood at the city's center, and when it ceased to operate, the Byzantines did not—as might have been expected—convert the compound into a church, as they did with other temples in Gerasa. Except for scattered workshops set up by artisans, they forsook the huge structures of the Artemis compound and left the quadrangle between them abandoned and neglected.[4] Understanding the situation in Jerusalem in similar terms, many scholars have argued that theo-

Fig. 15. Part of the famous mosaic map, known as the Madaba map (after the place were it was found in Jordan), depicting the Byzantine city of Jerusalem. At the left one can recognize the northern gate to the city leading to the main colonnaded street (the *cardo maximus*); at the center of the map stands (inversely) the Church of the Holy Sepulcher. The inscription at the top left reads in Greek "The holy city of Jerusalem." (Note that nowhere in the map is the compound of the Temple Mount to be found). From the Studium Biblicum Franciscanum Archive. Courtesy of Michele Piccirillo.

logical motives underlay the continued desolation of the Temple Mount. In their view, the destroyed Jewish temple symbolized the church's triumph and therefore demonstrated the validity of its Christological claims. Byzantine authorities, therefore, left the derelict site in the city as a testimony and monument.[5] The current chapter reexamines the first half of this syllogism—the physical state of the Herodian compound in the Byzantine period and its position within the urban framework. The city's layout and history are analyzed with a focus on the Temple enclosure. Chapter 5 then revisits the theological and ideological aspects of this issue.

The City Walls

The course of Jerusalem's walls holds the key to the baffling question regarding the inclusion (or seclusion) of the Temple Mount in (or from) the boundaries of Byzantine Jerusalem. If a fortified circuit reached the eastern retaining wall of the Herodian compound—in other words, if the city wall stretched to the southeastern and northeastern corners of the compound (as presented, for example in map 7)—this would clearly indicate the inclusion of the Temple Mount within the city. But if this was not the case, and the wall approached only the southwestern and northwestern corners of the Temple compound, then the Temple area remained, as it had, according to my claims, during the early Aelia Capitolina period (see map 6), outside the city. True, this is not an incontrovertible conclusion, since the compound may have been included in the city even if the walls reached only the western retaining wall. The Second Temple period offers a clear example of such an alignment, when the so-called Second Wall—the northern defense line of Jerusalem at that time—extended only to the Antonia fortress at the northwest corner of the Temple compound.[6] Yet Second Temple circumstances, in which the city developed organically from the southeast to the west, with the Temple Mount always constituting an integral part of its landscape, differ significantly from what existed in Jerusalem during the Roman and Byzantine periods. As I argued in chapter 3, Aelia resembled a new city that developed in the opposite direction (from the west to the east and southeast) and did not embrace the Temple area from the start. In this case, the run of the walls and their points of contact with the Temple compound can indicate the latter's position in relation to the city.

Two questions therefore ought to be addressed: (1) When did the rulers of Jerusalem/Aelia fortify the city? (2) At that time, did the walls encompass the ruined Temple compound? These two inquiries stem from, and build on, my conclusions of chapter 3 about Roman Jerusalem. During the first centuries of its existence, when Aelia Capitolina remained an unwalled colony, the Herodian compound was left outside the city's boundaries (which were marked by monumental gates). Following this long period as a wall-less city, the integration of the Temple Mount precinct into the city must be seen as a radical move that dramatically altered its landscape. Admittedly, the annexation of adjacent territories into civic space is a familiar and logical urban process, practiced in many Byzantine cities, Jerusalem included. During the fifth century, for example, the people of Jerusalem extended the city limits southward to bring in Mount Zion and the Siloam pool (who exactly was responsible for this move remains unknown, but it seems that the empress Eudocia's support or influence provided the incentive). Nevertheless, we must investigate whether such a course of action also befell the Temple Mount and, if it did, what factors brought it about.

When was Aelia delimited with a wall? At a number of points along the Ottoman fortifications of today's Old City—especially on the west side, in the area of the Citadel (David's Tower; see map 2: 19 and fig. 1) and to its north—excavators have identified courses of an otherwise unknown ancient wall. The relative chronology provided by the stratigraphy of these excavations, and some ceramic and numismatic finds (which provide a more accurate means of dating the strata) at those points where archaeologists were able to isolate sealed loci, date this wall to somewhere between the end of the third and the beginning of the fourth century.[7] Unfortunately, insufficient archaeological data preclude a precise date, and thus do not clarify whether a "Christian hand" such as Constantine's, with a possible religious agenda, initiated this fortification endeavor, or whether earlier Roman generations had carried out the project.

Written sources may assist here in pinpointing the date, but they must be studied with careful attention. For example, John Rufus's biography of his teacher, Peter the Iberian, a Georgian prince who became a monk and settled in Jerusalem in the 430s, indicates that in the early fifth century the city still lacked a wall.[8] But the temporal distance of this work from the days of Constantine and its legendary-hagiographic nature cast doubt on its credibility. Furthermore, more reliable sources contradict it. One of these is the *Onomasticon* of Eusebius. A Palestinian native and bishop of Caesarea in the days of Constantine, Eusebius composed this document as a gazetteer to biblical sites in Palestine. Scholars today are quite certain that Eusebius produced this text in the early stages of his career, certainly before Constantine's rise to power. In the *Onomasticon* Eusebius identifies the biblical site of the valley of Hinnom as "situated close to the wall of Jerusalem to its east."[9] The mentioning the city's wall is included in the account matter-of-factly; the biblical verses that Eusebius discusses provide no hint of such an element, and it serves no purpose in explicating the tradition that the author notes, namely that Hinnom marked the entrance to Hell. The lack of any internal reason for the reference to the wall, whether theological or exegetical, makes it reasonable to conclude that Eusebius knew of a wall when he wrote of it. We should keep in mind that this is a man who was personally acquainted with Jerusalem at the end of the third and beginning of the fourth century.

The traveler from Bordeaux, a famous and anonymous Christian pilgrim who toured the city in the 330s, also makes note of the city's fortification system. He encounters walls as he exits and reenters the city on his way to and back from the Siloam pool and Mount Zion (now in its Christian identity as the southwestern hill), as well as next to the site represented to him as Pontius Pilate's house. Although his description is not sufficiently lucid, and despite the fact that at times he blends reality with fiction in a way that can mislead the modern reader, the walls he alludes to seem quite real.[10]

Taken together, the information provided by Eusebius (and, to a lesser extent, the Bordeaux traveler, who confirms the existence of the wall but is unhelpful in determining its date) and the archaeological material support those scholars who suggest that the city walls were erected prior to Constantine (see n. 7), either at the end of the third century or the beginning of the fourth. According to this reconstruction, the evacuation of the city by the Tenth Legion at some point toward the end of the third century may have created the circumstances that required the construction of a defense system. This conclusion about the dating of the fortification (henceforth referred to here as the "third-century wall") requires a reexamination of the second question, about the inclusion of the Jewish Temple precinct within the boundaries of the walled city. After all, scholars have justified their claim that the compound was incorporated into the city by adducing its theological importance to the Byzantines, yet such an argument loses its validity for a wall built at the end of the third century (and, in any case, before Constantine's reign).

How can we know whether the new city walls embraced the Herodian enclosure? A passage from Eucherius's *Letter to Faustus*, which portrayed Jerusalem as he knew it in the first half of the fifth century, offers some indication. Seeking, like Eusebius a century and a half before him, to identify the location of Gehenna, the entrance to Hell, Eucherius explicitly states, "the east wall of Jerusalem is also the [east] wall of the Temple."[11] Apparently, he viewed the Jewish Temple area as part and parcel of the city. But was this always the case? Earlier sources remain ambiguous. The traveler from Bordeaux, for example, explores the enclosure of the ruined Jewish Temple, and vividly depicts the objects and sites he encounters there. At the same time he remains rather vague about the relation between the compound and the city. As a Christian pilgrim, he made inquiries about sites dear to his faith, both in and around Jerusalem, not limiting himself to the city itself. Just as he at other times exited the city to the south and then returned,[12] so he could have left the city to reach the site of the ancient Jewish Temple. Egeria, a female pilgrim from Spain who spent time in the city close to the end of the fourth century, remarks on an eastern city gate (*porta civitatis*) through which one proceeds to reach the Mount of Olives. She does not, however, specify its location.[13] Did the eastern gate of Egeria's time stand close to today's Lion's Gate (see map 2), thus embracing the Temple Mount? If so, this would have meant that by the late fourth century the eastern boundary of Jerusalem—which, as argued in chapter 3, was marked in the second century CE by the Ecce Homo arch—had shifted about a thousand feet eastward. Egeria and other sources provide no proof of such a move.

Archaeological material in this case also fails to provide sufficient evidence. Several excavations have examined the southeastern corner of the Herodian compound, as well as the line of the wall that runs from this point southward along the eastern slope of the City of David, a line of fortification called by scholars the Ophel Wall (map 7: 9). None of these digs yielded any evidence suggesting a fortification from the third and fourth centuries. The work of Eilat Mazar, who reexcavated one of the towers on the Ophel Wall, supports this conclusion.[14] Such finds allow the conjecture that the southern part of the third-century Roman wall of Aelia did not coalesce with the eastern retaining wall of the Temple compound. According to this line of thought, only in the fifth century, when the third-century circuit fell into disuse as a result of the expansion of the city southward, did a newly constructed wall—the so-called Eudocia's Wall (scholars have named the wall after the empress, wife of Theodosius II, who, while residing in Jerusalem for a few years in the fifth century, initiated and funded its construction)—bring Mount Zion and the City of David into the city and link up with the Temple compound at its southeastern corner.

Even more complicated is the situation at the northern end of the city. All scholars believe that, from the time of its construction—according to the foregoing conclusions, at the end of the third century—the northern line ran parallel to today's Old City wall and met the Herodian compound at its northeastern corner (compare maps 2 and 7).[15] Such a course would have encompassed the Temple Mount compound and incorporated its grounds into the city. In my opinion, however, the truth is not nearly so simple. Methodical archaeological excavations have yet to be conducted on the northern segment of the eastern city wall, from the northeastern corner of the Temple Mount, via the Lion's Gate, to the northeastern corner of the Old City. The question remains, therefore, whether the third-century wall continued all along the line of the current Ottoman wall up to what is today the northeastern corner of the Old City, from which point it turned south until it joined the eastern retaining wall of the Temple compound. Perhaps it followed a different path, but we do not today have enough archaeological evidence to answer this question decisively. It could very well be that the third-century wall did not continue along the entire line of the Old City wall visible today. Instead, it may have turned south at some earlier point, perhaps extending toward the Ecce Homo arch and the northwestern corner of the Temple Mount, thus leaving its compound outside the city limits (as was the case, according to my argument, in the days of Aelia; see map 6). Some recent, albeit limited, excavations point in this direction,[16] but only more comprehensive research will enable firm conclusions.

Today one might find it difficult to understand why anyone in the ancient world would want to leave the area north of the Temple precinct outside the city walls. But such a position stems from the manner in which the modern map of the Old City came to dominate our consciousness about Jerusalem. We find it hard to imagine the Old City of Jerusalem devoid of its major eastern limbs, the Muslim Quarter, that space to the east of El-Wadi (Ḥagai) Street (see map 2) and the Ḥaram (the Moslem designation of the Temple Mount). But from the point of view of people residing in the city during the Roman period, such a choice would hardly have been baseless. As noted, during most of the Second Temple period, until the construction of the so-called Third Wall, this area lay outside the city's circuit. And as claimed in chapter 3, the founders of Aelia Capitolina marked the city edge with the Ecce Homo arch, leaving all the area to the east outside its limits. So it would have been a natural choice for the builders of the wall at the end of the third century not to include this area within their fortified perimeter. In keeping with this conjecture, only the demographic and urban expansions of the city in the early Byzantine period, during the late fourth and fifth centuries, accelerated the habitation of the northeastern parts of the city and in the end justified its incorporation with the city walls.[17]

Taking all this into account, it seems more likely that the Jewish Temple compound did not become an organic part of the city at the end of the Roman period and the beginning of the Byzantine era. Such a proposal follows the conclusions reached in the preceding chapter, where I argued that the Roman founders of Aelia abandoned, to some extent, the traditional contours of Jerusalem and shifted the city center to the northwest, leaving the Jewish Temple platform outside the city limits. Why should we assume that they discarded this blueprint at the end of the third century by integrating the precinct into the city, with no apparent reason to do so?

Such a line of thought entirely overturns our understanding of the compound's role in the Byzantine city. No evidence, neither documentary nor archaeological, indicates that Constantine added to the third-century wall of Jerusalem. As far as we know, walls were not part of his architectonic repertoire in Jerusalem. Thus the Temple enclosure probably remained outside of Byzantine Jerusalem for the first four generations after Constantine, not to be annexed until at least the mid-fifth century. The compound stood next to the city but not within its limits.

According to this reconstruction, the first wall to bring the Temple precinct into the city was Eudocia's Wall. This wall responded to the natural growth of the city that became a central Byzantine hub. It expanded Jerusalem's border in the south by incorporating the southern part of Mount Zion and the Siloam pool, and it intersected with the southeastern corner of the Temple compound. This wall marks the first inclusion of the Temple Mount into the Roman and Byzantine cities since the destruction of the Second Temple.

A Ruined Temple Compound

By far the most important source of information regarding the situation that transpired on the Temple enclosure at the beginning of the fourth century comes from Eusebius's *Proof of the Gospel*. In a chapter meant to demonstrate the fulfillment of the prophet Micah's vision of the Temple's destruction, Eusebius provides an eyewitness account about the state of affairs in the area of the ruined Jewish Temple.[18] Modern scholars completely misread this portion.

Mislead by Eusebius usage of the appellation Mount Zion, these scholars associate the text with the area that Christians came to identify as Mount Zion, namely the southwestern hill of Jerusalem (see map 1).[19] Eusebius, however, clearly applies "Mount Zion" here to designate the site of the Jewish Temple. Admittedly, other writings of his attest to Eusebius's awareness of a new Christian application for this ancient biblical appellation, redirecting it to signify the city's southwestern hill, which retains the name Mount Zion to this day.[20] But in the section under discussion here Eusebius introduces Jerusalem and Mount Zion as the two "objects of Jewish reverence" targeted in Micah's prophecy, which Eusebius quotes at the beginning of the pericope. In keeping with this, he presents Mount Zion as "their [the Jews'] once-famous mountain" and as the site of the Temple, altar, and Holy of Holies.[21] In fact, Eusebius's entire chapter—aimed, as noted, at demonstrating the fulfillment of Micah's prophecy—loses all meaning if not understood as pointing to the location of the Temple. There can thus be no doubt that the Mount Zion in this chapter of *Proof of the Gospel* refers to the mountain on which the Jewish Temple once stood.[22]

In other texts Eusebius's use of the term "Zion" fluctuates among different connotations, assigning it both spiritual and physical meanings.[23] His writings thus represent a transition in the denotations and images associated with Zion. In its traditional usage (discussed in chapter 1 and again in chapter 5), common in the Second Temple period and in the early patristic literature of the second century, Zion always alluded to the space inhabited by the Jewish Temple. Later on, in the third century, Christian authors begin to identify Mount Zion with the city's southwestern hill. Eusebius knew and used both senses, but the context of the passage under discussion here unequivocally presents Mount Zion as the place of the Jewish Temple.

Eusebius seeks in this chapter to illustrate the devastation of the city and the site of the Temple (Mount Zion). He equates destruction with the city's settlement by pagans and sees its manifestation in the use of debris from the ancient Jewish edifices as building material for the pagan structures of the colony.[24] This description fits reality very well. In Eusebius's time, after all, Jerusalem no longer lay in ruins. Yet, regarding the wreckage of Mount Zion, Eusebius offers an entirely different portrayal:

> Their once famous Mount Zion, instead of being, as once it was, the center for
> study and education based on the divine prophecies, which the children of the

ancient Hebrews, their godly prophets, priests, and the teachers of all the nation loved to interpret, [is now] being farmed by Roman men, not different from the rest of the country. So I have observed with my own eyes—bulls plowing [there], and the place sown [with seed].[25]

This extract unmistakably contrasts the mountain's glorious past with the humiliating reality of the present. First, it commemorates the place's function in ancient times as a center for the study of the Torah, probably molding this facet on the verse from Micah (although reversing its time from the future to the past) that Eusebius quotes at the beginning of the chapter: "And many nations shall come and say: Come let us go up to the mountain of the Lord, to the house of the God of Jacob; that he may teach us his ways and we may walk in his paths. For out of Zion shall go forth the Torah and the word of God from Jerusalem" (4:2). To substantiate the degradation of the site Eusebius offers his own observation of the place. He claims to have encountered there farmland worked by Roman inhabitants of the colony, plowed and sown by oxen and human muscle. In another portion of the same work, devoted to a comprehensive theological homily denouncing the Temple Mount (see chapter 5), Eusebius depicts the place in the same way: "If our observation has any value, we have seen in our own time Zion, once so famous, ploughed with yokes of oxen by Roman men, and utterly devastated."[26]

The same chapter in Eusebius's *Proof of the Gospel* contains another description of the ruin in the compound of the old Jewish Temple, this time not focusing on the area as a whole but rather on the Temple structure itself: "And it is sad for the eyes to see stones from the Temple itself, its ancient inner sanctuary, and holy places, used for the building of pagan sanctuaries and spectacles for the public."[27] It should be noted that Eusebius makes no mention of a pagan temple on the site. Instead, he alludes to stones that were hauled from the debris in the Temple compound and used in the construction of pagan sanctuaries (in the plural!), apparently elsewhere. This account confirms one of my central arguments in chapter 3, namely that no pagan temple ever existed on the Temple Mount. Eusebius depicts a despoiled, abandoned area— mounds of stones that constituted the ruins of the compound and of the Temple edifice. Quite naturally, it attracted the attention of the builders in the adjacent Roman colony and came to function as a source for building material. It serves Eusebius's literary purpose to highlight the basest of all the new structures built from the Temple's stones: idolatrous temples (which were scattered around the city). There is an ideological undertone here, of course, but it does not make the description any less factual.

The same picture emerges from the *Theophania,* a later work by Eusebius that has come down to us primarily in a Syriac translation. In a chapter entirely devoted to the theological implications of the Temple's destruction, Eusebius interlaces several references to the state of the Temple site in his time. For example, alongside his assertion that God, as recorded in the prose of his prophets, condemned the Temple to obliteration, Eusebius writes: "To those who visit these places, the sight itself affords the most complete fulfillment of the prediction." Shortly thereafter he states: "The outcome that remains evident today is just as the prophecy said," and he then embarks on a detailed report from the field: "The whole shrine and its walls as well as those ornamented and beautiful buildings which were within it, and which exceeded all descriptions, have suffered desolation from that time to this." He concludes, "Anyone who desires may see [this] with his own eyes."[28]

Caution must be exercised before taking these descriptions at face value. Works as steeped in theology as *Proof of the Gospel* and *Theophania* are susceptible to manipulate reality to fit their agenda—all the more so, given that Eusebius's depiction of the area in *Proof of the Gospel* fits neatly with the sources he refers to, which foretell the site's fate: "Zion shall be plowed as a field" (Micah 3:12). But in order to refute Eusebius's testimony here, one must consider him an out-and-out liar, because he pronounces quite explicitly that he bases his report on firsthand experience. Time and again throughout this chapter, Eusebius emphasizes this point: that he is conveying details he gathered from personal encounters with the place. Toward the end of the section he explains why it was necessary to adhere to the facts in this account: "As this state of things was never achieved at any other time but during the Roman Empire, from our Savior's birth till now, I consider the proof irrefutable that the prophet refers to the time of our savior's coming among men."[29] The author's theological predilections resonate in the erroneous chronological framework he establishes for the destruction—from the birth of Jesus to his own time. Similar to other Christian thinkers who linked the destruction of the Temple to the death of Jesus, Eusebius overlooks the decades that separate the two events. But this does not detract from his fundamental argument, which amounts to the chapter's core—the landscape as we see it today, he claims, confirms the prophecy. He must, then, portray the reality that people are likely to encounter when they visit the location he describes.

Moreover, Eusebius's aspiration to tally his words with the facts in the field is evident in his insistence on formulating an unusual definition for the destruction of Jerusalem—rather than its literal reduction to ruins, Eusebius sees the city's destruction in its habitation by Gentiles (see n. 25). In doing so, he departs from the common discourse about the destruction many of his peers share. Christian writers tend to neglect the actual situation in the city and continue to evoke its destroyed state many generations after its restoration as a fully-fledged Roman town. The church historian Socrates, to mention one example, claims that Helena, Constantine's mother, found the city literally devastated,[30] although Jerusalem had been settled for two hundred years at the time. As is well known, religious perception may at times deviate from actuality. In contrast, Eusebius's portrayal seems intentionally to engage the actual situation. Furthermore, his insistence on the tangibility of the account makes fabrication highly unlikely. After all, many of the consumers of this text visited Jerusalem themselves and could vouch for its validity.

Allusions to the ruins heaped up on the Temple Mount emerge in many other sources as well, both Jewish and Christian. The Talmudic legend, cited at the beginning of the introduction, about the sages and Rabbi ʿAkiva who spotted a fox emerging from the rubble at the site of the Holy of Holies provides a clear example of a literary narrative constructed around the wreckage on the Mount. A similar example appears in Cyril of Jerusalem's *Catecheses,* the sermons that he, as bishop of the city, preached before candidates for conversion (the catechumens) and which are generally dated to the 350s. References to the demolished Temple area turn up in this text on more than one occasion. Cyril introduces these depictions not as an abstract symbol but as a concrete element, on display before the eyes of his audience.[31]

In the same vein, traditions that relate the attempt to restore the Jewish Temple in the days of the emperor Julian (in the 360s) mention the ruins of the Temple both before the project began and after it ceased abruptly.[32] For example, Gregory of Nazianzus, who as a youth spent some time in the Christian school in Caesarea and most probably visited Jerusalem, reports in his *Orations against Julian* that workers at the site during the days of Julian removed mounds of "dirt" that had built up through the generations. This detail also appears, matter-of-factly, in a homily by John Chrysostom on the same subject.[33] Jerome too maintains that when the Jews arrive in Jerusalem each year, they direct their mourning toward the "ruins of their Temple." In the course of his commentary on Isaiah, while attempting to demonstrate the fulfillment of the prophet's foretelling of destruction, he more than once stresses the visibility of the Temple's ruins, and at several points he even mentions a certain flight of stairs, a remnant of the Jewish Temple, that people can discern in the area.[34] Later in the fifth century, the biography of the monk Barsauma recounts that he and his company (gang) ascended to "the desolate Temple of Solomon."[35] Note that none of these descriptions contain any implication that city dwellers deliberately dumped garbage on the site. Even Jerome, whom scholars often cite as the source for the image of the Temple enclosure as a garbage dump, only portrays the site as a dung-pit (*sterquilinium*), in line with the general filth of the place.[36] All in all, even if the line between realistic depiction and religious perception in these sources remains blurred, the picture that emerges is one of visible ruin.

Finally, the Arabic sources on Omar's arrival in Jerusalem and his establishment of a mosque on the Temple Mount repeatedly refer to the refuse that covered the site of the rock, and they attribute the detritus to deliberate Christian actions from the time of Helena onward.[37] In general, these traditions lie outside the scope of the present work. Suffice it to say that such a radical picture, which shows the site operating as the city's official garbage dump, is not consistent with the testimony of visitors during the Byzantine period nor with the various Christian sites and activities there. Possibly, in the last decades of the era, with Jerusalem suffering repeated invasions and frequently changing hands, a great deal of filth amassed in the Temple compound. More than revealing the Byzantines' treatment of the compound, these sources reflect the large-scale cleansing of the Temple Mount initiated by the Arab conquerors before they commenced the construction of their new structures. It is only natural that, given the carting away of huge quantities of debris, legends would arise about the way this refuse came to be there.

Pilgrimage Attractions on the Temple Grounds

The compound of the ruined Jewish Temple attracted the attention of Christians and ignited their imagination throughout the Byzantine period. In the words of the great French scholar of the Dominican order Félix Abel: "The ruins were fertile [grounds] for legends. Every segment of wall, tunnel, and any piece worth pausing at became the material for fantastic interpretations."[38] Regardless of their judgment about the place and its past (a subject discussed at length in chapter 5), the Temple precinct fascinated Christians, those who lived in the city as well as their coreligionists from afar. They frequented the enclosure and engaged its landscape, mainly by identifying meaningful objects there and associating them with their Christian world.

Interest in the compound was neither static nor uniform; rather, it evolved in diverse and, at times, even contradicting trajectories. At its core, Christian relations with the space of the Temple involved a vexing paradox. On the one hand, the writings of some visitors to the city make no reference to the Temple area. The site does not appear among the places evoked in the Jerusalem liturgy described by Egeria at the end of the fourth century. It is also absent from Peter the Iberian's dream, which describes the course of an imaginary stroll through the city some one hundred years later.[39] Likewise, the representation of Jerusalem on the Madaba map fails to note the massive space of the Temple precinct.[40]

Yet other sources, throughout this period, recognize the Temple compound as a routine stop in the standard pilgrimage tour of the city. A comparison of the report produced by the Bordeaux traveler, who spent time at the site in the fourth decade of the fourth century, with the work known as *Breviarius de Hierosolyma* (A Short Account of Jerusalem), apparently dating to the beginning of the sixth century, demonstrates the process the site underwent in Christian consciousness. The pilgrim from Bordeaux applies the word "Temple" (*templum*) in the first sentence describing his arrival in Jerusalem. He introduces the Temple precinct as a familiar physical feature, known to all, which serves as a point of reference for the identification of other sites. He devotes long passages in his travel book to Christian points of interest, "tourist spots" of a sort, on the platform of the Temple precinct: the corner of a very high tower on which Satan tempted Jesus; a bulky cornerstone figuring in the explication of several biblical verses; rooms that had been part of Solomon's palace; the same king's chamber, tunnels, pools, and other locations. The writer knows exactly where the sanctuary itself stood, and next to it he locates the site of the altar, pointing to splotches of Zechariah's blood and nail marks from the sandals of the soldiers who killed him. Not far from there he makes note of statues of the emperor, the pierced stone (*lapis pertusus*), and the house of King Hezekiah.[41] Without revisiting the issue of the Bordeaux traveler's reliability, and without attempting to determine which of these things he saw with his own eyes and which through his "religious glasses," we can posit that the author perceived the Temple enclosure as a dominant feature in the city's vicinity, one worth a visit. Furthermore, he imbued the physical objects he encountered there with religious-historic significance.

Some two hundred years after the traveler from Bordeaux's visit, the author of the Breviarius summarizes his recollections from the site in a short phrase: "Nothing is left there" (*non inde remansit*).[42] This statement encapsulates the perspective of a sixth-century visitor to Jerusalem. On all sides of the Temple Mount a city flourished, adorned with myriad churches and public buildings, yet in the compound of the Jewish Temple "there is nothing."

But the fact that Jerusalem's growth left the Temple precinct untouched does not mean that the masses of pilgrims who swamped the city ignored it or removed it from their tour routes. Even the *Breviarius,* despite the quoted categorical sentence, does not neglect the site, nor does its author advise his readers to avoid visiting it. On the contrary, not only does he include the compound in his city tour, but he also uses the traditional rubric to identify it as, "the Temple built by Solomon." Despite his remark that there is nothing there, he makes note of two elements on the site: a kind of cave (*cripta*) and some sort of tower (*pinna*) on which Satan tempted Jesus. Another version of this text adds a cross-shaped basilica, which, if accepted verbatim (for reservations about this, see n. 50), makes one of the only two statements affirming Christian construction on the site of the Temple.

Throughout the Byzantine era, writers document their attraction to the physical fabric of the compound (I am not referring here to its notional status, which is discussed in chapter 5) and offer accounts of their visits there, even if not as exhaustively as in the report of the Bordeaux pilgrim. Many of the traditions he cites have parallels in the writings of his contemporaries, both Christian and Jewish. I have already noted (in chapter 2) the widespread accounts about Zechariah's blood, the site of Jesus's temptation by Satan, the tower (*pterygion*), and the large stone next to it, both before and after the time of the pilgrim from Bordeaux. Eusebius knew the house of King Hezekiah in the area of the Temple, and Jerome repeats the same tradition.[43]

More than one hundred years after the Bordeaux traveler, the panoramic view of the city produced by Eucherius in his *Letter to Faustus* includes the Temple site. Eucherius noted the site's position within the framework of the city, and in describing it as "magnificently built" he voiced the fascination, regardless of theology, that the compound elicited from visitors.[44] Out of the wealth of objects enumerated by the Bordeaux traveler, Eucherius preserves only the *pinna*—that is, even less than the *Breviarius* written about half a century later. Yet he also adduces a legend that relates how, when the walls of the Temple were shattered to their very foundations, this steeple miraculously remained in place. Given that no earlier references to the *pterygion/pinna* include such details, this instance probably reflects evolving folk tradition, more often than not catalyzed by tourists and their guides.

Neither the Bordeaux traveler nor Eucherius provides even the slightest support for the current scholarly consensus locating the *pterygion/pinna* tower in the southeastern corner of the Temple Mount wall (see map 4: 2).[45] As many have already noted, the Bordeaux pilgrim delineates a geographically sequential route. Within this framework, he situates the tower between the sites to the north of the Temple Mount—such as the Bethesda pool (Probatika) and others—and the spot of the (ruined) sanctuary itself. This sequencing, then, demonstrates that in his mind the tower too stood somewhere between the northern edge of the Temple platform and the ruins of the Temple more or less at the center of the compound—that is, very far from the southeastern location proposed by scholars and accepted by many others. He also places there the palace of Solomon, perhaps associating it with the imposing ruins of the Antonia fortress. Similarly, the legend recounted by Eucherius asserts that the *pinna* remained the only remnant of a wall (*paries*) otherwise shattered to its foundations. In this same passage, Eucherius distinguishes clearly between that wall and the wall of the enclosing fortification system (which he calls *murus*). Thus his characterization of the *pinna* rules out the possibility of associating it with the outer wall of the compound. The latter, while not standing (very) high at the time, was certainly not razed to its foundations. It seems more reasonable, therefore, to suppose, although the identification cannot be conclusive, that some, even if not all, in the Byzantine period continued to locate the tower associated with Jesus's temptation at the heart of the Herodian compound (map 4: 1), not at its southeastern corner.

The biography of Barsauma, a monk who visited Jerusalem about the same time Eucherius wrote his first letter, supports and complements this picture. He reached the city during Sukkot (the Feast of Tabernacles) in the year 438/9 in order to frustrate the Jews' intention of renewing their prayers "on the ruins of the Temple built by Solomon," as allowed by the empress Eudocia. On the first day of the holiday, Barsauma secretly entered the city and after praying at the Siloam spring, ascended, along with twenty monks, to "Solomon's desolate Temple" in order to see the Temple's "pinnacle" (*pterygion*), on which "Satan placed the Savior."[46] One might almost say that the Syrian monk toured Jerusalem in accordance with Eucherius's Latin letter. Of course, none of the evidence suggests any acquaintance between them, but their descriptions of the ruined Temple compound share many traits: they label the place with the same appellations and point to the very same spot (the *pterygion*) as worth a visit. The biography of Barsauma also contains no indication that the Temple's "pinnacle" stood anywhere near the compound's exterior wall. The opposite is true; he states explicitly that in order to reach this site it was necessary to climb to the desolate Temple, where they encountered the Jews who had come to pray at its ruins. It is thus more reasonable to assume that he envisioned the *pterygion* as at the center of the compound.

Later Byzantine sources allude to similar elements in the landscape of the Temple enclosure. The accounts of Theodosius and of a traveler known as the Piancenza pilgrim join the previously mentioned *Breviarius* as reliable narratives of the sixth century. Later sources, such as the depictions of Arculf, a pilgrim from Gallia, as recorded by Adomnan, as well as the nucleus of the book composed by Epiphanius the Monk, provide information about the site's appearance immediately before and after the Arab conquest (in 640). All these documents mention the Temple site, generally referring to it by its common name, "Solomon's Temple," as a place to be visited and comment on the various features that can be seen there. Some of these include previously known objects, in particular the tower or steeple rising at the Temple's *pterygion,* and others introduce new elements added over time, such as the convent mentioned by Theodosius or the "beautiful gate" mentioned by the Piancenza pilgrim.[47] To these may be added the "reservoirs" enumerated by the monk Strategius in his list of sites where bodies of those killed in the Persian conquest of the early seventh century were found and which Milik identifies with the Temple Mount cisterns.[48]

Despite its appeal to visitors, the urban growth that Jerusalem enjoyed in the Byzantine period passed over the space of the ruined Jewish Temple. No important churches were built there, nor did any impressive construction projects transpire on the site. Various circumstances explain this neglect. Tsafrir, for example, conjectures that Julian's actions in Jerusalem demonstrated to the Christian authorities the threats involved in developing the compound.[49] The ideological attitude toward the site, as formulated by patristic writers (analyzed in depth in chapter 5), certainly contributed to diminishing its status in the eyes of the Christian believers and perhaps affected the decision of municipal powers to avoid its development. My proposal, if correct—that the Temple Mount lay outside the city's boundaries until the fifth century—adds another, more mundane aspect to the rejection of the site. Naturally, a space that remains ruined outside the city will lose ground to sites located within the city or in its developing environs. To the question of causality—whether the desolate reality of the compound instigated the ideological expressions or vice versa—there can be no absolute answer.

Nevertheless, more than a few references attest to a small number of buildings on the Temple Mount. As noted earlier, one version of the *Breviarius* mentions a cruciform basilica adjacent to the *pinna templi* where Satan tempted Jesus. Theodosius writes that close to the same location stood a *monasterium castas*, a convent of "pure women" (virgins?).[50] We have no way of knowing whether the writers are referring to a single building or several, and it is also difficult to determine the location of these structures, because that depends on the position of the *pinna templi*. As stated before, I reject the common identification of this feature as occupying solely the southeastern corner of the Temple Mount enclosure.

Two physical elements supplement these two traditions. One concerns the Golden Gate, the now-blocked eastern entrance to the Temple precinct, which, at least according to some scholars, dates to the end of the Byzantine period.[51] Much smaller, but still significant, is a fragment of a staircase that Bagatti uncovered at the bottom of the Mount of Olives and which climbs toward the Temple Mount.[52] Even if this flight of steps cannot be linked to the Golden Gate, as Bagati has proposed, it nevertheless testifies to architectonic activity linked to the Temple enclosure. The stairs presumably continued on the west side of Jehoshaphat Valley and most probably led to some opening in the compound's walls.

These shreds of information can only loosely be formed into a coherent picture, but they provide two important insights into the story of the Temple Mount during the Byzantine period. First, the *pinna templi* (known also as the *pterygion* in Greek), wherever its location, surpassed in popularity any other site in the area of the ruined Temple, as the writings of pilgrims and visitors from this period indicate. The two sources cited here suggest that its reputation did not remain without architectonic expression. Second, chronologically, all the information adduced here about building activity in the Temple compound comes from the period after the inclusion of the site within the city's boundaries, which occurred according to my proposal in the fifth century. This chronology supports my claim that urban status affected architectural development. To put it another way, as long as the Romans and early Byzantines left the compound outside the city limits, and then walls, no one bothered to build there (even though many stopped to visit), but once the walls embraced the compound, building activity commenced as well.

The Days of Julian

Any discussion of the Temple Mount in Byzantine Jerusalem must include the reign of the emperor Julian (361–64). Julian instigated an anti-Christian religious reaction throughout the empire, earning him the epithet "the Apostate." His plan to rebuild the Jewish Temple, and the little that was accomplished, mark the only time during the entire Byzantine era during which the Temple Mount stood at the heart of activity in Jerusalem.[53] This scheme to restore the Jewish Temple, the crowning glory of the ancient city that had been relegated to the margins by historical, religious, and urban forces, failed in its nascent stages. It epitomizes, however, Julian's aspiration to turn back the clock and halt the ascent of Christianity to the pinnacle of worldly power. His belief that the rebuilding of the Jewish Temple could serve his purposes confirms the importance, if from the opposite standpoint, that the site held for Christians.

Scholars have extensively discussed Julian's ideology and the controversy it aroused.[54] In the essays and letters he sent to Jews and others, Julian expressed his desire to resurrect the Temple in Jerusalem and restore its ritual sacrifices.[55] As for the Temple Mount per se, Julian's writings, and the Christian responses to them, do not suggest any particular interest in it, except as the space on which he intended to rebuild the Jewish Temple. Indeed, if Julian's project had succeeded, the Temple Mount might very well have returned to the status it had in the Second Temple period—or, more precisely, to its lack of independent status at that time (see chapter 1).

What exactly took place in the Temple area at the time of Julian's enterprise? The sources all agree that some sort of activity commenced there. In one place Julian says only that he intends, in the future tense, to build the Temple, and his letter to the Jews discusses the rebuilding and resettling of the Holy City of Jerusalem without mentioning the Temple at all. But another fragment of a letter by Julian to the Jews—written just before he embarked on the war against the Persians and preserved in the writings of John of Lydia—states, "I raise with the utmost zeal the Temple to the Highest God."[56] This clearly implies that the work was in progress at the time of writing. Other sources, especially Ammianus Marcellinus—a contemporary Roman (non-Christian) historian whom scholars consider the most reliable source on this issue—confirm that Julian indeed began to carry out his plans for the Temple area. Ammianus reports that the emperor commissioned the restoration of the Temple in Jerusalem, issued instructions on how to execute this project, and appointed Alypius of Antioch, former vice-governor of Britannia, as the person in charge of the task. He also recounts the "terrifying balls of fire" that erupted near the foundations (of the Temple?) and stopped the work after it was already under way.[57]

Julian's sudden death at the early stages of his military invasion into Persia brought an end to the project. Writing close after, various Christian responses, although naturally tainted by polemics, tend to agree that the undertaking in Jerusalem was indeed set in motion. Gregory of Nazianzus, Julian's Cappadocian contemporary, writes in his second oration against the emperor that the Jews committed themselves to the project and performed the demanding tasks with zeal and enthusiasm.[58] The same details appear in hymns against Julian by the Syrian theologian and hymnographer Ephrem, produced at about the same time. Ephrem described the Jews' elation at length and very vividly. This may well have reflected the mood in the Jewish community of his hometown Nisibis, but at the same time he also suggests that the efforts in Jerusalem were progressing.[59] A few years later the Antiochean bishop John Chrysostom, in an anti-Jewish sermon reviling the Temple, stated explicitly, with respect to what had occurred in Jerusalem during Julian's blasphemy, that the workers "dug out a large pile of earth" and "exposed the old foundations" of the Temple.[60] Apparently, everyone recognized that the work was indeed ongoing.

Fifth-century church historians who discussed the events of this period all endorse the reports that Julian rebuilt the Temple in Jerusalem to some extent before his project came to an abrupt halt. Rufinus notes the tools that were set for the job, and the historians who followed him, Theodoret of Cyrrhus and Philostorgios, elaborated on this point. Another Byzantine historian, Socrates the scholastikos, refers to the building materials that were brought to Jerusalem. In the polemic essay just mentioned, Gregory of Nazianzus had already stated that the Jews had participated in this effort, and the fifth-century historians reiterate this detail in different versions. Philostorgios and Sozomen, after recounting the Jews' enthusiastic participation, also added that the pagans had helped them, whether by providing resources or carrying out some of the actual work.[61]

Finally, a fragment from Philostorgios, the fifth-century church historian from Cappadocia in Asia Minor, preserved in a ninth-century hagiographic composition on the martyrdom of Artemius (*Artemii Passio*), narrates the events in Jerusalem during Julian's reign. The text mentions a "synagogue of the Jews" in Jerusalem, which stood next to a certain stoa (i.e., a roofed colonnade, a portico) that collapsed and killed many Jews.[62] A Syriac letter attributed to Cyril of Jerusalem, which outlines the project of rebuilding the Jewish Temple in Jerusalem during those days, also adverts to a synagogue (*beit kanushtah*) in the city.[63]

Some modern scholars have accepted Philostorgios's report at face value. When examining the Jewish facet of the religious revolution initiated by Julian, they allude to this synagogue as part of Jerusalem's new fabric. They situate the synagogue on the Temple Mount, at or next to the ruins of the old Jewish Temple, thus reflecting, in their view, the rehabilitation of the Jews' status in the city after two centuries of rejection and humiliation.[64] But grave problems cast doubt on the reliability of this statement about the Jerusalem synagogue. As I demonstrate in detail elsewhere, the segment about the synagogue originates from a purely literary construction made up out of whole cloth by Philostorgios. This author stumbled upon vague reports about a site in which Jews were killed. Because these sources used terminology reserved for holy places, and one of them hints at a prayer that took place there, Philostorgios deduced the existence of a synagogue.[65]

All in all, these sources allow only a modest glimpse at the events that transpired on the Temple Mount at that time. Almost all we know is that some work commenced in the area and then ceased for some reason, most probably due to natural causes—a conflagration caused by gas that had accumulated underground (or possibly even arson), an earthquake, or some combination of both catastrophes. Nor do any of the writers tell us how far the project had progressed when it broke off, whether the builders actually erected any significant structures in the area, or what happened there after the work came to a halt. Julian's death reversed the course of events once again. When his venture died away, traces of the building project disappeared completely; neither writers nor visitors to the city speak of them in later years. Julian's enterprise reverberated in literature and debate, but it did not have any lasting effect on the physical texture of the Temple Mount.

The Temple Mount and the Byzantine City

Constantine's emergence as the sole ruler of the empire signaled the beginning of a process that in the long run transmuted Aelia Capitolina's cultural fabric and altered its physical appearance. The skeleton of the Roman city's urban layout, however, was preserved. Constantine and his local partners inherited the ready-made city plan modeled by the colony's Roman founders and radically reshaped it by eradicating some pagan monuments and incorporating new churches (compare maps 6 and 7). They integrated the main church, the Church of the Holy Sepulcher, into the city center, replacing the nearby pagan temples. Churches, monasteries, and other buildings were added to the city as well. Nevertheless, its initial, most basic, contours—the outline of its streets, squares, markets, walls, and gates—remained more or less untouched, as configured in previous generations by the Romans. This process altered the architectonic shell and metaphysical image of the city beyond recognition but all within the urban layout of its original form.

My major argument is that neither Romans nor early Byzantines integrated the site of the Jewish Temple into the Roman city. Because the early Byzantine builders of Jerusalem maintained the city's walls in their Roman circumference, the exclusion of the Temple Mount was, for Constantine, an established fact. Just as he let the southwestern area of the city, known by the Christians as Mount Zion and central to their religious landscape, remain for many years outside the city walls, so he left the area of the ruined Temple precinct untouched. In this, the situation in Jerusalem differed from that in Gerasa, where Artemis's temple and the compound around it were an integral part of the urban fabric that the Byzantines inherited.

For more than three hundred years, from the establishment of the colony in the 130s until the mid-fifth century, this space, a huge but desolate compound, remained outside the boundaries of Roman and then Byzantine Jerusalem. Only the second line of fortifications (known as Eudocia's Walls) finally integrated the Temple Mount precinct into the city of Jerusalem.

Throughout this period, the site was sprinkled with heaps of rubble, remnants from the Second Temple edifices. But desolation did not result in desertion. The piles of wreckage in such proximity to the city served as an inexhaustible source of building materials, and at the same time Jerusalem residents cultivated plots in the compound for agricultural use. It may be that garbage was dumped here and there, but we should not accept the Arab sources that speak of the site as the city dump. Most important, neither locals nor the many pilgrims who inundated Jerusalem shunned the Temple Mount. They frequented its grounds, "spotting" in the ruins various important sites for Christian heritage and elevating them as tourist attractions. Later in the Byzantine period they may even have erected certain structures on the site. Here the conclusion reached by this chapter differs from the common wisdom, cited at the beginning, which views the space of the Jewish Temple compound as an extraneous area that had no function in daily life. According to the evidence I have presented here, it was a ruin with quite a lively existence. This paradoxical character—as a lively ruin—represents the salient attribute of the Temple Mount during the Byzantine period.

To a certain extent, such conclusions challenge the accepted scholarly view about the Temple Mount's place in Byzantine Jerusalem. According to the common understanding among scholars, the Mount remained part of the city, but the Christian rulers deliberately left it in ruins for theological reasons. Apparently, both sides of this formula, the physical and the theological, need to be reevaluated. The current chapter has dealt with the former; the next moves to the role of this site in Christian thought.

CHAPTER FIVE

The New Mountain in Christian Homiletics

The Second Century: Turning Away from Jerusalem

The second century found Christianity's young communities beleaguered on two fronts, one external and one internal. In Stuart Hall's words it was an era of "defense and definition."[1] Christian scholars from this initial phase, contending with both the pagan and the Jewish world, carved their new theology onto rolls of papyri and sheets of parchment. Whereas the so-called first Christians, those of the first century CE, viewed themselves as part of the Jewish world, the second century witnessed the growth of a "third race," neither Jewish nor pagan, as many of the century's writers put it. But the new faith was not battling only forces on the outside. While, in the wake of Walter Bauer,[2] one cannot in the context of this period apply terms like "orthodoxy" and "heresy," this hardly detracts from the force of the internal divisions and opposing views that churned within Christianity during these years. Nearly everything was in dispute. At the same time, and sometimes in connection with theological disputes, institutions and frameworks took form: bishops, deacons, and ramified systems for initiation into the religion and for directing the community's way of life. Toward the end of the second century, Marcion and his views served as the foil against which the Christian canon more or less coalesced.[3]

For many (although not all) in the world of second-century Christianity, Jerusalem and the Temple no longer shone in their old glory. These two entities played a very real role in the experience of Jesus, his disciples, and their immediate followers, as reflected in the books that came to be the New Testament. But in the second century they were upstaged by more acute issues of developing Christian identity—Jesus's nature and the character of his gospel, the source of church authority, and the ritual and social obligations of its members. Geographically, the religion's focus migrated from Palestine and Jerusalem to the greater Roman dominion (a process that had begun in Paul's time). Antioch, Rome, the cities of Asia Minor, Alexandria, and a bit later the cities of Gaul and the western part of North Africa were now the arenas in which Christian issues were resolved. It is hardly surprising, then, that the theological prescriptions of the time neglected Jerusalem. A work such as the *Didache,* most of which belongs to the end of the first and beginning of the second century, fails to mention Jerusalem or the Temple even once. The more consolidated formulae of faith (*regula fidei*) from the last quarter of the second century, preserved in Irenaeus, are no different.[4] The crucifixion is central in all of them. They all refer to the man who sentenced Jesus, Pontius Pilate, by name but never specify the place in which the events transpired. Except for a few groups that clung to the city (such as the one that clustered around the image of James Brother of Jesus; see chapter 2), the Christians of the time apparently took no great interest in Jerusalem.[5]

Many facets of Christian life in this early stage, from liturgy to art, support this conclusion. In Jewish liturgies we find the image of Jerusalem incorporated into prayers and endowed with a special aura—for example, in the third benediction of the grace after meals.[6] The same would be true of the Christian liturgy that crystallized in the second half of the fourth century, which, as I will show shortly, embraced a wide range of similes associated with the city of Jerusalem. Yet the scraps of Christian ritual that have survived from the second century—in particular chapters 9 and 10 of the *Didache* and the fragments preserved in Justin Martyr's *First Apology*—give no sign that Jerusalem enjoyed any special status.[7]

No relics of Christian art have come down from the second century, but remnants from the third and especially the first half of the fourth century confirm my surmise. The artists who decorated the walls of the catacombs in Rome or the Christian house in Dura Europos took an interest in the figure of Jesus, as for example in the common motif of the good shepherd. They also gave their imagination free rein with the central events of his life (many of which took place in Jerusalem!) and of the lives of other characters in the Holy Scriptures (Jonah, Elijah, and so on). Yet they completely neglected Jerusalem and the Temple.[8] This disregard is especially notable when compared with motifs in Jewish art of the same period, which continued to be intimately tied to the Temple milieu—for example, in the symbols imprinted on the Bar Kokhba coins or in the art of the Jewish catacombs in Rome (and later in the mosaic floors of synagogues). A comparison with later Christian art from the second half of the fourth century onward, in which Jerusalem (even if in its heavenly guise) is given a significant place, further confirms my contention.[9]

Despite this apparent neglect, it would be a mistake to conclude that early Christians expunged Jerusalem and the Temple from their consciousness entirely. In fact, the opposite is true. It hardly needs to be said that the city and Temple figured prominently in the polemical literature against the Jews (*Adversus Judaeos*), which had its inception during this period. As part of the rivalry over who was the "true Israel," polemical works such as the *Epistle of Barnabas* and the *Dialogue with Trypho* repeatedly refer to Jerusalem and the Temple, claiming that their destruction expresses God's rejection of the Jews.[10] The initial stages of this trend can be discerned among the various authors of the Gospels, who often emphasize the destruction of Jerusalem and the Temple. Paradoxically, these early Christian polemicists, although suffused with an anti-Jewish attitude that did not naturally take to Jerusalem and the Temple, demonstrate the vitality of these Jerusalem-related issues in their own environment. This dialectical approach characterizes Christian writing in this period. On the one hand, it negates the textures of Judaism—for our purposes here Jerusalem, the Temple, and the practices associated with it (the priesthood, sacrifices, and so on)—but, on the other hand, it shapes its own world around these very same elements (after "converting" them, of course).[11]

This period lacks a uniform position about the destruction, there being as many shades of opinion about it as there are writers. Some stressed the aspect of divine punishment, while others focused on the predestination and symbolism of the destruction, which arrived precisely when the "old covenant" completed its function. Some writers emphasized the destruction of the year 70, while others addressed more contemporary events, giving prominence to the outcome of the Bar Kokhba revolt. They all repeatedly disputed and rejected the sacrificial system.[12] Consequently, modern scholarship too disagrees about the weight that ought to be given to the destruction of the Temple in the world of Christianity during this period. Some maintain that it was the most significant event in the development of the new religion, whereas others minimize its importance.[13]

But the polemical literature and its emphasis on the Temple's destruction represent only part of the picture. A careful examination reveals that the city of Jerusalem and elements associated with it continue to function on many levels of Christian consciousness, even if they do not occupy the same pivotal position as before. After all, the roots of second-century Christianity—as manifested in the Christian canon that was taking form during this period or, even more so, in the Jewish Scriptures that were accepted as a foundation of the new religion—lie deep in Jerusalem. Time and again, the apostolic traditions allude to the city and Temple, as do the writings of the prophets intended to be read "as much as time permits" (in the words of Justin Martyr) during Eucharistic gatherings or the psalms that believers chanted when they gathered for prayer, to baptize new converts, and at the Eucharistic ceremony. They are also salient in biblical quotations, especially from the so-called Latter Prophets, Psalms, and the book of Daniel, which second-century Christian writers so frequently invoked. That being the case, it is difficult to conceive that the beliefs and ideas shaped against the background of these writings could entirely ignore two elements that are so central to them.

Indeed, some groups within the Jesus movement remained closely tied to Jerusalem, and this may be one reason why modern scholars tend to identify them as "Judeo-Christian" sects. In chapter 2, I have discussed at length one of these groups, which coalesced around the figure of James Brother of Jesus. The members of another group, called Elkesaites, founded sometime in the reign of the emperor Trajan, prayed, in accordance with ancient Jewish custom, facing Jerusalem.[14]

Another expression of the connection with Jerusalem can be found in various millenarian trends, which embodied common and "actual" beliefs among Christians in the second century. They revolved around the anticipation, colored by eschatology, of a millennium, a thousand blessed years that would begin with the second coming (*parousia*) of Jesus (and, according to some views, even before this). A fundamental element in these approaches included the belief in the physical restoration of Jerusalem out of its ruins as the ultimate destination that Jesus prepared for his followers.[15] The Montanist movement provides an extreme expression of such positions, actively implementing this vision in Asia Minor and changing the name of two cities in Phrygia to "Jerusalem."[16] But millenarian propensities extended far beyond esoteric groups. Central writers from this period, such as Justin Martyr and Irenaeus, subscribed to such Jerusalemian tendencies in one form or another.[17] Some time later, at the beginning of the third century, Tertullian, one of the "chief speakers " of his time, joined the Montanist movement, confirming the wide distribution of its proclivities.[18]

On another, no less practical level, Jerusalem and its associated elements— Temple, sacrifices, and priesthood—influenced the era's conceptual world and its library of images. As a rule, the writers of the period walked the paths marked out by Christian scriptures. At the end of the first century, when Clement called for the unity of the church of Corinth, he drew on images of the Temple, the high priest, and the sacrifices in order to articulate the need to serve God in a particular place (the church) and in a particular way (in accordance with the official leaders and texts) in keeping with God's will.[19] His contemporary, Ignatius, compared the members of the Christian community to the stones in God's Temple and presented the Temple, together with Jesus the messiah and God himself, as the spiritual freight carried by the believer wherever he went.[20] A lost sermon by Melito (a bishop of Sardis in the second half of the second century), recently discovered in a Georgian translation, labels Jesus "the architect of Jerusalem."[21] This method of appropriating a certain element from the Temple 's vocabulary or pool of symbols and investing it with a "new spiritual life" in the Christian present was very common among early Christian writers. It can be traced back to books now part of the New Testament, in proverbs attributed to Jesus and to Paul,[22] but it reached a much fuller scope only in the second century. In the prevalent discourse of this period Jesus, the Apostles, and later also the bishops symbolized the priesthood; the Eucharist (and thus Jesus himself) was a surrogate for the Temple sacrifices; the individual or community, and later even the buildings that served as churches, personified the Temple in Jerusalem.[23] The same holds true in the so-called Gnostic texts. So, for example, Valentinian theology refers to "wisdom," the mother of the demiurge (the creator), as Jerusalem.[24] The martyrs' identification of themselves before their Roman interrogators as "men of Jerusalem" functions within the same conceptual framework.[25]

What does all this mean with regard to the status of Jerusalem and the Temple among Christians in the second century? Not much. The polemical niche and the members of the small groups that lived around the city or continued to reflect on it were exceptions. For most members of the rapidly maturing movement, represented by the writings just cited, Jerusalem remained an abstract concept that drew its substance solely from their sacred writings. At this advanced stage in the process of spiritualization, Jerusalem moves from the realm of the real into the realm of allegory, losing its vitality and its associated elements.[26] These tendencies are already evident in early books that later became part of the New Testament. They resonate also in the notion of "heavenly Jerusalem," which slowly became a fixture of Christian thought, until it later ensconced itself, largely at the encouragement of Origen, as a central strand of Christian consciousness.[27] Although I do not suggest that second-century Christians who uttered the word "Jerusalem" lacked a recollection of what it signified on earth, they were not far from such ignorance. The intangibleness of the term allowed these people to strip it of any precise geographical reference and thus to dissociate it from the actual location where the ruins of the Temple stood in the province of Judea. This vacuum of signification enabled the Montanists to "transfer" Jerusalem to Asia Minor.[28] Similarly, the millenarian view of Justin and others, which ostensibly centered on Jerusalem, was not accompanied by any specific interest in the physical city of that name.

A brief glance at later developments in the region will demonstrate the desolation of Jerusalem at this time. Unlike the multitudes of pilgrims that streamed into the city from the fourth century onward, Christians in the second century were, for the most part, not acquainted with the physical layout of Jerusalem and took no interest in its earthly appearance. Only the wishful thinking of modern scholars could turn Melito of Sardis's "innocent" theological pronouncement—which was part of an anti-Jewish polemic—into a "vivacious description" of Jerusalem from an eyewitness, "the first pilgrim."[29] It is nothing of the sort. According to Melito's letter, preserved in Eusebius, he traveled to the East, which he describes as "the place where it was proclaimed and done," as part of his efforts to collect details about the Holy Scriptures. But he does not disclose his destinations.[30] In his treatise on the Passover, Melito repeatedly insists (three times) that the Jews murdered Jesus "at the center of Jerusalem."[31] But these passages, if carefully examined, display no evidence that the author knew anything of the city's urban landscape. The expression "middle of the city" serves Melito as a literary device for magnifying the Jews' guilt, as if he wished to say: the Jews perpetrated this outrage in the full light of day and in plain view. Support for this reading comes from the contrast that Melito draws there between "night" and "deserted place" on the one hand and "in the middle of the street and in the middle of the city, at the middle of the day" on the other.[32] If so, "in the middle of the city" is no more than a rhetorical-polemical phrase, definitely not a literal geographic location.[33] The same usage appears in Eusebius's paraphrase of Josephus's testimony about murders that occurred in Jerusalem during the great revolt in "broad daylight." Eusebius replaces "broad daylight" with "in the middle of the city."[34] In short, without Melito, earthly Jerusalem remains desolate and unvisited by any who have left us documentation until at least the third century.[35]

Temple Mount Imagery in Second-Century Writings

Apart from the community that assembled around the figure of James Brother of Jesus, the picture drawn so far provides almost nothing for the study of the Temple Mount in the realm of second-century Christianity. The vacuum that the destruction of the Temple created had not yet been filled, and time would pass before the great centers of Caesarea and, later, Jerusalem flourished. A man like Irenaeus ranged from Asia Minor to Lyons (Lugdunum) in Gaul. His horizon and direction of interest both lay in the western parts of the empire. The great majority of writers during this period shared this axis of travel and attention—all their roads led to Rome. Another 150 years would pass before the rise of Constantine and subsequent waves of pilgrims to Palestine reversed this trend. Ignatius, Irenaeus, Hippolytus, Tertullian, and even Justin, who came from the Palestinian town of Flavia Neapolis, traveled of their own volition, or were constrained to move by imperial powers, in the same direction—west and away from Palestine. Melito of Sardis, who took the opposite route, was an exception. In the mind of these people Jerusalem signified an out-of-the-way corner, and it is reasonable to assume that most of them had no acquaintance at all with the physical reality that prevailed in the city after the Bar Kokhba rebellion. So it is hardly surprising that their writings provide no information about the urban texture of Jerusalem or the physical landscape of the Temple Mount.

In those instances in which some sort of portrait of Jerusalem can be detected in the consciousness of second-century writers, it largely coincides with the picture of Jewish Jerusalem of the Second Temple period in its biblical guise: a city with a Temple at its core. Clement's correspondence with the people of Corinth provides a classic example of this phenomenon. The layout he describes closely resembles the well-known Jewish ranking of the ten levels of holiness: sacrifices may be offered "only in Jerusalem; and there also the offering is not made in every place, but before the shrine, at the altar."[36] The only change—exchanging the Holy of Holies with the altar—derives from the writer's liturgical agenda to provide a foundation for the bishop's sole authority in Christian ritual by paralleling it to the exclusive ability of the priest to perform sacrifices on the altar. Such a scheme offers no trace of an additional entity that stands between the city and the Temple—the Temple Mount goes completely unrecognized.

Still, two works, the *Epistle of Barnabas* and Justin Martyr's *Dialogue with Trypho,* preserve an intimation of the Temple Mount's emerging status. Given what I have written to this point, it is hardly a coincidence that the writers of these two texts were much more familiar with the Jewish world than their colleagues, even if they were among its sharpest adversaries.[37]

The author of the *Epistle of Barnabas* includes a reference to the Temple Mount in a dense and meticulously crafted passage, formulated in the genre of midrash (utilizing biblical verses and endowing them with new, timely meaning). In this portion he polemicizes against the Jews' refusal to accept the rite of baptism and judges them harshly as a result, equating the Jews' denial of baptism with death.[38] Along the lines of biblical terminology, the author dubs the Mount—"His [i.e., God's] holy mountain." He then stamps the place with the image of destruction by linking it to the biblical motif of "desolation" (popular in many early Christian prooftexts, such as Daniel) and presents it as the living manifestation of the Jews' choice of "death pits" instead of the "living spring" (baptism).

This same desolation of the Temple Mount operates in the Jewish worldview of the time as well, making its best-known appearance in the famous legend of Rabbi ʿAkiva, who laughed when he saw a fox coming out of the ruins of the Temple Mount (I discuss this piece in the introduction). Barnabas and the midrashic legend of the rabbis draw on precisely the same two similes— "desolation" and "Mount Zion"—but imbue them with opposite meanings; whereas the rabbis instill optimism and hope, the Christian writer sees degeneration and despair.

Similar tendencies resonate in Justin Martyr's *Dialogue with Trypho.* Throughout this anti-Jewish manifesto Justin quotes biblical verses that include the term "holy mountain" or other similar expressions.[39] At first glance, these citations contain nothing out of the ordinary, simply attesting to Justin's fond-

ness for citing long sections from the Scriptures. Yet in one place he goes beyond routine quotation and develops his own ideas. Here he reveals the consciousness and concepts that had begun to pervade his world.

The subject matter of chapters 25–26 of *Dialogue with Trypho*—the redemption of Gentiles who believe in Jesus and the nonredemption of Israel—
is a central and frequent theme in the thinking of this era. Both Jewish and
Christian writers allude to it and discuss it from various vantage points on numerous occasions.[40] In the same vein, Justin's method of expounding his arguments on this matter contains nothing innovative. True to his line of reasoning through the entire work, here too Justin introduces the subject by
presenting the arguments of the Jews, in this case in his own voice and not in
that of his mouthpiece, Trypho (25:1). He follows this with an elaborate attack,
denying the validity of the Jewish argument by quoting sixteen verses from
Isaiah (2:5–25). Following this, he narrows the issue by having Trypho frame a
question (25:6) that simultaneously lays the foundation for an irrefutable answer and a final formulation of Justin's claims (26:1). Furthermore, via the dialogue's associative development, the question leads to the next subject of the
composition (26:2ff.).

But Justin's literary skill extends beyond this structural sophistication. He
designs the entire passage around a verbal motif, the verb "to inherit" (*klero-
nomein*), thereby sharpening the debate and marking its central axis of development. The passage begins with the Jews' desire to inherit the site (25:1). Justin
then adduces the central verse on which he wishes to focus, Isaiah 63:18 (in the
Septuagint version): "Inherit . . . your holy mountain" (25:3). Trypho's retort is
formulated in the language of this verse: "What is this you say? That none of
them shall inherit anything on the holy mountain of God?" (25:6). The conclusion delivers Justin's incontrovertible riposte: the Jews who will not repent
will not inherit anything on the holy mountain, whereas the Gentiles who convert to Christianity will inherit it (26:1).

This literary construction frames the conflict between Christianity and Judaism as a contest over "the inheritance of the holy mountain." Why did Justin
choose this paradigm for the rivalry between the two groups? Were his reasons
rhetorical—the presence of "the mountain" and the verb "to inherit" together
in a verse from Isaiah? Or does the juxtaposition echo the conceptual constituents that permeated the writer's world—concepts that he presents in order to reject? I lean toward the second possibility. The biblical books and their
phraseology hardly seem to be the sole influences on Justin in this case. In the

mind of biblical authors, more often than not (but by no means exclusively), the entire Land of Israel, not a specific holy mountain, constitutes the Israelite inheritance.[41] Later, in the traditions that came to form the New Testament and in other Christian writings of Justin's time, the verb "to inherit" expresses the spiritual bequest of the Christians in Jesus and in the kingdom of God.[42] Moreover, had Justin sought a rhetorical device to illustrate the Jews' claim that they are the ones who carry on in God's way, he could have selected among many possibilities, even in the very verses from Isaiah that he adduces, where Jerusalem, the Temple, and the Land of Israel all appear. But Justin neglects them all, and the mountain stands alone, as an independent element. Striking similarities link the status of the mountain here, whose inheritance symbolizes the rejection of Israel, and its position in the section of the *Epistle of Barnabas* discussed earlier, in which its desolation denotes the very same thing.

I conclude, therefore, that if we take Trypho's and Barnabas's negatively charged words and reformulate them in positive language, they reflect the Temple Mount's emerging status in the consciousness and spatial imagery of Palestinian Jews and Christians of this time. The Jews perceived the Mount as "the holy mountain of God," and its inheritance established them as the chosen people. Acquainted with many contemporary Jewish principles, even if he sometimes chose to distort them,[43] Justin devoted this section of his dialogue to disputing and ultimately refuting this Jewish claim. In doing so, he recorded another aspect of the Christian position about the Temple Mount. Unlike Barnabas, who emphasized the Mount's desolation, Justin stripped it of its realistic guise and turned it into a spiritual artifact of a different legacy—the Christian inheritance of God.[44] During the subsequent three hundred years, other church fathers elaborated these two approaches extensively.

The Maturation of Palestinian Christianity

Whereas in the second century Christianity was still in its initial stage, in the third century it metamorphosed into a coherent and well-structured religious movement. Spreading to the edges of the Roman Empire and beyond, it put down roots at all levels of society. Communities sprang up in major cities and towns, led by influential leaders and operating an elaborate network of prayer houses, charitable institutions, and other communal services. Simultaneously, the first real Christian scholars, later cherished as church fathers, fashioned a large body of theology and liturgy. These dynamics lasted for an extended period before the religious revolution that took place in the fourth century. But only the Edict of Tolerance of 313, the product of an agreement between Constantine and Licinius—redoubled in force when Constantine won sole suzerainty over the Roman world—finally legalized Christianity, allowing the movement to complete its process of institutionalization. The new religion now joined forces with the state. Soon the emperor explicitly identified himself with Christianity and became its chief advocate. It was then only a matter of time before the empire took on a new visage, and the Roman gave way to the Byzantine. Although paganism retained its strength and remained fairly widespread—and under emperor Julian (361–64) even achieved power in a brief reaction—it was already in an irreversible decline. After the reign of Theodosius I (379–95), who more than any other emperor imposed an orthodox dogma on the citizens of the empire, the Roman world had changed its face forever.[45]

The great upheavals that accompanied Constantine's accession to the throne did not leave Jerusalem unaffected. His initiatives restored to the city some of its primeval status as the stage on which many Scripture stories had been enacted. The seventh canon of the Nicene Council (325 CE) clearly reflected these tendencies when it formally recognized "the ancient tradition" that honors the bishop of Jerusalem and thus grants him certain "rights."[46] Modern scholars correctly note the vagueness of the document's wording, which leaves open to doubt whether it speaks of new rights or formally recognizes already existing ones.[47] Even if the latter is the case, official church recognition, under imperial sponsorship, of the city's unique status still differs notably from Jerusalem's absence from formulations of faith in previous centuries or from the ignorance of a Roman procurator in Caesarea who, at some point in the third century, did not even know its name (see chapter 3, n. 6). Constantine channeled the growing affection for Jerusalem into a large-scale reconstruction of the city, which radically altered its appearance (discussed in chapter 4). Another facet of the city's stature in Christian consciousness involves the seepage of Jerusalem motifs into the church's store of images. As I have shown in earlier chapters, Jerusalem, the Temple, and the destruction were not unfamiliar categories in the world of Christianity at the end of the first and throughout the second centuries, and they continued to play a role in the third century. But when Christianity assumed ascendancy in the Roman Empire and Jerusalem regained its lost honor, the use of similes and vocabulary relating to the city reached an unprecedented peak. Many studies have cast light on different aspects of this process—from the way such motifs were used in disputations with the Jews or in

Christianity's internal political struggles (such as the rivalry between Jerusalem and Caesarea) to the way they stimulated the world of pilgrims to the city and shaped a new Christian spatial consciousness. Within this new symbolic landscape, the emperor could resemble King Solomon, the legendary builder of the Jerusalem Temple; the establishment of a new church could be celebrated as the Temple's dedication; and notions and titles originally linked to the Jewish sanctuary could be reapplied to the church and its institutions, as, for example, in the architecture of the Church of the Holy Sepulcher, in art, and elsewhere.[48]

Nevertheless, the changes in Jerusalem should not be exaggerated.[49] The city did not become a major center—not even in Palestine, where it remained subject to the metropolis in Caesarea, and certainly not in the Byzantine Empire as a whole. Other than the pilgrimage phenomenon, all other significant events in the history of Byzantine Christianity occurred far from the boundaries of the Holy Land. Palestine was not the cradle of monasticism or of great schools of learning, and Christianity's great schisms—the Manichaean and Novatian in the third century, the Donatist and the Arian in the fourth century—erupted elsewhere. Jerusalem during this period recalls a ruler who had returned from captivity to discover that everyone honored him but that his powers had been abrogated and given to another. This tension, between the glorious past of the city and a respectable present lacking any real imperial status, holds the key to understanding the dynamic of Jerusalem's history in the Byzantine period. The ceaseless endeavor to reestablish Jerusalem's historical eminence as a dominant urban center underlies the various actions taken on behalf of the city during this period.

Palestinian Patristics

A fairly large body of information sheds light on Byzantine Palestine. Notable among these stands a not insignificant group of church compositions by individuals who were closely involved with life in Palestine. I label this corpus "Palestinian patristics" and define it as the writings of those Christian scholars, commonly known as church fathers, who had firsthand familiarity with the physical texture, geography, and local culture of Palestine. A work written on the basis of unmediated acquaintance with this "field data," allegorical and abstract as it might be, will nevertheless often contain, alongside information on the ideas that prevailed there, valuable material on the country's landscape and contemporary events, as well as on the writer's perception of both. As a result, these sources are fertile ground for the study of the encounter between physical reality and the realm of ideas and consciousness, the encounter that stands at the center of the present work.

If the conception of a Palestinian patristic corpus could be attributed to a single event, it would be Origen's departure from Alexandria and his decision to settle in Caesarea in the 230s.[50] Although Origen's tribulations in Egypt rather than his "love of Zion" brought him to Palestine, the importance of the move for the historiography of the region cannot be minimized. In establishing a library and a school in Caesarea, among whose graduates were Pamphilus and later his student Eusebius, Origin "founded" the Palestinian patristics. Central figures in this group included Origen and Eusebius in Caesarea and later Jerome in Bethlehem. These were prolific writers of the first rank in the Christian world: Origen in his biblical works, both allegorical and philological, as well as his philosophical and theological treatises; Eusebius in his historiographic project; and Jerome in his translation of and commentaries on the Bible. All three had direct contact with Palestinian scenery. Origen writes that he toured the country and examined its sites "in search of the 'footsteps' [whereabouts] of Jesus, his disciples and the prophets."[51] Eusebius's and Jerome's acquaintance with Palestinian geography is well known and is reflected in the large amount of information of this kind that they preserved, even if some of it falls short of accuracy.[52] All three knew Hebrew, some more (Jerome) and some less (Origen).[53] As one might expect, they all maintained some level of contact with Palestine's Jews and so documented many local customs and traditions in their writings.[54]

Several other figures can be added to these three central representatives of the "Palestinian school." Foremost among these are local Christian writers, such as the bishops of Jerusalem—Cyril in the fourth century and Hesychius in the fifth century—as well as Julius Africanus (c. 160–240), Epiphanius of Salamis (315–403), and the fifth-century church historian Sozomen, all of whom spent a significant portion of their lives in Palestine.[55] Others who arrived from abroad but resided in the region for a substantial amount of time should be included as well—Rufinus of Aquileia, a contemporary (first friend, then adversary) of Jerome, being a prime example.[56] The guidebooks and journals of pilgrims, although belonging to a different genre and obviously less erudite than the so-called church fathers, nevertheless fit the preceding definition of Palestinian patristics in that they are religious works growing out of an encounter with the physical texture of the region.[57]

Finally, the Palestinian Christian corpus also includes an intermediate class of works by church writers whose prime focus lies outside of the region. Yet some of these authors imbibed local information here and there, both from being present in Palestine and through indirect channels. Naturally, not everyone who passed through Palestine or acquired a certain proficiency in Hebrew should be included in this corpus. So, for example, Clement of Alexandria studied with a Hebrew teacher in Palestine and absorbed some local legends that also appear in rabbinic literature. Yet his writings do not display any evidence that the local setting, whether physical or spiritual, left its impression on him. The same can be said of the later writings of the Donatists from North Africa, who held the Holy Land in high esteem (according to Augustine) but remained far removed from its landscape.[58] In contrast, some works written elsewhere in the empire contain scraps of information of the "Palestinian" type, as here defined. These include renowned church scholars such as Gregory of Nyssa in Asia Minor, as well as less-known writers such as Optatus, the bishop of Milev in North Africa, both from the fourth century, and later in the sixth century even Gregory of Tours, in far-off Gaul.[59] Much remains hazy here, and in many cases to determine whether a given passage in a given work indeed exhibits a link to Palestinian reality, one must examine the source itself.

The Spiritual Mountain: From Origen to Eusebius

In book 23 of his *Commentary on the Gospel of John,* written after he had already settled in Caesarea,[60] Origen explicates the dialogue between Jesus and the Samaritan woman (John 4:19–24). In this conversation, both the Samaritan woman and Jesus contrast the Samaritan mountain with the city of Jerusalem. Following the sequence of the passage, Origen's commentary elaborates on the Samaritan mountain, Mount Gerizim, reflecting on its sanctity, and then moves to address the Jewish site. Yet, instead of adhering to the words of the verse in question, which explicitly refer only to Jerusalem as the site of Jewish worship, Origen inserts the designation "Zion" and asserts that the Jews "think Zion is divine and God's dwelling place." Immediately thereafter, when he paraphrases the positions of both sides, Origen states that each nation believes that its ancestors venerated the true God but "one on this mountain and one on the other."[61] By introducing "mountain" into the picture, Origen establishes symmetry between the two opposing positions of the Samaritans and the Jews and frames the dispute around the question of which mountain is the most sacred. But such a formulation is precisely what the biblical verse lacks. Neither is there any exegetical justification for creating such a parallel; the fact remains that other writers who dealt with the Jewish-Samaritan issue before Origen found no reason to configure the conflict as a contest between two mountains. No such contest can be found in 2 Maccabees or Josephus or in the Gospel of John (see chapters 1 and 2). Apparently, it is Origen's consciousness that depicts the Jewish cult site as situated on a "mountain."

Such an understanding may elucidate the image of the mountain that Origen interweaves into another work—his commentary on the Song of Songs. He uses the mountain theme numerous times throughout that text, which apparently also belongs to his post-Alexandria days.[62] On one occasion he names the true believer in God a "mountain," and soon thereafter he likens Jesus to a mountain—not an ordinary mountain but rather "the mountain of mountains" (*mons montium*).[63] Origen designates Jesus in three ways in the commentary: "the king of kings," "the priest of priests," and "the mountain of mountains." The first two bear clear connotations of the Temple and Jerusalem, and it turns out that the mountain metaphor belongs to the same conceptual field. On another occasion, Origen explicitly writes of the mountains of the Temple. This use of the plural to parallel the "mountains of Bethel"—about which the patriarch Jacob said in the book of Genesis, "This is none other than the house of God" (28:17)—serves the allegorical interpretation Origen bestows upon them. In his symbolic framework, they no longer function as the physical mountains on which the Temple stands, but rather as spiritual mountains *within* the Temple ("Montes . . . qui in domo Dei sunt"), which he interprets to represent the books of the Gospels and the Apostles.[64] In another context, Origen assigns "wisdom" to the mountains, and the mountain, this time in the singular, becomes God himself.[65]

As others have already noticed, Origen's commentary on the Song of Songs includes many Jewish motifs that the author attempts to adapt into Christian discourse. He achieves this here, as in other places in his writings, through an intricate exegetical maneuver in which he bestows upon them spiritual-allegorical meaning that neutralizes their Jewish content and, at the same, time transforms them into a Christian trope.[66] Accordingly, Origen presents King Solomon as a figurative predecessor of Jesus; casts Jerusalem, Solomon's capital, as the heavenly Jerusalem; and reconfigures the Jewish people, King Solomon's subjects, as the church.[67]

As is well known, this typological approach characterizes much, if not all, of

Origen's biblical commentary and resonates in many of his other writings as well. In book 4 of *On First Principles,* he expounds this notion in regard to Jerusalem at length. Founding his position on Paul's Letter to the Galatians (4:26) and the Letter to the Hebrews (12:22)—two of the earliest documents that embrace the idea of "heavenly Jerusalem" into Christian theology—Origen explicitly differentiates Christian views of the city from the Jewish understanding, which takes all the prophecies about Jerusalem literally. Rather, according to Origen, these prophecies refer to the spiritual city.[68] In keeping with this trend, Origen devotes an entire homily to an exhaustive exposition of the book of Exodus's description of the Tabernacle, showing how each detail in fact applies to the church (or to the Christian individual). Elsewhere he equates the church with Solomon's Temple or presents Jesus as the true Temple. Consistently using this method, he attributes spiritual significance to events that took place in the city. For example, Jesus's entry into the city is, in his gloss, an allegory for the entry of God's words into the human soul, and Jesus's tears over its destruction are directed at the Christian who has surrendered to those besieging him—that is, to the forces of evil.[69]

The "mountain" in Origen's commentary on the Song of Songs should be understood in the same exegetical context. His interpretation of the dialogue between Jesus and the Samaritan woman shows that Origen perceived the mountain in Jerusalem as an important factor in Jewish ritual and worship. That being the case, in his Song of Songs commentary he strips the mountain of its physical substance and revokes its religious status, only to endow it with spiritual essence. The mountain of the Temple no longer stands on its own. Instead, it becomes an allegorical symbol for Christian concepts.

I do not mean to argue that every time Origen uses the image of a mountain he has in mind the space around the Temple in Jerusalem. As I have already noted in other cases, "mountains" functioned as a common motif in the Greco-Roman culture of the ancient world in which Christianity operated. This motif also appears regularly in the Bible, which served as a literary substrate for Origen and other patristic writers. Many Christian works deployed "mountain" as a metaphor to bolster their arguments, without connection to any concrete reality. Comparing two North African Christian scholars from the second half of the third century and beginning of the fourth will illustrate the diverse spectrum of meaning that existed in Origen's literary milieu in regard to the symbolism of Mount Zion. In the midst of an anti-Jewish apologetic treatise, Lactantius, the "Christian Cicero," interprets the verse "For out of Zion shall go forth the Torah" (Isaiah 2:3) in a negative way. In other words, he takes it to mean that the Torah will leave Zion. He then explains that Mount Zion symbolizes Judaism, and God chooses to grant the real Torah on Mount Ḥoreb, not Zion. Contrast this with another work, *Concerning the Mountains Sinai and Zion,* attributed to Cyprian. Here the images are reversed. Mount Zion stands for Christianity, whereas Mount Sinai represents the old Judaism.[70] Apparently, in early Christian literature mountains shed and take on symbolic content independently of any physical reality the writers knew. Rabbinic literature is no different (see chapter 6). Indeed, Origen himself writes of mountains that are not necessarily in Jerusalem. He often alludes to biblical mountains, as in his statement that the mountains mentioned in the book of Isaiah are "the highest in the world" or the exegetical development he gives to the mountains and hills mentioned in Jeremiah. He also makes note of other mountains that received their own standing in Christian history, such as the mountain on which Jesus sat when he fled his disciples, which came to symbolize the church.[71]

Nevertheless, a number of considerations indicate that Origen's treatment of the mountain motif in his commentaries on John and on Song of Songs is fundamentally different from the examples just cited. Many Christian writers of the time imbued one of the mountains mentioned already in the Old or New Testaments (as they came to think of those texts) with their own, usually allegorical content or created an image from a neutral mountain not mentioned in Scripture. In contrast, Origen's integration of the mountain into the dialogue between the Samaritan woman and Jesus in the Gospel of John inserts the mountain into a place where it was absent. It never occurred to the author of the passage in John, or to other writers of his time who mention the Second Temple, to include a mountain in the landscape of Jewish worship. Of course, Origen was undoubtedly familiar with the many references to "the mountain of God" and similar expressions in the Bible. He acknowledges, in his letter to Julius Africanus, the widespread popularity of verses in Isaiah that mention this mountain.[72] However, as I have shown in great detail (in chapters 1 and 2 and at the beginning of the current chapter), others, both Jews and Christians, who knew of the same biblical terminology did not make the mountain part of their descriptions of Jerusalem's physical appearance. Just as the mountain's absence from works that grew out of the soil of Second Temple Judaism attests to its insignificance in their worldview, its inclusion by Origen signals the opposite. The mountain became an important element in the consciousness of this Christian scholar and resident of Palestine.

The resemblance between the approaches of Origen and Justin Martyr (discussed earlier in this chapter) is obvious. The author of the *Epistle of Barnabas* perceived the mountain as a Jewish entity, so he directed at it the arrows of his anti-Jewish polemic. The epistle emphasizes the mountain's destruction, using this as a means of assailing and confronting the Jews. In the case of Justin Martyr and Origen, however, this aspect of the mountain's destruction does not turn up at all. Origen's position also differs from that of Justin in one essential detail. While Justin rejects the mountain itself, seeing it as no more than a symbol of a part of Christianity's heritage, Origen "inherits" (to use Justin's terminology) the mountain altogether, transforming it into a Christian figure. Are these differences meaningful?

The destruction as a whole—that is, the devastation of Jerusalem and the demolition of the Temple—function as a key theme in Origen's writings, continuing a (relatively) long and ancient Christian tradition that views this event as one of the fundamental testimonies for the truth of Christianity. It serves as a cornerstone for the Christian claim that God imposed an absolute and irreversible punishment on the Jewish nation. Like his predecessors, Origen stresses that the Jews cannot observe large portions of the Torah's precepts without the Temple, and he sees this as a sign that the entire Jewish way of life has been annulled.[73] At the core of this claim lies a historical perspective on the salient fact of destruction and the consequential inability to comply with the statutes of the Torah. But alongside this historical discourse, Origen also formulates another set of ideas, inherent in his allegorical method, for example, in his commentary on the Song of Songs, cited earlier. There Origen lifts a long series of Jewish concepts relating to Jerusalem and the Temple out of their Jewish context and "baptizes" them with new spiritual meaning. Robert Wilken defined this approach as "anti-territorial."[74] In my opinion, it is also ahistorical, since it disregards the meaning that these notions bore in earlier times and neglects their past status. Allegory and history, which generally do not sit well together, collaborate in Origen's thinking.[75]

Wilken believes that Origen's spiritual method, like his approach to history, is driven by an anti-Jewish mind-set. For my part, I maintain that it also contains a pro-Jerusalem component.[76] Namely, by endowing these elements with spiritual substance, Origen facilitates their utility within Christianity without the need to polemicize against them (as the author of the Barnabas epistle felt compelled to do). As a result of Origen's transformation, Jerusalem and the Temple no longer represent only negative entities, whose destruction is to be rejoiced in, nor are they objects that he hopes will disappear and be replaced by others. He enables Christianity to adopt them, on the strength of the new spiritual meaning they have acquired. Both these approaches—the historical and ahistorical—exist in Origen's writings and, in my opinion, they epitomize the complexity of his religious outlook.

Origen's view thus emerges as a new stage in the history of the "Temple Mount" and the place assigned to it in Christian thinking. The mountain had come a long way from being disparaged, as it had been in the writings of Christians in the second century, an attitude that had existed even earlier in the traditions that found their way into the New Testament. Third-century writers modulated this judgmental tone. In the case of at least one central figure, Origen, the mountain operates as part of the Jewish cluster of concepts that can be taken into the bosom of Christianity via a spiritual "baptism."

Eusebius

Eusebius was well acquainted with Origen's writings and ideas, and they influenced him considerably, although not in all areas.[77] Addressing the Jewish-Samaritan dispute in one place in his *Theophany,* Eusebius construes the dialogue between Jesus and the Samaritan woman in a way that closely corresponds to Origen's innovative interpretation of the same incident. The discussion in *Theophany* revolves around the needlessness of observing the laws of the Torah, a common proposition in Eusebius's writings. One of the prophecies he cites to support this claim consists of Jesus's words to the Samaritan woman: "Woman, believe me, the hour is coming that neither on this mountain nor in Jerusalem will you worship the father" (John 4:21). In order to demonstrate the fulfillment of this prediction, Eusebius appeals to historical events. He contrasts the situation that prevailed when Jesus uttered these words, in the reign of the emperor Tiberius, when the Jews and Samaritans were ranged around their sanctuaries, with the situation in his own time, after the Roman emperors Vespasian and Titus and later Hadrian obliterated these sites. Relevant to our discussion is the manner in which he represents these two places of worship. Eusebius refers to the Samaritan and Jewish sites of worship as two mountains. When he speaks of their function, he disparages them as "Mounts [that are] anathemas of God," and after the deeds of the three emperors, "Both these mounts were, according to his [Jesus's] word, desolate." In time to come, Eusebius concludes, "No more on any mount . . . should the true worshipers worship the God."[78] Clearly, the picture Eusebius envisioned when he read these verses matches that of Origen. Both of them viewed the site of Jewish worship as a "mountain." This source joins other passages throughout Eusebius's work that plainly reflect the author's perception of the Jewish cult site as a "mountain." In one such instance (discussed in chapter 4), when Eusebius describes what he saw with his own eyes at the site of the Jewish Temple, he refers to the place with the biblical appellation "Mount Zion." In another case, which I analyze shortly, he goes as far as to apply the Jewish name for the site, calling it "the Temple Mount."

Eusebius's religious thought closely resembles that of Origen in broader matters as well. Take, for example, the significance of the destruction of Jerusalem and the Temple for the emergence of Christianity and the latter's superiority to Judaism. In addressing this subject, Eusebius follows a line of thinking similar to that of Origen. He does not restrict himself to denigrating Judaism by describing the physical destruction of the site. Rather, as many scholars have noted, his remarks add up to a well-honed theological line of reasoning. For him, the destruction marks the end of Jerusalem's religious significance, as well as that of Judaism as a whole. The historical event reveals God's will that the Jews cease to adhere to their mundane Temple. These assertions run through all his writings—not only when he addresses Jewish subjects, as in *Proof of the Gospel,* or in his biblical commentaries but also in works such as *Preparation of the Gospel,* which deals with the relations between the Christians and the pagan world.[79] In the same vein, the notion of "heavenly Jerusalem," a key concept in Origen's spiritual thinking, also occupies a central place in Eusebius's writings. More than once, both before and after the great changes that Constantine initiated in the city, Eusebius emphasizes that the true holy Jerusalem coincides only with the heavenly city. In his commentary on Psalms, for example, he claims that the "holy city" in the Gospel of Matthew refers unambiguously to the heavenly city. Accordingly, he diverts the application of the material promises in Isaiah from the earthly to the ethereal city.[80] Also like Origen, Eusebius frequently makes use of the model "the city of God," considering it a typological representation of the church.[81]

Given the conceptual proximity between the two church scholars, it is hardly surprising that the trope of the "spiritual mountain" that appears in the first emerges in a similar way in the second. Here are two examples, one from Eusebius's early writings and one from his later works. Eusebius first expresses his views about the "mountain" in one of his earliest works, *Selections of Prophe-*

cies, written in the early fourth century, many years before he was appointed bishop. In a collection of exegetical excerpts on Psalm 2, he includes a segment that deals with verse 6: "I have set my king on Zion my holy mountain." Eusebius presents what he calls the Jews' inferior ideas, which apply this verse to the carnal kingdom of the Messiah, whose seat will be on the earthly Mount Zion. But this position is without sanction, argues Eusebius, because the Apostles' understanding refutes it entirely (he apparently has in mind Hebrews 12:22), and the latter may also be supported with passages from the prophets. All these construe the Psalm's prophecy not as a physical kingdom on an earthly mountain but rather as a king "whose kingdom is not of the world" and a "heavenly Mount Zion."[82] More than a generation after he wrote this, Eusebius wove an identical view throughout his commentary on Isaiah. In one place he states that the Jews "fell" from Mount Zion; in another he proclaims that the Savior will establish his kingdom on the supernatural mountain in heavenly Jerusalem. In yet another place he maintains that the elect will inherit the holy mountain of God and dwell on it.[83] Throughout his writings Eusebius reiterates the concept of the "spiritual holy mountain" several other times, especially in his *Proof of the Gospel.*[84] Note the independent status of the mountain, which, in the passages cited, overshadows all other elements. The Temple is not mentioned, or even hinted at, leaving only two players on stage—Jerusalem and the mountain.

It hardly needs to be said that, like Origen, Eusebius was familiar with a wide range of "mountain" imagery not related to Jerusalem and that he often used such metaphors in his writings. As a well-versed scholar of the texts he called the Old Testament, he knew that in ancient times mountains served as cult sites. Because he was also closely acquainted with the New Testament, the allegorical motif of the church being as a city on a mountain (Matthew 4:15) was not foreign to him.[85] But we should not confuse these references with the notion of the "spiritual mountain," which differs from all other mountains in two ways: it is always situated in Jerusalem, and it never signifies a neutral entity. It always demarcates the line between Jews and Christians; the Jews comprehend it materially, as a real mountain that exists in their city, whereas the Christians endow it with spiritual substance.

An interesting parallel to Eusebius's conception of the spiritual mountain appears in the works of Numidian church writer Optatus, bishop of the North African town of Milev, in the second half of the fourth century. In the course of a treatise against the Donatists, Optatus speaks of not one Mount Zion, but two. He locates the first "in Syria Palestina, separated by only a small ravine from the walls of Jerusalem" and soon thereafter refers to it as "a material mountain" (*corporalis mons*). He clearly distinguishes this physical high spot from a second Mount Zion, "the holy mountain, that is the church," which he also sees as "the mount by which the church is spiritually signified."[86] Such formulations clearly resemble the spiritual mountain of Origen, and especially that of Eusebius. Optatus also has some idea, though admittedly a fuzzy one, about the physical layout of Jerusalem. He is familiar, for example, with the tradition about the seven synagogues on Mount Zion, which appears in the account of the Bordeaux pilgrim, and topographically he also knows that a small creek separates Mount Zion from the city.[87] I am unable to determine the source of Optatus's knowledge. But, characteristically, pilgrimage literature (*itineraria*) incorporated geographical knowledge and local customs. Optatus seems to have derived from one of these works, such as that of the Bordeaux traveler, both his physical details and the set of perceptions associated with them. If so, his writings offer one of the first examples of the dispersal of Palestinian conceptual frameworks about Jerusalem into the Christian world.

Along with the considerable resemblance between Origen's and Eusebius's "spiritual mountain," Eusebius also differs from his teacher in salient ways, especially in his polemic emphasis. For Eusebius, the discourse around the sacred mountain reaches far beyond the removal of some earthly features from a Jewish concept in order to allow its adoption by Christianity, as in the case of Origen. Eusebius launches a concerted attack on the Jewish alternative. This confrontational mode already reverberates in an early work, the *Selections of Prophecies*. The spiritual mountain is not presented there as a new and neutral Christian development, but rather as a mountain in opposition to another mountain that is earthly and Jewish. Indeed, the clamor of a war of ideas resounds between the lines that Eusebius devoted to the mountain on which the Temple stands, including in places where he does not address the mountain's spiritual aspect.

A Christian Midrash about the Temple Mount

In the previous chapter I showed one example of the barbs that Eusebius directs at the mountain of the Temple in his work *Proof of the Gospel*. In that text he refers to the physical reality of the mountain after the establishment of the colony Aelia Capitolina, and aims his polemic not at the mountain itself, except inasmuch as the place's desolation functions as one factor in a larger attack on Judaism in general. Elsewhere in this same text, Eusebius develops one of the most detailed homilies extant in the patristic literature against the Temple Mount.[88] To the best of my knowledge, it is also the only place in which a church writer calls the mountain of the Temple by its proper (Jewish) designation—the "Temple Mount." This excerpt, encompassing most of the thirteenth chapter of the sixth book of *Proof of the Gospel,* constitutes a complex but well-structured treatise. In its central section, the author addresses the Jewish destruction as an outcome of this nation's rejection of Jesus. Eusebius views the acme of the destruction as the demolition brought upon Jerusalem, Zion, and "the so-called Mountain of the house" (p. 264, lines 25–28). In order to provide a firm foundation for his claim that reality and prophetic vision are intertwined, Eusebius proceeds immediately to describe the destruction that he saw with his own eyes on the site of the Temple: "If our own observation has any value, we have seen in our own time Zion once so famous, plowed with yokes of oxen by the Romans and utterly devastated."

This excerpt provides important insights into the role of the Temple Mount in the author's worldview. First, Eusebius knows the appellation "Temple Mount." By referring to it as "the so-called Temple Mount," he demonstrates his awareness that contemporary Jews apply this name to a concrete location in Jerusalem. Likewise, in terms of terminology, Eusebius considers "Temple Mount" and "Mount Zion" interchangeable. He links the rubble on Mount Zion to the fulfillment of Micah's prophecy about the Temple Mount. In other words, Mount Zion matches the mountain that the Jews of his time call the Temple Mount. The importance of this identification goes beyond the light he casts on the history of the term "Mount Zion" in Christian circles (which I alluded to in chapter 4). To the best of my knowledge, no other Christian source explicitly adduces the name "Temple Mount." The absence of the term from Christian writings is rather surprising, especially given its frequent appearance in Jewish rabbinic writings, but Eusebius solves the vexing riddle. The Jewish character of "Temple Mount," as Eusebius considered it—a view apparently shared by other Christian writers—explains why these authors would shun the name.

Second, and even more important, the homily portrays the spatial dimension of Eusebius's consciousness. The mountain of the Temple, whether called Mount Zion or the Temple Mount, completely replaces the Jewish Temple alongside the city of Jerusalem. Throughout the treatise, Eusebius contends with the expressions of Jewish experience in all its aspects. The spatial layout that frames this experience includes Jerusalem and the mountain as the two principal elements, within which other Jewish institutions—leadership, teachers (rabbis?), and even sacrifices—take shape. There is no mention of the Temple itself anywhere in this text. This is especially notable when he states that the "the Jewish synagogues (were) established in all cities instead of Jerusalem and Mount Zion" (p. 263, lines 12–13)! Clearly, in Eusebius's view, Mount Zion—the Temple Mount—assumed a significant role in the Judaism of his day, functioning as a central and independent motif in its sacred landscape, a kind of twin to Jerusalem. For this reason, Eusebius directs the ammunition of his teaching against the mountain, condemning it to devastation and desolation. The destruction that Jesus's arrival brought on Judaism would be realized in the annihilation of the mountain, both the physical mountain and the Jewish institutions that it symbolizes. This represents one of the most notable expressions of the Christian polemic against the Temple Mount and what it signified at that time.

Finally, this "anti-mountain" ideology was not detached from reality. The treatise concludes with a view of the physical place. In the last section Eusebius presents his personal eyewitness account of the city. He mentions the Romans (p. 265, line 2) and, in a few short words, links their deeds in Jerusalem to the ideas he presented in his exposition. Reality and idea walk hand in hand.

The Mountain and the City before and after Constantine

Peter Walker has correctly detected the change in Eusebius's attitude toward Jerusalem and the Jewish Temple between the period prior to Constantine's accession to power (the reference here being to his final victory in 324) and thereafter.[89] Eusebius's positions on these issues weave political and religious considerations into a seamless fabric. I do not intend here to discuss these matters in general but will devote this section to addressing the points relevant to the role of the Temple Mount in early Christian thought and experience.

The degree to which Jerusalem and the Temple bond reflects the development in Eusebius's views. In his earliest years, writing before Constantine's rise, Eusebius addresses Jerusalem and the Temple together, in both positive and negative contexts. In speaking of the city's holiness, he presents a position close to that expressed in Jewish sources, in which the city and the Temple are irrevocably interwoven. In *Proof of the Gospel*, for example, he states that Jerusalem's sanctity derives from the Temple and altar within it, and a similar theme resonates in his commentary on Psalms, where he portrays the Temple as the prime constituent of the city.[90]Accordingly, when Eusebius condemns the Temple and city in his hostile mode, the two are also inseparable, as for example in the homily discussed in the previous section.

In one expression of the link between Jerusalem and the Temple in Eusebius's early worldview, he endorses the rise of a third element that replaces them—the Mount of Olives. Eusebius draws on Ezekiel's prophecy about the cherubs that bear God's glory and transport it from Jerusalem to the Mount of Olives (Ezekiel 11:22–23), reading it as proof of God's utter abandonment of the city. In his explication, the Mount of Olives prefigures the true church and replaces Jerusalem, which symbolizes Judaism.[91] Eusebius does not leave this formulation as an abstract idea but rather links it to what started to take place in the area.

> Believers in Christ gather from all parts of the world, not like old times because of the glory of Jerusalem, nor that they may worship in the ancient Temple at Jerusalem, but they come there so that they may learn both about the city being taken and devastated as the prophets foretold, and in order to worship at the "Mount of Olives opposite to Jerusalem" where the glory of the Lord migrated when it left the former city.[92]

This segment provides one of the earliest testimonies of Christian worship, perhaps involving prostration (*proskyneō*), that took place in Jerusalem before Constantine assumed control. But it occurs outside the traditional sites for the veneration of God. Jerusalem and the Temple combine here into a single religious unit that the Mount of Olives supersedes. The ridge to the city's east (see map 1) constitutes a new focal point of ritual, previously unknown in the sacred landscape of Jerusalem. The Mount of Olives never functioned as a locus of worship in the ancient Jewish city, nor did the Romans build any temples there. Its functional significance is precisely its externality, its location outside the city limits, and as such it both opposes and replaces the old spatial organization of Jerusalem. The important point for our discussion is that Jerusalem and the Temple are perceived as a single unit.

After Constantine's emergence, the unified pair was sundered. A variety of passages in the *Theophany* enunciate this new conceptual organization of space. For instance, in the course of his description of the prohibition against Jews entering Jerusalem, Eusebius distinguishes between "their city" and "their ancient place of worship." Shortly thereafter, he clearly separates the coupled places and asserts definitively that, while Jerusalem and its Temple were both destroyed at the same time, different futures await them. The city may be re-built, but the Temple must remain in ruins.[93] This distinction between the fu-ture fates of the ruined city and the ruined Temple runs throughout the later works of Eusebius. His early depictions of the destruction of 70 CE—such as those in *Proof of the Gospel* and *Preparation of the Gospel,* or even his early bib-lical commentaries in *Selected Prophecies (Eclogae propheticae)*—view the sites as one, and in his commentary on Psalms he explicitly states that the two shat-tered entities will have the same destiny.[94] In contrast, his later writings, such as his *Commentary on Isaiah,* consistently distinguish between the city and the Temple. On numerous occasions in these later works, Eusebius portrays the Temple as razed to its foundations, and thus irreparable, while the city is merely "destroyed in siege" and thus restorable.[95] Likewise, in the *Theophany,* another of Eusebius's later works, the author extols Jerusalem as a major metropolis su-perbly appropriate for a capital. He adds that, with the Jews removed, others can now take their place. The first replacements were pagans, but there is no reason that Christians should not also reside in the city.[96]

The clearest expression of the divorce between Jerusalem and the Temple in Eusebius's later writings resonates in the name he bestows upon the new real-ity that Constantine's actions created in Jerusalem. In a much-quoted passage from *The Life of Constantine,* Eusebius heaps praise on the Church of the Holy Sepulcher built by the emperor in Jerusalem. He refers to this edifice as "the New Jerusalem" and asserts that it was founded "over and against the celebrated ancient one, which [remains] . . . in extreme desolation."[97] In the same vein, Eusebius borrows images originally associated with the Jewish Temple and ap-plies them to the new church.[98] Together, the name and the images imbue his text with a strong sense of rupture between New and Old Jerusalem. The first stands in splendor and glory with a new Temple—a church—at its center, while the other, with the old Temple at its heart, lies in utter and irreversible ruin. True to his literary predilections, here too Eusebius interlinks physical re-ality and religious theology. The confrontation between the two Jerusalems bears a clear ideological subtext—the site that witnessed, and in a way partook in, the Savior's agonies flourishes, whereas the place that committed the crime of the Lord's murder lies in ruins. At the same time the author invokes the de-scription of the city's physical texture, underlined by his repeated references to the New and Old Jerusalems standing opposite each other.

It is hard to avoid the impression that, when Eusebius writes of the old city lying in ruins, he means the areas of the destroyed Temple, which in fact lay opposite the Church of the Holy Sepulcher (see fig. 16).[99] He is contrasting two sites that face each other, separated by only a few hundred yards; the Church of the Holy Sepulcher on one side, now blooming with Christian glory under the patronage of the emperor, and the demolished Temple Mount on the other. Such a paradigm negates the old unity of Jerusalem and the Temple. The two, which had gone a long way intertwined in the writings of the early church fathers, were now alienated forever (or at least until Crusader times), with an unbridgeable abyss between them. Standing in opposition, Jerusalem would become the beloved daughter of the Christian world, whereas the Temple would be rejected, banned, hated, and abandoned.

The first glimmerings of the view that estranged Jerusalem from the Temple in Eusebius's later writings became a bright glow, well formed and consistent, a generation later. It figures prominently in the sermons of Cyril of Jerusalem and later also in the writings of Jerome. The interval of years, coupled with the rapid changes that took place in early Byzantine Palestine—especially political interests that opposed Caesarea to Jerusalem and, in Jerome's time, also to Bethlehem—meant that these three church scholars did not see eye-to-eye on many issues. One of the major differences centered, quite naturally, on their attitude toward Jerusalem and what it represents.[100] Eusebius, although he recognized the "new Jerusalem" and formulated an entire ideology that allows its existence, never attributed sanctity to the earthly city. He reserves such virtue for the heavenly city, or at most for the city of the distant past.[101] In contrast, Cyril took the holiness of Byzantine Jerusalem for granted.[102] Jerome too, immediately after arriving in Palestine and settling in Bethlehem, preached Jerusalem's praises in his letter to Marcella, insisting that not only heavenly Jerusalem but also the earthly city is holy.[103] Nonetheless, when it comes to the separation between the city and the Temple—the first accepted, the second rejected—Cyril and Jerome follow in Eusebius's footsteps.

In the course of his sermons, Cyril more than once addresses the fate of the Jewish Temple. These references vividly illustrate the tension between the Temple and the Christian residents of Jerusalem. Cyril emphasizes that the Temple ruins signify the Christians' upper hand in their confrontation with Judaism. An unambiguous example of this approach appears in his tenth lecture, when Cyril draws the attention of his audience to the ruins of the Temple by exclaiming, "the Temple of the Jews opposite [*anti*] to us is fallen."[104] The Greek

Fig. 16. The complex of the Church of the Holy Sepulcher (at the bottom of the picture) faces the Temple Mount compound, just a few hundred yards to the east; the physical and symmetric proximity informed, so I argue, the theology and rhetoric of church fathers such as Cyril of Jerusalem. From Duby Tal and Moni Haramati, *Kav ha-Ofek* (Jerusalem: Ministry of Defence Publishing House, 1993). With permission from Albatross.

preposition *anti* induces a sense of confrontation between the Church of the Holy Sepulcher, in which Cyril and his audience gathered, and the ruined Temple, which indeed lay in an advanced state of decay just a few hundred yards to the east (fig. 16). Like Eusebius, Cyril's discourse combines physical reality with Christological ideology. He speaks not of abstract devastation but rather of the tangible ruin within arm's reach "opposite to us." By placing the reference to the actual ruins in the middle of the passage, bookended on one side with Jesus's prophecy ("There will not be left here one stone upon the other") and on the other with the sin of the Jews, Cyril instilled ideological content into the physical reality before the eyes of his audience. A similar, if less marked, approach to the ruins of the Jewish Temple can be traced in the many references to this subject in Jerome's writings.[105]

Liturgy and Art

Christian animosity toward the site of the ruined Temple rings out in two other spheres as well—liturgy and art. In the wake of the changes that took place in Jerusalem after Constantine's accession, the inhabitants of the city consolidated a system of worship that included not only the customary prayers and sacraments but also a number of unique ceremonies, known as the "Jerusalem liturgy." Much has been written about this rite, the many processions it involved, and its special commemorative days, many of them intended to preserve the memory of figures from the Christian past and important events from its heritage that are connected in one way or another to Jerusalem.[106] Yet it seems to me that one aspect of the Jerusalem liturgy has not received sufficient attention: the absence of the Temple.[107] This should not be taken lightly. Even though Christianity is generally seen as fiercely opposed to the Temple, making the exclusion of its site seem natural, the present study has adduced a great deal of evidence to show that the Christian attitude to the Temple, at least in the early centuries, was complex and ambivalent. The Temple and related issues functioned on many planes of Christian experience and influenced numerous elements of its worldview. Just as early Christian prayer continued to use some elements of Jewish prayer, including the memory of the Temple,[108] and just as the presence of the Temple in Christian hymns was so evident that "there is no need to prove it,"[109] so it is reasonable to expect that the Temple would find expression in the Jerusalem liturgy.

Furthermore, the very essence of the liturgical system that evolved in

Jerusalem synchronized Christian present and past by invoking the places in which past events occurred. The pilgrim Egeria, whose travel journal offers the most important account of the Jerusalem liturgy in the fourth century, frequently stresses the performance of ceremonies at the time and in the place (*apte diei et loco*) of the commemorated event. This close link to spatial layout facilitated the attempt to breathe life into the events being celebrated. It is the nature of the *imitatio* mentioned by pilgrims such as Egeria.[110] The bishops and community spared no effort to achieve this goal. Processions packed the various halls, chambers, and courtyards of the Church of the Holy Sepulcher compound and outside it at far reaches of the city as well—for example, on Mount Zion and at "Pilate's Palace" (the Saint Sofia Church). The participants did not hesitate to leave the bounds of the city to reach Gethsemane and the Mount of Olives; to mark the raising of Lazarus from the dead, they even went as far as Bethany. The only place they neglected was the Jewish Temple compound, which they could see below them as they ascended and descended the Mount of Olives, standing like a bull's-eye at the center of the arc of their route (see map 7). They did not set foot there during the ceremonies, and they expunged it from their prayers and rituals even at times when it almost demanded to be named, for example during Candlemas, the feast celebrating the presentation of Jesus in the Temple. Egeria describes the liturgy conducted on this day, but instead of at the Temple site, the obvious location, it took place in the Anastasis of the Church of the Holy Sepulcher.[111] Even if we accept the explanation scholars have offered for this phenomenon—that, in Christian consciousness, the Church of the Holy Sepulcher replaced the Temple[112]—this cannot exhaust the subject. After all, as I have shown in chapter 4, pilgrims frequently visited the site of the ruined Temple. They reported, some to a greater and some to a lesser extent, what they found there, and they preserved its traditions. In other words, Christian Jerusalem knew the Temple compound but avoided according it religious status. There is a manifestly spatial aspect to this: the Jerusalem liturgy, whose very essence derives from the profound connection between Christianity and Jerusalem, was alienated from the Jewish Temple. It thus laid out the boundaries of Christian conceptuality: Jerusalem—yes; the Temple and the Temple Mount—no.

Congruent with the liturgy, in its rejection of the Jewish Temple site, is the artistic rendering of Jerusalem in the sixth-century Madaba map (fig. 15). Studies of the map's portrayal of Jerusalem have highlighted the artist's precision in details (the gates, streets, and various structures) but at the same time recognized his (probably not her, but we cannot know for sure) imaginative and ideological "freedom" in their spatial arrangement.[113] For instance, he enlarged the dimensions of the Church of the Holy Sepulcher, displaced it from its actual location, and planted it in the center of the city. It is as if the artist were declaring: in our consciousness, this structure constitutes the spiritual core of Jerusalem. Such conceptuality of space accounts for the omission of the Temple Mount, the site of the Jewish Temple, from the Madaba map. Hostility toward the area of the Jewish Temple seems to generate this artistic exclusion.[114] One can hardly ignore the great similarity between this artistic statement, even if later than the sources discussed in this chapter, and the ideas expressed by Eusebius in relation to the "New Jerusalem." Both configure the Church of the Holy Sepulcher—in Eusebius's words, the physical witness to the Lord's suffering—as embodying the essence of Christian experience, and, no less significantly, both reject the site of the Jewish Temple.

The New Mountain

Alongside the confrontation with the "old" mountain—the traditional Temple area—a new mountain gradually "rose" in Jerusalem. The first faint signs of its existence can be found as early as Eusebius. On one occasion, in *Proof of the Gospel,* he speaks of the coming of a "New Mountain," which will arrive in conjunction with "another house of God," their mission being the salvation of Gentiles.[115] Eusebius grounds this idea in Isaiah's prophecy of the end of days, "The mountain of the house of the Lord shall be established as the highest of the mountains" (Isaiah 2:2). There are several important points here. First, the verse itself does not imply that the mountain in question is a new one—that notion comes independently from Eusebius. Second, the mountain in this passage significantly differs from the one discussed by Eusebius in the previous sections of this essay. It lacks the ethereal nature of the spiritual mountain and does not evoke the hostility that typifies Eusebius's attitude toward the Jewish mountain.

Constantine's reign marks a major turning point in the nature of the "new mountain." At this time it metamorphosed from an abstract idea into concrete form, reified in a specific site in Jerusalem, at Golgotha in the Church of the Holy Sepulcher. Sources from the second half of the fourth century onward convey the image of Golgotha as a holy mountain. A lucid expression of this view appears in the writings of Cyril of Jerusalem. Toward the end of his tenth catechetical lecture, as part of a long list of witnesses—both persons and natural forces—to Jesus's messianic vocation, Cyril includes Golgotha, which he characterizes as "a sacred [hill] rising above us here."[116] The use of the present participle as an adjective indicates that the speaker is pointing to a concrete feature visible to his audience. In addition, the taxonomy "sacred" fosters an image of "the holy mountain," even though Cyril does not state this explicitly. The author-speaker borrows the term "holy mountain" from the biblical lexicon, an appellation with a prestigious aura from the city 's distant (biblical) past. But during those primeval times, the location of this mountain was never Golgotha; certainly the Jews did not think so, and the early Christians show no sign of perceiving it in this way either.

This perception of Golgotha as a holy mountain had currency far beyond the writings of Cyril. It became a widespread theme that both residents of and visitors to Jerusalem associated with the site. The mosaic that decorates the apse in Rome's Saint Pudenziana Church, for example, positions Jesus at the head of the Apostles, with a panoramic backdrop of Jerusalem's buildings and a heavenly host shielding them from above (fig. 17). In the center, nestled like an opulent jewel, a mountain juts up from among the buildings, bearing a huge cross on its peak. This is the earliest artistic representation of Byzantine Jerusalem, dated to the beginning of the fifth century, and scholars are united in their opinion that the artist drew the details for his work from the actual architectural landscape of the city.[117] The mountain, which without a doubt corresponds to Golgotha, merges with the figure of Jesus beneath it and the cross on its top to marshal the composition's central axis. Its sanctity is obvious.

This new configuration of Jerusalem's sacred space in which Golgotha functions as a "holy mountain" was not entirely at odds with the physical morphology of the city. Certainly, the second component of the appellation ("mountain"), which relates to the site's topography, is anchored in reality. True, Epiphanius, the fourth-century native of Palestine and later bishop of Salamis, wondered at the mountain image, arguing that "it is not on a height, neither is it higher than the other places [in Jerusalem]."[118] Apparently, however, it was his wish to find another, more spiritual explanation for the site's name that caused him to downplay its altitude. The fact that the area rose several feet above the main traffic artery that lay to its east (the "Cardo"; see map 7) certainly provided a sense of elevation. Moreover, the various descriptions of the early church built on the site identify Golgotha with a large rocky outcropping that workers apparently uncovered during the razing of the pagan

Fig. 17. A mosaic decorating the apse of the Church of Saint Pudenziana in Rome; in the background, amid the urban architecture of Jerusalem rises the new sacred mountain—the Golgotha. Courtesy of Maja North Vredevoogd.

compound that occupied the place before Constantine's time. In fact, the Bordeaux pilgrim called the site "the small mountain Golgotha" (*monticulus Golgotha*). Egeria wrote of the cross that the local authorities erected on this boulder and about the various ceremonies that were held there, above all the *adoratio crucis,* conducted on Good Friday. Later sources, such as the *Brief Description of Jerusalem* and Theodosius's account of the Holy Land, referred to Golgotha as "rocky mount" (*mons petreus*), even making note of steps that ascended to its top.[119]

Despite these accounts, there is still a great distance between neutrally describing a topographic elevation and infusing it with holiness, thus etching it in people's consciousness as a central element of their sacred imagery. It is one thing to relate as an afterthought to the place's height and to mention that one must therefore climb to reach it; it is something entirely different to turn it into a "holy mountain" and to place it at the heart of Christian experience in Jerusalem (as in the mosaic from Saint Pudenziana). Of course, the very fact that Christian traditions located the crucifixion at Golgotha elevated its importance and perhaps even endowed it with holiness, but why perceive it as a "holy mountain"? It seems to me that the answer lies in broader considerations.

As noted, Byzantine Jerusalem witnessed a complex and convoluted process of cultural transformation. Guided by Emperor Constantine's will and the drive of his mother Helena, the newly Christian inhabitants and their leaders "borrowed" names, concepts, images, and ideas that were linked to the city's Jewish past, and especially to the Temple, and used them to inaugurate the new Christian space of the city. The Church of the Holy Sepulcher and the cluster of metaphors associated with it attracted much of the energy that arose from this practice. Modern scholarship has devoted a great deal of attention to these developments, revealing its various facets and documenting its numerous details.[120] It seems to me that the development of the new Christian "holy mountain" needs to be understood in this ideological context. The following example illustrates this claim.

A well-known Jewish tradition linking the binding of Isaac on Mount Moriah with the Jewish Temple compound was transferred in Christian Jerusalem to the Church of the Holy Sepulcher. Eusebius voices merely a typological parallel between Isaac designated for sacrifice and the crucified Jesus, thus implying but not asserting a connection between the site of the binding—the place where Solomon later built his Temple—and that of the crucifixion.[121] Unlike this minimalist approach, later writers, and especially pilgrims, explicitly maintain that the binding of Isaac occurred at Golgotha.[122] It is but a small leap between shifting a legend that people, for generations, associated with one place to another and going one step further to claim that the other properties of the first site actually belong to the second. Theodoret, the fifth-century Syrian bishop of Cyrrhus, offers one example of such hybridism. In the third dialogue of *The Beggar*, in the midst of a typological interpretation of the binding of Isaac and its comparison with the crucifixion, Theodoret claims that the deeds of Isaac and Jesus sanctified the "mountain peak."[123] A bit later, in the Syrian text called *The Cave of the Treasures*, the unification of the sites reaches its acme: the place of the binding, Mount Jebus, Mount Moriah, and the spot of the crucifixion are all identified as the same location.[124] Other traditions about the holy mountain, such as the belief that God created the world from the foundation stone (discussed in chapter 6) or the legend that this stone marks Adam's grave (see chapter 2), were also relocated to Golgotha. All these details facilitated a new imagery for Golgotha in the guise of the Temple Mount.

In order to complete the picture, we should view the figure of Golgotha as the "holy mountain" together with other important mountains that occupied Christian landscape and experience in Jerusalem. In the city's south, Christians began at some point to identify the southwestern hill (see map 1) as Mount Zion. The name attests to its religious status among the residents of the Byzantine city and suggests that its roots lie in earlier Jewish traditions that the Christians adopted and reshaped. In this it resembles the holy mountain of Golgotha. Many of the traditions about the new Mount Zion crystallized prior to Constantine's reign. Early Christians located there the site of the room in which the Holy Spirit descended upon the Apostles on Pentecost. In time, they placed the Last Supper there as well. Nearby, Christians could point to the home of the high priest Caiaphas, where Jesus was imprisoned and beaten before being handed over to the Romans. Pilgrims reported seeing various items connected to Jesus and his disciples, which were presented in the area as holy relics: the post to which Jesus was tied and flogged, the crown of thorns that was placed on his head, the spear that gouged him, the lamp with whose light he taught, and many other such objects. Sources tell us that, as early as the 340s, Maximus, bishop of Jerusalem, built a church on the site, although nothing remains of it. Some time later, Bishop John II (386–417) built the Basilica of Zion, which immediately became one of the city's most important churches (map 7: 7). Pilgrims, Egeria in particular, report on the ceremonies that local priests and deacons conducted there and the processions that traversed the new street stretching from the new Mount Zion to the Church of the Holy Sepulcher.[125]

Another mountain that attained exalted status in this period is the Mount of Olives. A passage from Eusebius, quoted earlier in this chapter, shows that as early as the third century the Mount served as a point of assembly and prayer for pilgrims, who saw it as a kind of stand-in for the city and Temple. In the wave of construction that swept through the city in the fourth century, the Mount of Olives gained two important churches, one at the point from which Jesus rose to heaven and the other around the cave in which he taught his disciples. The liturgical parades that took place in the city in those times frequently ascended to these churches to conduct prayers and ceremonies. From the second half of the fourth century onward, Christians applied the term "holy mountain" to this mountain as well,[126] and various traditions grounded this new image in verses from the prophets and in New Testament stories, as well as in sacred physical elements, such as the footprints of Jesus that were "revealed" there.[127]

A triangle of holy mountains thus emerged in Jerusalem, with its apex at Golgotha and two sides emanating from it—one running southward to Mount Zion and the other eastward up to the Mount of Olives. The churches erected on the hilltops, and the liturgies recited on the roads connecting them, defined this triangle and fixed it firmly in the conceptual picture of the city's residents and visitors. The new sacred layout of Byzantine Jerusalem coalesced within this space. It is hard to avoid noticing the absence of one mountain from the triad. The Temple Mount, which provided the names and images for the new framework of mountains, was not included. It remained out of the picture, like an irrelevant limb.

All in all, Christians and Jews of the time organized their religious geography around holy mountains, but different ones. As time elapsed and the new landscape became ensconced among the Christians, they entirely expunged the Jewish Holy Mountain from their memories. So, when the seventh-century pilgrim Arculf describes the space between (the new, Byzantine) Mount Zion at the south of the city and the Mount of Olives to its east, he asserts that only the Jehoshaphat Valley runs between them.[128] It was as if the Temple Mount had never existed.

Sacred Topography in Christian Jerusalem

This chapter has probed the consciousness and conceptuality of sacred space and their interaction with the textures of landscape. On one hand, consciousness absorbs physical reality as chiseled and shaped by conceptual and ideological frameworks. On the other, in an incredible reciprocal maneuver, the tangible environment also influences the content of ideas and beliefs. These three dimensions of human experience act on one another mutually, and the cultural energy produced by this process stimulates traditions, legends, ideas, and images. They can also be arranged as a narrative—as the history or, one might say, the story of a certain sacred space, in this case of the Temple Mount, in the worldview of Palestinian Christianity.

The views presented here, in particular those of Barnabas, Justin Martyr, Origen, Eusebius, Cyril, and Jerome, as well as some segments of early Christian liturgy and art, endorse a certain "mountain" in Jerusalem and integrate it into their shared organization of sacred space. Together, they represent the Christian parallel to the concept "Temple Mount," which appears contemporarily in rabbinic literature (and will be presented in the next chapter). The emergence of the Mount in the realm of Palestinian early Christianity stands out against the absence of such a concept in the writings that came to be the New Testament, corresponding to its similar insignificance in the world of Second Temple Judaism. While in Second Temple times Jews normally categorized the spatial dimension of their worship as conducted in a "Temple" or in a broader sense in "Jerusalem," at some stage the site of the Jewish Temple came to be perceived in Christian (as well as Jewish) writings as a mountain. The fact that the Christian authors discussed here rely to a large extent on biblical terminology, which frequently associates mountains with Jerusalem and the Temple, does not detract from the force of the argument. In the final analysis, after all, Second Temple literature also largely draws on the ancient books that came to be the Bible, yet the mountain goes almost completely unnoticed there. Palestinian Christian writers "revived" the mountain, assigning it a concrete place in their consciousness and integrating it into their ideological and theological frameworks.

These Christian authors do not display a uniform attitude toward the "mountain." At times they stripped it of its material features and tried to embrace it only as a spiritual entity. Others branded it a Jewish concept and aimed the polemical arrows from their theological quivers at it. Still others uprooted it from its Jewish location and planted it, as a new mountain, in the Christian space that took form in Jerusalem after the time of Constantine. However different, they all espouse the "mountain of the Temple" as an independent category, alongside and at times in contrast to Jerusalem and the Temple, and endow it with a unique status in the Christian discourse of Palestine during the first five hundred years of the common era.

The ideas about the mountain of the Temple that developed among Christians are closely linked to the physical reality they infused. Both the view of Origen, which links the mountain and Jerusalem to spiritual entities that may be absorbed into Christianity, and the position of Eusebius, according to which both represent Jewish substance to be scorned, are based on the pre-Constantine landscape, in which Christians had no real ownership of the city and its contents. Therefore, Jerusalem and its textures can either be brought close or pushed away. This equation strikes an even clearer note when the changes that took place in Jerusalem after Constantine's victory resonate in the background of the conceptions that separate the site of the Jewish Temple from "New Jerusalem" or in those views that draw the mountain into the heart of Christian experience.

The Palestinian church fathers were well acquainted with the space Jews recognized as the Temple Mount; they visited the site of the ruined Jewish Temple, and their writings exhibit intimate familiarity with both its physical features and conceptuality, yet they wrestled with it and what it represented in the arena of ideas. As a result, although not always traceable in direct lines, churches and their congregants performed no ceremonies there, preachers denounced it in their sermons, and artists omitted it from their compositions. The next chapter follows the same process but from the opposite direction in the writings of the rabbis.

CHAPTER SIX

The Temple Mount, the Rabbis, and the Poetics of Memory

Memory is always problematic, usually deceptive, sometimes treacherous.

YOSEF H. YERUSHALMI, *Zakhor: Jewish History and Jewish Memory*, 5

In a good deal of rabbinic literature—generally seen as spanning the first few centuries after the destruction of the Second Temple (70 CE) and usually subdivided into Tannaitic (c. 70–220) and Amoraic (c. 220–600) texts—the sages convey information, both directly and indirectly, about their past as individuals, a group, and a nation.[1] Scholars in the past century and a half have invested tremendous effort in weighing the credibility of these records. In particular the literature unearthed in Qumran (also known as the Dead Sea Scrolls) has proved many of the views ascribed by the rabbis to early opponents in the Second Temple period rather accurate.[2] Consequently, the pendulum of the so-called historicity of rabbinic literature debate has swung from a romantic, and rather naive, acceptance of most if not all the data transmitted in this corpus to extreme skepticism, and finally in recent years has settled somewhere in between, ruptured into a variety of approaches and methodological models.[3] In this chapter I wish not to return to this intriguing discussion but rather to explore a different angle, that of rabbinic collective memory, the set of conventions and images that organizes narratives and discourses about the past.[4]

Habits of remembering have received a great deal of attention in modern scholarship. Advances, especially in the fields of psychology and neurology, have clarified the elusiveness of this practice and, as a result, blurred what was thought to be a clear-cut line dichotomizing the present from the past.[5] We now know that these two seemingly separate elements of time (and factors of memory) constantly intermingle, influencing and reshaping each other. Memory is one product of such processes, and history, in the words of one scholar, is the "art of memory."[6] Taking shape in assorted channels of expression, whether vocal, visual, or written, memory is typified by its innovative character, which defines it as a separate entity, a third dimension of human experience. The following chapter explores the dynamics and nature of rabbinic memory regarding one feature of their life—an architectural structure called the Temple Mount. As in previous chapters, I begin by establishing the centrality of Jerusalem and the (now ruined) Temple in rabbinic thought, and clarifying the historical context for the sages' engagement with the landscape of Jerusalem in the centuries following the destruction of 70 CE. Then, I devote the rest of the chapter to refuting the deceptively neat set of notions that the rabbis seem to articulate about the Temple Mount, and to argue that lurking behind their statements on this issue is a fascinating and complex discourse on sacred space and its role in shaping identities.

Engaging Jerusalem and the Temple after 70 CE

It would be hard to overestimate the role of Jerusalem and the Temple in the worldview of the Jewish sages, also known as the rabbis, the famous group of Jewish intellectuals who produced the so-called rabbinic literature during the Roman and Byzantine periods.[7] Large portions of this corpus are devoted to these two places. Admittedly, the hexagonal structure of the Mishnah—the prime Tannaitic text, which, along with the biblical sequence, became the standard format for organizing rabbinic material—does not include a separate division of a "Temple Order," comparable with, for example, the "Orders of Damages" for financial issues or "Women" for family matters. The division entitled "Order of Holy Things" (number five in the mishnaic sequence), however, contains such tractates as "Daily Sacrifice" (*Tamid*) and "Dimensions of the Temple" (*Middot*). Likewise, although no ancient rabbinic text has ever been named "The Jerusalem Midrash," there is, for example, the composition *Lamentations Rabbah,* almost entirely devoted to contemplating the loss of Jerusalem and its sanctuary and consequently replete with motives that hinge on these two.

The rabbis produced innumerable passages relating to the reality, both physical and metaphysical, of Jerusalem, with the Temple at its core. This is true in the halakhic (legal) sections—regulating the heave offerings and the tithes, or the celebrations of the various holidays, and even the tiniest details of the laws of ritual purity and impurity—all closely associated with the Temple. In the haggadic (nonlegal) portions as well, legends about the scholars and great men of Jerusalem, vignettes depicting life in the city and the Temple, and the vast numbers of interpretations of biblical verses dealing with these localities all attest to the importance of the Temple-city paradigm in the collective memory of the rabbis. Time and again the sages of the Mishnah and the Talmud reilluminate various aspects of Jerusalem and the Temple, thus fixing them within the deepest layers of their consciousness and setting them as the perpetual background, if not the actual scenery, of their multifaceted literary enterprise.

This intense preoccupation of the sages with Jerusalem and the Temple occurs at a time when these places were in ruins or when a foreign regime—Roman and then Christian—presided over the area. At first, in the period between the destruction of the Temple and the Bar Kokhba revolt (70–135 CE), this paradox could be attributed to the genuine yearning to rebuild the city and its revered sanctuary and renew Temple worship—expectations that were a key factor leading to the revolt of 132.[8] This explanation cannot, however, account for the persistence of such attraction in subsequent years, when most, if not all, of the Jews in Palestine were remote from Jerusalem, many relocating to Galilee, and the palpable desire to renew the Temple cult gradually faded away.

It seems, therefore, that although the destruction of the Second Temple and its continued absence shook Judaism and its institutions, displacing some of its prominent spiritual and practical characteristics, this event did not by any means eliminate the Temple from Jewish experience.[9] Even when the hallowed shrine in Jerusalem no longer existed, and the physical basis for the way of life that centered around it had been eradicated, the vitality of the Temple, its practices, and its symbolism endured: they fostered a wide range of rituals and liturgies, shaped prayers, and nurtured a long list of behaviors and activities that were established as "commemoration of Jerusalem/Temple."[10] Artistic decorations of ancient synagogues feature close links with both Temple images and its paraphernalia.[11] Likewise, the writings of the sages perpetuate the city and its sanctuary in rulings commemorating practices from the days of its glory and in stories and traditions expressing nostalgia to the people and places of

Jerusalem. All these demonstrate that Jerusalem and the Temple remained part of these people's experience even after they had disappeared in reality.

This does not mean, however, that the city-temple image in this period was completely disembodied or that, for example, Jews were totally disengaged from the mundane features of its landscape. Many scholars in previous generations were of the opinion, maintained by some to this very day, that in the centuries following the Bar Kokhba revolt, an all-inclusive imperial ban forbade Jews from dwelling in the city and that, with short and limited exceptions, they were not even allowed to visit. Oded Irshay rightly rejected this view, showing at length that such a sweeping prohibition never really existed.[12]

One custom the Jews continuously maintained, although naturally on a diminished scale, was pilgrimage.[13] At least one Hebrew speaker, most probably a Jew, engraved the words of Isaiah 66:14, "And you shall see and your heart shall rejoice and your bones like the grass shall . . . ," on one of the stones of the Western Wall of the Temple Mount (fig. 18).[14] Other Jewish visitors bought numerous glass-vessel souvenirs decorated with a *menorah*, a seven-branched lamp-stand known to be a Jewish symbol par excellence, which archaeologists unearthed in Jerusalem and dated to the centuries prior to the Arab conquest.[15] The same exclusively Jewish symbol also appears on lintels of houses from the same period that were excavated near the southwestern corner of the Temple Mount, and in some cases it even replaces erased crosses.[16]

Complementing the physical evidence are sporadic literary reports about Jewish life in the city. One such piece of information is the famous account by the anonymous fourth-century Christian pilgrim from Bordeaux, who visited Jerusalem in the 330s and described a ceremony in the area of the ruined Temple during which Jews anointed a "pierced stone" (*lapis pertusus*) with oil.[17] The same author speaks of "seven synagogues" on Mount Zion (the southwestern hill), one of which was still accessible in his day.[18] Based on the information discussed here pertaining to the Jewish presence in the city, the "Jewish-Christian" label ascribed to those structures by some modern scholars (mainly from the so-called Testa-Bagatti school) seems rather misleading.[19] In subsequent generations, Jerome too refers to Jewish visitors in Jerusalem.[20] Similarly, the biography of Barsauma, the zealous Nestorian monk who came to the city in the middle of the fifth century, reports a large gathering of Jews on the platform of the ruined Temple, which was authorized by the empress Eudocia, at the holiday of Tabernacles.[21]

Such evidence provides a concrete backdrop for the famous rabbinic legend

Fig. 18. An inscription found on one of the stones of the Western Wall of the Temple Mount. A Hebrew speaker engraved the comforting words of Isaiah 66:14, "And you shall see and your heart shall rejoice and your bones like the grass shall . . ." Scholars date the inscription to the fourth century CE. From Ronny Reich, Gideon Avni, and Tamar Winter, *The Jerusalem Archaeological Park* (Jerusalem: Israel Antiquities Authority, 1999), p. 22. Courtesy of Israel Antiquities Authority.

about the Tannaim who "arrived at the Temple Mount and saw a fox coming out of the [ruins of the] Holy of Holies,"[22] as well as for a similar, but less familiar, statement by a fourth-century Amora who "affirms" seeing some rabbis visit the Temple Mount, take off their sandals, and store them "under the ʾ*agof* [i.e., in the doorway]."[23] This is not to claim, in the old-fashioned positivistic manner, that these particular anecdotes are based on real historical events but only that the authors were not compelled to invent the very possibility that they occurred. Jews were visiting Jerusalem throughout the Roman and Byzantine periods, and perhaps some even resided in the city.

The available sources do not fully illuminate this phenomenon, and much remains unknown. It is difficult to determine the extent or frequency of such visits, and details about their substance, such as the length of stay in Jerusalem or the places where the visitors lodged, are rather scarce. The few sources that hint at the number of people who participated in these events, such as the traveler from Bordeaux and Jerome, make it clear that they were not isolated individuals but relatively sizable groups. Barsauma's gathering, for example, is huge, although his descriptions may be somewhat exaggerated. It can therefore be concluded that the arrival of Jews in Jerusalem during the Roman-Byzantine period is well documented and not a one-time event. Whether there were hundreds or even thousands (as the biography of Barsauma suggests) of visitors on each occasion, however, or only a few dozen; whether Jewish residents were present in the city at all times, or whether they assembled there only on certain occasions, such as the Ninth of Av or the pilgrimage festivals—these questions, as well as others, do not have definite answers at present.

Even if various rabbis were at least somewhat familiar with Jerusalem and the area of the ruined Temple, they were not simply bystanders reporting what they observed. As is well known, rabbinic literature seamlessly amalgamates fiction and reality with perception, ideology, and hermeneutics, and those are just as central in their writings as actuality itself. In accordance with the richness and diversity of the sources, modern scholars have devoted considerable effort to decoding the multifaceted function of Jerusalem and its Temple as reflected in the works of the rabbis. The inviolability of the city and the sanctuary, both in terms of the halakhot intended to preserve it and the ideas and concepts associated with it, have all been repeatedly surveyed.[24] Other studies have examined developments in the rabbinic stance toward Jerusalem, the Temple, and a whole line of closely related categories (such as the priesthood and the sacrifices) against the background of the great historical changes that befell their society following the destruction of the Second Temple and the Bar Kokhba catastrophe, and, even later, as a result of Christianity's rise to power.[25]

But what about the Temple Mount? Here the picture is surprisingly different. The number of scholarly studies seems to be in inverse ratio to the frequent occurrences of this designation in rabbinic literature. The sages, as we shall see, adverted to the Temple Mount dozens of times in their work and in miscellaneous contexts. Yet, even though modern scholars have made occasional references to one or another of these sources (and some of their insights are quite important), the phrase "Temple Mount" has not received the same attention as its fellow terms—"Jerusalem" and "the Temple." To the best of my knowledge, there is still no comprehensive collection of rabbinic references to the Temple Mount that tries to assess the significance of this entity for those who used it. One exception is the repeated attempt to delineate the geographical boundaries of the mountain, especially by utilizing the Tannaitic halakha that defines it as a square each of whose sides is 500 cubits long.[26] Such deficiencies the present chapter aspires to rectify.

My concern here extends beyond the physical realm to the sphere of consciousness, images, and ideas. Obviously, from a topographical standpoint, the summit that housed the Temple, and the architectural structure in a shape of a huge compound that occupied its top still stood visible in the days of the rabbis, on the ridge that divided the two eastern tributaries of the Kidron Valley—the Jehoshaphat Valley to the east and what is known as the Tyropoeon Valley to the west (see map 1). But how was this mountain crest or the compound perceived by the sages, and what role did this space play in their lives? As we shall see, the answers to these questions are far from being simple. Following the rabbinic (literary) engagement with the Temple Mount unveils an absorbing process in which sacred space is reorganized, and both physical and spiritual landscapes are redefined through memory and literature.

Spatial Consciousness and Historical Context

Portrayals of the Temple Mount in Tannaitic literature create the impression that they derive from the milieu of Second Temple Judaism. Tractate *Middot*, for example, refers to the Mount as an established territorial entity within the larger Temple landscape: it clearly surrounds the central edifice (i.e., the Temple itself), its dimensions are meticulously demarcated ("The Temple Mount is 500 cubits by 500 cubits"), and the names of its gates are well known ("The Temple Mount had five gates"). The text also mentions some etiquette for visitors, such as the route people were required to follow when attending the site, along with the salutation for greeting other people they encountered along the way. Also mentioned is "the officer of the Temple Mount" (*'ish har ha-bayit*), an official overseeing security and order whose duties included supervision of the Levite guards who were stationed at the five gates of the compound.[27]

The content of these passages implies that their authors wished to represent them as taken from Second Temple reality—in other words, articulations of rabbinic memories about the past. In addition to the various details, these traditions portray a certain spatial layout, in which the Temple Mount operates as an integral element of Second Temple topography. For a reader of rabbinic texts, this organization of space comes as no surprise as it is documented in numerous other rabbinic sources. For example, when the rabbis speak of ceremonies and feasts that allegedly took place in Jerusalem before the destruction of 70 CE, they constantly mention the Temple Mount as a reference point and take for granted its familiarity to their audience. In one case, they locate the Temple Mount as the final station along the route of the oxen that brought the ritually pure children who carried water from the Siloam fountain for the ceremony of slaughtering the red heifer; in another, the Temple Mount functions as the point of departure for a procession, headed by a priest who set out from the city to burn the red heifer at the nearby Olive Mount.[28]

The vibrant description of the sacramental banquet celebrating the bringing of firstfruits provides another example. The rabbinic text follows the pilgrims' route and enumerates various details of the festivity: the ox "whose horns were overlaid with gold and a wreath of olive branches on its head" leading the flocking visitors; the flute "playing in front of them"; the biblical verses they recited, and the various personae that were involved in the ceremonies. One of the parade stations, after the pilgrims had already entered Jerusalem but before they arrived at the inner court of the Temple (the ʿazarah), features the Temple Mount: "The flute plays in front of them until they arrive at the Temple Mount. When they reached the Temple Mount even King Agrippa would take a basket on his shoulder and enter."[29]

Fitting well with this spatial arrangement, other halakhot also place the Temple Mount at the hub of daily life in Jerusalem at the time when the Temple still stood. One halakha prescribes that after the pilgrims in the first group completed their Paschal offering (which, due to the vast number of participants, was carried out according to the Mishnah in three consecutive shifts), "they went out . . . to the Temple Mount."[30] A position attributed to the Tanna R. Eliezer b. Yaʿakov locates on the Temple Mount the biblical reading that the Jewish king performed at the public convocation (haqhel) on the holiday of Tabernacles following the Sabbatical year.[31] In the same vein, the Mishnah rules about lost money found in the city of Jerusalem, "Coins that were found before cattle-dealers are always [considered to be second] tithe [coins]. [If they were found] in the Temple Mount [they are considered] profane [regular coins that were not sanctified for second tithe use]. And in Jerusalem—[if found] during the rest of the year [they are considered] profane, and [if found] on a pilgrimage festival all [are considered second] tithe [coins]."[32] Tannaitic literature also records a considerable number of customs and policies pertaining to the Temple Mount during the Second Temple period. Hand in hand with the entrance directives in tractate *Middot* mentioned earlier, another halakha regulates the dress code on the mountain, forbidding certain objects (such as shoes and walking sticks) to be brought in, and imposing a number of other restrictions on those who enter (dust on one's feet is not allowed nor is using the Temple Mount as a shortcut).[33]

On the literary level, the Temple Mount frequently appears in stories about Second Temple Jerusalem that the Tannaim introduce into their literature. The Tosefta, for example, tells "of R. Gamaliel and the elders who were sitting on the top of the stairs in the Temple Mount," from which they dispatched epistles to all the "nation of Israel" about the removing of tithes from their houses and the intercalation of an additional month into the yearly system.[34] To be sure, the source does not specify which R. Gamaliel this was (a few rabbinic characters held this name), so it might have been R. Gamaliel of Yavneh, in which case the account would be about the time after the destruction of the Temple. But since it is unlikely that the sages who configured this tradition thought Jews still occupied official positions in Jerusalem at that time, we can assume that the R. Gamaliel mentioned here was the so-called R. Gamaliel the Elder and that the author, therefore, attributed the incident, whether authentic, fictional, or just through confusion on the part of its transmitters, to the Second Temple period.[35] In other instances, the Tannaim extend the chronological boundaries even further, depicting the Temple Mount as part of Jerusalem's reality in much earlier periods. Illustrating this tendency, the Mishnah preserves a tale about Ḥoni the circle drawer, a saintly figure known to be active in Jerusalem toward the end of the Hasmonaean period (60s BCE), which at one point refers to heavy showers persisting "until the Israelites went up from Jerusalem to the Temple Mount."[36]

The conjunction of the Temple Mount with the Second Temple era extends beyond halakha and "historiography." A string of rabbinic sources also interweaves this feature into the physical landscape of the predestruction period by juxtaposing it with other architectural elements that existed at the time. One such case features the stoa on the Temple Mount, which modern scholars justifiably interpret as deriving from the Greek and denoting either the royal basilica erected by Herod on the southern portion of the compound or the porticoes that encircled the compound (see map 3).[37] Also mentioned in rabbinic literature are a synagogue, a study house, and a lawcourt on the Temple Mount, although it is not clear whether the references are to architectural structures or, at least in the case of the last two, merely to the gatherings of people for such purposes.[38] Other tangible elements, diminutive as they might seem, are scattered throughout rabbinic texts, such as the step and tier used by R. Gamaliel for burying copies of the translation of Job that he withdrew from circulation,[39] or the tops of pillars in the Temple Mount, of which R. Eleazar b. Zadok said "that artisans sit on them and polish the stones."[40]

Culminating the Tannaitic presentation of the Temple Mount as a Second Temple element is the famous halakha in tractate *Kelim* that maps the hierarchy of spatial holiness by dividing it into ten consecutive degrees. Within that arrangement, between the city of Jerusalem ("within the city walls") and the Temple structure itself stands the Temple Mount, which "is still more holy [than the city], for no man nor woman who has the flux, no menstruant, and no women after child birth may enter therein."[41] Apparently, the Tannaim considered the Temple Mount an integral part of Second Temple reality, and as such they were required to rank it among the holy features of that time. At the center of this calibration of sacred space shines the Temple of Jerusalem, the focus and peak of holiness, as an accessible and functioning institution. Accentuating its elevated status other architectural elements of this time—the inner courtyards, Temple Mount, and the city of Jerusalem—envelope the house of God. Characteristically for the rabbis, they refrain from conveying such a concept in spiritual terminology but rather anchor it in mundane daily practices. They formulate sacredness through halakhic prohibitions regarding ritual purity, known to be widely observed at the time. By applying such language, the passage creates the impression that the various components on its list, including the Temple Mount, were fundamental to the awareness and experience of Jews during the Second Temple period.

Amoraic literature proceeds along the same lines. The Amoraim too considered the Temple Mount to have been an established entity as well as a functioning site during the Second Temple period, constituting an essential factor of Jewish consciousness at that time. They show concrete knowledge of the physical layout of the place—for example, when referring to "the *'agof* [doorway] of the Temple Mount" in relation to the sanctuary's halakhic boundaries.[42] In a debate regarding a Paschal sacrifice that had become ritually impure, they evoke the scenery at the site. The Mishnah stipulates that such an offering must be burned "in front of the *birah* [castle or fort]." The Amoraim in the Palestinian Talmud differ about the identification of this structure;

R. Yoḥanan claims, "There was a tower on the Temple Mount that was called *birah*," while R. Simeon b. Lakish contends, "the entire Temple Mount was called *birah*."[43]

Like the Tannaim, the Amoraim preserved "memories"—whether real or imagined—of scenes from the Second Temple period that had occurred on the Temple Mount. For example a tradition in the Palestinian Talmud tells of Bava b. Buta, a disciple of the Second Temple sage Shammai, who in his aspiration to follow the halakha of the rival school of Hillel, mustered three thousand animals intended for ritual offering, stood them on the Temple Mount, and called upon the Jews to "place their hands on the animals' heads," an action consistent with the ruling of the school of Hillel.[44] Also presented by the Amoraim as associated with the Temple Mount are some official practices from the days of the Temple. The post-Amoraic compilation *Midrash Tanḥuma*, for example, details a regulation that forbids a priest to leave the Temple Mount while dressed in his vestments.[45] Furthermore, the Amoraim resembled the Tannaim in considering the Temple Mount to have been in service even during the earliest days of the Second Temple period. For example, one version of the Amoraic legend about Alexander the Great's alleged arrival in Jerusalem maintains that when the Hellenistic king entered the Temple Mount, the Jewish protagonist of the story—a character named Gabiah (the Hunchback)—coaxed him to replace his shoes with some socklike slippers (from the Greek *empilia*).[46] Quite clearly, the author shaped this segment of the story in accordance with the Tannaitic halakha mentioned earlier, which prohibits walking in the Temple Mount with shoes on.

Distorting a Seemingly Harmonious Picture

At first glance, then, rabbinic sages in the post-70 era place the Temple Mount in the realm of the Second Temple. They seem to communicate memories that picture the Temple Mount as an essential element of Second Temple Jewish experience and an inseparable part of reality in that earlier generation's consciousness. These memories suggest that, during the time of the Temple, Jews were both familiar with and used the term "Temple Mount." They abided by customs linked to the Mount as well as the laws governing the area. People were also acquainted with its physical details. But a more careful examination of the traditions regarding the Temple Mount in rabbinic literature—one that investigates the various versions of and changes in the texts over time—reveals deep fissures in the picture delineated here. Such an analysis raises serious doubts about the historical reliability of relating the term "Temple Mount" and its conceptual content to the Second Temple period. I argue that the conclusions of this inquiry should reverse this model of the Temple Mount as a Second Temple feature and present it as a conceptual innovation of the rabbis.

David Weiss-Halivni was, as far as I know, the first to point out the problems involved in the sources about the Temple Mount and to note that this term does not fit smoothly with the halakhic fabric of the Mishnah.[47] Halivni directs his attention to *Mishnah Bikkurim,* which presents the limits of firstfruits liability. The Torah commands to bring the earliest harvest to the Temple and to offer it to God as a token of thankfulness. Developing this statute into a scrupulous legal system, the rabbis demarcate the line beyond which the legal responsibility of the person bringing the offering does not extend. It reads as follows:

> If they [the firstfruits] contracted uncleanness while in the Temple Court [ʿazarah], he must scatter them and he may not make the Avowel [a liturgical reading of some biblical verses related to this offering]. From where do we learn that a man is liable for them until they are brought to the Temple Mount [*har ha-bayit*]? Because it is written "The first of the firstfruits of your land you shell bring into the house of the Lord thy God" [Exodus 23:19, 34:26], which teaches that one is liable for them until they are brought to the Temple Mount.[48]

Halivni is very much aware that the two designations in this passage—Temple court (ʿazarah) and Temple Mount (*har ha-bayit*)—signify different parts of the Temple complex (map 3): the first stands for the inner courts (B, C), whereas the latter marks the outside precinct (D). Therefore, he notes, the change in name—from "Temple court" at the beginning of the halakha to "Temple Mount," appearing twice in the exegetical (midrashic) segment following it ("From where do we learn . . . Because it is written . . .")—creates legal incongruity. The first part of the halakha specifies that only when the pilgrim brings the firstfruits to the inner Temple court is he no longer responsible for them, and so if they became ritually impure, "he scatters them" but is not required to bring "others instead of them [as demanded from someone whose fruits became invalid prior to his fulfillment of the obligation]." The closing, midrashic, part, however, implies that as soon as he has brought the offering to the Temple Mount, his obligation is fulfilled. Thus a person who has brought the offering to the Temple Mount maintains his liability according to the first part of the halakha but is no longer responsible according to the last part. Halivni correctly observes that this last section contradicts not only the first section but also the accepted halakha in rabbinic literature elsewhere. He calls attention to a midrashic excerpt in the *Mekhilta of R. Simeon b. Yoḥai,* which is practically identical to the one in the preceding Mishnah, except that it ends, "'thou shalt bring into the house of the Lord thy God' teaches that people are bound to look after the bringing of [the firstfruits] until they reach the chosen house [*beit ha-beḥirah;* the Temple]."[49]

Halivni then attempts to resolve this legal contradiction: "Clearly, during the time when the continuation of the Mishnah Bikkurim [i.e., the midrashic segment in the second part] was composed, the Temple proper too was referred to (as in the Bible) as the Temple Mount." Halivni claims that this time was the period before the reign of King Herod (37–4 BCE).[50] Underlying his interpretation is the assumption that the meaning of the term "Temple Mount" has changed over time. With this insight, Halivni provides the methodological foundation for a historical study of the expression "the Temple Mount" and its development in both rabbinic literature and Jewish civilization in general. His chronological model, however, may not be the only possible solution. A priori, there could be two possible, chronologically different, origins for the Temple Mount image in rabbinic literature. According to one option, the one embraced by Halivni, the sages really did capture the essence and experience of the previous era—that is, the Second Temple period—and they preserved and documented it in their literature. According to this line of thought, the writings of the Tannaim and Amoraim genuinely display the Temple Mount as part of the Second Temple world. Consequently, Halivni proposes that the authors of the Mishnah retrieved the source about the Temple Mount from early layers of Second Temple literature, namely pre-Herodian times.[51]

An alternative possibility, however, should also be considered. Perhaps the sages offer a new picture of the past based primarily on the concepts and images that were prevalent in their own time. If this is so, when the rabbis present the Temple Mount as an essential feature of Second Temple experience, they are actually projecting their own images backward and sketching the past according to the accepted notions of their own time. This view, the one I argue for, accepts Halivni's distinction between the various layers of the Tannaitic literature dealing with the Temple Mount but differs with his historical conclusion. According to this view, "the Temple Mount" in rabbinic literature is not an early conceptual entity that the rabbis incorporated into their writings but rather a later invention that was plotted into these texts by those who created them, namely the rabbis themselves.

How then is *Mishnah Bikkurim* to be understood? The midrashic segment at the end of the passage, which fixes the limits of firstfruits liability at the Temple Mount, has a parallel in two other Tannaitic works: the Tosefta and *Sifre to Deuteronomy*. These texts, however, cite R. Judah's view, which demarcates the line of liability at a place called "the well [cistern] of the *Golah*," known from other sources to be located in the Temple, between the Israelite and priestly courts (map 3: B).[52] The *Sifre* discusses the liability limits of all offerings in general. It interprets the verse, "But such sacred donations that are due from you, and your votive gifts you shall bring to the place that the Lord will choose" (Deuteronomy 12:26), as, "One is bound to take care of the bringing [of the offerings] until they are brought to the Chosen House [*beit ha-beḥirah*]." Following this general statement R. Judah locates the line of liability more specifically in the well of the *Golah*.

Clearly, the general boundary for liability set by the *Sifre*, as well as the more specific location noted by R. Judah, agrees with the first part of *Mishnah Bikkurim*. Both ʿ*azarah* (inner courtyard), and *beit ha-beḥirah* (chosen house), even if not identical, point to the inner structures of the Temple, which stood at the time as a detached architectural unit, physically removed from the compound by a fortified wall and legally separated by a whole series of halakhot.[53] R. Judah's remark too, although a more specific clarification that marks the boundary for responsibility in exact terms, shares the view of the *Sifre* and the first part of *Mishnah Bikkurim*. All three disagree with the boundary designated by the midrashic segment in the second part of the Mishnah—"Temple Mount"—which denotes the outer precinct (map 3: D) and therefore reduces the extent of liability in comparison with that of the other sources.

The question is the relation between the three formulations that locate the boundary of liability at the inner structure of the Temple, on the one hand, and the midrashic segment at the end of the Mishnah, which sets the boundary at the Temple Mount, on the other. At first glance it might seem that the sources simply disagree about the liability boundary—one locates it in the Temple, the other at the Temple Mount. But, as Halivni already showed, the phrasing of the Mishnah does not seem to indicate a difference of opinion between the first part and the second; rather, it seems to be presenting one view. Moreover, the use of a very precise designation, "the well of the *Golah*" (as opposed to naming a broader vicinity such as "the Temple" or "the Temple Mount"), seems to demonstrate familiarity with the layout of the Temple area, thus attesting that this version is probably an early one.

It may thus be suggested that the expression "the Temple Mount" represents a later reformulation of the halakhot about the boundary of liability, reflecting a distant viewpoint from which this term came to encompass, and consequently replace, the particularities of the Temple reality. According to this interpretation, ʿazarah (inner courtyard) and the well of the *Golah* had been germane when they were well known to everyone but lost their relevance once the Temple had been destroyed. The sage who coined this term in the midrashic segment of the Mishnah adjusted its phrasing to the common vocabulary of his own day. From this point of view, he may not even have noticed the contradiction that this change created between the two parts of the Mishnah because in his time the term "Temple Mount" stood for a general, all-inclusive name of the Temple space.

This is a theoretical model. Although it may be correct, alternative proposals can be offered as well. In what follows I therefore bring evidence in support of this thesis, demonstrating that the "Temple Mount" constitutes a later expression taken from the worldview of the Tannaim and Amoraim. It represents their own unique spatial organization, which they then applied to earlier times.

The Direction of Prayer

Numerous sources from the Second Temple period attest to an ancient custom of praying in the direction of Jerusalem and the Temple. The embryonic phases of this practice may already be spotted in the prayer attributed by the biblical book of 1 Kings to King Solomon, said to be delivered at the dedication of the First Temple: "Hear the plea of your servant and of Your people Israel when they pray toward this place."[54] In accordance with this tradition, the early halakha, preserved in *Sifre to Deuteronomy* and in the Tosefta, as well as in a series of Amoraic parallels and some fragments in the Geniza, calibrate the various directions of prayer:

> Those who stand outside the Land direct their hearts toward the land of Israel . . .
> Those who stand inside the land of Israel direct their hearts toward Jerusalem . . .
> Those who stand in Jerusalem direct their hearts toward the Temple . . . Those who stand in the Temple direct their hearts toward the Holy of Holies.[55]

The Mishnah presents an abbreviated form, mentioning only the final destination but with a similar orientation: "He should direct his heart toward the Holy of Holies."[56] One source, however, deviates from this conventional pecking order and introduces a slight change into the hierarchy of places. A baraita (an "external Mishnah," i.e., a Tannaitic pericope not included in the final edition of the Mishnah) cited by the Palestinian Talmud replaces "the Temple" with "the Temple Mount": "Those who pray in Jerusalem turn their faces toward the Temple Mount . . . Those who pray on the Temple Mount turn their faces toward the Holy of Holies."[57] Even those scholars who noticed this change paid no attention to its significance;[58] indeed, from a practical viewpoint it makes no difference because people in prayer continue to face the same direction. But from a conceptual point of view, the change in the designation of the location suggests an essential development.

All versions of the hierarchal list of places, including the baraita in the Palestinian Talmud, coincide stylistically. Even more so, they concur about the identity of the various places, with only one exception—the Temple Mount in the baraita. The closeness of both style and wording makes it unlikely that the two versions were formulated concurrently. It is also rather implausible that the early version was "the Temple Mount" and that it was later changed to "the Temple." More probably, most of the sources in this case preserved the ancient and obvious version in which the direction of prayer points toward the Temple, as is also evident in all early Second Temple sources. Only the Tannaitic source that was preserved in the Palestinian Talmud alters the location to "the Temple Mount."

A clue to the reasons for this modification may be found in the portion of the Palestinian Talmud following the baraita. In that passage, R. Joshua b. Levi interprets the verse, "For my House shall be called a House of Prayer for all the nations" (Isaiah 56:7), as follows, "It is the inner sanctuary towards which all faces turn [to pray]." When the Talmudic author challenges the eternal veracity of this statement due to the realities of the time—"This applies when the Temple was standing, but how do we know [it is true when the Temple] is destroyed?"—the sugya (the Talmudic passage) introduces an alternative understanding. R. Bon discerns a play on the biblical image, "shapely built [*talpiyot*]" (Song of Songs 4:4). Splitting the Hebrew noun in two, he reads "the hill [*tel*] toward which [literally in Hebrew—on top of which!] all mouths [*piyot*] pray." Even without solving all the textual uncertainties that arise from other versions of this segment,[59] the gist of its textual moment is clear. It deals with the situation that came into being after the destruction of the Temple. In R. Bon 's formulation, the word *tel,* denoting the Hebrew hill or mountain, substitutes for the word *heikhal* in R. Joshua's interpretation, which means shrine or Temple. Precisely the same change took place in the baraita: "the Temple" turned into "the Temple Mount."

To unpack the narrative embodied in this passage: in the wake of the destruction of the Temple the sages were compelled to contemplate the issue of the direction of prayer and asked themselves if it still had any significance, now that the sanctuary was annihilated and the sacrificial process had ceased to exist. Shifting the destination of prayer from the Temple to the Temple Mount can easily be seen as part of this consideration. The baraita in the Palestinian Talmud thus provides a glimpse at the process by which "the Temple Mount" replaced "the Temple." In the earlier era, rendered by the sources from the Second Temple period, people directed their prayers to Jerusalem and the Temple. Only later, when the spatial arrangement involved in the prayer activity changes, "the Temple Mount" took the place "the Temple." Most of the sources dealing with the direction of prayer did not absorb this change and they remain faithful to the original hierarchy of locations. But the baraita quoted by the Palestinian Talmud preserved the new orientation for us.

This partial shift in the prescription for direction of prayer and the new configuration of space that it embodies is by no means an isolated case. In the following, I wish to support my argument by showing that the same phenomena circulated throughout rabbinic literature. Discerning similar literary and epistemological developments in seemingly unrelated instances reinforces the plausibility of such a change.

Innovative Perception: Remembering Physical Reality

The mechanism laid out in the previous example for the evolution of both the term and image of the Temple Mount recurs throughout rabbinic literature. In some cases the change is readily apparent. One example from the sphere of biblical hermeneutics comes in the course of a rabbinic discussion about places that are exempt from the requirement of having a *mezuzah* (a parchment scroll containing some biblical passages, which the halakha requires to be affixed to the doorpost of rooms in Jewish buildings). Based on the scriptural verses that are commonly associated with affixing a *mezuzah* (Deuteronomy 6:9, 11:20), the Palestinian Talmud renders a Tannaitic midrash on the word *uvishe'arekha* ("and on your gates")—"except for the gates of the Temple Mount and the inner Temple courts."[60] Early Tannaitic versions of this midrash, however, preserved in *Sifre to Deuteronomy* and in the Tosefta, do not mention the Temple Mount at all but rather make it explicit that the issue at hand refers to the gates of the Temple.[61]

In a second example, a Mishnaic passage detailing some rituals that were performed on fasting days include one view that limits the observance of these practices to what took place "at the Eastern Gate and in the Temple Mount."[62] So says the printed version of the Mishnah, as well as the version in the Munich manuscript of the Bavli (short for Babylonian Talmud), which quotes the Mishnah, the Babylonian Talmud too cites this tradition in this way.[63] But none of the Palestinian textual witnesses, known to represent the more original versions of the Mishnah, mention the Temple Mount in this passage—not the so-called Kaufmann manuscript, or the one from Parma, or the Cambridge manuscript published by Lowe. Citations of the Mishnah by the Palestinian Talmud show no awareness of this reading either. Most of these sources refer to "the eastern gates," in the plural, not to the Temple Mount.

According to all available evidence, this decisive change occurred between the days of the Tannaim and the time when the Babylonian Talmud alluded to this source (since the quotation of the Mishnah in the Bavli already has the Temple Mount). It seems plausible that "and the Temple Mount" represents a type of gloss—annotations commonly added by scribes to the margins of manuscripts (although here it could have been added orally)—meant to cope with the fact that the "gates" in the original version appear in the plural. According to this explanation, the later reader assuming only one eastern gate added the Temple Mount to sustain the Mishnaic version of "gates" in the plural. Although it is difficult to reconstruct exactly the changes in wording that led to the one preserved in the printed edition of the Mishnah as we have it ("at the Eastern Gate and in the Temple Mount"), the main stages of the process are quite clear, and it is fairly obvious that the expression "the Temple Mount" was not part of the original account.

A third case features similar developments but this time within the narrative framework of a fictional story. A legend transmitted twice in the Palestinian Talmud (see n. 44) recounts the measures taken by Bava b. Buta to reinvigorate the deserted inner courts of the Temple complex and revive the neglected sacrificial process. According to the story, the fact that the procedures in the Temple regarding the laying of hands on sacrificial animals accorded with the school of Shammai resulted in people avoiding animal offerings altogether. Troubled by the empty inner court of the Temple—the ʿazarah—but not dismayed, Bava b. Buta decided to reinstate the law according to the school of Hillel. The story concludes with the protagonist b. Buta bringing thousands of animals to display in the Temple Mount and calling upon the nation to renew the sacrificial process in accordance with the more popular Hillelite halakha.

The literary structure of the Palestinian Talmud passage shows the final location, "Temple Mount," to be out of place. The motif that shapes the plot centers on "the empty inner court [ʿazarah]" and thus generates the expectation that Bava b. Buta's actions will fill this void and that the story will conclude in the inner courtyard itself. Indeed, in another, apparently earlier version of this legend in the Tosefta, the plot culminates with "he placed them [the animals] in the ʿazarah."[64] It seems that the process described previously, in which "the Temple Mount" replaced early terms associated with the Temple, occurred here as well.

Finally, a fourth example of placing an authentic structure within a spatial setting that did not prevail at the time involves the previously mentioned Amoraic debate about the identification of the *birah*. R. Yoḥanan maintains, "There was a tower on the Temple Mount that was called *birah*," while R. Simeon b. Lakish contends, "the entire Temple Mount was called *birah*." Undoubtedly, an architectural structure (tower, fortress, garrison?) by that name stood somewhere in the vicinity of the Temple during the Second Temple period; the Mishnah mentions it a few times; Josephus confirms it and also provides its Greek transliteration *baris*. Its earliest usage in relation to the Temple in Jerusalem reaches back to the book of Nehemiah.[65] But all early sources establish the location of the *birah* as simply next to the Temple—both in rabbinic literature, including the passage in the Mishnah about whose interpretation the Amoraim were debating, as well as Josephus. It is entirely possible, as Paul Mandel claims in his study of the term *birah*, that at a certain stage during the Second Temple period the denotation of this term was extended to include the entire Temple area.[66] This, however, only underscores the absence during that time of the name "Temple Mount," which would have obviated the necessity for finding another term (*birah*) to describe exactly the same area. Apparently, here too the designation "Temple Mount" entered rabbinic discourse only at a later stage, and the Amoraim introduced it into earlier depictions of the Temple area. To be sure, the *birah* represents an authentic structure of Second Temple landscape; the "*birah* on the Temple Mount," however, was an artifact of Amoraic memory.

These four cases (and many others I left out here) [67] shed light on how the rabbis shaped their memory of physical space. How do architectural elements or spatial arrangements from the past register in the mind of the individual or in the collective consciousness of a group? Unlike the earlier example discussed in this chapter about the direction of prayer, the Temple Mount in the last few cases does not take center stage. Rather the gates and *birah* are the important features, either as halakhic categories or as venues for certain rituals and stories. The Mount is mentioned in passing and therefore in a way that allows a neutral glimpse into the inventive process of memory. Clearly gates existed in the Second Temple complex as well as inner quads and other structures such as the *birah*, but later generations listed them in their literature in a very inventorial way. That is to say: out of the countless physical elements that occupied the world of Second Temple Jews, only those that hinge on an issue worth remembering earned a spot in later traditions, whether written or oral. The terminology that later generations, in this case the Tannaim and Amoraim, utilized to present this area, however, dramatically altered with the addition of the Temple Mount. There is no hint that the people of the Second Temple period thought about the site on which these rituals and practices took place as "the Temple Mount." In all early versions of the traditions cited here, the area is never called by this appellation. The "eastern gates," for example, probably pointed to the space between the two eastern gates leading to the Temple, the eastern entrance to the women's court, and the gate leading from it to the Israelites' court (often incorrectly called "the Nicanor gate"; see map 3).[68] The same holds true for the *birah* and the ʿ*azarah*. Only at a later stage in the transmission of these halakhot, either in the Tannaitic period or sometime between that time and the following Amoraic era, were the traditions reworded and the location "Temple Mount" introduced. Whereas in the early literary strata they were simply gates—eastern gates or the gates of the Temple—and a structure named *birah*, they were transformed over time into something new, the gates and *birah* of the Temple Mount. As a result, a new space emerged that had not been part of the original cluster of memories. The same process marks the shift of consciousness from the ʿ*azarah* as the physical destination of offerings to the Temple Mount. The story of Bava b. Buta shares common traits with the first-fruits liability case, analyzed by Halivni, as well as with the destination of prayer case discussed earlier. Here too the introduction of the Temple Mount gives the memory of the physical layout of the Temple another form.

All in all, these sources indicate that a variety of physical elements, all remembered as associated with the Temple, changed at a certain stage to the realm of the Temple Mount. I have provided evidence to substantiate the claim that this change had a chronological dimension as well: at first these elements were all seen as related to the Temple and over time reallocated to the Mount. I call this process "innovative perception."

The Mountain Image

As in earlier literary circles, the sages well recognized the topography of Jerusalem as a city nestling among hills and frequently alluded to this image in their prose. When a rabbinic commentator states, "The Temple is called possession," supporting his assertion with a verse from Psalms (78:54), "The mountain [*har*] His right hand had acquired," he reveals his regard for the place as a *har*.[69] The same outlook fuels a midrash on the verse, "Bless the Lord your God for the good land" (Deuteronomy 8:10), which claims that "the good" refers to Jerusalem and then associates with this clearly non literal interpretation the verse "this good mountain [*har*]" (Deuteronomy 3:25).[70] The very possibility of performing such exegetical maneuvers points to the position of Jerusalem in the rabbinic mind-set as situated in a hilly setting. A passage in the Targum (Aramaic translation of the Bible) attributed to Jonathan on the same verse in Deuteronomy expresses the same notion when it construes it as, "That good hill on which is built the city of Jerusalem,"[71] as does an extract from *Sifre to Deuteronomy*, which puts it simply, "Everyone called it a *har*."[72] Whether such scenery came to the rabbis from biblical verses that depict this landscape or from firsthand encounter is of no concern to this study.

But it is important to note that such literary passages relate to the mountain as a neutral topographical elevation with neither a special name nor a particular location. In this regard they follow Second Temple representations, especially Josephus's, who spoke of Jerusalem and the Temple as being situated on a hill, mostly without endowing this physical fact with any conceptual significance (see chapter 1). These and similar examples demonstrate an acquaintance with the topography of Jerusalem and its surroundings but fall short of alluding to an entity called "Temple Mount" or any of the ideas associated with this image. This, however, is not the case in all sources.

Here is one example from the legal discussions concerning a certain aspect of pilgrimage. To prescribe the celebration of the three major pilgrim festivals—Passover, Shavuᶜot (the holiday of Weeks or Pentecost), and Sukkot

(Booths-Tabernacles)—the Bible uses the term "appearing" (*re'iyah*). One is charged to appear in the chosen place: "Three times a year all your males shall *appear* before the Lord your God at the place that he will choose" (Deuteronomy 16:16; Exodus 23:17). What is that place? In the context of recording a Tannaitic dispute about the obligation of a minor to embark on a pilgrimage journey, the Mishnah outlines the route that visitors take when approaching the Temple. It describes the final portion of this itinerary as "going up from Jerusalem to the Temple Mount."[73] Quite clearly, this constitutes an imaginary schematization of Jerusalem's topography; people climb to the Temple Mount only when approaching the Temple from the so-called Lower City of Jerusalem (also known as the city of David). Anyone who has ever stood in the section of town known as the Upper City (the so-called southwestern hill, which now occupies the area between the Tower of David and Jaffa Gate, on one side, and the Jewish Quarter, on the other; see map 1) would recognize that it is higher than the Temple area. And so, reaching the Temple from the Upper City in the days of the Temple would have necessitated descending rather than ascending. The same holds true for the northern neighborhoods of Jerusalem. It would thus seem that the use of the term "mountain" and the application of the verb "going up" in the preceding Mishnaic formula accentuated an already existing image of a high place for the Temple that does not necessarily correspond with the actual terrain of the city. Such a fantastic topography of Jerusalem and its sanctuary could be traced back to early texts such as the *Letter of Aristeas,* which depicts Jerusalem's landscape as a high mountain with the Temple on its top. The roots of this picture lay in the concept of the cosmic mountain that various First and Second Temple authors bestowed upon Jerusalem and the Temple (see chapter 1).

But in addition to the fanciful topography, the preceding Mishnah on the pilgrimage route provides an inaccurate picture of Tannaitic halakha. According to its formula, in order to fulfill the biblical precept to appear, which, as mentioned, was the foremost manifestation of pilgrimage, one needs to arrive merely at the Temple Mount.[74] But as Halivni already pointed out, appearing at the Temple Mount (map 3: D) did not satisfy the obligation of pilgrimage according to rabbinic halakha. The very essence of pilgrimage ritual was fulfilled only when the individual entered the inner court of the Temple (the *ʿazarah;* map 3: B), where the first stages of the sacrificial process (known as the burnt offering of appearing—*ʿolat re'iyah*) took place. One of the Amoraim, R. Bun b. R. Ḥiyya, already recognized the halakhic inconsistency implied by this

Mishnah, as if the injunction to appear could be achieved by arriving at the Temple Mount. He therefore questioned, "Where did they show their face [fulfill the injunction to appear]—in the Temple Mount or in the inner Temple courts?" The expected answer bounced back: "In the inner Temple court they [were required] to show their face [fulfill the injunction to appear]."[75]

If so, why did the Mishnah present the Temple Mount as the final destination on the pilgrimage route? Recall that Halivni claims that this Mishnah reflects an early situation in which the appellation "Temple Mount" was synonymous with "the Temple." In his view, when the Tannaim spoke of "the Temple Mount," they actually meant "the Temple." I accept the essence of this solution but reverse the time frame he suggests. In my opinion, it is not an earlier lexicon that reverberates in the Mishnah but rather a later one. According to this reconstruction, the initial version of the halakha presented the inner court of the Temple—the *ʿazarah*—or the Temple itself as the final destination for accomplishing the biblical command to appear. Echoes of such an early form of the halakha can be found in other sources that instruct about pilgrimage. A midrashic segment preserved in the Tosefta about the biblical directive, "You shall go there and you shall bring there [your burnt offerings and other sacrifices]" (Deuteronomy 12:5–6), reads, "Those that are fit to enter the inner court [*ʿazarah*]."[76] It shows the mind of its author to be set on the Temple and its inner courts rather than the Temple Mount. A passage in the *Mekhilta* articulates a similar inclination when it discusses the same pilgrimage halakhot as in the Mishnah (but this time in the literary mode of halakhic midrashim), but never mentions the Temple Mount.[77]

It seems to me that the writer (or the oral producer) of the halakha in the Mishnah under discussion rephrased the topographic designation according to what was accepted in his day, from Temple or inner court to Temple Mount. In his mind the Temple Mount functions as a legitimate representation of everything associated with the Temple. Especially so in this case, since the word *har*, "mountain," fit the content of the issue at hand, which deals with the arduous conditions involved in the pilgrimage (literally, "going up for the festival") of a minor child. What could be more strenuous for a child than to climb a mountain? By making this substitution, the author misrepresented both the topographical texture of the site and the halakhic provisions regarding the injunction to appear. At the same time, he also reveals to us how the place is registered in his mind.

Many other examples illustrate the same process. A similar paradigm lies be-

hind the famous legend cited earlier about the rain that fell on Jerusalem in response to Ḥoni the circle drawer's prayer. According to the version in the Mishnah, when the heavy rain became unbearable, "they went up" (according to the
good textual witnesses) to the Temple Mount. Here too, the Tannaim endorse
the mythic figure of the Temple Mount as a high place, as well as the literary
model in which people climb from Jerusalem to the Mount.[78]

These minute details of halakha, biblical hermeneutics, and legendary narrative accumulate to form a new sacred figure—the Temple Mount. The rabbis meticulously inscribe it into the spatial organization of ancient Jerusalem;
they mold it to be part of the Temple and dress it in the customs, vocabulary,
and traditions of their ancestral holy place. But if I am right in my analysis, this
entity prevailed only in their time, functioning in their consciousness and literature. The destruction of 70 CE stripped the Temple from its glory, leaving
its compound orphaned and desolate. In the following generations, rabbinic
literature imbued the ruined site of the Temple with a new life. Resuscitating
its image with Second Temple oxygen, the rabbis endowed the place with an
ancient biblical name taken from the works of the prophet Micah (see the introduction), and configured its shape as a holy, towering mountain. The Temple Mount therefore should be seen in this context as a sacred space in the landscape of memory. The following sections follow the rabbis in their innovative
process.

Conceiving a Sacred Image; Ideating the Mount

More than any other source, *Mishnah Tractate Middot* formulated the Temple Mount's conceptual shape for future generations and established its image
as an inseparable constituent of Second Temple Jewish experience. Time and
again it focuses the reader's attention on this space, defining its dimensions and
boundaries, listing its gates, detailing its customs, and stationing its guards. Its
descriptions lend more than just graphical flavor, as if invoking their addressees
to shut their eyes and envisage the Mount in their minds. Consider the following passage:

> The Temple Mount measured five hundred cubits by five hundred cubits. The
> largest [open] space was to the south, the next largest to the east, and the third
> largest to the north, and its smallest [open] space was to the west. The place where
> its measure was greatest was where its use was greatest.[79]

The precise measurements inscribe a perceivable, tangible unit. Next, the reader embarks on a panoramic tour of the grounds. The Mishnah stipulates the proper rules for entering and behaving in this area: "Everyone entering the Temple Mount enters from the right and circles [the compound] and exits on the left." It goes on to specify who the exceptions are (mourners and the excommunicated), and it even regulates how people engage these individuals, laying down a set of formulae for inquiring as to their welfare and wishing them relief from their sorrow. Elsewhere in the same tractate, the text enumerates five gates that were on the Temple Mount and details the protocol for its guards—the Levite sentinels who were stationed at the gates and at other places around the Temple Mount, as well as the "Temple Mount man" who was in charge of them.[80] The outcome of this literary discourse is a tangible image, which is seemingly remembered from earlier times—a physical structure named the Temple Mount that the Mishnah weaves into Second Temple landscape.

But Tannaitic literature takes its audience far beyond the physical dimension of the place. The sages consider the Temple Mount not only a piece of land but hallowed grounds—a sacred space. Expressing this notion is one of the most famous sources, often mentioned to support scholarly opinion about the dominant status of the Temple Mount in the worldview of Second Temple Jews. Although I think its association with the earlier periods is unfounded, it can nevertheless tell us much about the rabbis and their association with the space of the Temple Mount. An excerpt in *Mishnah tractate Kelim*, seemingly communicating Second Temple notions, enumerates ten gradations of holiness and features the Temple Mount as a centerpiece of this hierarchy. "The Temple Mount is still more holy [than the city of Jerusalem]. For no man or woman that has a flux, no menstruant, and no woman after childbirth may enter there." A second, more condensed, three-tiered ladder of the sacred realm also appears in rabbinic texts. This classification equates the topography of Second Temple Jerusalem with the three camps of the wandering Israelites in the Sinai desert—priestly, Levite, and Israelite. The Temple Mount serves as a key factor in this list as well: "From the entrance to Jerusalem till the Temple Mount is [considered] the Israelite Camp; from the entrance to the Temple Mount till the inner Temple court is [considered] the Levite Camp."[81]

It is only natural that these texts drew most of the attention of scholars who investigated the Temple Mount. Archaeologists and historians as well as other people, mainly contemporary rabbis committed to disentangling matters of practical halakha, spared no effort in trying to locate the exact site of the 500-by-500-cubit square mentioned in *Mishnah Middot*. The main obstacle for these inquiries lies in the fact that the compound encircled by the wall that is visible today, and that everyone agrees corresponds by and large with the work of King Herod (see chapter 1), does not fit the dimensions of the Temple Mount as delimited by the Mishnah. The varied creative ideas proposed for reconciling this discrepancy, and the perplexing geometric shapes that were drawn in an effort to locate the square, 500-by-500 "Temple Mount" of the Mishnah within the existing trapezoidal Herodian enclosure, deserve a study of their own. The common view among modern scholars interprets the Mishnaic measurements as belonging to what scholars call the "early Temple Mount, " from before the time of Herod's endeavor, and it is therefore customary to label them as marking the "Hasmonaean Temple Mount." As for why the sages should have preserved the dimensions of a place that had become insignificant even when the Temple still existed since Herod had built a much larger enclosure, the prevalent answer surmises that even in Herod's time the early sacred zone continued to play an important role in the halakhic system that served the Temple.[82]

It seems to me that these conjectures should be rejected for a number of reasons. First, the schematic nature of the formula "five hundred cubits by five hundred cubits" ought to arouse doubt in the mind of anyone trying to apply it to a particular historical moment. Second, several considerations call attention to the unrealistic disposition of these figures. The exact correlation with the dimensions in Ezekiel's vision provides one example. Prophesying the ideal Temple of the future, Ezekiel exclaims, "He measured it on four sides. It had a wall around it, five hundred cubits long and five hundred cubits wide, to separate between the holy and the non-holy."[83] A second example is the use by the author of the Qumranic *Temple Scroll* of these same numbers for his utopian "middle court" of the Temple.[84] Reverberations of a mythic square surrounding the Temple may also be found in Josephus's description of Solomon's Temple, in which he portrays the court as "in the form of a quadrangle."[85] Schematic dimensions betray a lack of reality.

Third, the sources already discussed in this chapter make it plain that rabbinic literature too is ignorant of these dimensions. When the sages relate to the Temple Mount, they always presume a Temple compound whose boundaries were the walls surrounding the enclosure, not some other 500-by-500-cubit square within this enclosure. Take, for example, the story of R. ʿAkiva and the other sages who visited the Temple Mount and saw a fox coming out of the Holy of Holies (quoted in full in the introduction): the narrator does not hint that the sages were sojourning at a 500-by-500-cubit square within the larger complex; the story simply says that they entered the ruined compound which he calls Temple Mount. Or consider the tradition (quoted earlier in this chapter) about the sages who left their sandals under the *'agof* of the Temple Mount; is it conceivable that in the mind of the narrator some kind of an entrance stood in the middle of the ruined area, at some imagined 500-cubit line? The same applies to all the many passages cited previously, in which it is clear that the appellation "Temple Mount " signifies the entire enclosure surrounding the place where the Temple had been; people approach it, entering and exiting its gates, and colonnades embellish its encircling walls. None of these texts (and many others) hint at any 500-by-500-cubit square in the middle of this compound. The suggestion that a certain space called "the Temple Mount" operated within the Herodian complex and that only later on was this name extended to include the full area bounded by the walls is hermeneutic hairsplitting intended only to reconcile the words of the Mishnah with the obvious reality that does not match it. It cannot withstand criticism.

I claim that a 500-by-500-cubit square called "the Temple Mount" never really existed. Only after the designation "Temple Mount" was fashioned and began to play a significant role in the worldview of the Tannaim was it necessary to demarcate its space in exact measurements, especially since the rabbis wished to present it in tractate *Middot,* which devotes much attention to dimensional and spatial organization and was designed to depict the ruined Temple and features associated with it. At this point, the sages turned to the representation of the ideal Temple in Ezekiel, borrowing from it the numerical figures for the Temple Mount's size. In other words, the biblical, mythic dimensions set down for this space were purely imaginary. The outcomes of these maneuvers were far-reaching; the rabbis established here a new (imaginary) sacred space—they gave birth to the conceptual space of the Temple Mount.

It is precisely the second part of *Mishnah Middot* cited earlier that scales the level of activity in the various sectors of the Mount according to their size— "The largest [open] space was to the south, the next largest to the east, and the third largest to the north, and its smallest [open] space was to the west; the place where its measure was greatest was where its use was greatest"—that evinces some of the real asymmetries of Herod's enclosure. This genuine layout was then squeezed into Ezekiel's schematic dimensions, resulting in two disparate landscapes that do not necessarily overlap, the area of the Herodian compound and the invented image of the sacred space of the Temple Mount.

Imaginary Landscapes, Taxonomy, and Epistemology

In light of this reconstruction, other facets about the Temple Mount in *Mishnah Middot* deserve reexamination as well. One such feature is "the officer [the Hebrew *'ish*] of the Temple Mount," who "used to track every watch" and oversee its performance. This clearly portrays a security position, responsible for the safekeeping of the sanctuary. The question is, however, whether rabbinic sources preserve the original title for this vocation. Second Temple sources speak of various posts with responsibilities similar to those of the Mishnah's "officer." 2 Maccabees, for example, assigns one Simeon "from the tribe of Benjamin" the position *prostatēs* of the Temple, a Greek title very close in meaning to "officer" or "guardian." Although the book does not spell out the extent of his authority, he is ranked high enough to challenge the high priest.[86] In the same vein, Josephus introduces the *stratēgos*, explicitly reporting that the Temple guards (the *phylakes*) were subordinate to him.[87] The book of Acts also mentions this same position twice, unequivocally referring to it as the *stratēgos* of the Temple.[88]

Rabbinic literature adds to the list of officials who are potentially associated with guarding the Temple.[89] Some of the rabbinic epithets may well have been the Hebrew equivalent of the Greek titles. One example involves the "officer [*'ish*] of the *birah*." Mentioned rather obscurely in *Mishnah tractate 'Orlah*, it brings to mind a similar title in the book of Nehemiah, from the early Second Temple period—"the commander [*sar*] of the *birah*."[90] As recognized by previous scholarship (see n. 60), the *birah* clearly embodies military characteristics—sort of a stronghold or a fort contiguous to the Temple complex—and so it would be appropriate for the "officer of the *birah*" to oversee the picket of the Temple enclosure. Even if the *birah*, at least in the later Second Temple period, may be identified with the Antonia fortress, known to house a Roman garrison, it is still plausible for the Jewish officer responsible for maintaining order at the Temple compound to be identified with it. A second candidate for correlation with the Greek *stratēgos* may be the hero of the legend related earlier about Alexander the Great's visit to the Temple. The story's hero, Gabiah, who encountered the king upon his arrival and made sure his entrance would conform to rabbinic regulations, is said, according to one version, to hold the office of "guardian [*shomer*] of the house."[91]

On the basis of these sources I contend that the title "officer of the Temple Mount" in *Mishnah Middot* mirrors a later formulation for one of the positions that prevailed early in the Second Temple period. Linguistically, the shift from "guardian of the Temple" to "guardian of the Temple Mount," or from "officer of the *birah*" to "officer of the Temple Mount," is not radical. Conceptually, however, it represents the transmutation of post–Second Temple public memory. The same holds true with regard to the holiness of the Temple Mount. On a literary basis, we should note that the extract in *Mishnah Kelim* introduces a list consisting of ten gradations yet actually records eleven—a problem noticed and endlessly debated by scholars throughout the centuries.[92] Such an inconsistency tempts me to speculate that the Temple Mount is the eleventh item, which was added to the hierarchy of holiness only at a later stage. A more substantial argument against the authenticity of the Temple Mount in the hierarchy list stems from content and comparative considerations. Structuring the realm of holiness in hierarchal terms, focusing on Jerusalem and the Temple, patterns on an ancient model: its roots are anchored in the prophecies of Ezekiel, and it can be traced to many Second Temple sources, especially the Qumranic *Temple Scroll*.[93] A comparison of the names bestowed by the various sources upon the places associated with the degrees of holiness reveals, however, important differences. All documents attest to certain restrictions that applied to the populace beyond the limited space of the Temple, excluding people with insufficient ritual purity from the vicinity of the sanctuary so they cannot defile the sacred. But as I show in chapter 1, Josephus, the *Temple Scroll*, and other sources of the Second Temple period refer to the precinct surrounding the Temple edifice as part of the Temple complex itself; it did not have a special name or a different status from other parts of the compound. When Josephus, for example, lists the names of the places that certain people were forbidden to enter, he asserts that people suffering from venereal diseases were excluded from the entire city of Jerusalem, and menstruating women were not allowed to enter the Temple. Josephus does not mention any intermediate entity between Jerusalem and the Temple. This sharply contrasts the Mishnah, which deems it illicit for people with these two impurities from entering the Temple Mount. Thus, although the area might be physically the same, it is registered in the mind of the authors rather distinctively. Josephus perceives it as the Temple enclosure, part and parcel of the Temple, while the Mishnah sees it as the "Temple Mount."

The transition from an external "innocent" area surrounding the Temple in

Josephus's writings, which, important as it might be, had no name of its own or special halakhot, to a separate unit with an independent title, unique laws, and customs of its own in the Mishnah marks the turning point at which the Temple Mount came into being as an independent category in the worldview of the rabbis. According to this analysis, the Mishnah's authors innovatively changed the name of the area around the Temple and in doing so crafted a totally different conceptual view of its space.

The sources discussed thus far are neither of the same type nor uniform in their conclusions. Some articulate legal pronouncements and accordingly present their content in definite terms, while others stemming from the hermeneutical practice known as midrash preserve the dissonant yet vibrant atmosphere of disputing intellectuals. Several sources convey traditions about customs; others communicate memories; a third group depicts topographic and architectural details from the monumental to the diminutive, not to mention the purely fantastic. Other cases involve haggadic (i.e., nonlegal) material, whether interpretations of difficult biblical verses or legends relating fictitious stories. The chronological spectrum of the material ranges quite broadly as well. Some date to the Tannaitic period, others to the days of the Amoraim, and some to as late as the medieval commentators.

Despite their generic diversity, I have tried to show that these texts partake in the same epistemological development, which may be discussed in both literary and conceptual terms. From the perspective of textual criticism, the documents examined in this chapter exhibit a process by which their authors added a later designation—the Temple Mount—to early material. At times, these emendations are plain to see, with conspicuous differences distinguishing earlier versions lacking the Temple Mount from later versions including it. In other cases, however, the process has left only faint traces, with primitive readings concealed beneath more mature and elaborated formulations. In these instances considerable research is required to reveal the early phases of the literary process. At times, it must be admitted, the early version may not be altogether recoverable, and one can only hypothesize about its existence.

But the essence of the phenomenon explicated in this chapter involves more than terminological developments. Philological changes are linked here to conceptual evolution. As mentioned before, by conceiving the name "Temple Mount," shaping it as a sacred space, and then projecting it backward to describe the earlier period, the sages redrew the bounds of Second Temple landscape. Consequently, they have ushered in a new infrastructure for their shared memory. The many passages in rabbinic literature that refer to the Temple Mount lend the impression that this spatial entity was a central component of Second Temple consciousness and experience. But this impression is only ostensibly true. It was only part of the rabbis' perception of Second Temple times.

All in all, the evidence presented so far suggests that the "Temple Mount" is not an ancient term stemming from, and representing, the worldview of Second Temple Judaism but a mostly unused phrase (although with ancient biblical roots that surfaced sporadically) that the Tannaim, followed by the Amoraim, applied to the old landscape of the ruined Temple area, thus reshaping how it was remembered and crafting for it a fresh image. The preceding discussion sets to reveal this process and locate places where traces of the older conceptuality still resonate.

It is worth reiterating that this phenomenon has to do with the term and the cluster of images and notions associated with it rather than the events described in the sources. That is, even if the comings and goings related in rabbinic literature as happening in Second Temple times actually occurred (just as they might be purely fiction), the sources need not also have preserved the vocabulary used by the people of the Second Temple to describe these events and the places in which they took place. The heart of the issue here is whether rabbinic literature faithfully reflects the consciousness of previous eras. I have suggested answering this question in the negative.

Finally, this process of shifting imagery was by no means an all-encompassing reform. Obviously, no guiding hand supervised the penetration of the phrase and image "Temple Mount" into traditions produced and transmitted by the rabbis about the Second Temple period. On the contrary, many rabbinic passages follow earlier paradigms, which preceded the imagery, symbolism, and language of the Temple Mount and remain congruent with Second Temple writings. Examples of these earlier layers are presented throughout my discussion in this chapter, which argues that, in later stages of transmission, rabbinic traditions substituted the new term "Temple Mount" for expressions describing the area during the Second Temple period, such as "Temple" or "inner Temple court." The early formulations, in which the "Temple Mount" does not appear, reflect the consciousness and terminology of the Second Temple era.

But the story of the Temple Mount in rabbinic literature goes a step further. Not only did the rabbis craft a new image of a holy mountain and implant it in the memories of the glorious past of their nation, but they have also used this image to redefine their sacred landscape, thus instilling the religious experience that defined their lives as Jews with new substance. The following discussion explores this aspect of the Temple Mount story.

The Individualization of the Temple Mount

Many rabbinic texts present the Temple Mount as an independent element, distinguished from both the Temple and the city of Jerusalem. To be sure, the Temple towers in the background—as part of the name (the Temple Mount; *har ha-bayit*) as well as the ultimate goal in some accounts and the decisive purpose in others. For example, in the halakhot laying out the itinerary for the bringing of firstfruits or the route for transporting the pure water for burning the red heifer, discussed earlier in the chapter, the mountain rests beside the Temple, which is both the final destination and the objective behind the whole venture.

But even in cases of this sort, the two are clearly distinguished, with the mountain presented as an area adjacent to but separate from the Temple. This is evident, for example, in the halakhot prescribing the obligation of pilgrims to "appear" at the Temple Mount rather than at the Temple itself (n. 73). In this source the independence of the Temple Mount strikes a clear tone because the Temple is no longer to be found, so the Temple Mount cannot be subordinate to it. Other sources adhere to similar patterns. Consider, for example, the halakha regulating the procedures for treating misplaced coins found on the Temple Mount (see n. 32). The measures in that passage pertain to both Jerusalem and the Temple Mount with no sign of the Temple. Clearly the Temple provides the immediate context, because the incident adduced by the halakha—bringing second tithe money to Jerusalem (and then losing it)—would not have come about in the first place but for the decree that this offering had to be eaten in the vicinity of the Temple. Nevertheless, although implied by the context, the Temple lacks any concrete role in the literary piece itself. The passage endows the space called "Temple Mount" with a life of its own and provides it with its own halakhot, without any explicit relation to the Temple.

The same phenomenon can also be discerned in the stories about Rabban Gamaliel that are said to take place on the Temple Mount and do not disclose any sort of connection with the Temple (nn. 34–36) or in the traditions about a synagogue and a study house located there (n. 38). In the same vein are halakhot such as the prohibition against planting trees in that enclosure or the ruling against using stones for construction on the Temple Mount if they had been prepared for another purpose.[94] All of these sources feature the independence of the Temple Mount; they maintain no direct connection with the Temple, nor do they make any reference to its existence.

This stand-alone status of the Temple Mount epitomizes an essential difference between rabbinic consciousness and that of Second Temple times. Not only are there no hints of the name "Temple Mount" in the period when the Temple was up and running (as shown in chapters 1 and 2), but Second Temple writers always present the various components of the sanctuary as subordinate to the Temple itself. As I showed in the extended discussion of Second Temple sources, Jerusalem and the Temple monopolized the entire conceptual gamut, leaving no room for anything else between them. Strikingly different is the stance voiced in rabbinic material, where many times Jerusalem and the Temple disappear altogether and the Temple Mount functions independently; or at other times these traditions link the Temple Mount directly to the city of Jerusalem, with the Temple being practically ignored. Such trends could not be dismissed as a mere literary nuance; revealed here is a change in the way people engaged the landscape of their sacred places.

Replacing the Temple

The rabbinic notion of the Temple Mount involves a rather complex relationship with the Temple. In many texts, the Mount functions not just as a plot of land that happens to be next to the Temple and inferior in status but as an independent structure that occasionally even supersedes the Temple. At some point, the rabbis rephrased the ancient halakha that had directed all prayer toward the Temple and the Holy of Holies, and shifted the focus from the Temple to the Mount; the Palestinian Talmud termed it "the mount to which all mouths pray" (see nn. 57–59).

A similar amendment affected the rules prescribing the proper "reverence for the Temple," which over time were modified into "reverence for the Temple Mount."[95] Dissociating the procedures of reverence from the Temple, this source treats the Mount as if it were a sacred site for its own sake. The same views seem to be at work when the sages apply the ruling "utensils that were originally made for [the use of] an ordinary person cannot be converted to [the usage of] the High" to the previously mentioned decree, "stones and beams which one originally quarried [and hewed] for a synagogue should not be used for building on the Temple Mount." Normally one would read "the High" (*gavoha*) as the common, almost technical term for the Temple, yet here, surprisingly and very much unnoticed, the halakha directs it to the Temple Mount instead. Striking the same chord, the rabbis denounced a person negligent about pilgrimage rites as sinning against the Temple Mount rather than, as seems expected, the Temple itself: "And when you do not celebrate [the three pilgrimage festivals] properly, I consider it as if you unlawfully used [*me'ilah*] the Temple Mount and the [Temple] inner courts."[96]

Along the same lines, other anomalous halakhot also fall into place. One such example involves the proscription, rendered by *Midrash Tanḥuma-Yelamdenu,* forbidding priests to leave the Temple Mount dressed in their priestly attire and inadvertently allowing them to wear their hallowed vestments while in the Temple compound.[97] No early source on the distribution of the sacrosanct wardrobe and the various limitations associated with it contains a halakha of this sort, as they all focus on the Temple itself. Thus, for example, in relation to the biblical laws of *Kil'ayim* (the prohibitions against mixing certain "different kinds," in this case fabrics), the Tosefta stipulates that "garments of the high priest—he who goes out [while dressed] in them to the provinces [i.e., outside the Temple] is liable, but [he who wears them] in the Temple, whether [he does so] to serve or not to serve is exempt [from liability] because they [the garments] are for the Temple service."[98] And the same holds true in the Yerushalmi's assertion that "The [consent] for temporary wearing of *Kil'ayim* [does not take form] in the Temple."[99] Indeed, given the wide range of "secular" activities that took place in the large enclosure around the Temple, it does not make sense to allow holy garments to come in contact with the mundane nature of the area. Apparently, as in all other cases discussed previously, here too the original version, although not preserved in any of our sources, forbade priests to leave the Temple in these clothes. In the rephrasing of these guidelines the author of the *Tanḥuma-Yelamdenu* passage replaced the Temple with the Temple Mount, thus raising it to the status of the Temple. More important, by doing so he rearranged the conceptual mapping of Jerusalem's sacred grounds.

Haggadic sources express this same phenomenon when their authors dismiss the Temple and introduce the Temple Mount. Legends produced by the sages allow this change quite decisively. The tale cited earlier about the three hundred sacrifices brought by Baba b. Buta, provides a typical example of this process in which the rabbis shifted the destination of the animals from the "inner Temple court" to the "Temple Mount." An equally emblematic example occurs in a story in *Genesis Rabbah* about a certain Joseph Meshitha "when enemies desired to enter the Temple Mount. They said: 'Let one of them [the Jews] enter first.' . . . So he went in and took out a golden lamp [the candelabrum?]."[100] The plot in this brief fable centers on the verbs "entered" and "left," which are used no fewer than five times in such a short passage. The story explicitly names the place being entered as the Temple Mount, yet when Yosi leaves the site, he carries out an object that clearly belongs to the Temple—the candelabrum. Even if the author assumed basic knowledge of the site's layout, in which the Temple rests on the Temple Mount, one cannot ignore the fact that the narrative fails to provide this detail and that the literal meaning of the tale situates the holy vessels on the Temple Mount itself. The Temple Mount had taken the place of the Temple in the perception of the storyteller who formulated this version of the legend.

The process by which the Temple Mount supersedes the Temple extends beyond halakhic and haggadic passages to excerpts pertaining to more spiritual issues as well. The passage cited in which the *tel* (hill) replaces the Temple as the place "toward which all mouths pray" clearly expresses such conceptual changes in the status of the Temple Mount. It is in this light that one must understand the better-known sources expounding the notion that God's divine presence (*shekhinah*) never left the locality of the Temple, even after its destruction. The Amoraic sages disputed over this issue: Samuel b. Naḥman opined that "until the destruction of the Temple the Divine Presence resided in the shrine [*Heikhal*] . . . and from the time of the destruction of the Temple he [the Lord] removed his Divine Presence to the heavens." R. Eleazar b. Pedat, however, argued, "Whether [the Temple is] destroyed or not destroyed, the Divine Presence does not move from its place." In support of his position he cited the verse, "I raise my voice unto the Lord, and he answers me from his holy mountain" (Psalms 3:5).[101] The rabbinic teaching, "even when destroyed it retains its holiness," comports well with this view, as does the well-known saying of R. Aḥa: "The Divine Presence shall never move from the western wall of the Temple."[102]

As many modern scholars have correctly pointed out, these sources are not referring to the present-day "Western Wall," which is not a direct component of the Temple building but belonged to the outside walls encircling the Temple Mount compound (see fig. 19).[103] The sages were concerned with the site of the

Fig. 19. The Western Wall of the Temple Mount compound, also known in Jewish tra-
dition as the "Wailing" Wall, and held as a sacred remnant of the Temple. From Duby
Tal and Moni Haramati, *Kav ha-Ofek* (Jerusalem: Ministry of Defence Publishing
House, 1993). With permission from Albatross.

Temple itself, maintaining that the holiness of that space did not depend on the
existence of the Temple. It is fair to say that such ideas laid the foundation for
the rise of the Temple Mount image as a sacred space in post–Second Temple
Judaism.

'Even ha-shetiyah (the Foundation Stone) and the New Mount Moriah

The central example demonstrating the configuration of the Temple Mount
as an independent holy space has to do with the increased attention given by
the rabbis to the so-called Foundation Stone. Rabbinic literature first mentions
this feature in a segment in *Mishnah tractate Yoma* that describes the high priest
entering the Holy of Holies: "After the Ark was taken away, a stone was there

from the days of the early Prophets, called 'foundation' [*shetiyah*], three fingers above the ground, and upon it he [the high priest] would put [the incense fire pan]."[104] The Tosefta recounts the tradition about the stone nearly verbatim, but its conclusion includes a passage absent from the Mishnah: R. Yose interprets the name "foundation stone," claiming that "from it the world was founded."[105] Many modern scholars identify R. Yose's statement as a manifestation of the ancient idea about the Omphalos—the "navel of the earth" (discussed in chapter 1). Meant to elevate a certain space or site and glorify its centrality, this conceptual paradigm can be found, in different forms, in ancient Semitic and Greek cultures. As such, it was also adopted by some Second Temple Jewish writers, such as the author of the *Letter of Aristeas,* Josephus, and perhaps even earlier in the book of Ezekiel.[106] Indeed, considerable similarities link the two notions—the navel of the earth and the foundation stone. Focusing, however, on this comparative aspect of R. Yose's statement has apparently inhibited scholars from appreciating its uniqueness, and from distinguishing between his remark and other Jewish models of spatial centrality that preceded it. Unlike R. Yose, the *Letter of Aristeas* and Josephus unequivocally associate the Omphalos with the man-made city of Jerusalem and the Temple, describing them as being located at the center of the earth. These Second Temple authors articulated their ideas within the framework and terminology of ancient Near Eastern and Hellenistic discourse about the Omphalos, either by defining a particular element in Jerusalem as being the Omphalos or by locating the city itself at the center of the universe. R. Yose, on the other hand, underscores the natural quality of a stone whose presence at the site predates the establishment of any mundane structures. He crafted a shrewd explication playing on the ancient name of the stone by taking the noun *shetiyah* (foundation) and changing it into the verb *shatat* (to found or create). He mentions neither "navel" nor "center" nor is there explicit reference to the city and the Temple, but only that the stone sits where the world was created.

Admittedly, in the ancient period all these expressions belonged to the same family of ideas, and many defined the Omphalos as both the center of the world and the place of the creation. Nevertheless, one cannot ignore the fact that R. Yose created a different terminological and ideological gamut. To stretch this argument a bit, the perception of the Temple as Omphalos and as center of the earth was widespread in Jewish circles, and R. Yose was therefore probably familiar with it. Why, then, did he decide not to name the concept explicitly by either using the terms "Omphalos" or "naval" or by referring to one of the elements that had been tied to it in the past (Jerusalem and the Temple)? Sometimes omissions can be as significant as inclusions.

Although the silence of the source does not provide firm ground to reconstruct R. Yose's stance, his interpretation quite evidently emphasizes a new element: the foundation stone, which does not appear in any of the previous works. Significantly, the two presentations of the stone, in the Mishnah and in R. Yose's formulation in the Tosefta, are essentially different.[107] The Mishnah portrays it as an ancient rock whose name simply derives from the fact that it served as the foundation on which the Ark of the Covenant stood in the Holy of Holies until right before the destruction of the First Temple. Although such a formulation grants the stone certain significance—after all, the Ark was placed on it—it nevertheless measures the stone's importance within the framework of the Temple and the hierarchy of its articles. In contrast, R. Yose's formulation removes the stone from its Temple setting and grants it a value in and of itself, calibrating it in relation to the entire universe. To him, this is the most important stone in the world.

This transition from the "Temple" stone of the Mishnaic tradition and the Temple-city domination of the Omphalos image in Second Temple writings to the "cosmic" stone in Rabbi Yose's presentation develops along the same conceptual contours discussed already. The Temple's territory—and, in this case, a natural, physical element that occupied the area, a stone—replaces the actual edifice of the Temple. The foundation stone endows the space of the Temple Mount with its own value.[108] Later on, the stone continued to play a central role in Christian imagery during the Byzantine era. The essence of the stone and the scope of ideas and tropes associated with it remained similar to its Jewish counterpart, but Christian writers relocated its actual spot to Golgotha, in the Church of the Holy Sepulcher. Early Muslim traditions embraced these notions as well but restored the stone to its original location.[109]

Other traditions reflect similar conceptual dynamics, focusing on the space on which the Temple had stood rather than the Temple itself and picturing it as a mountain, as well as shifting images and symbols originally linked with the Temple and reassociating them with the Temple Mount. For example, the notion of Mount Moriah—identified as the site of the ʿaqedah (Isaac's binding) and considered to be the place where the Temple had been built—was well known during the Second Temple period and even earlier (see chapter 1). Yet it was only Rabban Simeon b. Gamaliel, when discussing the dust from which Adam was created, who presented Mount Moriah as the source of this soil and described it as a place of "worship" and "atonement," two terms that had generally been reserved for the Temple itself.[110] The traces of a legend that Adam was buried under the foundation stone, discussed in chapter 2, should be seen in the same light. Similar to the creation of the universe in R. Yose's formulation about the foundation stone, both the commencement and the conclusion of Adam 's life are thus placed on Mount Moriah.

Another source, a tradition cited in the name of R. Simeon b. Yoḥai, recounts the process by which God elected the people of Israel: "The Holy one, blessed be he, considered all mountains [*harim*] and found no mountain on which the divine presence [*Shekhinah*] should dwell other than Mount Moriah. The Holy one, blessed be he, considered all towns and found no city in which the Temple should be built other than Jerusalem."[111] Although the text enumerates all three elements—Mount Moriah, Jerusalem, and the Temple (and later on the Land of Israel as well)—the two key factors that both frame the segment and lie at its nucleus are Mount Moriah and Jerusalem. It appears that this passage too endorses the new outlook that was taking shape as the Temple Mount gained import. A conceptual context of this sort sheds new light on the sages' intense preoccupation with the Temple Mount and Mount Moriah. The various interpretations of the name "Moriah" and the legends expanding on the biblical stories about events that allegedly occurred there even before the Temple was built—such as the binding of Isaac or the story of the purchase of the place from Araunah the Jebusite—are all connected, as I see it, with the ideological trend consolidating the independent status of the site.[112]

Practicing (on) the Mount: Customs and Liturgy

This discussion has so far focused on the consciousness of the Temple Mount and the ideas and symbolism that were derived from it. The place of the Mount in post–Second Temple Jewish experience, however, was not limited to such abstract terms. It had more practical dimensions as well, which were expressed in the era's liturgy. A liturgical system spells out many intangible, and at times elusive, concepts for day-to-day life by channeling them into rituals, prayers, and customs. Characterized by its decentralizing tendencies, Jewish liturgy of the post-destruction period took place within the dispersed localities of Jewish communities. Its prime institution was the synagogue, which left little room for the Temple Mount. The Mount did play an important part in rabbinic thought, historical memory, and conceptual landscape. Along the

same lines, the direction of Jewish prayer as formulated by the rabbis centered
on the Temple Mount, which obviously inscribed this site in the minds and
hearts of at least some people. Beyond that, however, no records survive of any
prayers referring to the Mount or ceremonies connected to it that were carried
out in the synagogue. The reasons for this absence seem quite natural and derive from the very thesis presented in this study. The Temple Mount achieved
a significant life of its own only when it was bereft of its place of worship, the
Temple. In the realm of day-to-day liturgy, the synagogue essentially filled the
vacuum that was created by the destruction,[113] leaving no need for a "Mount."

Predictably, then, the liturgy that did develop around the Temple Mount targeted those occasions when Jews were immediately confronted with the absence of their Temple—that is to say, on visits to the site of the ruined Temple
in Jerusalem. As described earlier, during the first centuries after the destruction a steady stream of Jews regularly frequented the demolished compound of
the Temple, interrupted only rarely by occasional local bans. These visitors
were not mere tourists in the modern sense of the word, and such excursions
took on a religious dimension that was accompanied by customs, prayers, and
liturgical rituals.

Various sources, discussed at the beginning of this chapter, clearly refer to
the practice of a Jewish liturgy at the place of the ruined Temple. The anonymous pilgrim from Bordeaux describes a ceremony that the Jews conducted
every year at the site next to what he calls the "Pierced Stone" (the foundation
stone?), in which they anointed the stone with oil. This clearly portrays a ritual practice, although its exact nature remains uncertain.[114] Four generations
later, the monk Barsauma similarly reports that the Jews came to celebrate the
Feast of Tabernacles on the grounds of the ruined Temple. Jerome's account of
the gathering of Jews on the Ninth of Av (the fast commemorating the destruction of both the First and Second Temples) to mourn the destruction also
testifies to Jewish rituals at the site.

Jewish sources also contain explicit liturgical information. Elaborating on
the motivation to travel to Jerusalem, the rabbis speak of the desire either to
fulfill the biblical requirement of pilgrimage or simply to come and pray. Ad-
ditionally, they detail some of the mourning customs that visitors observed at
the site, mainly the tearing of clothing and perhaps even fasting.[115]

These traditions, then, do indicate certain Jewish liturgical activities on the
Temple Mount, but the picture remains incomplete. Aside from the basic fact
that Jews indeed attended the ruined Temple Mount, performed some cere-

monies there, and observed certain customs of mourning (which seems to go without saying), we know little about what transpired there. What sort of gatherings did they have? How often did they occur? What was said there? Were prayers uttered? Did other customs aside from the act of mourning for the destruction of the Temple develop on the site as a result of these visits? The answers to these questions together with many of the liturgical details are wrapped in mystery.

Nevertheless, some rabbinic sources that mention the Temple Mount contain explicit evidence that the customs they render were observed, or at least were meant to be observed, in the period following the destruction of the Temple. Typical examples are the halakhot prescribing the proper reverence for the Temple Mount (see n. 94). The *Sifra* cites these rules to illustrate the dictum that "reverence for the Temple is for ever"; the context indicates that "forever" (*le'olam*) implies "even when the Temple is not in existence."[116] The same conclusion can be drawn from the closing line of the passage in *Deuteronomy Rabbah,* which states, "And you must not say that since the Temple has been destroyed he treats it [the Temple] in an unseemly way, but [rather the law is the same] if it is standing or destroyed."[117]

Such an understanding places this set of laws in the realm of post–Second Temple environment and presents them as a series of regulations whose purpose was to create a norm of respectful behavior at the site of the ruined Temple: it was illicit to enter the area with shoes on, with one's walking stick, with one's traveling bag and money belt; one must clean the dust off his feet before entering; and it is forbidden to spit there or to use the area as a shortcut. Evidence that these rulings were seen as potentially in effect, not to say actually carried out, in the period of the Mishnah and the Talmud can be found in the Amoraic tradition cited earlier, according to which the fourth-century scholar R. Pinḥas attests that he saw sages taking off their sandals and leaving them at the entrance to the Temple Mount.

The ban against using the Temple Mount as a shortcut concurs with my conclusions regarding the location of the site within the urban layout of the Roman colony Aelia Capitolina. As argued in chapter 3, the grounds of the Temple Mount remained outside the colony's municipal borders. Over time, as the population increased and the town expanded along its southern and northern sides, cutting across the Temple Mount would have considerably reduced the walking distance for anyone who traversed the city from south to the north or vice versa.

Another post-Temple custom may be reverberating in the legend about Gabiah, who persuaded Alexander the Great to take off his shoes before entering the Temple Mount (n. 91). The story mentions a certain type of footwear, *empilia* (felt shoes), that Alexander wore in place of the shoes he had taken off. It is worth considering, even without decisive evidence, whether this detail registers an actual practice that the Tannaim and the Amoraim implemented on the Mount.

It is possible that an artistic source also displays post-70 awareness of the laws prescribing the proper reverence for the Temple Mount. Two panels from the mosaic floor of the excavated synagogue in Sepphoris portray scenes associated with the binding of Isaac. One of the panels, although not well preserved, clearly depicts a ram tied to a tree, and two pairs of shoes, one large and one small, bunched underneath that tree. Zeev Weiss and Ehud Netzer, the archaeologists who excavated and studied the mosaic, rightly identify the shoes as belonging to Abraham and Isaac (fig. 20).[118] They interpret this artistic representation of the footwear, which has no parallel in the iconography of the binding of Isaac, in light of the general assertion that "any contact with a higher power necessitates the removal of shoes." Their evidence spans the biblical accounts of Moses and Joshua taking off their footwear at sacred sites all the way up to what was, and still is, conventional in Islam. As they see it, views such as those expressed in *Midrash Genesis Rabbah* that Abraham "saw a cloud enveloping the mountain" required the removal of one's shoes in this case as well.

It seems to me, however, that the conclusions of the present chapter allow for a slightly different reading of the mosaic. As mentioned, the rise in the status of the Temple Mount in the Roman-Byzantine period generated intense preoccupation with the biblical associations of the site. A central piece in this endeavor was the story of the binding of Isaac. Coinciding with this literary disposition, everyday visitors to the site of the ruined Temple adapted to removing their shoes. This custom originated before 70 CE but only within the confinements of the Temple itself, and after the destruction it was transferred to the Temple Mount. The collections of shoes awaiting their owners' return "under the *ʾagof*" (the doorway) or in other corners outside the Temple Mount created a visual effect that was very likely etched into popular lore, as in the case the Yerushalmi details about R. Pinḥas. It is therefore quite possible that the mosaic of the binding of Isaac at Sepphoris reflects this actual practice, and not only the symbolism stemming from the literary sphere, although admittedly the two are closely related.

Fig. 20. The binding of Isaac in a mosaic floor from the synagogue in Sepphoris dating to the Byzantine period. Note the two pairs of shoes at the bottom left of the right panel, a detail not mentioned in any of the biblical traditions of the story. Courtesy of the Sepphoris excavations, drawing by Penina Arad. Courtesy of Zeev Weiss.

Finally, liturgical activities of the sort described thus far are also attested in a fragment of prayer collections from Palestine discovered in the Cairo Geniza. The text reads:

> If you have the good fortune to go up to Jerusalem, when you look at it from Mount Scopus, if you are riding on a donkey step down, and if you are wearing shoes take them off, and rend your garments . . . and enter in mourning. When you arrive in the city make another tear [in your garments] for the Temple and for the nation of Israel. Then, say the following prayers: "'Exalt the Lord our God and prostrate yourselves at His footstool . . .' [Psalms 99:5]; 'Exalt the Lord our God and prostrate yourselves at His holy mountain . . .' [Psalms 99:9]; 'Come let us prostrate ourselves, kneeling down before the Lord . . .' [Psalms 95:6]; 'And the king will desire your beauty; he is your lord, prostrate yourself before him' [Psalms 45:12]; 'I prostrate towards Your holy Temple and give thanks to Your name' [Psalms 138:2]; 'We thank you, you are the Lord our God who has given us life and assisted us and given us the good fortune to come near your House which you have chosen from all the dwelling places of Jacob, which your eyes and your heart focus on when it is in ruins and when it is built up. Just as we have seen it

in its ruins, let us have the good fortune to see it built up. And give us a good portion . . . with the ones who bring sacrifices and first-fruit offerings to this mountain which your right hand has acquired, the Temple of the Lord which your hands have built. . . . And may You shake its dust off it and cleanse it of its impurities and fence it off from its breaches and restore it to its place of honor and its holiness and its built-up state, and then may you dwell in it as in the days of old, as it is written 'I will bring them to my sacred mountain' [Isaiah 56:7]." . . . And then, return and circle all the gates and all the corners, as it is written, "Walk about Zion, circle it; count its towers" [Psalms 48:13].[119]

Without making any firm commitment about the nature of this text or the time of its composition (which would require a separate study), it would seem that something of the liturgical order I have attempted to reconstruct here materializes in this passage as well. Through the clutter of details, excerpted biblical verses, and explicit or implicit references to rabbinic halakhot, a number of points stand out as directly relevant to the issue at hand. First, the concluding clause, "And then, return and circle all the gates and all the corners," suggests some sort of liturgical procession. Second, the author negotiates the mountain imagery by repeatedly choosing verses alluding to it. Third, the document explicitly lists two of the practices mentioned here—rending one's garments and removing one's shoes—although admittedly not in direct relation to the Temple Mount. Finally, prostrations are the common thread that crisscrosses the various quotations from Psalms, which might signal some actual behavior in this ceremonial context.

The Temple Mount and Jewish (Rabbinic) Experience after 70 CE

Lurking behind the appearances of the "Temple Mount" in rabbinic literature is an absorbing conceptual process that came to pass in Jewish circles during the generations following the destruction of the Temple. The sages revived the term "Temple Mount" whose roots lay in the primordial layers of Israelite biblical literature, and applied it to the now ruined compound of the Temple. Accompanied by a set of fresh notions and imagery, it gradually crystallized into a distinctive sacred space and acquired an important place in the worldview of the sages and, it would seem, that of other Jews as well. This innovative development led the rabbis to redesign their view of the present and at the same time remake their memory of the past.

How did the rabbis perceive the Temple Mount? First and foremost, they identified it as a concrete, earthly place. In contrast to the Temple and the city of Jerusalem, which in the sages' mind became only partly earthbound—thus the expressions "heavenly Jerusalem" or "heavenly Temple[120]—they did not attribute any ethereal characteristics to the Temple Mount. Rabbinic literature formulates the Mount's essence not as a spiritual notion floating in the upper regions of abstract thoughts but as a worldly, tangible entity that could be seen and visited. Thus, the rabbis regulated everyday encounters with this area through a set of practical, detailed rules. A new consciousness emerged around this experience. The Temple Mount supplanted the Temple in the conceptual framework of the time: vocabulary originally associated with the Temple was reassigned to the Temple Mount, halakhot that had been observed in the former were ascribed to the latter, and themes that had been part and parcel of the Temple repertoire were redefined as relating to the Temple Mount.

As I have stressed throughout this chapter, this was by no means an absolute transformation, with the notions about the Temple obliterated overnight from Jewish consciousness and totally replaced by the spatial conceptuality of the Temple Mount. The sanctuary in Jerusalem and the elements associated with it—its paraphernalia, sacrifices, and priests—did not evaporate from Jewish experience of the Roman and Byzantine periods but rather maintained great significance and continues to affect numerous facets of life. The argument here makes the case that, alongside these Temple-oriented features, a new factor had now come into being—the Temple Mount. The claim that the Temple Mount became an important entity in and of itself is not meant to imply that it was completely detached from its Temple foundations. It is implausible to think that people who visited or contemplated the Temple Mount were unaware that this was the place where the ruins of the Temple were to be found.

In a convoluted process, most of which is now obscured, the Mount inherited several of the Temple's characteristics and acquired a status of its own. It was a dialectical paradigm in which the new and the old both competed with and supplemented each other at the same time. The various formulations used by the rabbis to negotiate this complexity—in halakhot, customs, legends, and ideas—are detailed throughout this chapter. The outcome of this process was the reconfiguration of spatial organization in Jerusalem. By defining a new space, endowing it with the vocabulary and images of the past, the rabbis redesigned their landscape of the sacred. Previously, in Jewish experience of the Second Temple period; it was centered on the city-Temple pair, after the destruction it shifted to the Temple Mount.

Another aspect of the consolidation of the Temple Mount's image, and perhaps the most fascinating one, relates to its impact on shared Jewish memory. According to this cognitive model, people projected the new spatial model backward in time, reshaping their picture of the past. Inculcating a certain idea or image in the world of the present is often achieved by fixing its roots deep in the past. Applying this method, the sages of the Mishnah and the Talmud perceived their past in keeping with the concepts prevailing in their own time. Because the Temple Mount had become a prominent category in their experience, they also wove it into their historical memories, as if it had always existed. I devoted most of the investigative energy in this chapter to unveil this process.

My arguments here are also supported by the conclusions of chapter 1; indeed, the present chapter should be seen as accompanying that chapter, which dealt with Jewish experience of the Second Temple period. Comparing the great body of Second Temple literature with the rabbinic corpus bears out my claims about the Temple Mount even more fully. The nearly total absence of the "Temple Mount" from Second Temple writings, except for some faint traces toward the end of that period, stands in sharp contrast to the countless references to this feature in Tannaitic and Amoraic traditions, which are later than most if not all of Second Temple material.[121] The claim that the conceptuality of the Temple Mount came into being at a certain time between the production of these two bodies of literature can explain this discrepancy.

Who is behind this development? Who was the first person to apply the appellation "Temple Mount" to a concrete strip of land and mark by it the Temple enclosure? Who worked to introduce it into Jewish worldview and experience—into halakhic formulations, legends, and everyday speech? I have no answers to these questions. My inability to resolve such issues derives from the nature of conceptual dynamics, which can be identified only once an image is sufficiently consolidated, making the stages of its formulation hard to follow. Evidently, the process under discussion was already in full force during the time of the Tannaim, that is, during the second century CE. But rabbinic material in itself provides no terminus a quo for the process. As a result, this discussion suggests only a relative chronology for the evolution of the Temple Mount conceptuality in rabbinic literature, namely that it is not an ancient concept inherited from predecessors. It cannot, however, provide an absolute chronology, and consequently the question of who coined the expression remains unresolved.

It nevertheless seems feasible to identify one important element in the process, namely the source of the expression and the literary context that produced it. As mentioned already in the introduction, the phrase "Temple Mount" appears exactly once in the writings that came to form the Bible, in Micah's prophecy. Other biblical authors also make use of the image of the mountain in connection with Jerusalem and the Temple. The rabbis were well aware of such imagery, and it seems quite plausible to assume that this was the source from which they drew the name "Temple Mount." Striving to fill a vacuum in their suddenly crippling world, people frequently turn to their foundational writings, their ancient sacred texts, for both inspiration and terminology. I believe this is what happened in the case of the Temple Mount. I cannot say, however, why the specific expression "Temple Mount" was chosen rather than other biblical names with similar imagery, such as "Mount Zion" or "My Holy Mount."[122]

Finally, tracing the various stages in the evolution of the Temple Mount image also requires a consideration of the relations between the views attributed here to the sages and those of both other Jewish groups, for instance the early believers in Jesus or the followers of James his Brother, and non-Jews such as the Palestinian Christians from the third century on. It is clear that all frequented the site. But, in contrast to the writings of the church fathers, for example, rabbinic literature contains no hints associating the Temple Mount with the religious dispute that stirred the public debate in Palestine at that time. Still, two basic facts should not be ignored. First, the same nomenclature, "the Temple Mount," is found in both sets of writings. Second, a similar concept and a parallel set of images were formulated by both groups, although rather differently, and perhaps even in opposite terms.

In view of the substitution of the Temple Mount for the Temple in Jewish perception, the Christians' diatribes against it acquire a new, more concrete meaning. It seems clear to me that the Jewish sages' preoccupation with the Temple Mount did not occur in a vacuum. No less intriguing is the question of whether the eminence of the Temple Mount among the followers of James Brother of Jesus (discussed in chapter 2) induced the sages in any way. It could very well be that the effort by the Tannaim and the Amoraim to anchor the Temple Mount in their historical heritage and to determine its character as a real, concrete mountain, existing in one particular place, could be linked to their rivalry over its "possession" with other groups of their countrymen or their religious debates with the Christians. Although no explicit reference in rabbinic texts indicates that this was the case, the similar phenomena occurring among different groups at the same time in the same geographical setting make it more than plausible.

So, does rabbinic literature provide us with an accurate picture of the past? Are portrayals of the Second Temple period in this later corpus to be trusted? The answer of the current study is both yes and no. But isn't that what memory is all about?

Afterword

A Mount without a Temple

It was a Monday afternoon, some time in the winter of 638 CE. Caliph Omar ibn al-Kitab, who by then held most of the Middle East under his sway, entered the gates of Jerusalem riding on a haggard beast of burden, his body draped in a simple robe of camel hair. This was in keeping with Islamic mores—modesty, humility, and frugality. It also corresponded fully to a long tradition of messiahs and redeemers of previous centuries who had considered Jerusalem their highest joy. Immediately upon his arrival, so say the fragments of legends that passed from mouth to mouth in those days, the caliph inquired about the location of "the Temple of the Jews that Solomon built." He spent his first night in the Tower of David in prayer and in study of the relevant suras of the Quran, especially the *surat sad,* which mentions David and Solomon, Abraham, Isaac, and Jacob, and the *surat al-asra,* which relates the prophet Moḥammed's night journey. At dawn, ʿOmar walked to the *Ḥaram,* the Arab name for the Temple Mount. The many versions of what took place there differ in their details—about the finding of the foundation stone, about the caliph's prayer there, and about the establishment of a house of prayer on that spot. But no one questions the outcome. The Islamic conquerors commenced a large-scale clearing operation on the Temple Mount, and at the end of a convoluted process they canonized the place as the location from which Moḥammed ascended heaven-ward during his renowned night journey. With the sweep of a hand, the Temple Mount platform, with its new mosques and other sites, again became a focus of religious belief and practice, subordinate in Islam only to Mecca and Medina.

Great narratives never grow obsolete. The end of the earlier story sets the beginning of a new chapter, and many of the old elements—physical features, notions, and images—seem to have been carried over. The issue, then, is not the materials from which the story is built but rather the way in which they are arranged and how they relate to one another. This book began with a presentation of the "sequential development" model, which constitutes the basis of standard scholarly understanding of the space we call "Temple Mount" and its conceptual substance. Scholars concatenate the various phases in the site's history into a long chain of interlocking links. The present research has called that chain into question. It examined the links and found numerous breaches. It has shown that the principle of continuity that lies at the foundation of the sequential pattern does not exist, at least not in its commonly understood sense.

The accepted view fixed the beginnings of the Temple Mount's renown in earliest Jewish-Israelite history, in the First Temple period, and presumed that the idea of the Temple Mount developed continuously from those times into the Second Temple period and thereafter found a place in rabbinic literature. The present study has suggested that the Second Temple period is not, in this case, a prolongation of the earlier era, because a conceptuality of sacred space associated with the Temple Mount did not materialize in any meaningful way in Jewish consciousness and experience during the greater part of the first millennium BCE. Thus the sequence is interrupted.

The accepted view also holds that the days of Aelia Capitolina represent but another stage in the continuum, even if in a negative sense. The Romans, so goes the *communi consensu,* aware of the site's stature for the Jews, concurred in its importance by constructing a pagan temple to Jupiter at the spot of the demolished Jewish sanctuary. Yet the present study has undermined this claim as well. It has argued that the Romans in fact never built a pagan temple on the Temple Mount. Instead, I have proposed that the compound remained desolate, entirely outside the limits of the Roman colony. The Mount's position in Byzantine Jerusalem demands reexamination as well. The common wisdom attributes the site's neglect in this period to the theological polemic that Christian thinkers engaged in with Judaism. This scholarly paradigm fails to stand up to examination, at least not in its widespread formulation. Both sides of the equation must be reevaluated. On the one hand, it seems quite possible that the reason Christian rulers refrained from including the Mount in the Byzantine city stems from the situation they inherited from their Roman predecessors. On the other hand, it turns out that the Mount was much less forsaken than we have been accustomed to think.

Finally, this study refutes the notion that the traditions about the Temple Mount in rabbinic literature reflect the site's position in the Second Temple period. I have shown that the conceptual category "Temple Mount" was not, in any salient way, a part of Jewish consciousness during most of the Second Temple period. Only the Tannaim and Amoraim retrieved this relatively peripheral biblical appellation, endowed it with new substance, sanctified it as a holy place, and made it into a concept. They made the space of the Temple Mount part and parcel of their religious landscape and reshaped their view of the past accordingly. It should be emphasized that I am not suggesting that the rabbis *invented* the notion of the Temple Mount out of whole cloth. As I show in chapter 1, similes and symbolism relating to the holy mountain in Jerusalem, opaque as they might be, pervaded Israelite-Jewish discourse centuries before the rabbis. More important than pinpointing the precise time of invention, many times a futile task, is to determine the period in which a certain entity (or set of ideas) became meaningful and significant in the life of the people who engaged them.

Aside from this discontinuity of the links on the sequential development chain, this study has also drawn attention to other chapters in the story of the Temple Mount that have not hitherto been taken into account. It turns out that this space (and not the Temple itself) played a very real role in the life of the Jewish group centered on James Brother of Jesus, serving as its holy place and pilgrimage site. In contrast, passages preserved in what came to be the New Testament contain echoes of the polemic over the significance of the Temple Mount space (although not calling it by this name), conducted among the different streams of the Jesus movement. It goes without saying that the sequential development approach provided no room for these links.

After rejecting the sequential development paradigm, subsequent chapters of this book offered an alternative reconstruction for the story of the Temple Mount and its various incarnations. I argue for a multifaceted model that encompasses both radical changes in the function of the Temple Mount site within the urban landscape of Jerusalem, and a dialectical, cultural-religious discourse involving the variety of groups that resided in Palestine during the Late Roman and Byzantine periods. Anthropologists and linguists have attempted to follow the birth of new concepts, and their conclusions suggest that in many cases these concepts develop after a major change in reality. A shift in the surrounding environment forces people to address the new situation, and their adjustment involves the coining of terms that define the way in which they perceive and engage with the new circumstances around them. These insights inform my thesis that ties physical landscape to consciousness.

Such were, according to this study, the urban dynamics that shaped the tangible appearance of the "Temple Mount." It originated in the colossal reconstruction project that King Herod (37–4 BCE) devised and carried out in the Temple and the compound surrounding it; and continued with the changes that occurred on the site in the wake of the destruction of the Temple in 70 CE, when the Mount lay in ruins, forever decapitated from the shrine on its top. The process culminated in the new municipal layout that emerged in Jerusalem with the establishment of the colony Aelia Capitolina (132–35 CE) and with its conversion, in time, into a Christian-Byzantine metropolis. Both Roman and Byzantine cities did not include the Temple Mount within their boundaries, at least until the middle of the fifth century. Herod transformed the space of the Temple Mount beyond recognition, and crafted the huge compound that at the time functioned as part of the Temple complex. But in subsequent stages the Herodian compound was left barren, without the structure for which it was established. It would eventually lie outside the city whose heart it had always occupied. This paradoxical urban process resulted in an independent, stand-alone space. Its detachment from the pagan Roman city only enhanced its accessibility, both physical and even more so ideological, for Jews and early Christians.

Consciousness grew along with the transmuting landscapes. The early seeds of this process may be located in the final generations of the Second Temple period but it fully matured only during the centuries following the destruction. From a Temple enclosure serving the sanctuary at its center and devoid of any independent value, this space evolved into the Temple Mount, an autonomous entity with the stature of a holy mountain in every sense of the word. Ironically, then, the space became the Temple Mount only when it no longer had a Temple—the Temple Mount is a Mount without a Temple.

The process by which a place becomes a holy site remains a thorny riddle difficult to solve. Recent scholarly studies on this issue have emphasized that no single model can account for all cases and that a variety of factors—social, political, and spiritual—instigate and impel this process, each making its own special contribution. This book argues that a variety of Jewish factions that had engaged the landscape of the "Mount without a Temple" integrated this space into their experiences, developed its imagery and symbolism in different, at times contrasting, ways, and in the long run assigned it their own form of sanctity. This is especially true of the community that formed around James Brother of Jesus and later of the circle of Jewish scholars that came to be known as the rabbis.

During the course of this study, I surmise that there may well have been mutual influences among the various groups that established a connection to the Mount. To illustrate this possibility, imagine the following scene. Jewish believers in Jesus, members of the coterie that consolidated around his Brother James, ascend to visit the holy tomb of their leader, which their traditions located on the Temple Mount, close to the ruins of the Temple. As they pray and conduct their ceremonies, a clique of rabbis appears on the site. As Rabbi ʿAkiva and his company did, they visit the ruins of the Temple and the Holy of Holies. They, too, recite prayers, observe customs, and conduct rituals there, some of them not unlike the ones performed by the first group. The first group kneels and prays, and the members of the second group prostrate themselves as well. What did one assembly say to the other? What relations developed between the two parties, and, more important, how did they influence each other, if at all? Such a scene, although imaginary in nature and with no precise information corroborating its occurrence, is nevertheless based upon historical evidence about what transpired in Jerusalem during the hundreds of years after the destruction of the Second Temple (at least until Christianity's rise to power in the fourth century). In other words, even if we have no accounts of such meetings, they probably did take place.

This fictional but nevertheless realistic situation introduces the model I apply in deciphering the early story of the Temple Mount. It illustrates a dynamic discourse that affected the shaping of the conceptual category "Temple Mount" by the different groups. By nature such processes conceal more than they reveal. Hundreds of years of confrontation between Jews and Christians in the Middle Ages, and consequently disconnected scholarly fields, contributed to the artificial dichotomies between these closely related, at that time seamless, communities.

Bringing together all the sources of Jews, Christians, and those in between leads to the following conclusions. It is a solid fact that the Temple Mount functioned as an independent entity in the experience of the sages as reflected in rabbinic literature. It also clearly operated in the world of the community of James Brother of Jesus and later also in the Christian milieu of Palestine, as evidenced by the writings of the church fathers who lived in the region and by the descriptions provided by pilgrims who visited the Temple Mount. Each of these factions perceived the Temple Mount in different, sometimes opposing, ways. A Temple Mount that continues the "Temple experience," standing in for, at times replacing, the destroyed sanctuary and inevitably reshaping it, is unlike the Temple Mount as the site of a sacred tomb. Nor is the physical and historic Mount of the Jewish sages like the spiritual and allegorical Mount that could be uprooted from its original site and transferred to Golgotha, as happened in Byzantine Jerusalem. Common to all these notions is the existence of an entity that registered in the mind of these people as a "Mount." Streams within Judaism, as well as in Christianity, all related to this space and viewed it as an essential part of the formula that defined their identity. It was their sacred space. Naturally, they each shaped their own image of the mountain and developed the traditions, memories, and symbolism that anchored the site in their lives. If I am right in this reconstruction, there was not one Temple Mount but rather many Temple Mounts. Understanding these "mountains," and the place they occupied in the worlds of these different groups, brings to light another chapter of Jerusalem's history.

Abbreviations

AB	Anchor Bible
ABD	David N. Freedman, ed., *The Anchor Bible Dictionary* (6 vols.; New York: Doubleday, 1992)
ACW	Ancient Christian Writers
AION	*Annali dell'Instituto Orientale di Napoli*
AnBib	*Analecta biblica*
ANF	Alexander Roberts and James Donaldson, eds., *Ante-Nicene Christian Library: Translations of the Writings of the Fathers down to A. D. 325* (25 vols.; Edinburgh: T&T Clark, 1867–97)
ANRW	Hildegard Temporini and Wolfgang Hasse, eds., *Aufstieg und Niedergang der römischen Welt: Geschichte und Kultur Roms im Spiegel der neueren Forschung* (Berlin: De Gruyter, 1972–)
ASOR	American Schools of Oriental Research
ATLA	American Theological Library Association
BA	*Biblical Archaeologist*
BAR	*British Archaeological Reports*
BARev	*Biblical Archaeology Review*
BFCT	Beiträge zur Förderung christlicher Theologie
BHT	Beiträge zur historischen Theologie
Bibl	*Biblica*
BJRL	*Bulletin of John Rylands University Library of Manchester*
BJS	Brown Judaic Studies
BLE	*Bulletin de littérature ecclésiastique*
BR	*Biblical Research*
BSOAS	*Bulletin of the School of Oriental and African Studies*
BWANT	Beiträge zur Wissenchaft vom Alten und Neuen Testament
CahRB	Cahiers de la Revue biblique
CBQ	*Catholic Biblical Quarterly*
CCSG	*Corpus Christianorum: Series graeca*
CCSL	*Corpus Christianorum. Series latina*
CQ	*Classical Quarterly*
CRINT	Compendia rerum iudaicarum ad Novum Testamentum
CSCO	*Corpus scriptorum christianorum orientalium*
CSEL	*Corpus scriptorum ecclesiasticorum latinorum*
CSHB	*Corpus scriptorum historiae byzantinae*
DACL	Fernand Cabrol, ed., *Dictionnaire d'archéologie chrétienne et de liturgie* (15 vols.; Paris: Letouzey and Ané, 1907–53)
DHGE	Alfred Baudrillart et al., eds., *Dictionnaire d'histoire et de géographie ecclésiastiques* (28 vols.; Paris: Letouzey and Ané, 1912–)
DJD	*Discoveries in the Judaean Desert*

DOP	*Dumbarton Oaks Papers*
DSP	Marcel Viller et al., eds., *Dictionnaire de spiritualité ascétique et mystique: Doctrine et histoire* (16 vols. in 18; Paris: Beauchesne, 1937–50)
EHR	*English Historical Review*
EJ	*Encyclopedia Judaica*
EL	*Ephemerides Liturgicae*
ETR	*Etudes théologiques et religieuses*
FC	Fathers of the Church
FRLANT	Forschungen zur Religion und Literatur des Alten und Neuen Testaments
GCS	Die griechische christliche Schriftsteller der ersten Jahrhunderte
GNT	Grundrisse zum Neuen Testament
HAR	*Hebrew Annual Review*
HSM	Harvard Semitic Monographs
HTKNT	Herders theologischer Kommentar zum Neuen Testament
HTR	*Harvard Theological Review*
HUCA	*Hebrew Union College Annual*
ICC	International Critical Commentary
IEJ	*Israel Exploration Journal*
JECS	*Journal of Early Christian Studies*
JJS	*Journal of Jewish Studies*
JLCRS	Jordon Lectures in Comparative Religion Series
JQR	*Jewish Quarterly Review*
JR	*Journal of Religion*
JRA	*Journal of Roman Archaeology*
JRS	*Journal of Roman Studies*
JSJ	*Journal for the Study of Judaism in the Persian, Hellenistic, and Roman Periods*
JSNT	*Journal for the Study of the New Testament*
JSNTSup	Journal for the Study of the New Testament: Supplement Series
JSOT	*Journal for the Study of the Old Testament*
JSOTSup	Journal for the Study of the Old Testament: Supplement Series
JSP	*Journal for the Study of the Pseudepigrapha*
JSPSup	Journal for the Study of the Pseudepigrapha: Supplement Series
JSQ	*Jewish Studies Quarterly*
JSS	*Journal of Semitic Studies*
JTS	*Journal of Theological Studies*
LASBF	*Liber annuus Studii biblici franciscani*
LCL	Loeb Classical Library
MGWJ	*Monatschrift für Geschichte und Wissenschaft des Judentums*
MUSJ	*Mélanges de l'Université Saint-Joseph*
NEAEHL	Ephraim Stern, ed., *The New Encyclopedia of Archaeological Excavations in the Holy Land* (4 vols.; Jerusalem: Israel Exploration Society, 1993)
NHS	Nag Hammadi Studies
NovTSup	Novum Testamentum Supplements

NPNF	Philip Schaff et al., eds., *A Select Library of the Nicene and Post-Nicene Fathers of the Christian Church* (14 vols.; New York: Christian Literature, 1886–90)
NT	*Novum Testamentum*
NTOA	*Novum Testamentum et Orbis Antiquus*
NTS	*New Testament Studies*
OBO	*Orbis biblicus et orientalis*
OCA	*Orientalia christiana analecta*
OCP	*Orientalia christiana periodica*
OWA	One World Archaeology
PAAJR	*Proceedings of the American Academy of Jewish Research*
PEQ	*Palestine Exploration Quaterly*
PEFQst	*Palestine Exploration Fund Quarterly Statement*
PG	Jacques-Paul Migne, ed., *Patrologia graeca* [= *Patrologiae cursus completus: Series graeca*] (162 vols.; Paris: Migne, 1857–86)
PL	Jacques-Paul Migne, ed., *Patrologia latina* [= *Patrologiae cursus completus: Series latina*] (217 vols.; Paris: Migne, 1844–64)
PO	*Patrologia orientalis*
PPTS	Palestine Pilgrims' Text Society
PrOrChr	*Proche-Orient chrétien*
PTS	Patristische Texte und Studien
PWRE	August Friedrich von Pauly, *Paulys Real Encyclopädie der Classischen Altertumswissenschaft* (49 vols.; new ed.; Munich: G. Wissowa, 1980)
QDAP	*Quarterly of the Department of Antiquities in Palestine*
RA	*Revue d'assyriologie et d'archéologie orientale*
RB	*Revue biblique*
RBPH	*Revue belge de philologie et d'histoire*
REAug	*Revue des études augustiniennes*
REJ	*Revue des études juives*
RHR	*Revue de l'histoire des religions*
ROC	*Revue de l'Orient chrétien*
RQ	Römische Quartalschrift für christliche Altertumskunde und Kirchengeschichte
SAOC	Studies in Ancient Oriental Civilizations
SBF	*Studium Biblicum Franciscanum*
SBLDS	Society of Biblical Literature Dissertation Series
SBLMS	Society of Biblical Literature Monograph Series
SBLSP	*Society of Biblical Literature Seminar Papers*
SBLTT	Society of Biblical Literature Texts and Translations
SC	*Sources chrétiennes*
SCI	*Scripta Classica Israelica*
SecCent	*Second Century*
SJLA	Studies in Judaism in Late Antiquity
SJOT	*Scandinavian Journal of the Old Testament*
SP	*Studia patristica*
STDJ	Studies on the Texts of the Desert of Judah

StPB	*Studia post-biblica*
StTh	*Studia theologica*
SVTP	*Studia in Veteris Testamenti pseudepigraphica*
ThZ	*Theologische Zeitschrift*
TLZ	*Theologische Literaturzeitung*
TSAJ	Texte und Studien zum antiken Judentum
TU	Texte und Untersuchungen
UNT	Untersuchungen zum Neuen Testament
VC	*Vigiliae christianae*
VT	*Vetus Testamentum*
WHJP	World History of the Jewish People
WUNT	Wissenschaftliche Untersuchungen zum Neuen Testament
ZAW	*Zeitschrift für die alttestamentliche Wissenschaft*
ZDMG	*Zeitschrift der deutschen morgenländischen Gesellschaft*
ZDPV	*Zeitschrift des deutschen Palästina-Vereins*
ZNW	*Zeitschrift für die neutestamentliche Wissenschaft und die Kunde der älteren Kirche*

Notes

INTRODUCTION

1. See, e.g., Eliade, *The Sacred and the Profane*, 20–65; J. Smith, *To Take Place;* Arnold and Gold, *Sacred Landscapes and Cultural Politics.*

2. For instance, Goodman, *Mission and Conversion*, 41–48, which rejects the notion of a "break" at the end of the first century CE.

3. Studies on the Temple Mount are listed in the general bibliographies on Jerusalem. The most important of these are Purvis, *Jerusalem;* Bieberstein and Bloedhorn, *Jerusalem.* Many of the (few) works that have the term "Temple Mount" in their titles deal in fact with the Temple that was located there. When they address the Temple Mount, they only repeat the physical data, with an emphasis on a comparison of Josephus's description with that of *Mishnah tractate Middot;* or they discuss current issues, such as the customs associated with the Mount, the areas Jewish law permits Jews to enter, and so on; see also n. 7. After I completed this book, David Goodblatt published a short, though important, study on the terminological history of the Temple Mount; see Goodblatt, "The Temple Mount," 91–101.

4. *SifreDeut* 43 (Finkelstein, 95; trans. Hammer, 91–92). And with slight variations: *LamR* 5:18 (Buber, 80a); *bMak* 24b; *Yalkut Makhiri*, Mic 3:12 (Greenup, 19).

5. For a similar reading of the biblical text and the function of the various terms within it, see Goodblatt, "The Temple Mount," 92–93.

6. The full expression "Mountain of the Temple of God" has parallels in other First Temple texts, and may in fact represent one of the names given to the mountain on which the First Temple stood. On this, on other names given to the location of the Temple in ancient Israelite literature, and on the status of mountains in general in the ancient Near East, see chapter 1.

7. Illustrating this approach is B. Mazar, *The Mountain of the Lord*, which surveys the history of the Temple Mount in all periods. For a handful of other examples (out of many), see Bickermann, *Der Gott der Makkabäer*, 2; Avi-Yonah, "Jerusalem in the Hellenistic and Roman Periods," 212–19; J. Levenson, *Sinai;* Cohen, *From the Maccabees to the Mishnah*, 106; Ritmeyer, "Locating the Original Temple Mount," 26, which more than once makes use of the term "earlier Temple Mount"; Wharton, *Refiguring the Post Classical City,* 98: "The Temple Mount was the physical center of the Jewish cult and, for centuries, the most sacred site in the city." As a result of the application of the term, the idea of the Temple Mount's deep roots in Jewish consciousness has found its way into various encyclopedias, e.g., *NEAEHL* 2:699 (which freely applies the term to the First Temple) and the maps on pp. 707, 718, 737, 738. It has also been adopted by popular publications, such as Mann, *Jerusalem, Judea and Samaria,* 119–26; Peters, *Jerusalem,* 31 (First Temple), 68 (Second Temple map), 84–87. Dozens of other examples could be added to this random list. Its variety—including works by archaeologists, historians, textual scholars, and popular writers—shows that this misunderstanding of the Mount transcends disciplines and dominates both scholarly and public discourses.

8. On this term, see Abler, Adams, and Gould, *Spatial Organization.*

9. For a thorough analysis of these aspects of his work and abundant bibliography on recent trends, see, e.g., Branham, "Vicarious Sacrality," 2:323ff. See also the following note.

10. For one example out of many, see the collection of studies in Carmichael et al., *Sacred Sites, Sacred Places.* Also, directly focusing on the historical periods discussed here, J. Smith, *To Take Place;* Nicolet, *L'inventaire du monde.*

11. For reviews of these issues, see, e.g., Sturtevant, *An Introduction to Linguistic Science;* Hayakawa, *Language in Thought and Action,* esp. 150–90; Nelson, *Naming and Reference,* 1–143. For a good introduction to these questions in modern scholarship and to prevalent approaches, see Blackburn, *Spreading the Word.* On Derrida, see the next note. I have gleaned the main points of Saul A. Kripke's thinking from his *Naming and Necessity.* For a critical view of this approach, see Linski, *Names and Descriptions,* 42ff. For a comparison of these approaches, see the introductions to Blackburn's and Nelson's books. I would like to express my gratitude to Daniel Statman and to Yossi David, who have helped me clarify these issues in my theoretical discussion.

12. Derrida, *Of Grammatology,* 158 (emphasis in original).

13. Compare with the term "Jerusalem," which includes both the earthly and divine cities. On metaphysical descriptions of mountains, especially in the apocalyptic literature of the Second Temple period, see my discussion in chapter 1.

14. See, for example, the many instances collected and discussed in Lévi-Strauss, *Structural Anthropology.*

15. For a short survey of these developments in rabbinic studies, including bibliographical references to the various views, see Eliav, "Realia, Daily Life, and the Transmission of Local Stories during the Talmudic Period," 235–65. See also the beginning of chapter 6.

16. See Boyarin, *Dying for God,* who also examines these developments at length (quotations from pp. 8–9).

17. On the application of deconstruction principles to the study of the New Testament, in accordance with the major spokesmen in the field (Michel Foucault, Jacques Derrida, and others) see, e.g., Moore, *Poststructuralism and the New Testament.*

18. Aram Veeser, *The New Historicism,* xi; see also Fineman, "The History of the Anecdote: Fiction and Fiction," 49–76; Greenblatt, *Learning to Curse,* esp. 14; Kermode, *The Genesis of Secrecy,* 1–21.

19. A concise presentation of these methods, along with a basic bibliography, can be found in Hayes and Holladay, *Biblical Exegesis.*

O N E : Transmuting Realities

1. *Let. Aris.* 83–84 (Pelletier, 142; trans. R. J. H. Shutt in Charlesworth, 2:18).

2. The unrealistic quality of Jerusalem's depiction in the *Letter of Aristeas* is sharpened by contrast with his later portrayal of the city (100; Pelletier, 152–54). While the picture here places the Temple on the peak, at the highest spot of the city, it is the citadel that the author locates in that same place in the latter description; see Vincent, "Jérusalem," 531, who discusses the problems involved in Aristeas's account and detects the biblical influence on this description.

3. The question of their historical authenticity is beyond the scope of this research.

4. 2 Kgs 19:31; Isa 37:32. Many have missed these simple facts. For just one example, see J. Levenson, *Sinai*, 92; although Levenson notes that "It is not clear that 'Zion' always referred to the same spot in ancient times," he nevertheless takes an harmonistic approach and reads the prophetic books of the Bible as well as the poems of the Psalms together with the books of Samuel and Kings, and thus concludes that "In any event, most of the biblical references to Zion have in mind what is today known as the Temple Mount."

5. 2 Sam 24:18–25.

6. 2 Sam 6:17–18; 1 Kgs 2:28; 1 Chr 21:20. Contra J. Levenson, *Sinai*, 95.

7. For a concise presentation and further bibliography, see Zakovitch, "The First Stages of Jerusalem's Sanctification under David: A Literary and Ideological Analysis," 16–35.

8. Compare the later efforts of Alexander, who established many Alexandrias in an attempt to unite the Semitic East and Greek civilization, and of Constantine, who tried to bring together the crumbling Roman Empire by building a new Rome—Constantinople.

9. 1 Kgs 8:16, and see, again one study out of many, Japhet, "From the King's Sanctuary to the Chosen City," 3–15.

10. 1 Kgs 12:26–27.

11. See, e.g., the juxtaposition of "the House of the Lord" with "the King's house" in 1 Kgs 9:1–10. The physical proximity between the two structures is apparent in the account of Athaliah, who sits in the king's house and hears the comings and goings from the house of the Lord (2 Kgs 11). It still appears, however, that from a topographical standpoint the king's house was on lower ground (e.g., Jer 26:10; 36:12). House of the People—Jer 39:8; House of the Forest of Lebanon—1 Kgs 7:2, 10:17–21; Isa 22:8.

12. Isa 2:2–3; Mic 4:1–2.

13. This generalization does not apply to the latter prophets. In Jeremiah, for example, none of the terms appears even once, and an expression like "holy mountain," which in most of the prophetic writings almost always refers to the location of the Temple, is used in Jeremiah as a neutral name for the entire Judean mountain ridge (Jer 31:22).

14. Ps 2:6.

15. E.g.: "Nevertheless David took the strong hold of Zion: the same is the City of David" (2 Sam 5:7); "Then Solomon assembled the elders of Israel, and all the heads of the tribes, the chief of the fathers of the children of Israel, unto king Solomon in Jerusalem, that they might bring up the ark of the covenant of the Lord out of the city of David, which is Zion" (1 Kgs 8:1).

16. 2 Chr 3:1.

17. For a summary of the scholarship on this issue, see Davila, "Moriah," 905.

18. Because the editor of Genesis already knew of the association between the story and the place of the Jerusalem Temple, he closed the account with a note about it; see Gen 22:14.

19. Pointed out, but interpreted differently by Goodblatt, "The Temple Mount," 92.

20. See Clements, *God and Temple*, and Clifford, *The Cosmic Mountain*.

21. See Parry, "Sinai as Sanctuary and Mountain of God," 482–500.

22. Bousset, *Die Religion des Judentums*, 91–102. Much has been written in rejection of this view; see especially Townsend, "The Jerusalem Temple in the First Century," 48–65.

23. Cohen, *From the Maccabees to the Mishnah*, 106. In the present work I do not intend to detail the people's attitude toward each of the elements of the Jerusalem-Temple pair, as, for example, Schwartz did in his discussion of Diaspora Jewry; what I am concerned with is only the presence of the various elements in the consciousness of people, so it makes no difference here if their attitude was favorable or unfavorable. See D. Schwartz, "Temple or City: What Did Hellenistic Jews See in Jerusalem?" 114–27. Finally, the bibliography on Jerusalem in the Second Temple period is so vast that throughout this chapter I can only refer the reader to major studies. For a comprehensive bibliography, see Purvis, *Jerusalem*, 1:163–99, 2:158–97.

24. Nikiprowetzky, "La spiritualisation des sacrifices," 97–116; Barker, "Temple Imagery in Philo," esp. 90–100. On Josephus's views of the Temple, see my detailed discussion later in this chapter.

25. Vincent, "Jérusalem"; Hayward, "The New Jerusalem," 123–38; Stadelmann, *Ben Sira als Schriftgelehrter*, 55–67. On Jerusalem and the Temple in the writings from Qumran, see, e.g., Schiffman, *Reclaiming the Dead Sea Scrolls*, 385–94. The uniqueness of the latter survey is that it clarifies the ambivalence that characterized the ideas that sprang up in Qumran, and in its claim that affinity to what Jerusalem and the Temple represented (or were supposed to represent) formed the basis of the sharp criticism by the Qumranic people.

26. Himmelfarb, *Ascent to Heaven*, esp. 9–46; Böcher, "Die Heilige Stadt," 55–76.

27. Eusebius, *PE* 9:24 (Mras, I, 517, line 16). The status of Jerusalem and the Temple among the Jews of the Hellenistic Diaspora—a major topic in the discussion of their self-identity, with various scholarly opinions being expressed on the issue—extends beyond the scope of this study.

28. 2 Macc 2:22 (Kappler and Hanhart, 53).

29. See Mendels, *The Rise and Fall of Jewish Nationalism*, 107–59, 277–331; Schwier, *Tempel und Tempelzerstörung*, esp. 55–201.

30. There is no need to expand on the enormous influence the Bible (although then not compiled into the homogeneous composition we know today) had on the concepts and literary works of Second Temple Jews; see, e.g., Mulder, *Mikra*, esp. chaps. 10–14. Böcher, "Die Heilige Stadt," is an excellent example of the way one can trace the transformations of early biblical motifs into Second Temple literature.

31. Jdt 5:19 (Hanhart, 76).

32. *4 Bar.* 3:21 (Kraft and Purintun, 18).

33. 4Q372 frag. 1, lines 8, 11, and 13 (Schuller, 352); Josephus, *BJ* 5:137 (Thackeray, III, 238–40), 184 (ibid., 254). Hilly landscapes appear in other texts as well—for example, the beginning of *1 Enoch*, also known as the "Book of the Watchers," takes place against a backdrop of mountains, and Jerusalem is apparently alluded to. Yet it is difficult to establish the source from which the writer drew this scenery.

34. Dan 9:16; verse 20 is also to be understood in this way. And see the expression "holy mountain of beauty" (11:45), which signifies the entire territory of Judah. On the date of Daniel, see Schürer, *History*, 3.1:245–50.

35. 4Q171 frag. 1 (Allegro, 44); Wis 11:37 (Ziegler, 124); 1 Macc 11:37 (Kappler, 119); *Jub.* 1:2 (VanderKam, II, 1), 18:13 (ibid., 107–8).

36. *Jub.* 1:28 (VanderKam, II, 6), 4:26 (ibid., 28–29), 8:19 (ibid., 53), 18:13 (ibid., 107–8); 1 Macc 4:37, 60 (Kappler, 72, 74), 5:54 (ibid., 81), 6:48, 62 (ibid., 88, 90), 7:33 (ibid., 94), 10:11 (ibid., 108), 14:26 (ibid., 136); *2 Bar.* 13:1 (Dedering, 6), 40:1 (ibid., 20); *4 Ezra* 13:35

(Klijn, 84). But compare this with the absence of the term in Josephus, as discussed in the next section.

37. Jdt 9:13 (Hanhart, 108); Josephus in the references in n. 33.

38. E.g., *Jub*.18:13 (VanderKam, II, 107–8); Josephus, *JA* 1:226 (Thackeray, IV, 112).

39. My analysis here follows Seeligman, "Jerusalem," 203 (Heb.); Talmon, "TABUR HAAREZ and the Comparative Method," 163–77 (Heb.). Talmon proved that even the biblical image of "navel of the earth" should not be interpreted as the Hellenistic "Omphalos." These fundamental distinctions of Seeligman and Talmon have not received proper attention, and scholars continue to err in discussing this lengthy period—from the Book of Judges until the late Midrashim—as if nothing had changed throughout this entire time. See, e.g., Hayman, "Some Observations on Sefer Yesira," 176–82. See also my discussion of the "foundation stone" in chapter 6.

40. *Jub.* 1:28 (VanderKam, II, 6), 4:25–26 (ibid., 28–29), 8:19 (ibid., 53).

41. *1 En.* 26:1 (Knibb, II, 114). See Grelot, "La géographie mythique d'Hénoch," 42–44; Black, *The Book of Enoch, or, 1 Enoch*, 172–73. On the Temple in this composition, see Himmelfarb, "The Temple and the Garden of Eden," 66–72.

42. Studying this issue separately, Goodblatt has reached the same conclusion; see Goodblatt, "The Temple Mount," 95–99.

43. Wis 9:8 (Ziegler, 124); *1 En.* 26:1 (Knibb, II, 114). The fact that the phrase was not used to refer to some concrete geographical entity is also clear from its application in the apocalyptic portion of Daniel (9–12), where the author uses it to refer to other entities as well, such as the city of Jerusalem and the entire land of Judea.

44. Philo, *Legat.* 294–95 (Colson, 148); Josephus, *BJ* 3:52 (Thackeray, II, 590); *Sib. Or.* 5:250 (Geffcken, 116). Cf. Chester, "The Sibyl and the Temple," 59–62. Chester's approach, which links the fifth Sibyl with the earlier compositions, misses the basic difference deriving from the absence of the mountain image in the Sibyl. The very nature of the place as connecting humans with the deity in the heavens necessitates the link with the heavens motif that appears there. But this cannot serve as a replacement for the theme of the mountain, which exists in all the ancient texts but is absent in the later ones, including the Sybil.

45. On the time and place of these compositions, see the summaries of Nickelsburg, "Stories of Biblical and Early Post Biblical Times," 45, 51–52; and, with slightly different emphasis, Schürer, *History*, 3:1:218–19, 223–25.

46. Tob 1:3–8 (Hanhart, 60–64). See Deselaers, *Das Buch Tobit*, 328–30, who convincingly argues for the ambivalence of the author of Tobit toward Jerusalem but nevertheless agrees that he places the city at the center of Jewish experience.

47. Tob 13:11–18 (Hanhart, 170–75).

48. Put forward again recently by C. Moore, *Tobit*, 281.

49. Jdt 4:2 (Hanhart, 66), 10:8 (ibid., 111), 13:4 (ibid., 128), and see also 8:24 (ibid., 101).

50. Jdt 3:4 (Hanhart, 67), 8:24 (ibid., 101).

51. Schürer, *History*, 3.1:292–93; Nickelsburg, *Jewish Literature*, 315–16.

52. City walls—*4 Bar.* 3:1 (Kraft and Purintun, 16); Agrippa's vineyard—3:14, 21 (ibid., 18); markets—6:19 (ibid., 30); Temple—2:1–2 (ibid., 14).

53. See, e.g., Stambaugh, "Functions," 562.

54. Josephus, *JA* 12:145–46 (Marcus, VII, 74–76). Another official letter sent by the Seleucid king Demetrius II to Jonathan, which I discuss in note 81, mentions "the sacred mountain," but as I show there, the authenticity of this letter's wording remains doubtful.

55. See, for example, the words of the Greek author Hecataeus of Abdera, in a fragment preserved in Josephus, *Ap* 1:198 (Thackeray, I, 242). See also Neh 13:7–9; 8:16; *Jub.* 49:20 (VanderKam, II, 323–24); *Let. Aris.* 100 (Pelletier, 154). These territories, with their components and contents, were frequently described in studies devoted to reconstructing the Temple and its environs. See especially Busink, *Der Tempel*, 2:904–1016, 1178–1200.

56. E.g., *ḥaṣer*—Neh 13:7–9; 8:16; for numerous references in the *Temple Scroll*, see Yadin, *Temple Scroll*, 1:200–276. Regarding the term *ʿazarah*, see Hurvitz, "The Evidence of Language," 41–43. *aulē*—1 Macc 9:54 (Kappler, 105). *peribolos*—Sir 50:2 (Ziegler, 357); Josephus, *JA* 12:145–46 (Marcus, VII, 74–76); 2 Macc 6:4 (Kappler and Hanhart, 70); 4 Macc 4:11 (Rahlfs, 1162); Philo, *Legat.* 212 (Colson, 110). *Temenos*—3 Macc 1:113 (Hanhart, 43); Philo, *Legat.* 296 (Colson, 148). On Josephus's application of all these, see my discussion later in this chapter.

57. For an extensive discussion of this topic, see Stambaugh, "Functions," 554–608, esp. 562–63, 575–77. Concerning the roots of the phenomenon in the Greek world, see Marinatos and Hägg, *Greek Sanctuaries*, 228–33. See also Wilken, *The Land*, 103–4.

58. See Stambaugh, "Functions."

59. 2 Macc 6:4 (Kappler and Hanhart, 70); *Temple Scroll* (*11Q19*) 45:7–8 (Yadin, 135).

60. The Temple and the areas associated with it, as described in this text, have been studied by scholars time and again. For a partial review, see Wise, *Critical Study*, 14–15. For further references, see the index of García-Martínez and Parry, *A Bibliography of the Finds*, 558–60, s.v.

61. Schiffman, "Architecture," 279–80; Maier, "Architectural History," 49.

62. Yadin, *Temple Scroll*, 190–92; Schiffman, "Architecture," 280–82.

63. E.g., Schiffman, "Exclusion from the Sanctuary," esp. 317–18.

64. 1 Macc 13:49–52 (Kappler, 133–34); Josephus, *JA* 13:215–17 (Marcus, VII, 334–36) See Schürer, *History*, 1:154–55 and n. 39, 1:192 and n. 10.

65. E.g., 1 Macc 6:18 (Kappler, 85).

66. *Megillat taʿanit* to the 23 of *ʾiyyar* (Lichtenstein, 327). For a survey of the scholarly debates about the historical reconstruction of the events, see Schürer, *History*, 1:154–55, 192; Sievers, "Jerusalem, the Akra, and Josephus," 201–2.

67. 1 Macc 13:49–52 (Kappler, 133–34), but cf. 1 Macc 14:37 (Kappler, 138), which seems to imply that the citadel remained in place and was even fortified by Simeon. This is precisely the contradiction that led to the doubts discussed in the studies cited in the previous note regarding the authenticity of Josephus's description. For the present study the actual occurrence is of less importance because the major focus here is on how the event was perceived by observers, both at the time it occurred and many years later.

68. The details about Herod's endeavor, which come from both literary sources, mainly Josephus, and the extensive archaeological excavations that were carried out around the compound, have been collected and examined time and again in the last few decades. The best, most comprehensive studies are Vincent and Steve, *Jérusalem de l'Ancien Testament*, 2:526–610; B. Mazar, *Excavations*; B. Mazar, *The Mountain of the Lord*; Busink, *Der Tempel*, 2:904–1016, 1178–1200; Ben-Dov, *Shadow*; Ritmeyer, "Reconstructing Herod's Temple Mount in Jerusalem," 23–53; Ritmeyer, "Locating the Original Temple Mount," 25–45; Geva, "Jerusalem: The Second Temple Period," 2:736–44.

69. The data and comparisons were collected in Geva, "Jerusalem: The Second Temple Period," 737.

70. Numerous scholars over the years have studied this literary material in an attempt to reconstruct the Temple; for a recent discussion, see Busink, *Der Temple*, 2:1062ff. For an exhaustive bibliography, see Purvis, *Jerusalem*, 1:178–92, 2:170–75.

71. Sulpicius Severus, *Chronicon* 2:30:6 (Halm, 85, line 8); trans. Stern, *Greek*, 2:64; for a summary of the questions concerning this passage, as well as a bibliography, see Stern, *Greek*, 2:64–67.

72. *bBB* 4b.

73. Concerning the basilica, see Ben-Dov, *Shadow*, 124–25; Busink, *Der Temple*, 2:1200–1232. On the Antonia—Busink, *Der Temple*, 2:1233–49.

74. A summary of the finds and various reconstructions may be found in Mazar, *Excavations*; Ben-Dov, *Shadow*, 122–33.

75. Josephus, *JA* 20:219 (Feldman, X, 116); John 2:20. According to these two sources the construction work continued for years after Herod's death; this may also be hinted at in *tShab* 13:2 (Lieberman, 57 and the parallels he cites there).

76. 1 Macc 1:37 (Kappler, 52).

77. 1 Macc 3:45 (Kappler, 66–67), 4:44 (ibid., 72), 6:7 (ibid., 84).

78. 1 Macc 9:54 (Kappler, 105).

79. 1 Macc 4:36–38 (Kappler, 72), 4:60 (ibid., 74) compared with 6:7 (ibid., 48).

80. 1 Macc 5:54 (Kappler, 81), 7:33 (ibid., 94), 14:26 (ibid., 136) compared with 14:84 (ibid., 139).

81. Other references to the Temple Mount in this text are rather doubtful, and serious problems assail their authenticity; in all likelihood they were later additions, possibly from the period after the destruction of the Temple. The closing pericope in a letter sent to Jonathan, the second Hasmonaean leader, by the Seleucid king Demetrius II insists that the recipients set it up "in the Holy Mount"; near the end of the book, in a description of Simeon's reign, the expression "the Mount of the Temple" appears twice—the first in connection with Simeon's fortification of the site, the second in the narration of the rebellion of Ptolemy son of Abubus, who reportedly intended to capture Jerusalem and the Mount of the Temple. See 1 Macc 11:37 (Kappler, 119), 13:52 (ibid., 134), 16:20 (ibid., 145). In regard to the letter from Demetrius II to Jonathan, Josephus (*JA* 13:128 [Marcus, VII, 288]) provides an alternative reading for this document. Although most of its language is practically identical, Josephus's text uses *hieron* (Temple) instead of 1 Maccabees's *oros* (mountain). This change fits the epithet given to the Temple in another letter from Demetrius I in 1 Macc 10:43 (Kappler, 111) as well as another official letter in 1 Macc 15:9 (ibid., 140). Evidently in this case Josephus preserved the more original wording of the document. Another possibility is that *oros* (mountain) mistakenly took the place of *horos* (the surrounding area), which in Greek are spelled with the same consonants, distinguished only by the pronunciation of the first vowel (*spiritus lenis* in mountain; *spiritus asper* in the surrounding area). *Horos* (the surrounding area) is used in this sense in the letter from Demetrius I (1 Macc 10:43). The use of *horos* to denote the space around sanctuaries has parallels in official Hellenistic writing (letters, edicts, decrees, and the like), whereas *oros* is never to be found; see, e.g., Welles, *Royal Correspondence*, 129, line 12; 260, line 12. The difficulty with this last suggestion is that the suffix of *oros* here is *ei* (indicating a dative), while according to my suggestion it should have been *wi*, yet such inconsistencies are quite frequent. The pos-

sibility that the closing segment of this document was reworded by a Jewish scribe was raised years ago by Starcky; see Abel and Starcky, *Les livres*, 176. See also Bartlett, *Maccabees*, 156. This line of interpretation, which argues for a later Jewish interventions in the original formula of the documents, tallies with Stern's general observation, "The various translations and the attempt to fit the language of the document with biblical figures of speech has somewhat blurred the original Hellenistic terminology"; see Stern, *Documents*, 85 (Heb.).

As for the mention of "mountain of the Temple" in two instances (13:52; 16:20), it is rather surprising that the author of 1 Maccabees deviates from his consistent practice of refraining from calling the Jewish Temple *hieron* (unless he is quoting an official document like the ones cited here). Scholars debate the status of the last chapters in 1 Maccabees—primarily because Josephus, who was acquainted with the rest of the book, makes no use of them. Some scholars claim that these chapters are not an integral part of the book but were added to it later, perhaps even after the destruction of the Temple. The usage of the epithet *hieron* for the Temple in these chapters, which was common in late Second Temple writers, supports this view. For a review of the various scholarly considerations and bibliography, see Feldman, *Josephus*, 219–25. If this is indeed the case, then there is no evidence here for Hasmonaean terminology but rather for the vocabulary of someone who lived after the destruction of the Temple. However, the whole issue is still up in the air; cf. Goodblatt, "The Temple Mount," 99.

82. 1 Macc 4:46 (Kappler, 72).

83. Mulder, *Mikra*, chap. 12; Abel and Starcky, *Les livres;* Bartlett, *Maccabees.*

84. Goldstein, *1 Maccabees*, 284. Compare with other suggestions, e.g., Bartlett, *Maccabees*, 64, which overlooks the aspect of destruction and desolation that the text emphasizes.

85. The relevance of the verse in Micah to this passage had already been noted in the nineteenth century; see Keil, *Commentar*, 92. Keil, however, did not recognize the uniqueness of the expression Temple Mount in contrast to the other names that appear in the book, and therefore he harmonizes this expression with the name Mount Zion. A century later the same categories still apply; see Dommershausen, *1 Makkabäer, 2 Makkabäer*, 37.

86. Following Neuhaus, *Studien*, 30–31.

87. For example, the forest motif in *2 Baruch* is linked with the destruction, but in itself it stands for the government, and therefore it is the uprooting of the forest that represents the destruction; see *2 Bar.* 36–39 (Dedering, 18–19). In another part of that work the forest indicates the place of origin of jackals and demons that come to live in the ruins; see *2 Bar.* 10:8 (ibid., 5). See also *2 Bar.* 77:14 (ibid., 43), where the forest is a place in which people get lost. See also Josephus, *JA* 12:317 (Marcus, VII, 164), which is based on the passage in 1 Maccabees under discussion but omits the motif of the thicket. For many other examples of this sort, see Botterweck and Ringgren, *Theologisches Wörterbuch*, 3:785–87.

88. Following Bickermann, *Der Gott der Makkabäer*, 31–32, 145–46; But compare other views that delay the composition of this text to early in the first century BCE—Schürer, *History*, 3.1:181.

89. A fortified place—4:60, 6:48, 6:62, 10:11, 13:52, 16:20. Indirect connection to fortification—4:36, 7:33. Without any connection to fortification—4:64, 5:54, 11:37, 14:26.

90. For an overview of the parts of the building and their names, see Busink, *Der Temple,* 2:810–38; S. Safrai, "Temple," 865–70.

91. S. Safrai, "Temple," 866–67.

92. Josephus, *BJ* 5:136 (Thackeray, III, 238); following Thackeray's translation on p. 239; see also 149–50 (ibid., 244).

93. Josephus, *JA* 15:397 (Marcus, VIII, 192); *BJ* 5:184 (Thackeray, III, 254).

94. Acra—*JA* 13:215 (Marcus, VII, 334); Bezetha—*BJ* 5:149 (Thackeray, III, 244); Mount of Olives—*JA* 20:169 (Feldman, X, 92); Givʿat Shaul—*BJ* 5:51 (Thackeray, III, 216).

95. E.g., Josephus, *JA* 12:316 (Marcus, VII, 162–64) compared with 1 Macc 4:36 (Kappler, 72) and many more.

96. Simeon—Josephus, *JA* 13:213–17 (Marcus, VII, 332–36) compared with 1 Macc 13:52 (Kappler, 134); Judas Maccabeus—Josephus, *JA* 12:326 (Marcus, VII, 168) compared with 1 Macc 4:60 (Kappler, 74), 6:7 (ibid., 84).

97. Josephus, *JA* 11:310 (Marcus, VI, 464), 12:10 (Marcus, VII, 6).

98. 2 Macc 6:2 (Kappler and Hanhart, 70); John—see chapter 2.

99. The many references to each of these can be found in the appropriate entries in the concordance; see Rengstorf, *Concordance,* 1:8 (*hagios*); 1:265–66 (*aulē*); 2:373–78 (*hieron*); 3:132–35 (*naos*); 3:387–88 (*peribolos*); 4:178–79 (*temenos*).

100. See, e.g., Simons, *Jerusalem in the Old Testament,* esp. 92–93; Busink, *Der Temple,* 2:1005–16; and again recently Kaufman, "The Temple Compound Made Rectangular," 46.

101. Josephus, *BJ* 5:184 (Thackeray, III, 254).

102. E.g., Josephus, *BJ* 4:196 (Thackeray, III, 58); *JA* 15:409 (Marcus, VIII, 196); *Vit.* 419 (Thackeray, I, 152).

103. Josephus, *BJ* 1:351 (Thackeray, II, 164), 4:343–44 (Thackery, III, 100); *JA* 15:419 (Marcus, VIII, 202), 18:19 (Feldman, IX, 16).

104. Clermont-Ganneau, "Une stèle du Temple de Jérusalem," 220. For an analysis of the inscription and its parallels, as well as bibliographical references, see Schürer, *History,* 2:285 and n. 57.

105. Josephus, *JA* 18:19 (Feldman, IX, 16), 18:82 (ibid., 58); animal sacrifices—11:336 (Marcus, VI, 476), 14:66–67 (Marcus, VII, 480), 20:191 (Feldman, X, 102).

106. Destruction—Josephus, *JA* 18:8 (Feldman, IX, 8), 20:123 (Feldman, X, 66), *BJ* 5:362 (Thackeray, III, 312), 6:110 (ibid., 406); other temples—*JA* 18:65 (Feldman, IX, 50), 19:7 (ibid., 218), 19:161 (ibid., 288), 19:248 (ibid., 328), *BJ* 2:81 (Thackeray, II, 352).

107. Clear examples for the implementation of this systematic terminology can be found in the two major passages Josephus devotes to the description of the Temple: Josephus, *JA* 15:417–19 (Marcus, VIII, 202); *BJ* 5:184ff. (Thackeray, III, 254ff.).

108. Josephus, *BJ* 4:313 (Thackeray, III, 92), 5:207 (ibid., 262).

109. Josephus, *BJ* 4:388 (Thackeray, III, 112–14); trans. based on Thackeray, III, 113–15, with some changes for accuracy.

110. See, e.g., Ps 84:3; 92:24. *Temenos* is used in the Septuagint to signify idolatrous sanctuaries, and the same holds true for 1 Maccabees; see the references in Hatch and Redpath, *Concordance,* 2:1345. For the beginnings of the use of this term in reference to the Temple in Jerusalem, see n. 99.

111. The most comprehensive summary of the issue remains Mayer, "Temenos," cols. 435–58 (with many examples).

112. Aristophanes, *Pl* 659 (Rogers, 424).

113. DS 5:58:2 (Oldfather, III, 254), 2:238:2 (Oldfather, I, 442); Polyaenus, *Stratgemata* 8:52 (Wölfflin and Melber, 413, line 16); *Sib. Or.* 5:493 (Geffcken, 128), and see on this passage Collins, *The Sibylline Oracles*, 93–94. I discuss the passage from Dio in detail in Eliav, "Hadrian's Actions," 141–43.

114. Josephus, *BJ* 7:158 (Thackeray, III, 550). All references to *temenē* are listed in the appropriate entry in Rengstorf, *Concordance*. Another example in Josephus appears, according to some of the textual witnesses, in the passage in which he quotes Menander of Ephesus concerning the *temenē* that were built in Tyre honoring Heracles and Astarte; see Josephus, *Ap* 1:118 (Thackeray, I, 210), based on codex Laurentianus.

115. Josephus, *BJ* 6:271–76 (Thackeray, III, 454–56); all translations in the following discussion are based, with minor changes, on Thackeray (ibid.).

T W O : *Locus Memoriae*

1. Nora, "Entre mémoire et histoire," in Nora, *Les lieux*, 1:xvii–xlii.

2. Luke 2:22–29, 41–50; 4:9–13; Matt 4:5–11. The author of the Gospel of John relocated many of Jesus's deeds from Galilee to Jerusalem. The explanation for this change has to do with the relation between the fourth Gospel and the synoptics; for an apt summary, see R. Brown, *The Gospel according to John*, 1:xli–li. A more updated bibliography can be found in Van Belle, *Johannine Bibliography*, 135–37, 140–42. For a detailed and updated summary regarding Jerusalem and the Temple in the documents that came to be the New Testament, see Walker, *Jesus*; Han, *Jerusalem*.

3. I discuss the Temple experience of the Second Temple period at length at the beginning of chapter 1. It was Sanders who stressed the need to investigate the New Testament's attitude to the Temple in light of the Jewish attitudes of that time; see Sanders, *Jesus and Judaism*, 61–90. However, he emphasizes mainly the unfavorable aspect of these notions; see also Evans, "Opposition to the Temple," 235–353; Walker, *Jesus*, 269–326; Han, *Jerusalem*.

4. Heavenly Jerusalem—Heb 12:22; Gal 4:26. Concerning this concept and its development in Christian literature from the second century on, see the conclusion to this chapter. Many scholars have studied the roots of this term and its underlying notions in the milieu of Second Temple Judaism; see, e.g., Klauck, "Die heilige Stadt," 129–51; D. Schwartz, *Studies*, 15–26. The Temple as an epithet for the Christian community— 1 Cor 3:16; 2 Cor 6:16; Eph 2:19–22; 1 Pet 2:5.

5. See Brandon, *Fall;* Walter, "Tempelzerstörung," 38–49; Gaston, *No Stone*. For some more recent discussions on this topic, see the various studies collected in Hahn, *Zerstörungen des Jerusalemer Tempels*.

6. *Prot. Jas.* 1–10 (de Strycker, 64–86). For the Jewish characteristics in this work, alongside its ignorance of Palestine's geography, see Smid, *Protevangelium Jacobi*, 20–22. Later works also preserve the motif of Mary's life in the Temple; see, e.g., *Quaestiones Bartholomaei* 2:15 (Wilmart and Tisserant, 324).

7. *Poxy* 840 (Grenfell and Hunt, 6–7).

8. *Acts Thom.* 79 (Bonnet, 194, lines 9–10). Both the Greek translation, which provides the most ancient extant version and uses the familiar combination with the verb *prospherō* (to offer) and the object *dōron* (gift or offering to deities), and the Syriac, *'azal leheykhalah veqarav qorbanah* ("went to the sanctuary and offered a sacrifice"; Wright,

I, 248), are quite clear as to the nature of this deed. The parallels from the New Testament that Drijvers suggests for this passage should therefore be rejected, because both lack the essence of the act—Jesus offering sacrifice; see Drijvers, "The Acts of Thomas," 2:408 n. 119; Klijn, *The Acts of Thomas,* 262.

9. For the traditions in the Letter to the Hebrews, see the extensive discussion later in this chapter; the same image also resonates in the writings of second-century early Christian writers, as discussed in chapter 5.

10. Eusebius, *HE* 1:13:6 (Schwartz, 86).

11. *Apoc. Pet.* 70:14:6 (*Nag Hammadi Codices* VII.3; Robinson, 373).

12. See, e.g., Bernard, *Commentary,* 1:93; Schelkle, *Theologie des Neuen Testaments,* 4.1:36–51. These are only two examples, one a commentary and the other an introductory textbook, but many New Testament scholars hold this view. Aside from the studies listed in n. 3, see esp. Bachmann, *Jerusalem;* Biguzzi, *Il tempio di Gerusalemme;* Renwick, *Paul, the Temple, and the Presence of God.* A variety of new essays investigating the many-sidedness of the episodes associated by the Gospels with Jerusalem can be found in Horbury, *Templum Amicitiae.*

13. Matt 4:5; 27:53. The expression is absent from the other synoptics. The importance of this phrase is demonstrated by Eusebius's efforts to avoid it; see Walker, *Holy City,* 364–65; Rev 11:2; 21:2, 10; 22:19; John 2:16.

14. Mark 11:15–17, and its parallels Matt 21:12–13; Luke 19:45–46. It also appears in John 2:14–16, although in a different phase in the sequence of events and lacking the verse from Isaiah.

15. Heb 13:12–14, but cf. Acts 1:4; John 4:20–21.

16. Davies, *The Gospel and the Land,* 188–93; Townsend, "The Jerusalem Temple in the First Century," 48–65. The Tübingen school at the height of its popularity voiced the opposite approach; see Gaston, *No Stone,* 4–5. But many scholars still hold this view; see Brandon, *Fall;* Walker, *Holy City,* 9 n. 16; Chadwick, *The Early Church,* 20–21. I do not delve into the continuing debate about Paul's attitude to Judaism here, even though the "Jerusalem question" might contribute to this dispute as well.

17. E.g., Bachmann, *Jerusalem;* Barrett, "Attitudes to the Temple," 345–67.

18. For a recent example, see Larsson, "Temple-Criticism and the Jewish Heritage," 379–95. It is worth noting that the "anti-Temple" paradigm is still alive, although it has changed form since the days of the Tübingen school. Currently its main advocates are in the American scholarly group known as the "Jesus Seminar." For a summary of the views and origin of this school, along with a bibliography of its major spokespersons, see Fredriksen, "What You See Is What You Get," 82–91.

19. Highlighting the differences in approach toward Jerusalem and the Temple among the various groups within early Christianity are Cullmann, *Der johanneische Kreis,* 43ff.; and Hengel, *Zur urchristlichen Geschichtsschreibung,* 63–70; and now Han, *Jerusalem.* Hans Conzelmann expressed the view that the early Christians's disappointment at the delay in the *parousia* caused their ideological posture toward the city/ Temple; see Conzelmann, *Die Mitte der Zeit,* 66–71. Finally, for a literary approach to this question, see Schneider, *Die Apostelgeschichte,* 1:452–75.

20. Nibley, "Christian Envy of the Temple," 97–123, 229–40.

21. On mountains in the New Testament, see the summary in Balz and Schneider, *Exegetical,* 3:533–34.

22. John 4:7–42; see also *Ps.-Clem. Recognitiones* 1:57:1 (Rehm, 40).

23. Vincent and Steve, *Jérusalem de l'Ancien Testament* 2:467.

24. Mark 11:15–17, and parallels; John 2:16 names the *hieron* "my father's house"; Luke 2:22ff.; Acts 21:23–27, 24:17; 1 Cor 9:13. See Kittel, *Theologisches Wörterbuch*, 3:230–47; Balz and Schneider, *Exegetical*, 2:175.

25. Mark 13:1–2, and the synoptic parallels in Matt 24:1–2; Luke 21:5–6. Translations here and throughout this chapter are based, with slight changes, on the second edition of the Revised Standard Version (RSV).

26. For bibliography and summary of this question, already discussed in many studies, see Gaston, *No Stone*, 10–11. Differences in form, structure, and content also dissociate the stone-upon-stone passage from the adjoining little apocalypse passage—the place, characters, and subjects in the two passages are all different. In addition, in the Apocryphal parallel to this chapter, the *Apoc. Pet.*, preserved in Ethiopic, the story of the Mount of Olives appears in and of itself, and the stone-upon-stone prophecy is missing. See Buchholz, *Your Eyes Will Be Opened*, 162.

27. Voiced already in Meyer, *Kritisch*, 173. And see on this explanation n. 31. Gaston lists others who have adopted this understanding of the text; see Gaston, *No Stone*, 65–66, and n. 1, for his extensive bibliography. Also, Schlosser, "La parole de Jésus sur la fin du Temple," 398–414; Evans, "Predictions of the Destruction of the Herodian Temple," 89–91. Cf. the scholars brought together in Beasley-Murray, *A Commentary on Mark Thirteen*, 23, who deny the authenticity of these verses but nevertheless agree that it was produced in regard to the Temple. This understanding cuts across the board in New Testament scholarship; I encountered no one who denies it.

28. Eusebius, *Theoph.* 4, end of chap. 18 (Lee, no page numbers; trans. Lee, 248).

29. So claims Bultmann, *Die Geschichte der synoptischen Tradition*, 36.

30. Determining the chronological order among synoptic passages of the Gospels has been a complicated task. Although Mark is generally considered to have preceded the other two, this is not definitive for individual passages, especially where quotations attributed to Jesus are involved. For an up-to-date bibliography on this issue, see Neirynck et al., *The Gospel of Mark*, 643–44. Regarding the current segments, some linguistic features may shed light on their development. The modus of the verbs in the prophecy (2b) differs among the gospels. In Mark both verbs (*katalyō; aphiēmi*) are in the subjunctive (*coniunctivus*); in Matthew the first verb remains in that mood, but the second is in the future indicative, whereas in Luke both are in the future indicative. It seems that this difference can help us understand the internal development of the three versions. The similarity between the subjunctive and the future indicative (morphology, content, and more) caused them to be frequently confused in Hellenistic Greek; see Blass and Debrunner, *Greek Grammar*, 166–67, 183. Here, however, the verbs are in the aorist passive and in the future indicative; thus the morphological similarity, resulting from the suffix sigma (which is missing from the aorist passive), is not as strong (I owe this last point to Martha Himmelfarb). It is nevertheless hard to imagine that Mark, with his rough, simple language, would have taken a simple sentence in the future indicative, as found in Luke and Matthew, and changed it into the more complicated subjunctive construction. Moreover, the degenerate morphology of the verb *aphethēi* in Mark, in which the iota is left out—which is also preserved in Matthew—indicates that the direction of development was from the more complicated version in Mark to the simpler one in Matthew and Luke. On this aspect of the iotacism, see Moul-

ton and Howard, *Grammar*, 2:65. These details support the conclusion that the versions in Matthew and Luke belong to a second stage in the development of the text.

31. Three examples, spanning a century and a half of research, illustrate this claim: (1) Meyer, *Kritisch*, 173, who relates the stones in Mark to those of the Temple described in Josephus, did not take into account that in Josephus's case the subject is the inner sanctuary (*naos*), whereas in Mark the subject is what they saw when exiting the *hieron*. (2) Juel, "The Messiah and the Temple," notices the text deals with many buildings and finds this peculiar (p. 192), but he does not draw the appropriate conclusion and keeps identifying the prophecy as dealing with the Temple (p. 203; cf. to the "Temple complex" on p. 210). (3) Twenty years later, Sweet argued the same point; see Sweet, "A House Not Made with Hands," 374 n. 11. His argument, that writers in late antiquity did not discern the different terms, refutes itself. If, as he claims, Mark said "buildings" (structures) but actually meant "temple," then why did Matthew and Luke feel it necessary to add a specific identification?

32. Eusebius, *Theoph.* 4:18 (Lee, no page numbers; trans. Lee, 247–48).

33. On this story and its interpretations, see Wright, "The Widow's Mites," 256–65.

34. Opening the stone-upon-stone passage with the linguistic model known as *genetivus absolutus* is meant to serve the same purpose; see Moulton and Howard, *Grammar*, 1:74. These points become even more salient when comparing the passage in Mark with the parallel in Matthew 13. In Matthew the story about the widow's mite does not appear before the prophecy, so there is obviously no need to link the two. Indeed, in Matthew the two syntactic elements just noted do not appear; the passage begins as a new story, calling Jesus by his full name.

35. Cf. other suggestions that attempt to link the stone-upon-stone segment to different parts of the literary context, e.g., Lauverjat, "L'autre regard Marc 12:37b–13:2," 416–19, or, alternatively, studies that claim that this segment carries no specific context of its own but rather functions merely as a connecting limb; see S. Smith, "The Literary Structure of Mark 11:1–12:40," 111. It is hard to determine whether the background for the passage as interpreted here is eschatological or rather a social statement. I leave the door open for both sides in the current debate.

36. Matt 21:1–11; Mark 11:1–11; John 12:12–19. Note that the verb here is identical to the one in the other stone-upon-stone segment (*aphiēmi*), and its future tense here matches what is first found in Luke's version of that segment.

37. Cf. Gaston, *No Stone*, 12; Dupont, "Il n'en sera pas laissé pierre sur pierre (Marc 13,2; Luc 19,44)," 301–20. I find it hard to accept Gaston's assertion that Luke's pericope about Jerusalem represents the earliest version; he himself does not provide any evidence to support this claim, and even more importantly he does not recognize the linguistic and content nuances I have specified above (n. 30) that suggest the opposite. Dupont's view that the version in Luke is an independent tradition stems from the fact that he assumed, like his predecessors, that the prophecy in Mark was about the destruction of the Temple, on which basis he constructed his thesis that there were two versions of the prophecy—the destruction of the Temple and the destruction of Jerusalem. But if this assumption is refuted, his thesis has no leg to stand on.

38. Hatch and Redpath, *Concordance*, 1:177 s.v.

39. As described by Josephus, *BJ* 4:196ff. See Wellhausen, *Skizzen und Vorarbeiten*, 6:221–23; Wellhausen, *Analyse der Offenbarung Johannis*, 15.

40. For a recent survey and discussion of the various dates offered by scholars, which concludes in this way, see Marshall, *Parables of War*, 88–97.

41. This part of the chapter appeared in an earlier version as Eliav, "The Tomb." For a comprehensive and updated bibliography on this figure and the sources dealing with him, see Pratscher, *Der Herrenbruder;* Ward, "James," 779–812. For James's place in later Christian thought—in the Byzantine and medieval periods—see my discussion later in this chapter, with n. 81.

42. The origin of this dispute goes back to the 1840s, to the publications of Ferdinand Baur and the Tübingen school, with its most recent manifestation being the debate about the theories of the Franciscans Testa and Bagatti. For a fairly comprehensive bibliography, see Manns, *Bibliographie du Judéo-Christianisme*, and "A Survey of Recent Studies on Early Christianity," 17–25. Also see the papers collected in Everett Ferguson et al., *Early Christianity and Judaism*.

43. As articulated by K. Carrol, "The Place of James in the Early Church," 49, 56ff.

44. For some reason this point has been blurred in studies of the theology of the various Christian groups in those days; see, e.g., Schoeps, *Theologie und Geschichte des Judenchristentums;* Daniélou, *Théologie du Judéo-Christianisme;* Conzelmann, *Geschichte des Urchristentums;* Testa, *The Faith of the Mother Church.* Perhaps these scholars considered the emphasis on Jerusalem to be self-evident, since it was, after all, the site where the group lived, but it seems to me that the following discussion will demonstrate that the city and the Temple exceeded the technical sense of residence. In contrast, the studies of Pratscher and Irshai highlight this aspect, giving it the place it deserves; see Pratscher, *Der Herrenbruder*, 110–14; Irshai, "Historical," 1:4–34 (Heb.). See also Bauckham, "James," 417–27.

45. Acts 1:4; 1:12ff.; 2:5ff. (prophesying during Pentecost); 3:1; and more. Cf. *1 Apoc. Jas.* 25:15–18 (Parrott, 70), where, on the contrary, Jesus orders James to leave Jerusalem. For various explanations of the commands in the Apocalypse of James, see Schoedel, "A Gnostic," 161–62, and see also the following note. Obviously the status of Jerusalem in Acts can be seen as part of Luke's theology, and the verse is indeed explained in this way by most commentators; see, e.g., Conzelmann, *Acts of the Apostles,* 6; but the comparative material about the site presented here shows that, apart from the literary and theological uses of Jesus's instruction made by the author of Acts, these verses also reflect a certain authentic position of some members of the community.

46. But cf. *Ps.-Clem. Recognitiones* 1:71:2 (Rehm, 48), which hints that the supporters of James had some sort of center in Jericho and that he was brought there after he was injured at the Temple, although the same sentence also says that his home was in Jerusalem; also see *Prot. Jas.* 49 (de Strycker, 188), which explicitly states that James the "Jerusalemite" left the city for a while and went to live in the desert. On this passage, see Ward, "James," 800.

47. *Ap. Jas.* 16:9–10 (Attridge, 52).

48. *1 Apoc. Jas.* 25:15–18 (Parrott, 70), 36:16–18 (ibid., 90–92). Cf. Schoedel, "A Gnostic," 174–78.

49. *2 Apoc. Jas.* 44:15 (Parrott, 110), 45:24–25 (ibid., 112), 60:14–22 (ibid., 140), 61:21–23 (ibid., 142).

50. *Ps.-Clem. Recognitiones* 1:55:2 (Rehm, 40; Frankenberg, 60, line 28), 70:6–8 (Rehm, 48; Frankenberg, 74).

51. Eusebius, *HE* 2:23:4–18 (Schwartz, 166–70). I am not delving here into the com-

plex, and mostly unresolved, issue of Hegesippus's identity and sources. See, e.g., Gustafsson, "Hegesippus," 227–32; Irshai, "Historical," 8 (Heb.).

52. See also Bauckham, "James," 448–50.

53. Epiphanius, *Haer.* 29:4:2 (Holl and Dummer, I, 324, line 19); see also 78:13:5–78:14:2 (Holl and Dummer, II, 464–65). Views differ on the source of Epiphanius's data; some scholars believe that his information was based on another version of Hegesippus, independent of Eusebius, whereas others claim that Epiphanius developed and expanded the very same version. On all this, see already Lawlor, *Eusebiana*, 10–56.

54. *Ps.-Clem. Recognitiones* 1:70:6–8 (Rehm, 48; Frankenberg, 74, line 25).

55. Eusebius, *HE* 2:23:18 (Schwartz, 170, lines 23–24). For the tradition in Josephus (*JA* 20:200) and the enormous research literature about it, see Feldman, *Josephus,* 704–7. An interesting parallel to such a view can be found in the legend about the fall of Bethar, the final refuge of Bar Kokhba (*yTaʿan* 4 [68c] and parallels). This legend too links the killing of R. Eleazar ha-Modaʿi, who sat and prayed every day, and the capture of the town by Hadrian. A similar conception is expressed by the midrash in R. Yoḥanan ben Zakkai's answer to Vespasian concerning R. Tṣadok, "If there is one like him in a city, you would not be able to conquer it forever." See *LamR* 1:5 (Buber, 34b). The same line of thought is offered by that story's version in *bGit* 56a, which states, "R. Tṣadok sat in fast for forty years so that Jerusalem shall not fall." In a nutshell the idea that the presence of a pious man safeguards the city appears already in the biblical sequence about Sodom (Gen 18:23ff.), and from there it was adopted by some Second Temple apocryphal writers; see *2 Bar.* 2:1–2 (Dedering, 1); *4 Bar.* 1:2 (Kraft and Purintun, 12). The cited rabbinic portions continue this same notion; see also *PRK* 13:13 (Mandelbaum, 238, line 2:4); *PesR* 26 (Friedmann, 131a). All these confirm the Jewish origins of Hegesippus's tradition about James.

56. *1 Apoc. Jas.* 36:16–18 (Parrott, 90–92). Brown's claim that this association can also be found in the Second Apocalypse of James is rather doubtful; see K. Brown, "Jewish and Gnostic Elements," 228. The passage only asserts that Jerusalem would be destroyed, as Jesus had said, but does not establish any connection with James's death.

57. Origen, *Comm. in Mt.* 10:17 (Klostermann, 22, lines 7ff.); Origen, *Cels.* 1:47 (Borret, I, 198–200), 2:13 (ibid., 324); Eusebius, *HE* 2:23:20 (Schwartz, 172). A discussion of the source of the passages and a bibliography can be found in Pratscher, *Der Herrenbruder,* 119–20; Baras, "The Testimonium Flavianum," 338–48. This fragment should not be confused with Josephus's famous passage about James (in n. 55). Most of the scholarly attention has been devoted to the latter, while the one discussed here has gone mostly unnoticed.

58. On these matters, see Pratscher, *Der Herrenbruder,* 229–60; Feldman, *Josephus,* 704–7; Ward, "James"; Irshai, "Historical," 5–13 (Heb.); Böhlig, "Zum Martyrium des Jakobus," 207–13; Beyschlag, "Das Jakobusmartyrium," 149–78. A more recent source-critical examination of the various traditions, which exhaustively discusses the vast scholarly opinions that were offered on this topic, may be found in Jones, "Martyrdom," 322–35. Not all sources about James emphasize these aspects of his life pertaining to Jerusalem and the priesthood; on the contrary, some of them seem to be deliberately ignoring these features and highlighting opposing ones. See, e.g., the fragment from the *Gospel of the Hebrews* adduced by Jerome, which is cited by Ward, "James," 793. Even though the theological picture stemming from these early layers of the Jesus movement

is very complex, it is hard to ignore the fact that the fragmentary details mentioned here join up to form one fairly well-grounded facet of their discourse.

59. Eusebius, *HE* 2:23:11 (Schwartz, 168, line 18). A bit later in the passage (line 22) some textual witnesses read *naos*, which usually denoted the inner shrine of the Temple (fig. 2:A), instead of *hieron*. I discuss this variant in n. 99.

60. *2 Apoc. Jas.* 61:20–23 (Parrott, 142).

61. Eusebius, *HE* 2:23:18 (Schwartz, 170, lines 21–22).

62. For a summary of the various proposals, see Jeremias, "Die 'Zinne,'" 195–205; Balz and Schneider, *Exegetical*, 3:191–92, s.v.

63. Matt 4:5–7; Luke 4:9–12.

64. About this unique textual tradition, see Montgomery, *Commentary*, 386–88. The date of this translation is commonly fixed in the second half of the second century; see Collins, *Daniel*, 10–11.

65. *T. Sol.* 22:8 (McCown, 66, line 11).

66. To the best of my knowledge, no one has yet collected the various documentations about this site from the literature of the pilgrims and other writings of the Byzantine period and discussed them critically. Partial references may be found in Jeremias, "Die 'Zinne,'" 201–5.

67. Jeremias, "Die 'Zinne,'" 205–6 and his summary on p. 208. More on this conjecture below, n. 70.

68. Josephus, *JA* 15:412. For scholars who hold this position, see Balz and Schneider, *Exegetical*, III, 191–92.

69. *yPes* 7:11 (35b). For this proposal, see the extensive discussion in Jeremias, "Die 'Zinne,'" 201–5. For the *'agof*, see chapter 6.

70. Indeed, sharp criticism of the various suggestions has been expressed time and again in scholarly literature; ironically, however, the various critics have suggested hypotheses that are no less astonishing than the ones they condemned. Jeremias, for example, argues extensively against the positions that were prevalent in the literature before him, yet he himself bases his interpretation on the *Testament of Solomon*. And Hyldahl, who disapproves of Jeremias's thesis (and also repeats the criticism against all the other scholars), presents an equally ill-founded view in which the *pterygion* is presented as the official execution site of Jerusalem. See Hyldahl, "Die Versuchung," 113–27.

71. Enumerated in Hatch, *Concordance*, 1238, s.v.

72. Eusebius, *HE* 2:23:11 (Schwartz, 168, lines 18–19; trans. Lake, 173).

73. Eusebius, *HE* 2:23:18 (Schwartz, 170, line 21–22). Lake translates *naos* as "Temple" and thus misses the subtle nuances of the writer, who differentiates between *hieron* and *naos*.

74. So claim, e.g., Vincent and Abel, *Jérusalem nouvelle*, 842; McGiffert, *Church History*, 1:127 n. 30; Jeremias, "Die 'Zinne,'" 201 n. 1.

75. *2 Apoc. Jas.* 61:20 (Parrott, 142–44). The pericope that might be considered to hint at a burial is 62:8–11 (Parrott, 144), and one author who understood it that way was K. Brown, "Jewish and Gnostic Elements," 228 n. 10. In contrast, Brown's (230) suggestion that the description of James being dragged along the ground after he was thrown off (62:2 [Parrott, 144]) implies that the body was taken out of the Temple area is doubtful, if only because there is no hint of it in the text. On this whole issue, see also Funk, *Die zweite*, 176–80.

76. *Ps.-Clem. Recognitiones* 1:70:6–8 (Rehm, 48; Frankenberg, 74).

77. These segments and others are gathered in Abel, "La sépulture," 482–83. Abel, like the scholars discussed already, assumed that the tomb could not have been located on the "sacred Mount," as he calls it, and so was compelled to suggest other readings of these passages. Concerning the later versions of James's martyrdom, see Schneemelcher, *New Testament Apocrypha,* 2:478–79.

78. *Itinerarium Burdigalense* 589:12–590:2 (Geyer and Cuntz, 15). See also *Breviarius de Hierosolyma* 6 (Weber, 112). Many have missed this point; see, e.g., Maraval, *Lieux,* 261. Maraval lists the references to the *pterygion* in the pilgrimage literature, adding incidentally that this is also the place from which James was thrown ("ce pinacle est aussi l'endroit d'où fut précipité Jacques, frère du Seigneur"), but this is precisely the detail that is not mentioned at all by any of the pilgrims!

79. Cf. Wilkinson, *Egeria's,* 183. Wilkinson suggests that parts of the description of Jerusalem in the writing of the so-called Peter the Deacon of the twelfth century are taken from lost fragments of Egeria's writings. But the information about James in the passage he cites there is far too similar to the fragment of Hegesippus, and it seems much more likely that Peter, a librarian in the Monte Casino monastery, took them from Eusebius (perhaps through Rufinus's translation or Jerome's citations of the passage in his *De viris inlustribus* 2). For more about this, see Abel, "La sépulture," 499.

80. Irshai, "Historical," 86–87 (esp. nn. 35–36; Heb.).

81. Abel collected the various sources describing this site and its functions during the Middle Ages and discussed them at length; see Abel, "La sépulture," 480–99; and a somewhat shorter version in Vincent and Abel, *Jérusalem nouvelle,* 845–50. For a more recent discussion of this site, see Verhelst, "L'Apocalypse," 81–104. Other famous Christian characters received similar attention in Jerusalem of those days; see, e.g., Limor, "Christian Sacred Space and the Jew," 63–65.

82. To the literature enumerated in the previous note, add Wilkinson et al., *Jerusalem Pilgrimage,* 44.

83. Jerome, *De viris inlustribus* 2 (Richardson, 8, lines 26–27). See also Theodosius, *De situ Terrae sanctae* 9 (Geyer, 119, lines 10–12), and another tradition from the same period in Gregory of Tours, *De gloria beatorum martyrum* 27 (Ruinart, cols. 727–28). Cf. Hunt, *Holy Land,* 155 n. 1. Hunt's interpretation of the first two texts presented here, as saying that James's tomb was located in the Kidron Valley, has no foundation. Jerome and Theodosius both clearly say "the Mount of Olives" (*in monte Oliveti*); moreover, Theodosius distinguishes explicitly between the sites on the Mount of Olives (par. 9) in which he locates James's tomb and the site in the Jehoshaphat Valley. See also Abel, "La sépulture," 491. Concerning the "cornerstone" on Mount Zion, see the second version of the so-called *Itinerarium Antonini Placentini* 22 (Geyer, 165). For Gregory of Tour's sources, see the detailed discussion in Hen, "Gregory of Tours and the Holy Land," 47–64.

84. *Armenian Liturgy, lectio* for 25 December (Renoux, 367). Note Renoux's comment (ibid.) that the original version referred to the biblical patriarch Jacob and not James. On these ceremonies, see Limor, "The Origins of a Tradition," 457–62. It is worth noticing that this particular feast was still unknown to Egeria in the late fourth century. For additional, later "holy days" that were devoted to James in the various Palestinian liturgies, see Abel, "La sépulture," 494 and n. 3.

85. Reproduced in Williams, *The Holy City,* plate 1, following p. 196.

86. Abel, "La sépulture," 499: "La vénération de la mémoire du premier évêque de Jérusalem ne s'éloignait pas beaucoup du lieu de son martyre."

87. Abel's attempt (ibid., 485) to explain this difference between the early and Byzantine sources by arguing that at a certain point James's body was moved from one grave to another is nothing but a harmonizing effort lacking any evidential basis. Clear examples of this process of "reading backward" are Jeremias, "Die 'Zinne,'" 201 and n. 1; Hunt, *Holy Land*, 155 n. 1; Donner, "Der Felsen und der Tempel," 1–11. The same process is reflected in remarks of John Wilkinson on the Byzantine pilgrims, e.g., his comments on the description of the Temple Mount in the writings of the traveler from Bordeaux: Wilkinson, *Jerusalem Pilgrims*, 173, s.v. "Temple"; and Wilkinson, "Christian Pilgrims," 86. From here it is but a short step to a "new reality" in the guides and introductory books; see, e.g., Kopp, *The Holy Places of the Gospels*, 287 (map); Maraval, *Lieux*, 33, 264.

88. Abel, "La sépulture," 495–99; Wilkinson et al., *Jerusalem Pilgrimage*, 44; Schein, "Between Mount Moriah and the Holy Sepulchre," 175–95.

89. *Itinerarium Burdigalense* 589:11–590:4 (Geyer and Cuntz, 15).

90. *T. Sol.* 22:7–8 (McCown, 66), 23 (McCown, 69–70). For another later version of this legend, see Duling, "Testament," 1:985, verse 24 note a.

91. For some of the more popular examples, see Duling, "Testament," verse 23 note b; McKelvey, "Christ the Cornerstone," 352–59. An additional interesting parallel is *Barn.* 6:3–4 (Lake, 358), which alludes to this verse in the context of its criticism of those people who interpret it literally and put their trust in an actual stone. This may echo the identification of a particular stone in Jerusalem as indicated by the Bordeaux pilgrim. See also *Ap. Jer.* 28 (Kuhn, 302–3), a late (fourth or fifth century) text that conveys a fully developed legend about the cornerstone in the Temple with no connection to the other features discussed here (I owe this reference to Kirstie Copland, and I am also grateful for her help and advice on the Coptic throughout this chapter). Concerning the motif of the stone in biblical imagery, which undoubtedly affected the religious thinking of whoever shaped the traditions about Jesus and James, see Gruenwald, "God the 'Stone/Rock,'" 428–49. Gruenwald's study complements my presentation here. It examines the picture from the abstract aspect of ideas, while my own remarks reflect the way these ideas encountered the real world (with thanks to Professor Gruenwald for referring me to this study of his).

92. *2 Apoc. Jas.* 61:21–22 (Parrott, 142). For the various alternative translations from Coptic, see Crum, *A Coptic Dictionary*, 421. See also the editor's hesitations in the notes of Parrot, 142–43.

93. I discuss the early Christian attraction to Solomon's Temple in chapter 5.

94. Scholars who did not recognize the realistic dimension of these documents have missed this point entirely; Funk, *Die zweite*, 175 n. 1, although noticing that all three texts share the "great stone," nevertheless returns to Jeremias's view (see nn. 69 and 95). But at the time when Jeremias produced his study, the *Second Apocalypse of James* was still buried in the ground at Nag-Hammadi, and Funk did not consider the possibility that this new discovery could highlight aspects unrecognized by Jeremias. Funk's claim that Hegesippus's story was shaped by the verse about the "cornerstone" in Psalms 117 (118):22 compounds the wrong since the two major features—the great stone and the verse from the Psalm—are precisely what is missing from Hegesippus, surfacing only in the *Testament of Solomon* and the *Second Apocalypse of James*. This point was also missed by Brown, "Jewish," 227.

95. So Jeremias, "Die 'Zinne,'" 200, and many more.

96. Matt 4:5–7 = Luke 4:9–12. The elements of the episode constitute an independent literary unit: an exposition presenting the site of the event, followed by a hermeneutic contest between Satan and Jesus, both of whom substantiate their positions with Bible verses. The author of Mark does not include such a pericope in his temptation sequence at all; see Mark 1:12–13. In Luke, although the author treats the whole cycle of temptations rather freely and interchangeably, the inner structure of the *pterygion* experience as well as its content nevertheless remains intact (except for some minor details).

97. Hyldahl, "Die Versuchung."

98. Eusebius *HE* 2:23:18 (Schwartz, 170, lines 21–22). Contra Groh, "The Onomasticon of Eusebius," 27, who ascribes the remark "his gravestone still remains by the shrine" to Eusebius and compares it with this writer's habit in his *Onomasticon* of concluding a geographical account with the statement that the situation at a particular site continues "until this very day." Groh's reading of the passage stumbles on both linguistic and literary grounds. Eusebius consistently uses the expanded, biblically rooted and therefore almost formal formula *eti nyn* (until this very day), not the ingenuous temporal adverb *eti* (still). See also Wilken, *The Land,* 100. Furthermore, in the absence of distinguishing punctuation such as colons and quotation marks, competent writers like Eusebius utilized literary techniques to distinguish a quotation from their own words. This could not be clearer than in the current passage, where Eusebius brings Hegesippus's segment to a close with the statement, "This account is given at length by Hegesippus . . ." (23:19).

99. Noting this, Schwartz in his notes to Eusebius's text (p. 170) concluded that the two endings of the story cannot function together (i.e., come from the same author: " . . . wei Schlüsse der Erzählung, die neben einander nicht stehen können"). On the other hand, his assertion in the apparatus criticus that the phrase locating the site "next to the shrine" is a scribal error due to *homoioteleuton* (the same phrase *para tōi naōi* appears once before in the same context, which could signal that the eyes of the manuscript copier skipped from one to another) does not seem persuasive. This version is documented in all the Greek manuscripts as well as by the Syriac translation (Wright and McLean, 104, line 8), which shows that it already existed in the fifth century. The entire pericope about the tombstone was omitted from Rufinus's text, perhaps because of his inaccurate translation, which Mommsen called "arbitrary" (*wilkürliche*) and "strongly reducing the original" (*verkürzende Behandlung der Urschrift*); see Mommsen, "Einleitung zu Rufin," ccli. But cf. Murphy, *Rufinus of Aquileia,* 164ff. An alternative reason might be that the monument was no longer known in the fifth century.

100. *Mart. Pol.* 18:2–3 (Lake, II, 336; trans. Lake, II, 337).

101. The most detailed discussions of the early traditions about this tomb are still those of Vincent and Abel, *Jérusalem,* 1–2: 89–104; Jeremias, "Wo lag Golgotha und das Heilige Grab?" 141–73; Jeremias, "Golgotha und der heilige Felsen," 74–128 (these two papers were published later as a short monograph: *Golgotha* [Leipzig: E. Pfeiffer, 1926]). I do not want to delve here into the debate about what exactly the early Christians remembered or what transformations and developments these memories underwent. But it is hard to accept extreme positions such as that of Parrot, *Golgotha,* 49–59. There is still some basis for the claim that the early members of the Jesus movement preserved some memory whose early layers are reflected in the various Gospel accounts of the Resurrection (Matt 27:59ff. = Luke 23:52ff.). For a more moderate view, see Coüasnon, *The Church of the Holy Sepulchre in Jerusalem,* 6–14. On the entire issue, see the bal-

anced, persuasive discussion of Walker, *Holy City,* 241–47 (including an updated bibliography).

102. A. Grabar, *Martyrium,* esp. 1:27–44; P. Brown, *The Cult of the Saints.* Even though most of Grabar's and Brown's discussions are devoted to later periods than the one at issue here, they too assert that the beginning of these processes was very early. For a discussion concentrating on Palestine, see also Wilkinson, "Jewish Holy Places," 41–53.

103. The mutual relations between sites and saints were extensively discussed in Delehaye, *Les légendes hagiographiques,* 45–51, 190–201; see also 253–56.

104. See, e.g., Schneemelcher, *New Testament Apocrypha,* 1:396; Chapman, "Zacharias Slain," 398–410; Blank, "The Death of Zechariah," 327–46; Dubois, "La mort de Zacharie," 23–38. The similarities between Zechariah and James were discussed in detail in Irshai, "Historical Aspects," 8–12 (Heb.). There is not yet a complete summary of the tradition and the site in the writings of the pilgrims and later authors; in the meantime, see Wilkinson et al., *Jerusalem Pilgrimage,* 173, who for some reason did not include *Itinerarium Burdigalense* 591:2 (Geyer and Cuntz, 15), and now Verhelst, "L'Apocalypse."

105. E.g., the Martyrdom of Tabitha in *Apoc. El.* (c) 6 (Steindorff, 120–25; chap. 4 in Charlesworth's enumeration).

106. *LamR* 4:14 (Buber, 149). Other sources on Zechariah are listed in n. 104.

107. Gafni, "Pre-Histories of Jerusalem," 12–16.

108. *mEduy* 8:5; *yPes* 9:1 (36c); *ARN* version a 26 (Schechter, 41b). See Krauss, *Qadmoniot ha-Talmud,* 1.1.109–11, who deduces from these sources that burial was indeed practiced on the Temple Mount (or in the numerous tunnels underneath its surface).

109. Recently the research and a bibliography on this topic were reviewed in Satran, *Prophets,* 22–25.

110. Ibid., 118–20. For a view opposing these inclinations, see, e.g., Matt 23:29.

111. Heb 2:17, 3:1, 5:1–10, 6:19, 7:11ff.; see Attridge, *Hebrews,* 97–103. Oddly, even when Attridge cites parallel Christian sources outside of the New Testament (Attridge, *Hebrews,* 102 n. 263), he does not mention James.

112. Himmelfarb, *Ascent to Heaven,* 30–31.

113. Heb 7:27; Epiphanius, *Haer.* 30:16:7 (Holl and Dummer, I, 354–55).

114. Noticed by Gustafsson, "Hegesippus," 229ff. See also Pratscher, *Der Herrenbruder,* 110–14; Frederick F. Bruce, *Peter, Stephen, James and John,* 116–17.

T H R E E : Delusive Landscapes

1. Josephus, *BJ* 7:1–2 (Thackeray, III, 504). On Jews visiting the city during this period, see chapter 6.

2. Not much, if at all, could be extracted from the legend in *GenR* 64:9 (Theodor and Albeck, 710–12) about a Roman plan to rebuild the Temple. No one now endorses claims such as that promoted by Adolf Schlatter in the nineteenth century that the Romans indeed restored the Jewish Temple prior to the Bar Kokhba revolt; see Schlatter, *Die Tage Trajans und Hadrians,* 59–67. For a balanced assessment of this source, see Schäfer, *Der Bar Kokhba-Aufstand,* 29–34.

3. For a comprehensive and critical review of the sources relating to this period, see Schäfer, *Der Bar Kokhba-Aufstand.*

4. See Isaac, "Roman Colonies," 31–54; Millar, "The Roman *Coloniae*," 8, 23–30.

5. For a detailed study of this community, see Irshai, "Historical Aspects," 4–43 (Heb.).

6. Eusebius, *De martyribus Palestinae* 11:8–12; this story appears in both the short Greek version (Schwartz, 936–38) and the long one preserved in Syriac (Cureton, 40–41).

7. This part is based on a previous study of mine; see Eliav, "Hadrian's Actions," 125–44.

8. Cassius Dio, *Hist.* 69:12:1 (Cary, VIII, 446; trans. Cary, VIII, 447).

9. So claims Gregorovius, *Der Kaiser Hadrian*, 212: "Für den neuen Tempel des Römergottes konnte keine Stelle geeigneter sein, als die von Riesenmauer gestützte Felsenfläche Moria."

10. Wartensleben, *Jerusalem*, 156: "An edleren Formen und reinerem Style übertraf dieser Jupiter-Tempel vielleicht sogar die drei Jehovah-Tempel, die nach der Reihe an demselben Flecke gestanden hatten." See also E. Robinson, *Biblical Researches*, 1:437; Williams, *The Holy City*, 214; Thrupp, *Antient Jerusalem*, 202–5; Pierotti, *Jerusalem*, 1:43, 57; Derenbourg, *Essai sur l'histoire*, 6, 419–20; Couret, *La Palestine*, 3; de Saulcy, *Jérusalem*, 87–89; Schlatter, *Zur Topographie*, 142; Schick, *Die Stiftshütte der Temple*, 216–19; Graetz, *Geschichte der Juden*, 4:152–53; Reinach, *Histoire des Israélites*, 9, and many more.

11. Schlatter, *Zur Topographie*, 152–56.

12. Germer-Durand, "Aelia," 369–87; Schürer, *Geschichte*, 1:700–701. The latter stayed practically unchanged in later editions; see Schürer, *History*, 1:554. And the same in C. Wilson, *Golgotha*, 62.

13. Vincent and Abel, *Jérusalem nouvelle*, 33–35. Although Vincent stops short of asserting that the shrine is a Capitoline, he does not doubt its existence and location; Avi-Yonah, *Historical Geography of Palestine*, 98 (Heb.). See also Henderson, *Life and Principate*, 219; Watzinger, *Denkmäler Palästinas*, 2:79–80.

14. For some examples, see Bahat, *Illustrated Atlas*, 59 (map); Littell, *The Macmillan Atlas History of Christianity*, 19 (map); Geva, "Jerusalem: The Roman Period," 2:758 (map); Richard Z. Chesnoff, "God's City," *U.S. News and World Report*, 18 December 1995, 68; The Tower of David Museum of Jerusalem in the permanent display titled "Aelia Capitolina: A Pagan City"; Israeli Supreme Court verdict, *Piskey Din* 47/V/6 (1993) 240 (Heb.). For a fuller list, see Eliav, "Hadrian's Actions," 126–27.

15. I first learned of this doubt from Professor Benjamin Isaac, during a lecture at the Institute for Advanced Studies, Jerusalem 1993 (see his "renewed" translation of Cassius Dio: Isaac, *The Limits*, 353, but cf. Isaac, "Roman Colonies," 48 at the end of n. 78). But it seems that he was preceded by several other scholars: Grelle, *L'autonomia*, 227–28, and following him Bowersock, "A Roman Perspective," 137–38. This approach was cited in some other works, such as Wilken, *The Land*, 41–43 (cf. p. 82); Schäfer, "Hadrian's Policy," 288–89. Others, though not explicitly stating their doubts, left the Capitoline temple out of their descriptions of the Temple Mount in the days after the Bar Kokhba revolt; e.g., Wilkinson, *Egeria's*, 36, who asserts that the mountain remained in ruins from Hadrian's time onward. See also Peters, *Jerusalem*, 129–30; Stemberger, *Jews and Christians*, 53–54 (cf. p. 51, where he claims that large parts of the Jewish temple walls remained standing until the end of Byzantine times!); Millar, "The Roman *Coloniae*," 29 n. 95.

16. Bowersock, "A Roman Perspective," 137–38; for a detailed analysis and critique of Bowersock's reading, see Eliav, "Hadrian's Actions," 132–33.

17. For all the details, see Eliav, "Hadrian's Actions." Preceding me in this idea, although without offering any proof to substantiate it, were Boissevain, *Cassii Dionis Cocceiani*, 3:232, in his note to line 14; Grelle, *L'autonomia*, 227–28; Murphy-O'Connor, "The Location," 407–15.

18. Cassius Dio, *Hist.* 73:23:5 (Cary, IX, 118). For a detailed discussion on Dio's methods, see Millar, *A Study*, 28–72; Barnes, "The Composition of Cassius Dio's Roman History," 240–55.

19. On the *Epitomai* in general and in the Byzantine period in particular, see Brunt, "Historical Fragments," 477–94; R. Browning, *The Byzantine Empire*, 129–38. On the works of Xiphilinus and Zonaras in Dio, see Brunt, "Historical Fragments," 487–92; Millar, *A Study*, 1–4, who also provides further bibliography.

20. See Eliav, "Hadrian's Actions," 131 and n. 21.

21. *Barn.* 16:4 (Lake, I, 396; trans. Lake, I, 397).

22. For a survey of the various suggestions, see D. Schwartz, *Studies*, 147–53; Paget, *The Epistle of Barnabas*, 17–28.

23. Schwartz, *Studies*, 152.

24. *Itinerarium Burdigalense* 591:1 (Geyer and Cuntz, 15).

25. E.g., Stewart and Wilson, *Itinerary*, 21 n. 4; Donner, *Pilgerfahrt ins Heilige Land*, 56 n. 86; Mango, "The Temple Mount," 1:3; Belayche, "Du Mont," 398.

26. See Vincent and Abel, *Jérusalem nouvelle*, 16–17, and esp. n. 4.

27. *Aedes* in relation to the Temple Mount appears also in Rufinus, *HE* 10:39–40 (Momsen, 998). Rufinus does not offer any additional details about the nature of the site or the source of its name, which makes it difficult to draw any firm conclusions from his remarks. It is quite clear, however, that he does not see any connection with a pagan temple, which he would undoubtedly have mentioned in his discussion of Julian's enterprises if it had existed or if he had any knowledge about it. Also unclear is whether the *aedes* mentioned by Rufinus can be identified with the one mentioned by the traveler from Bordeaux.

28. *Chronicon Paschale* (Dindorf, 474, lines 10–17). The references are to the lines in the Dindorf edition. On the date of this document, see Whitby and Whitby, *Chronicon*, ix–xi.

29. Schlatter, *Zur Topographie*, 142; following Germer-Durand, "Aelia," 380–81; Belayche, "Du Mont," 397. See also Vincent and Abel, *Jérusalem nouvelle*, 7, 14–15; Tsafrir, "Topography," 157 (Heb.), and many more.

30. For some doubts about the trustworthiness of this source, see Bowersock, "A Roman Perspective," 135; Isaac, *The Limits*, 353.

31. Flusin, "L'esplanade," 17–31.

32. Ibid., 28; Mango, "The Temple Mount," 2–3.

33. Murphy-O'Connor, "The Location," 414–15.

34. *Itinerarium Burdigalense* 591:4 (Geyer and Cuntz, 16). The clause about the statuary is missing from the Madrid manuscript Matritensis (Arc. Hist. Nac. 1279) and from manuscript 1007 D (254).

35. Jerome, *Comm. in Mt.* 4, 24:15 (Hurst and Adriaen, 226).

36. Jerome, *Comm. in Isa.* 1, 2:9 (Adriaen, 33). On the dates of these compositions, see Kelly, *Jerome*, 222, 299.

37. E.g., Germer-Durand, "Aelia," 373 (map); Vincent and Abel, *Jérusalem nouvelle,* 15–18, 33–55; Schürer, *History,* 1:554–55; Bahat, *Illustrated Atlas,* 59 (map); Geva, "Jerusalem: The Roman Period," 765.

38. See Wilkinson, "Christian Pilgrims," 77–79; Lifshitz, "Jérusalem," 484; Stemberger, *Jews and Christians,* 54; Murphy-O'Connor, "The Location," 410–11; Belayche, "Du Mont," 399–401; Tsafrir, "Topography," 157 (Heb.).

39. Eliav, "The Desolating Sacrilege."

40. For a more detailed version of the discussion on Aelia's urban framework, see Eliav, "The Urban Layout of Aelia Capitolina," 241–77.

41. The most up-to-date comprehensive treatment of this subject is Tsafrir, "Topography," 115–66 (Heb.). A good English summary of the material may be found in Geva, "Jerusalem: The Roman Period," 758–67. In what follows I refer mostly to Geva's English study.

42. Of all these, only the coins have been documented and studied in detail. See Kindler and Stein, *Bibliography,* 22–37; Meshorer, *The Coinage.* For typical examples of stamped roof tiles, see Geva, "The Camp," 245. The inscriptions have now been collected and translated by Isaac, "Inscriptions from Jerusalem after the First Revolt," 167–79 (Heb.).

43. Geva, "Jerusalem: The Roman Period," 761–62; Wightman, *The Walls,* 199–200. Contra: Magness, "The North Wall," 331. The written sources do not provide unambiguous evidence on this issue. On the one hand, one of the later traditions about the exclusion of Jews from the city during Hadrian's reign uses the Greek *sēmeia* to mark the city limits, without mentioning any city walls. See Alexander Monachos, *Inventio crucis* (Gretser, col. 4068). However, he may be rephrasing his earlier sources on this issue (such as Aristo of Pella), making it difficult to determine what the original wording was in this case. On the other hand, it would be problematic to rely on the mention of the city wall built during Hadrian's reign in *The Dialogue of Timothy and Aquila* 130 (Conybeare, 98), as historians tend to date this source to a much later period (apparently the sixth century); see Robertson, *The Dialogue of Timothy and Aquila,* 372–83. The same holds true for the report about a city wall built by Hadrian in Orosius, *Historiarum adversum paganos* 7:13:5 (Zangemeister, 469). Orosius, who visited the city in the fifth century, was probably influenced by its Byzantine scenery. See also Smallwood, *The Jews under Roman Rule,* 461 n. 130.

44. Wightman, *Damascus Gate.*

45. E.g., Pierotti, *Jerusalem,* 2: pls. 12–13; Clermont-Ganneau, *Archaeological Researches,* 1:49–77.

46. One of Vincent's students summarized and extensively discussed the excavations and findings in her doctoral dissertation; see Aline, "La forteresse."

47. Bagatti, "Resti romani," 309–52.

48. The attribution of the pavement to the Antonia fortress is based on the nineteenth-century "Great Antonia" concept, which received its fullest expression by Vincent and his students; see Aline, "La forteresse," 88–142. It was reiterated, with certain variants, by Blomme, "Faut-il revenir sur la datation de l'arc de l'Ecce Homo," 244–71. For a summary of Coüasnon's findings, see *RB* 73 (1966) 573–74. Benoit's arguments are laid out in Benoit, "L'Antonia," 145–47.

49. Cf. Arnould, *Les arcs romains de Jérusalem.* Although I find her general conclusions about the date and function of the two entrance structures rather convincing, her

attempt to pinpoint the date of each structure to specific years seems too particular in light of the available evidence.

50. Benoit, "L'Antonia," 162–63, and following him (and at times placing the arch erroneously in their maps) Geva, "The Camp," 249 (map); Geva, "Jerusalem: The Roman Period," 764; Bahat, *Illustrated Atlas*, 59 (map); Bar, "Aelia Capitolina," 14–16; Avigad, *The Upper City of Jerusalem*, 227 (map; Heb.); Segal, *From Function to Monument*, 136 (but cf. n. 139, where he asserts that "we know too little about the city plan of Jerusalem in this period in order to be certain that the arch was in fact the entrance to the forum"); Magness, "The North Wall," 332 (map).

51. Vincent already offered to view the Ecce Homo arch as the eastern gate of Aelia; see Vincent and Abel, *Jérusalem nouvelle*, 24, and Wightman, *Damascus Gate*, 197, 199. See also Tsafrir, "Topography," 156.

52. Clermont-Ganneau, *Recueil d'archéologie orientale*, 6:188–99, who believed that the inscriptions were etched in the "city walls" (*mur d'enciente*, 196); Savignac, "Inscription romaine," 90–99; Vincent and Abel, *Jérusalem nouvelle*, 36.

53. For a succinct summary of the findings and their various interpretations, see Geva, "Jerusalem: The Roman Period," 763.

54. Ibid., 762–64.

55. Ibid.

56. B. Mazar, *Excavations*; B. Mazar, *The Mountain of the Lord*, 237–43.

57. E. Mazar, "The Roman-Byzantine Bathhouse," 87–102 (Heb.).

58. Geva, "Jerusalem: The Roman Period," 766. In his map of Aelia, Geva includes the lower aqueduct as well, and there seems to be some logic to this, since no reasonable person would want to give up such a source of water.

59. Eusebius, *Chronicon* year 136 (Helm, 201, lines 18–19). Whether this detail was taken form the original writings of Eusebius or supplemented by Jerome is not clear, since it does not appear in the Armenian version (Karst, 221), but in any case it may well refer to a gate from the days of Aelia.

60. *Itinerarium Burdigalense* 591:7 (Geyer and Cuntz,16). The clue comes from the use of the verb *exeo* (to exit), and it was already understood in this way, as alluding to an ancient gate, by Wightman, *The Walls*, 207; Tsafrir, "Topography," 142.

61. *Itinerarium Antonini Placentini* 24 (Geyer, 141, lines 19–20). Here too this conclusion was previously reached by Tsafrir, "Muqaddasi's Gates of Jerusalem," 159–60; Wightman, *The Walls*, 220–22.

62. Cotton and Eck, "Ein Ehrenbogen für Septimius Severus."

63. Cf. Meshorer, *The Coinage*.

64. Eusebius, *VC* 3:26 (Heikel, 89–90).

65. For a possible Mithraeum a bit to the west of that area, see Magness, "A Mithraeum in Jerusalem?" 163–71.

66. Germer-Durand, "Aelia," 369–87. His view of the city contours underlies all the reconstructions that have been put forward since then. It was taken *ad absurdum* by Wilkinson, who dates the road system even earlier, claiming that it was built in the Second Temple period. See Wilkinson, "The Streets of Jerusalem," 118–36. A more balanced reconstruction based on Germer-Durand's principles has recently been presented, exhaustively and fully referenced, in Tsafrir, "Topography."

67. O. Grabar, "Jerusalem," 524.

68. The two most recent studies that express this all-encompassing view are Geva,

"Jerusalem: The Roman Period"; Tsafrir, "Topography." A more popular summary, intended for the general public but based on the same principles, is Bahat, *Illustrated Atlas*, 58–67.

69. Germer-Durand, "Aelia," 373; C. Wilson, *Golgotha*, 144; Vincent and Abel, *Jérusalem nouvelle*, chart 1.

70. Avigad, *Discovering Jerusalem*, 225–28; Magness, *Jerusalem Ceramic Chronology*, 28–29, 119–37.

71. Avigad, *Discovering Jerusalem*, 206–7; Geva, "The Camp"; Reich, "Four Notes on Jerusalem," 164–67; Magness, "The North Wall"; contra: Tsafrir, "Topography," 132–34, 144–45.

72. A survey of those who locate the camp on the southwestern hill can be found in Geva, "The Camp"; the Christian Quarter—Bar, "Aelia Capitolina"; the northern part of the city—Isaac, *The Limits*, 427–28; the Temple Mount—Isaac, *The Limits*, 427–28; Cohn, *New Ideas about Jerusalem's Topography*, 122–24. The area adjacent to the Temple Mount on its southwestern corner—E. Mazar, "The Camp of the Tenth Roman Legion," 52–67 (Heb.).

73. Josephus, *BJ* 7:1–2 (Thackeray, III, 504).

74. Geva, "The Camp."

75. Some of the intricacies involved in such reconstructions were highlighted by Ward-Perkins, "Survival of an Ancient Town-Plan," 223–29.

76. As mentioned earlier (n. 51), in my inclination to see the Ecce Homo arch as marking the eastern boundary of the city, I am joining other scholars who have already suggested this, each for his or her own reasons. I discussed the phenomenon of entrance structures delineating city limits in another context; see Eliav, "Pylè-Puma-Sfat Medinah," 5–19 (Heb.). In addition to the familiar parallels to this phenomenon in neighboring regions—in Tiberias, Gadara, and the southern gate in Gerasa, not to mention the Hadrianic gate in Athens, which its inscriptions explicitly note was intended to mark the border between the old and new cities—another parallel has recently been discovered in Beit She'an-Scythopolis. Two gates, dated to the second century, were uncovered, in the northern and western parts of the city, while the city wall that connects them belongs to the Byzantine period. At the time the gates were constructed, Scythopolis had no city walls, and the gates stood as markers of the city boundaries. I thank Gabi Mazor for providing me with this information and sharing his conclusions with me.

77. Cf. n. 50 for several studies that failed to acknowledge this point, placing the arch too far east. In reality, topographical constraints involving the hefty boulders in the northwest corner of the Temple Mount made it necessary to shift the arch somewhat west of the line of the Temple Mount wall.

78. Working separately on this issue, Magness has reached a similar conclusion; see Magness, "The North Wall," 331, end of n. 3. But this has led her to reconstruct the Roman colony far north of the current Old City of Jerusalem. In general, I am not convinced by her arguments, mainly because I do not see a reason that would lead to extending the border of Aelia so far north only to come back south in the Byzantine period. If at all, the prosperity of the Byzantine period would suggest an expansion of the city's limits.

79. Challenging this view now is Bar, "Aelia Capitolina's Main Street Layout," 159–68 (Heb.).

80. In general, the transversal roads in Aelia have not been studied sufficiently due to the lack of archaeological findings. It is not clear, for example, how the street continued west of the Ecce Homo arch, but it is not impossible that the route along the modern St. Francis–el-Khanqah streets is a remnant of such a road. This line of streets, which travels west to east along a fairly straight line north of the Church of the Holy Sepulcher, is parallel to the more southern route of David-Chain streets and makes a right angle with Khan ez-Zeit Street near what is now called "the Seventh Station." If this thoroughfare indeed traces Aelia's transversal *decumanus,* or at least one such road, it was not reconstructed correctly in the various scholarly discussions of the city because of the attempt to compress the Roman colony into the space of the current Old City. To be sure, this analysis of the traffic routes is not meant to imply that old, Second Temple roads were not included in the new plan of Aelia. The el-Wad road continued to function as an important path, even if it was secondary to the one west of it (pace Bar, "Aelia Capitolina's Main Street Layout"). Another road from the Second Temple period, the one that descends eastward along the route of David-Chain streets, continued to exist and, according to the evidence of the latest excavations, even reached the wall of the Temple Mount, which was the eastern boundary of Aelia. See the short and only summary of this excavation in *Ḥadashot Arkheologiyot* 97 (1991) 66–67. But the existence of these routes is not enough to negate the fundamental change that occurred in Jerusalem.

81. The fullest reconstruction was made by Aline, "La forteresse" (esp. chart 34). For others who hold these views see, e.g., Vincent and Abel, *Jérusalem nouvelle,* chart 1, but cf. their arguments below, n. 95; Wilson, *Golgotha,* 144; Bahat, *Illustrated Atlas,* 63; 67; Geva, "Jerusalem: The Roman Period," 764–65.

82. Benoit, "L'Antonia," 147–58.

83. Ibid., 152.

84. The details about these findings are summarized in Aline, "La forteresse," 88–142; Bagatti, "Resti romani." An analysis of the sort offered here accounts for the asymmetry of the Ecce Homo arch and the pavement adjacent to it, which troubled various scholars; see, e.g., Benoit, "L'Antonia," 163; Wightman, *The Walls,* 199. According to what has been argued here, the reason for this asymmetry is that these two elements, even if built at the same time, were intended for different purposes: the pavement for covering the pools and blazing the trail, and the arch for marking the boundary and functioning as the city's gate.

85. Geva, "The Tenth Roman Legion *Did* Camp on the South-West Hill," 184 (Heb.); Benoit, "L'Antonia," 162—"petit forum ornant la sortie orientale d'Aelia Capitolina."

86. Mauss, *La piscine.* The excavations were carried out a little at a time and without any systematic publication for many years. An important tool for following the findings and the suggestions that were made for interpreting them can be found in the reports delivered from time to time by Conrad Schick, Claude Conder, and others to the British Society for Near Eastern Studies; see *PEFQst* 20 (1888) 115–34, 259–60; 22 (1890) 18–20; 33 (1901) 163–65; 53 (1921) 91–100. The research of the "White Fathers" in the first third of the twentieth century, which Vincent was involved with almost throughout, is summarized in Van der Vliet, "*Sainte Marie où elle est née,*" 176–207. Concerning the Dominicans' excavations in the 1950s, see Rousée, "L'église," 169–76; Pierre and Rousée, "Sainte-Marie," 23–42. For a good summary of the whole project, see also Jeremias, *Rediscovery of Bethesda,* 28–56.

87. Meshorer, *The Coinage*, 56–57. Meshorer himself associates the coins with the Siloam pool, but the links to the findings cited here make it at least plausible that the coins depicting a cultic-healing center and the other votive objects are related to each other.

88. Vincent and Abel, *Jérusalem nouvelle*, 669–98.

89. But the use of the word "temple" in the discussions of this site should not lead us to infer that it consisted of a Roman temple in the full sense. There is no evidence for this. Pace Rousée, "L'église"; Duprez, *Jésus*, who reconstructed the site as a temple to Sarapis. Modern scholars have adopted this "extended" approach far too literally and placed a full-size temple at the site. The material, if closely examined, does not offer any evidence to support this claim.

90. The most comprehensive study of Asclepius and the health installations associated with him are Edelstein and Edelstein, *Asclepius*; Miller, *The Birth of the Hospital*, esp. 30–49.

91. Avalos, *Illness*. This sort of continuity does not, however, necessitate the conclusion that pagan rituals permeated Second Temple Jerusalem, as claimed decisively by Benoit, "L'Antonia," and even more by Duprez, *Jésus*, but this issue is beyond the scope of the present study.

92. MacMullen, *Paganism*, 27.

93. Avalos, *Illness*, 48–54; Edelstein and Edelstein, *Asclepius*, 2:233 and n. 2; Fritz Graf, "Heiligtum und Ritual," 168–78, 201–2.

94. Acts 14:13.

95. Vincent had already suggested that the Temple Mount enclosure was left out of the colony; see his discussion in Vincent and Abel, *Jérusalem nouvelle*, 24, and chart 1 of that study, where the city map he produced places the eastern boundary of Aelia in a line stretching south from a point east of the Damascus Gate to the Ecce Homo arch. On this issue our views concur, but from this point onward we develop our arguments in totally different directions, since he locates the *kodra* mentioned by the *Chronicon Paschale* on the Temple Mount and accordingly reconstructs there some sort of a sanctuary; see his elaborate discussion, Vincent and Abel, 35. But such a view leads to a paradox: Why should anyone build a monument of this sort and then leave it outside the city? (The same difficulty applies to Wightman, *The Walls*, 179.) Vincent does attempt to resolve this problem, however, saying, "Dans la restauration de Jérusalem par Hadrien, le Temple et ses abords immédiats formaient une sorte de quartier à part que l'on distinguait de la cité proprement dite d'Aelia" (Vincent and Abel, *Jérusalem nouvelle*, 671 n. 2). But this answer only strengthens the question: Why do such a thing? And what proof is there that it was actually done?

96. Three recent studies voicing this widespread view are Heribert Busse, "Temple, Grabeskirche und *Haram as-sarif*: Drei Heiligtümer und ihre gegenseitigen Bezeihungen in Legende und Wirklichkeit," in Busse and Kretschmar, *Jerusalemer Heiligtumstraditionen*, 9; Wilken, *The Land*, 83; Wharton, *Refiguring the Post Classical City*, 98–99.

97. As this issue cannot be elaborated here, see the summary in Isaac and Oppenheimer, "The Revolt of Bar Kokhba," esp. 35–36, 44–48.

98. Illuminating surveys of both old conceptions and current tendencies can be found in Mattingly, *Dialogues* and, more specifically for my suggestion here, Whittaker, "Imperialism and Culture," esp. 144–48.

99. For concise summaries regarding urban developments throughout the Roman

world, see Gros and Torelli, *Storia.* On Corinth: ibid., 391–96. The best comprehensive summary is still Wiseman, "Corinth and Rome I," 438–548.

100. *NH* 5:24 (Rackham, II, 236). Extensive archaeological excavations that were carried out in Carthage confirm Pliny's contemporary testimony against the later second-century writer Appian, who, in an attempt to mediate between the actions of Augustus and the famous curse (*consecratio*) of Scipio, asserted that the city was built "quite near" the original site. See Appian, *Historia romana: Pun.* 136 (White, I, 644); Gross and Torelli, *Storia,* 284–91; Friedrich Rakob, "The Making of Augustan Carthage," esp. 79, about the Roman temple's location on top of its Punic predecessor.

101. For summaries and bibliography, see Ottaway, *Book of Roman York,* esp. 11–44; Fentress, *Numidia and the Roman Army,* 126–32; Gross and Torelli, *Storia,* 331–38.

102. Gross and Torelli, *Storia,* 237–64; 373–83; Levick, *Roman Colonies,* summarized most explicitly on pp. 189–90; Mitchell, *Anatolia,* 1:80–98 (esp. 90), 198–226. In Gallia, even cities that were thought by scholars for many years to be Roman innovations turn out to be continuations of pre-Roman settlements. Arelate (modern Arles sur Rhône) in Gallia Narbonensis is a good example; see Arcelin, "Arles protohistorique," 325–38.

103. Jerusalem's uniqueness in this regard was accentuated by Millar, "The Roman *Coloniae,*" 28. For a detailed comparative study of Aelia and other colonies, which reaches similar conclusions regarding the uniqueness of the Aelia's case, see Isaac, "Roman Colonies."

104. For a good up-to-date summary and bibliography, see Bechert and Willems, *Die römische Reichsgrenze,* 65–70 (bibliography, 75–76).

105. See Hinz, "Colonia Ulpia Traiana I," 825–69.

106. The urban dynamics and shifts in the locations of towns in Lower Germany are discussed in detail by Bloemers, "Lower Germany," 72–86.

107. The complex questions about the Samaritans's relations with the Jewish community and the Roman Empire in the period of the Bar Kokhba revolt are extremely complicated matters, on which various contrasting opinions have been expressed. See Mor, "The Samaritans," 19–31, and the references there. Only one chronological fact is important for the present purpose—namely, that the Romans established two pagan temples, the one in Jerusalem and the other on Mount Gerizim, around the time of the Bar Kokhba revolt. The connection between the construction of the temples and the revolt, if indeed there was such a link, is yet to be resolved and makes no difference here.

108. For the first view, which is the one accepted by most scholars, see, e.g., Mor, *The Bar-Kochba Revolt,* 179–80 (Heb.). For the view relying on the coins, which dates the construction to a later time, see Magen, "Mount Gerizim and the Samaritans," 126–27.

109. Magen, "Gerizim, Mount," 484–87. For a good bibliography on the rivalry between Jews and Samaritans and the tension between the two temples, and other topics involving the Samaritans, see Crown, *Bibliography* (on the issue under discussion here, see his index, 1003.4).

110. Regarding the status of Jerusalem and the Temple among the Jews after 70, see the discussion in chapter 6. On the prominence of Mount Gerizim after the destruction of the Samaritan temple, see, e.g., Schürer, *History,* 2:19.

111. On the subject of Shechem-Neapolis, see Magen, "Shechem-Neapolis," 1354–55. Clearly the foundation of Neapolis preceded Aelia by many years, but this does not change the principles underlying these activities, which are the essence of the comparison presented here.

112. This is one of the most salient new conclusions arising from Magen's excavations on the peak of Mount Gerizim; see Magen, "Gerizim." It refutes the theory presented by Bull, who excavated the site in the 1960s, that the Samaritan temple was underneath the pagan one—a hypothesis based on an erroneous interpretation of the ceramic findings; see Bull, "The Excavation of Tell er-Ras on Mt. Gerizim," esp. 70–71.

113. Scholars at some point have expressed all these views. See, e.g., Mor, "The Samaritans," 28–31; Avi-Yonah, "The Samaritan Revolts against the Byzantine Empire," 127–32 (Heb.).

114. For the coins, see Meshorer, *City Coins*, 48–52, esp. coin no. 135. For written sources representing the close ties between the city and the temple on Mount Garizim, see, e.g., *Chronicon Adler* (Adler and Séligsohn, *REJ* 45 [1902] 82); Damaskius Diadochos, *Vitae Isidori reliquiae* 141 (Zintzen, 196, lines 1–2).

115. Meshorer, *City Coins*, 48–52.

116. The calculations about the city's area were carried out by Broshi, "Estimating the Population of Ancient Jerusalem," 10–15. My inference about the small size of the colony agrees with that of other recent scholars, who nevertheless reconstructed the contour of the city differently; see, e.g., Bar, "Aelia Capitolina"; Wightman, *The Walls*, 196–97. As far as I know, the only study that comes to almost exactly the same conclusion as mine is that of Lifshitz, "Jérusalem," 484, who claims about Aelia: "Le tracé de l'enceinte de la colonie laissait en dehors de la ville le Bézétha, l'esplanade du Temple, l'Ophel et le quartier du Cénacle."

117. Britain: Collingwood and Richmond, *The Archaeology of Roman Britain*, 95–100; Timgad and North Africa: MacDonald, *The Architecture of the Roman Empire*, 2:5, 25–27; Asia Minor: Levick, *Roman Colonies*, 42–43, and n. 2.

118. Holum et al., *King Herod's Dream*, 163–65.

FOUR: A Lively Ruin

1. Following Amnon Linder, "Ecclesia and Synagoga," esp. 1024–25. On Constantine's "Holy Land policy" and its practical implication, see Telfer, "Constantine's Holy Land Plan," 696–700; Hunt, *Holy Land*, 1–49. On Helena's activity in the city and the legends that rose around her, see Holum, "Hadrian and St. Helena," esp. 80 n. 43; Drijvers, *Helena Augusta*, esp. 55ff.

2. The most recent summaries are Geva, "Jerusalem: The Byzantine Period," 768–85. Many valuable studies are collected in Tsafrir and Safrai, *History of Jerusalem*. The reconstruction presented in the following paragraphs is based on these studies. For a more popular summary, see Bahat, *Illustrated Atlas*, 58–67.

3. E.g., Geva, "Jerusalem: The Byzantine Period," 769 (map; he does not discuss this compound again later in the chapter!); Tsafrir, "Byzantine Jerusalem," 144; Bahat, *Illustrated Atlas*, 69 (map), 78.

4. This comparison was made recently in great detail by Wharton, *Refiguring the Post Classical City*, 64–104. On the history of the Temple of Artemis and its fate in the Byzantine period, see Kraeling, *Gerasa*, 137–38; I. Browning, *Jerash and the Decapolis*, 163–65.

5. E.g., Stroumsa, "Mystical Jerusalems," 351; Maraval, *Lieux*, 261. For a more complex position, see Wilkinson, *Egeria's*, 37–38. On the same subject, see also chapter 5 below, regarding the Palestinian church fathers.

6. That scholars disagree on the precise route of this wall is not relevant to this point. On the various reconstructions, see Wightman, *The Walls*, 181–84, and his own reconstruction on p. 190 (map).

7. For a comprehensive summary, see Wightman, *The Walls*, 200–206; Geva, "Jerusalem: The Byzantine Period," 770–72.

8. John Rufus, *Vita* (Raabe, 44, lines 17–18): "At this time, the holy city of Jerusalem was . . . being deprived of walls, since the former walls had been destroyed by the Romans"; trans. in Lang, *Lives and Legends*, 65–66.

9. Eusebius, *Onomast.* (Klostermann, 70, lines 3–4). On this shift of the valley of Hinnom to the eastern side of the city, see in greater detail Newman, "Jerome," 251–53 (Heb.). I have no answer to the question of why Eusebius chose to use the designation "Jerusalem" here and not his more common name "Aelia." Cf. Walker, *Holy City*, 5 n. 9. The rule established by Walker—that, in the *Onomasticon*, Eusebius applies "Jerusalem" only in speaking of the biblical city or that of the Second Temple—is not accurate. See, for example, the entry "Fuller's Field" (Klostermann, 38, lines 2–3), where Eusebius states explicitly that he is discussing his own time but uses the term "Jerusalem." On the early date assigned to this work, to the beginning of the fourth century (and perhaps even earlier), see Barnes, "The Composition of Eusebius' Onomasticon," 412–15. For an opinion dating the work later, to the 330s, see Klostermann, p. xii; Wallace-Hadrill, *Eusebius of Caesarea*, 55–57. Barnes's convincing considerations have been accepted by scholars; see, e.g., Walker, *Holy City*, 42–43.

10. *Itinerarium Burdigalense* 592:1, 5; 593:1–2 (Geyer and Cuntz, 16–17). For the various attempts to fit these descriptions with what is known of Jerusalem of that time, especially with regard to the identification of the wall he mentions next to the Siloam pool, see, e.g., Hamilton, "Jerusalem in the Fourth Century," 85–86; Wilkinson, *Egeria's*, 157–58; Wightman, *The Walls*, 207–8. Later in the fourth century, Jerusalem's wall is mentioned also by the North African bishop Optatus of Milevi when he refers to Mount Zion as lying outside the city walls (*monte Sion, quem in Syria Palaestina a muris Hierusalem parvus disterminat rivus*); see Optatus, *Adversus Donatianae* 3:2 (Ziwsa, 70, lines 9–10). Optatus's reliability is questionable, as there is no evidence that he ever spent time in Jerusalem. He may have retrieved this information from other visitors, such as the Bordeaux pilgrim. I return to discuss this text in chapter 5.

11. Eucherius, *Epistula ad Faustum* 9 (Fraipont, 238, lines 46–47; trans. Wilkinson, 53).

12. On his exits and entries, see *Itinerarium Burdigalense* 591:7, 592:4, 5 (Geyer and Cuntz, 16).

13. *Itinerarium Egeriae* 36:3 (Franceschini and Weber, 80, line 22), 43:7 (ibid., 86, lines 58–59).

14. For a summary of the findings and conclusions, see Wightman, *The Walls*, 214–15; E. Mazar, "The Ophel Wall," 48–63. But cf. Geva, "Jerusalem: The Byzantine Period," 769 (map), 770.

15. E.g., Bahat, *Illustrated Atlas*, 68 (map); Geva, "Jerusalem: The Byzantine Period," 769 (map), 771; Wightman, *The Walls*, 201 (map), 205.

16. For a brief summary and bibliography, see Baruch et al., "The Northern Wall," 175–82 (Heb.). I wish to thank Dr. Gideon Avni, one of the excavators, who showed me around the excavations and shared his views on this topic with me.

17. The only piece of information that is inconsistent with this proposal comes from

the comment by the Bordeaux traveler locating the Bethsaida pool (map 2: 8) "inside the city" (*Itinerarium Burdigalense* 589:8 [Geyer and Cuntz, 15]). But, as I hope to demonstrate elsewhere, this pilgrim cannot be trusted on the subject of this pool. His tendency to shape the report about the Probatika site in light of the New Testament's account of the curing of the lame man may have caused him to locate the pool inside Jerusalem, which seems to be the case in the Gospel account. See for now, Eliav, "A Mount," 90–93 (Heb.).

18. Eusebius, *DE* 8:3 (Heikel, p391–94).

19. Tsafrir, "Zion," 94–96 (Heb.); Groh, "The Onomasticon of Eusebius," 28; Walker, *Holy City*, 302–3; Bar, "Aelia Capitolina and the Location of the Camp of the Tenth Legion," 10. These scholars have assumed, without thoroughly examining the textual context of this segment, that the "Mount Zion" mentioned here by Eusebius is the southwestern hill (see map 1). This reading thus became the accepted scholarly wisdom. Walker did discern that Eusebius's "Zion" carries a variety of meanings, and he even agrees that it sometimes designates the Temple Mount (see *Holy City*, 198–99), but his opinion of the case in point is that Eusebius means the southwestern hill. This position cannot stand up to critical evaluation. First, Walker bases his principal evidence on Christian writers postdating Eusebius, who describe the southwestern hill as farmland (Walker, *Holy City*, 302 n. 78) and therefore assumes that every cultivated "Mount Zion" in Eusebius must be that place. The failing here is obvious: what people thought after the term "Mount Zion" became associated unalterably with the southwestern hill, and to which they therefore attributed all passages mentioning that name, cannot be applied to Eusebius. In his time, the identification was not absolute. One cannot first determine the nature of Mount Zion in accordance with its later image and then draw conclusions regarding every earlier reference by adjusting it to the later identification. This is the fallacy of *petitio principis*. Second, despite Walker's opinion, the Bordeaux traveler (*Itinerarium Burdigalense* 592:7 [Geyer and Cuntz, 16]) does not say that Mount Zion is a cultivated area. He rather expounds a verse in Isaiah (apparently 1:8) to apply to the destruction of synagogues. The term *reliquae* there refers to the six synagogues that were destroyed, excluding the one that survived. Thus, "sown and plowed" serves him as a literary expression, meaning "destruction as the prophet foretold" and no more. Wilkinson noticed this (*Egeria's*, 158) and therefore put these expressions in quotation marks. Third, the use of the plural "mountains" does not mean that Eusebius was aware of the term's multiple connotations and certainly cannot be taken to mean that he used only one specific meaning. Fourth, in reading Eusebius, Walker makes no distinction between purely literary passages, which have no connection at all to reality (such as *Demonstratio evangelica* 2:3), and the passage under discussion here. In this portion, as I intend to show shortly, Eusebius repeatedly emphasizes that he is writing of reality as he sees it. Finally, the most difficult aspect of Walker's proposal is that he ignores the specific content of the passage, which indicates unambiguously that Mount Zion in this case is the mountain on which the Temple stood.

20. In the *Onomasticon*, for example, although in the entry "Zion" he states, vaguely, "a mountain in Jerusalem" (Klostermann, 74), with regard to Golgotha he knows that it is "in Jerusalem north of Mount Zion" (Klostermann, 162), obviously referring to the new, Christian Mount Zion.

21. Eusebius, *DE* 8:3:6 (Heikel, 392, lines 21–24), 10 (ibid., 393, lines 11–12; trans. Ferrar, II, 140–41).

22. The text has already been read this way by Wilken, *The Land,* 83.

23. Vincent and Abel, *Jérusalem nouvelle,* 449–50: "Toute église, selon Eusèbe, peut s'appeler Sion, et tout lieu saint Jérusalem," and see in particular p. 450 n. 2. And following them Walker, *Holy City,* 298–99.

24. Eusebius, *DE* 8:3:11 (Heikel, 393, lines 22–23).

25. Eusebius, *DE* 8:3:10 (Heikel, 392, lines 11–18; trans. based with slight differences on Ferrar, II, 140–41).

26. Eusebius, *DE* 6:13:17 (Heikel, 264–65; trans. Ferrar, II, 15).

27. Eusebius, *DE* 8:3:12 (Heikel, 393; trans. with slight differences Ferrar, II, 141). This motif, the use of stones from the Temple's ruins in other buildings, appears also in the *Dialogue of Timothy and Aquila* 98 (Conybeare, 79), 130 (ibid., 98). However, as noted earlier, this work has not been dated beyond question, and some scholars suggest moving it up to the sixth century.

28. Eusebius, *Theoph.* 4:18 (trans. Lee, 246–47).

29. Eusebius, *DE* 8:3:15 (Heikel, 394).

30. Socrates Scholasticus, *HE* 1:17:1 (Hansen, 55).

31. Cyril of Jerusalem, *Catech.* 10:11 (Touttée and Maran, 676–77).

32. The sources mentioning the ruins have been collected by D. Levenson, "Source," 263–65. Levenson casts doubt on the authenticity of the description. He tends to see it as no more than a literary motif and even tries to identify the source from which the writers drew this image. Pace Levenson, it cannot be ruled out that natives of Palestine such as the church historian Sozomen may have described the removal of the Jewish Temple's vestiges based on the sight of the ruins etched in their memory, not on a literary convention. See Sozomen, *HE* 5:22:7 (Bidez and Hansen, 230, line 20).

33. Gregory of Nazianzus, *Or.* 5:4 (Bernardi, 298); John Chrysostom, *Adversus Iudaeos orationes* 5:11 (Migne, col. 901). On possible connections between Gregory and Chrysostom, see D. Levenson, "A Source," 31–32 n. 47. Levenson believes here as well that the removal of the earth is not a description of reality but rather, perhaps, a literary motif.

34. Jerome, *Comm. in Seph.* 1:16 (Adriaen, 673, lines 680–81); *Comm. in Isa.* 17, 64:8–12 (Adriaen, 740, line 53); *Homiliae in Psalmos* 119 (Morin, 247, lines 37–38). For further instances in which Jerome mentions the remains of the stairway in the Temple area, see Newman, "Jerome," 246–48 (Heb.). Unlike Newman, I do not think we should read too much into Jerome's identification of these or other stairs, and we should certainly not conclude that he knew the Temple's rampart or the latticework fence that encircled it. Erudite visitors familiar with the sources will always conflate their previous knowledge with what they see. It is hard to believe that in Jerome's day, hundreds of years after the destruction and after the activity that took place on the site in Julian's day, there were still identifiable remains of any type. At most the area would have been strewn with ruins that visitors identified as they liked.

35. Nau, "Résumé," 120. Because this edition is abridged and the full manuscript has not been published, I have been unable to examine the Syrian source. On this passage, see more in n. 46.

36. Jerome, *Comm. in Isa.* 17, 64:8–12 (Adriaen, 740, lines 53–55).

37. For a collection of the Arabic sources, see Assaf and Mayer, *Sefer Ha-Yishuv,* 2:16–21, and a discussion of them in Gil, *A History of Palestine,* 65–74. From time to time additional texts that express the same features are discovered. Two of these, in Georgian

and Greek, have been published recently and present the cleaning operation in an authentic way, as well as the experience and the traditions that came into being around it. Naturally, they also emphasize the dirt and filth on the site. See Bernard Flusin, "L'esplanade," 1:17–31, and my discussion of these sources in chapter 3.

38. Abel, "Saint Jérôme ," 142: "Les ruines sont fertiles en légendes. Chaque pan de mur, chaque souterrain, chaque fragment digne d'attention devient matière aux plus fantaisistes interprétations."

39. John Rufus, *Vita* (Raabe, 98–99). The route of the visit proceeds from the Martyrion of Stephen in the northern part of the city to Golgotha, continues eastward to Pilate's house, from there along the walls of the compound (which are not mentioned) north and east to the Church of the Paralytic (the Probatika), and from there crossing to Gethsemane and the Mount of Olives. After the Mount of Olives, the path turned south to Bethlehem and completes the circle at the city's south, at the Siloam pool and Mount Zion. The work clearly ignores the Temple Mount.

40. Avi-Yonah, *The Madaba Mosaic Map*, pl. 7, and cf. p. 59. The many attempts to identify a specific element on the map as representing the site (as with Avi-Yona's element no. 23) do not change the fact that this realistic map does not represent the area of the compound properly. On possible reasons for this, see, e.g., Tsafrir, "The Maps Used by Theodosius," 129–45 (with references and a discussion of previous proposals). See also my discussion in chapter 5.

41. *Itinerarium Burdigalense* 589:7–591:7 (Geyer and Cuntz, 14–16).

42. *Breviarius de Hierosolyma* 6 (Weber, 112).

43. Eusebius, *Comm. in Isa.* 2:14 (38:4–8) (Ziegler, 242, line 22); Jerome, *Comm. in Isa.* 11, 38:4–8 (Adriaen, 445).

44. Eucherius, *Epistula ad Faustum* 7 (Fraipont, 238, line 35).

45. Contra Herbert Donner, "Der Felsen und der Tempel," 7; Donner, *Pilgerfahrt ins Heilige Land*, 55 n. 83. Donner identifies the Bordeaux traveler's *pinna* with the Temple Mount's southeastern corner and consequently questions the traveler's route. Yet Donner does not consider that this is precisely the point missing from the traveler's account. Such confusion, in which a baseless convention becomes fixed in scholarship and causes a distorted understanding of the sources themselves, characterizes modern discussions on this minute, though significant detail. See also my discussion of the *pterygion* in chapter 2.

46. Nau, "Résumé," 119–20. Here, too, I am basing my discussion on Nau's abbreviated translation. For the entire story, see Nau, "Deux épisodes," 194–201. The debate over the historical reliability of this work is not within the purview of this study, since in any case its author preserved the way in which the Temple site was perceived in his day. For an opinion opposing Nau's, see Honigmann, *Le couvent de Barsauma*, 17–18. Supporting Nau is Holum, *Theodosian Empresses*, 217–18.

47. Theodosius, *De situ Terrae sanctae* 9, 11 (Geyer, 119); *Itinerarium Antonini Placentini* 17 (Geyer, 138), 23 (ibid., 141); Adomnan, *De locis sanctis* 1:14 (Bieler, 186); Epiphanius the Monk, *De locis sanctis* 2:17–19 (Donner, 69).

48. Milik, "La topographie," 178–79.

49. Tsafrir, "Byzantine Jerusalem," 144.

50. *Breviarius de Hierosolyma*, version B, 6 (Weber, 112) But see Milik, "La topographie," 173–74, who reconstructs a different textual witness that locates this church at the Siloam pool. I find it hard to choose between the two versions, but the more difficult

rendering, which thus may be the more original, seems the version that links the church and the *pinna*.

51. The strongest advocate of this position is, I believe, Bagatti, who makes this gate the central entrance to the city from the east; see Bagatti, *Recherches*, 13–19. Others reject these approaches categorically and support a later dating, associating the gate with the Arab period. See, e.g., Ben-Dov, *Shadow*, 282–86. But see also Cyril Mango, "The Temple Mount," 7–16.

52. Bagatti, *Recherches*.

53. For a detailed summary of this subject, see Stemberger, *Jews and Christians*, 185–216.

54. The most comprehensive study of Julian's projects involving Jerusalem is D. Levenson, "Source," which includes a detailed discussion of the development and transmission of the information on this issue. See also D. Levenson, "Julian's Attempt to Rebuild the Temple," 261–79; Adler, "The Emperor," 591–651; Aziza, "Julien et le Judaïsme," 141–58.

55. The clearest articulation of these goals surfaces in his letter to a pagan priest; see Julian, *Ep.* 89 (Wright, 312). The ideological foundation of this position is laid out in his essay *Against the Galileans;* see, e.g., Julian, *Galil.* 305D–306A (Wright, 404–6); 343C–D (ibid., 416–18). See also the following note.

56. Referring to the future: Julian, *Ep.* 89 (Wright, 312); Letter to the Jews, *Ep.* 51 (Wright, 180). For an incisive summary of the controversy about the authenticity of this epistle, see Stern, *Greek,* 2:508–10. Adler, "The Emperor," deduced from these two sources that the project was never carried out and that the whole thing is a Christian invention, but his view can easily be refuted, as the sources listed in the following notes clearly demonstrate; see also D. Levenson, "Source," 264 n. 14; John Lydus, *De mensibus* 4:53 (Wünsch, 110, lines 6–7); trans. Stern, *Greek,* 2:569.

57. Ammianus Marcellinus, *Res gestae* 23:1:2–3 (Rolfe, II, 310).

58. Gregory of Nazianzus, *Or.* 5:4 (Bernardi, 298). Levenson offers a detailed presentation of the chronological sequence of the various sources for Julian's reign, and in general I accept his dates for the sources on the issue at hand.

59. Ephrem, *Hymns against Julian* 4:19–24 (Beck, 89–90). And see Griffith, "Ephraem the Syrian's Hymns," 258–60.

60. John Chrysostom, *Adversus Iudaeos orationes* 5:11 (Migne, col. 901; trans. Maxwell, 160).

61. Rufinus, *HE* 10:38–40 (Momsen, 997–98); Philostorgios, *HE* 7:9, 14 (Bidez and Winkelmann, 95–96, 99–100); Socrates, *HE* 3:20 (Hansen, 215–16); Theodoret of Cyrrhus, *HE* 3:20:1–5 (Parmentier, 198–99); Sozomen, *HE* 5:22:5–8 (Bidez and Hansen, 230–31). Levenson's study demonstrates in detail that most of the material used by these historians did not consist of original sources but was a literary expansion of reports by the fourth-century authors—Gregory, Chrysostom, Ammianus, and even Julian himself; see D. Levenson, "Source," 43–72. At the same time, Levenson also admits that some of these historians—mainly Rufinus and Philostorgios—did have access to what he calls "local Jerusalem traditions" (pp. 47–48, 61). It is quite clear that all these historians, whatever sources they may have used, agreed that the work of restoring the Temple had indeed begun.

62. Philostorgios, *HE* 7:9a (Bidez and Winkelmann, 96, line 30).

63. Brock, "A Letter," 270. But scholars rightly consider this a later document (of the

fifth or sixth century) based on Philostorgios, at least as far as the synagogue is concerned. The publisher dates it to the early fifth century; see Brock, "The Rebuilding of the Temple under Julian," 103–7. D. Levenson ("Source," 82–94) delays its production even later to the late fifth or early sixth century. Both agree that it was not Cyril who wrote it.

64. See J. Schwartz, *Jewish Settlement in Judaea,* 180 (Heb.); Schwartz, "Gallus," 11.

65. See for now Eliav, "A Mount," 134–36 (Heb).

F I V E : The New Mountain in Christian Homiletics

1. Hall, *Doctrine,* 48ff. In general, this chapter opens with the second generation after the destruction of the Jerusalem Temple. For the purposes of orientation, the beginning of the period can be identified with the fall of the Flavian dynasty in 96 CE.

2. Bauer, *Rechtgläubigkeit und Ketzerei,* and in additional editions since then. But compare also to a comprehensive critique of his thesis: T. Robinson, *The Bauer Thesis Examined.* And see, now, Desjardins, "Bauer and Beyond," 65–82.

3. My understanding of early Christianity of the first century onward, including its social and theological elements, follows the path laid down by the British school of William Frend, Henry Chadwick, Frances Young, Stuart Hall, and others (except for certain reservations, largely on questions relating to Jews and Judaism). A good summary and basic bibliography of their thinking can be found in the jubilee book in honor of Frend; see Hazlett, *Early Christianity.*

4. Such as Irenaeus, *Haer.* 1:10:1 (Rousseau et al., 154–58), 3:4:2 (ibid., 46–48). See Kelly, *Early Christian Creeds,* 62–99, esp. 76–82. See also the principal formulation of the faith in Ignatius, *Epistula ad Smyrnaeos* 1 (Lake, 252). It mentions the House of David and Pontius Pilate, but there is no trace of Jerusalem.

5. Cf. Wilken, *The Land,* 62–63. As a rule, even though my argument here is consistent with several of Wilken's conclusions, overall the current discussion presents a different view.

6. On this prayer, see Heinemann, *Studies,* 3–11 (Heb.). I do not discuss here the dating of this liturgical formula. Sufficient for our purposes is the accepted view that locates its origin in the Tannaitic period (first and second centuries CE).

7. The relevant passages are gathered in Jasper and Cuming, *Prayers of the Eucharist,* 20–38. For a comprehensive introduction and up-to-date bibliography on these issues, see Bradshaw, *The Search.* I have chosen the "Building of Jerusalem" (*boneh yerusha- layim*) benediction as a case in point for Jerusalem's centrality in Judaism because of the great similarity between the Jewish grace after meals and the Eucharist (see, e.g., Bradshaw, *The Search,* 132ff.), but of course it is possible to bring other examples from the various appearances of this formula in the ʿ*Amida* prayer, in the bridegroom's benediction (*birkat ḥatanim*), and elsewhere. On these, see Heinemann, *Studies,* 3–11 (Heb.). On the Jerusalem liturgy that became consolidated in the fourth century against the background of the large changes in the city, see the discussion later in this chapter.

8. The absence of Jerusalem from the common depictions of Jesus's entry into the city has already been noticed by Mathews, *The Clash of Gods,* 28, with other bibliography and references.

9. On the Temple in coins from the Bar Kokhba rebellion, see Meshorer, *Ancient Jewish Coinage,* 138–54. On an example of a Jewish catacomb with Temple motifs, see

A. Grabar, *Early Christian Art*, 110; J. Stevenson, *The Catacombs*, 61. Jerusalem's place in later Christian art (from the end of the fourth century onward) is discussed at length in Kühnel, *From the Earthly*. On the Temple in Jewish art of late antiquity, see Kühnel, *From the Earthly*, 107–11. And see also Rosenau, *Vision of the Temple*. On the Temple's role in the design of synagogues from the high empire and Byzantine periods, see Fine, *This Holy Place*.

10. I devote the next section of this chapter to these two texts. See also in the following two notes.

11. Three examples to illustrate this claim: (1) The writer of the *Epistle of Barnabas* (*Barn.* 2:4–7 [Lake, I, 344]) objects sharply to sacrifices, but a few chapters later, in 5:1 (Lake, 354), he bases his arguments on this very system, contending that Jesus's death is a sacrifice of atonement. But if God had abhorred the sacrificial system, why would a human on the cross be any different from a slaughtered beast? (2) A similar tension surfaces in the relation between what Justin Martyr writes in *Dial.* 13 and 22 (Archambault, I, 58–64, 96–102) and 41 (ibid., 182–86). (3) At the end of the period under discussion here, in Irenaeus, the fundamental tension still remains, although its content had changed somewhat. Instead of Jesus as a sacrifice, he presents an organized church system, including donations for the Eucharist, which replaces the Temple system. Compare Irenaeus, *Haer.* 4:16 (Rousseau et al., 558ff.), which consists entirely of proof texts against the sacrificial system, with *Haer.* 4:18 (ibid., 596ff.), which argues that the true sacrifice is the observance of church ritual, and also 20:2 (ibid., 628–30), which presents Jesus (in accordance with Revelations) as a sacrifice.

12. Punishment: Justin Martyr, *Dial.* 16 (Archambault, I, 72–78). Justin's position on the destruction is complex, and a discussion of it goes beyond the scope of this study. For other passages of his that address this event, see *Dial.* 40:2 (ibid., 178–80), 46 (ibid., 202–8), 52:4 (ibid., 234); *1Apol.* 47 (Marcovich, p. 98). See Skarsaune, *The Proof*, 288–95. Predestination: Irenaeus, *Haer.* 4:4 (Rousseau et al., 416ff.). Against the sacrifices: This approach is common to all the writers; see, e.g., *The Epistle to Diognetus* 3 (Lake, II, 354–56), although its date has not been determined unequivocally; and Melito of Sardis, *De Pascha* 44–45 (Hall, 22). See also the position of the Ebionites, in chapter 2.

13. For the role modern scholars assign to the destruction, a fascinating and thorny subject, compare the maximalist view taken in Brandon, *Fall*, with the moderate position that appears in Gaston, *No Stone*. Kühnel, *From the Earthly*, 10–11, already surveys most of the bibliography.

14. Epiphanius, *Haer.* 19:3:5–6 (Holl and Dummer, I, 220). On this group and its views about the Temple and Jerusalem, see Luttikhuizen, *The Revelation of Elchasai*, 121–22, 202–3.

15. The basic study of the millenarians and their roots remains Gry, *Le millénarisme*. And on the period discussed here, see his discussions on pp. 62–86. See also Daley, *The Hope of the Early Church*, 5–32.

16. Eusebius, *HE* 5:18:2 (Schwartz, 472); see also Epiphanius, *Haer.* 48:14:1–2 (Holl and Dummer, II, 238–39). For a summary and bibliography about this movement and its position regarding Jerusalem, see Irshai, "Historical Aspects," 30–31 (Heb.).

17. Justin Martyr, *Dial.* 80–81 (Archambault, II, 30–42), 138:3 (ibid., 296). On Justin's approach, see Barnard, *Justin Martyr*, 157–68, and esp. 164, where he states: "There is no doubt that Justin held that Jerusalem would be *physically* rebuilt"; Irenaeus, *Haer.* 5:34–36 (Rousseau et al., 420ff.). See also Wilken, *The Land*, 61.

18. On Tertullian and the Montanist developments in his thinking, see Barnes, *Tertullian*, 42–56, 130–42. On traces of the Montanist approach in his treatment of Jerusalem, see, e.g., Tertullian, *Adversus Marcionem* 3:24 (Evans, 246–48).

19. Clement of Rome, *Ep.* 1:40–41 (Lake, I, 76–78).

20. Ignatius, *Epistula ad Ephesios* 9 (Lake, I, 182–84). On the roots of this approach in the Christian Scriptures, see the commentary by Schoedel, *Ignatius of Antioch*, 66–67, where there are also additional examples postdating Ignatius.

21. Hall, *Melito*, 93, line 179, and see also there n. 45.

22. On the sources in the New Testament, see chapter 2.

23. Priesthood: *Didache* 13:3 (Lake, I, 328); Melito of Sardis, *De Pascha* 68 (Hall, 36, line 477); Irenaeus, *Haer.* 4:8:3 (Rousseau et al., 472). The image of Jesus as a priest is very common in Justin Martyr; for a few examples, see Justin Martyr, *Dial.* 33 (Archambault, I, 144–46), 34:2 (ibid., 148), 42:1 (ibid., 186). This last passage is of particular importance for the development of these images, since Jesus is described here as the eternal priest, and his twelve Apostles are likened to the twelve bells on the hem of his robe. Temple: *Barn.* 4:11 (Lake, I, 352), 6:15 (ibid., 362); Irenaeus, *Epideixis* 96 (Smith, 106); Irenaeus, *Haer.* 5:6:2 (Rousseau et al., 80–82). And also see Kittel, *Theologisches Wörterbuch*, 4:894–95. Sacrifices: Justin Martyr, *Dial.* 41 (Archambault, I, 182–86), 117 (ibid., 198–204). Other descriptions of the Eucharist found in Justin's two apologetic works pass over this image; see on this: Barnard, *Justin Martyr*, 148. See also Irenaeus, *Haer.* 4:18 (Rousseau et al., 596ff.), 20:2 (ibid., 628–30, lines 37ff.); *Barn.* 5:1 (Lake, I, 354). On this image, see Rondorf, "Le sacrifice eucharistique," 335–53; Bradshaw, *The Search*, 15 n. 32. On the entire issue, see also Bauckham, "James and the Jerusalem Church," 444–46. Of course, all three of these motifs continued to exist in the later period as well, as I plan to show later in the chapter.

24. Irenaeus, *Haer.* 1:5:3 (Rousseau et al., 82, line 55), 4:1:1 (ibid., 394, line 21). On additional Temple motifs in Valentinian literature, see Pagels, *The Johannine Gospel*, 66–82; Pagels, *The Gnostic Gospels*, 116.

25. E.g., in the *Acta Martyrum* of Justin; see Musurillo, *Acts*, 54, line 16; Eusebius, *De martyribus Palestinae* 11:8–12 (Schwartz, 936–38; Cureton, 40–41).

26. Elaine Pagels and Paul Bradshaw discerned this, each in their own field; see Pagels, *The Johannine Gospel*, 66–68; Bradshaw, *The Search*, 15 n. 32. At greater length, see also Schmidt, "Jerusalem," 207–48, as well as the next note.

27. Cf. Wilken, *The Land*, 65–72; Schmidt, "Jerusalem"; Kühnel, *From the Earthly*, 74–81. Minor, though significant, variations distinguish my view from these approaches, especially my emphasis on the *process* of shaping the concept. This leads to a blurring of the dichotomy between the writers of the second century and the innovations in Origen's time and later. In my opinion, we are speaking of a gradual process the roots of which lie deep in the Second Temple period, and the notion of "heavenly Jerusalem" highlights only one of its products.

28. On this, see nn. 16 and 18.

29. The first to offer such a proposal was Harvey, "Melito and Jerusalem," 401–4. It has since been endorsed by many; see, e.g., Hunt, *Holy Land*, 3–4, 83; Maraval, *Lieux*, 33; G. Kretschmar, "Festkalender und Memorialstätten Jerusalems in altkirchlicher Zeit," in Busse and Kretschmar, *Jerusalemer Heiligtumstraditionen*, 64–65; Walker, *Holy City*, 242 n. 9.

30. Eusebius, *HE* 4:26:13–14 (Schwartz, 386–88) = Hall, *Melito*, 66, lines 14–15.

31. Melito of Sardis, *De Pascha* 72 (Hall, 38, lines 505–6), 93 (Hall, 52, lines 692), 94 (Hall, 52, line 704).

32. Melito of Sardis, *De Pascha* 94 (Hall, 52, lines 701–5). For a concrete example of the difference between an expression devoid of geographical substance and one that resembles the physical landscape, compare Melito's words here with the text known as *Breviarius de Hierosolyma* (A Short Account of Jerusalem), which has a sentence almost identical to Melito's—"*At the center of Jerusalem* there is the Basilica of Constantine" (Weber, 109, lines 5–6)—but is entirely permeated by the city's physical reality (even if not accurate).

33. Here I accede to the opinion of Perler, *Méliton de Sardes*, 177, who deems this expression a "rhetorical exaggeration." On Melito's rhetorical aptitudes and his use of them to amplify the guilt of the Jews, see S. Wilson, "Melito and Israel," 91–96.

34. Eusebius, *HE* 2:20:4 (Schwartz, 158–60); Josephus, *BJ* 2:254 (Thackeray, II, 422).

35. Pace Hunt, *Holy Land*, 4, and the literature cited there in n. 15. In describing the motives of ancients who supposedly attended Jerusalem, later writers, such as Jerome (cited in Hunt, *Holy Land*), apply arguments familiar to them from their world, a time when pilgrimage flourished. Thus, it should not in any case be seen as "testimony" of earlier pilgrims.

36. Clement of Rome, *Ep.* 1:41:2 (Lake, I, 78–79; trans. Lake).

37. For the scholarly debate about the Jewish character of the *Epistle of Barnabas,* see Paget, *The Epistle of Barnabas,* 7–9. Like him, I do not feel the evidence provides a definite solution, but the familiarity with the Jewish world as well as the hostility are easy to discern.

38. *Barn.* 11 (Lake, I, 378–80). For a detailed discussion and analysis of this passage, see Eliav, "'Interpretive Citation' in the Epistle of Barnabas," 353–62.

39. Ps 99(98):9—Justin Martyr, *Dial.* 37:4 (Archambault, I, 168); Isa 63:18 (discussed in detail below); Isa 65:25—*Dial.* 81:2 (Archambault, II, 38); Isa 65:11—*Dial.* 135:4 (Archambault, II, 286); Mic 4:1—*Dial.* 109:2 (Archambault, II, 160–62); Ps 96(95):9—*Dial.* 73:4 (Archambault, I, 352). The latter follows the Septuagint, which apparently rendered "holy courts" (ḥaṣerot qodesh) rather than "holy array" (haderat qodesh) as the Masora has it.

40. Justin Martyr, *Dial.* 25–26 (Archambault, I, 110–18). The references in the body of the discussion here are to this edition. On the "election of Israel" in this period, see Helfgott, *The Doctrine of Election,* 8–36. On this subject in Justin's thinking, see Skarsaune, *The Proof,* 326–34; Hirshman, *A Rivalry of Genius,* 31–41, 55–66. Justin's words here correspond to Hirschman's "exegetical Debate" between the religions.

41. Well shown by Wilken, *The Land,* 1–19.

42. See Kittel, *Theologisches Wörterbuch,* 3:758–64.

43. Many scholars have pointed out that Justin was aware of the stands his Jewish contemporaries took on theological issues and that his dialogue with Trypho offers many authentic Jewish positions. See already Harnack, *Judentum und Judenchristentum,* 47–92; recently this claim, proved from a number of angles, has been restated by Horbury, "Jewish-Christian Relations," 315–45; Skarsaune, *The Proof.*

44. Justin took the same approach in other instances as well; see Shotwell, *Biblical Exegesis,* 38–47.

45. Among the many book-length introductions that survey this fateful era in the history of the church, I base my discussion primarily on Frend, *The Rise of Christianity,*

and Chadwick, *The Early Church* (both contain long bibliographies). For a concise and up-to-date summary, see Hazlett, *Early Christianity*, esp. 81–132.

46. Joannes D. Mansi, *Sacrorum conciliorum nova et amplissima collectio*, II, Florentiae (Paris: Bibliopolae, 1903; repr., Graz: Verlagsanstalt, 1960), col. 672.

47. See already in Hefele, *Christian Councils*, 1:404–9; Walker, *Holy City*, 54–55 (which includes previous bibliography).

48. See, among others, Walker, *Holy City*; Fascher, "Jerusalems," esp. 87–98; Busse and Kretschmar, *Jerusalemer Heiligtumstraditionen* (especially Busse's article and Kretschmar's appendix). This work develops most interesting directions of thought about the extent to which elements from the Jewish Temple influenced Christian Jerusalem, even if it is difficult to agree with the status that it awards them. For example, Busse's position that a desire to imitate the Jewish Temple was the most important consideration ("schwerer wiegendes Argument") in the choice of the Church of the Holy Sepulcher's contours (p. 8) seems unjustified, as do other such claims. For a similar position (that does not acknowledge Busse's studies) on the architectural links between the Church of the Holy Sepulcher and the Temple, see Ousterhout, "The Temple," 44–53; J. Schwartz, "The Encaenia," 265–81; Kühnel, *From the Earthly*; Wilken, *The Land*, 65–125.

49. Wilken, for example asserts (*The Land*, 88): "As grand and sumptuous as Constantinople was to be, it was soon to have a rival in Palestine (meaning Jerusalem)." At the other extreme, Gedaliyahu Stroumsa, in one of his early studies, claims that: "Jerusalem played no important role in the thinking of the Church Fathers." See Stroumsa, "Which Jerusalem?" 120 (Heb.). The approach presented here lies between these two poles.

50. This event has been the subject of no few scholarly investigations. For a summary, see especially Crouzel, *Origen*, 17–33.

51. Origen, *Comm. in Jn.* 6:40 (Preuschen, 149, lines 15–17). See Walker, *Holy City*, 12 n. 27 with references to scholars who disagree on how to evaluate this information.

52. On Eusebius's familiarity with Palestine and the sources of information he had available to him on this subject, see the discussion in Barnes, *Constantine*, 108–11. On Jerome's knowledge of the land and the various scholarly opinions on this issue, see the recent study by Newman, "Jerome," 232–78 (Heb.). Even Wilkinson, who takes a minimalist position on Jerome's acquaintance with the Holy Land's geography and on his interest in the subject, sums up by recognizing his credence on these issues; see Wilkinson, "L'apport de Saint Jérôme à la topographie," 257.

53. On Origen's Hebrew, see de Lange, *Origen*, 22–23; Nautin, *Origène*, 336–39. See also McGuckin in the next note. On Eusebius's Hebrew: Nestle, "Alttestamentliches aus Eusebius," 57–62; Hollerich, *Eusebius*, 81–86. On the Hebrew of Jerome, see Barr, "St. Jerome's Appreciation of Hebrew," 281–302; Kelly, *Jerome*, 50–51.

54. Much ink has been spilled over this issue since the classic studies that discuss it, for example, Graetz, "Hagadische Elemente bei den Kirchenvätern"; Krauss, "The Jews in the Works of the Church Fathers." The accepted view holds that in the absence of direct evidence it is difficult to determine how close the connections were; see, e.g. McGuckin, "Origen and the Jews," 1–13. And see further below, n. 66. Newman's study ("Jerome") presents a comprehensive picture of Jerome's knowledge in this area.

55. For up-to-date biographical surveys on these figures, see Nautin, "Épiphane (10)," cols. 617–31. Nautin is correct to argue that the later references to Epiphanius be-

ing Jewish are difficult to credit, and Jerome's statement that this church father was fluent in Hebrew is far from the truth; Yarnold, *Cyril*, 3–64; J. Kirchmeyer, "Hésychius de Jérusalem," *DSP* 7, cols. 399–408. One could add to these three John II, the bishop of Jerusalem after Cyril, if indeed some of the sermons attributed to Cyril are actually his; on this, see Yarnold, *Cyril*, 24–25.

56. On his tangled stay in Palestine, see Murphy, *Rufinus of Aquileia*, 28–81.

57. A summary and detailed list of all pilgrims before and after Constantine, up to the Arab conquest, can be found in Leclercq, "Pélerinages aux lieux saints," cols. 65–176. See also Hunt, *Holy Land*; Maraval, *Lieux*.

58. On Clement, see Lange, *Origen*, 19–20. On the Donatists, see Wilken, *The Land*, 303 n. 96.

59. On Gregory of Tours, see Hen, "Gregory of Tours and the Holy Land." On Optatus, see here below. On Gregory of Nyssa's visit to Palestine, see Hunt, *Holy Land*, 88–90.

60. Origen testifies to this explicitly; see Nautin, *Origène*, 377–80; Crouzel, *Origen*, 24–25.

61. Origen, *Comm. in Jn.* 13:12 (Preuschen, 237, lines 6–7, 11; trans. in Heine, 84).

62. Nautin, *Origène*, 380–84.

63. Origen, *Comm. in Cant.* 3:12:11 (Brésard, II, 618).

64. Ibid., 13:51 (Brésard, II, 652).

65. Ibid., 13:42–43 (Brésard, II, 646–48)

66. See Kimelman, "Rabbi Yohanan," 567–95. Even if one does not accept Kimelman's extreme claim that the two learned men actually knew each other's teachings (p. 569), he is certainly convincing when it comes to the close (and antagonistic) interpretative and ideological connection between them. See also de Lange, *Origen*, 103–21. A great deal has been written on Origen's exegetical methods, its roots and its motives; for a concise summary, see Torjesen, *Hermeneutical Procedure*.

67. Origen, *Comm. in Cant.* Prologus (Baehrens, 38, lines 20ff.). On the relation between "typology" and "allegory" and on the correlation of their meaning for the church fathers in general and for Origen in particular, see Crouzel, "La distinction de la 'typologie' et de 'l'allégorie,'" 161–74; his discussion of Origen on pp. 172–73.

68. Origen, *De principiis* 4:3:4–9 (Koetschau, 328–37). And more or less similarly in 2:1 (Koetschau, 306). When Origen presents the error of the Jews, who comprehend the Bible's prophecies literally, his first examples are those of the building of Jerusalem. On this approach of Origen's, see Schmidt, "Jerusalem," esp. 220–21, 240ff.; Wilken, *The Land*, 70–71.

69. E.g., the Tabernacle and the Temple as the church: Origen, *Hom. in Ex.* 9 (Borret, 278–305); *Comm. in Jn.* 10:39 (Preuschen, 215–16). Jesus as the Temple: Origen, *Hom. in Lev.* 10: (Baehrens, 441, lines 21–22). The entrance of Jesus into Jerusalem as an allegory for God's entrance into the soul: Origen, *Comm. in Jn.* 10:28 (Preuschen, 201). Jesus's cry as an allegory for the cry on evil forces: Origen, *Hom. in Lc.* 38 (Rauer, 213–14); *Comm. in Lc.*, frag. 238 (Rauer, 329). Of course, these sources are but a sampling, and each one of these expressions can be found in many other parallels in Origen's writings.

70. Lactantius, *Divine institutions* 4:17:1–8 (Monat, 152–54); Pseudo-Cyprian, *De montibus Sina et Sion* (Hartel, 104–19). On the popularity of these verses from Isaiah and Micah in early Christian exegesis, see Wilken, "*In novissimuis diebus*," 1–19.

71. Origen, *Comm. in Jn.* 1:10 (Preuschen, 16, line 3); *Comm. in Mt.* 11:18 (Klostermann, 65–67), and many other similar examples.

72. Origen, *Ep.* 1:21(15) (de Lange, 568, lines 10–11).

73. See Fascher, "Jerusalems"; Bammel, "Law and Temple in Origen," 464–76.

74. Wilken, *The Land*, 69.

75. This has been noted by Boer, "Allegory and History," 15–25.

76. Likewise, there were those who interpreted Origen's *Hexapla* as deriving from anti-Jewish motives, while the background and causes of the project were in fact broader; see de Lange, *Origen*, 50–51.

77. Many have noted the complexity of this matter. For a concise summary, see Wallace-Hadrill, *Eusebius of Caesarea*, 72–99; Barnes, *Constantine*, 94ff. On Eusebius's method of integrating allegory, which is the cornerstone of Origen's exegetical method, with his fundamentally historical inclinations, see Hollerich, *Eusebius*, 87–93.

78. Eusebius, *Theoph.* 4:23 (Lee, n.p.; trans. with slight changes Lee, 257–58).

79. Among the many citations for this matter, see especially Eusebius, *DE* 1:1:7 (Heikel, 4), 16:36–37 (ibid., 28), 2:1:2 (ibid., 53), 5:23:3 (ibid., 245). What is important in all these examples is Eusebius's heterogenic use of the motif. In the first two examples, he integrates the destruction as evidence for the end of the Jewish religion's role. The third example deals with the inclusion of the Gentiles in divine benevolence, and the subject of the fourth example is the prophets' acquaintance with Jesus. For additional examples, see Eusebius, *PE* 1:3:13 (Mras, I, 13, line 16); *HE* 3:5:4 (Schwartz, 196–98), 7:5–6 (ibid., 212–14). On the destruction in Eusebius's later writings, especially the *Theophany* and the commentary on Isaiah, see nn. 93, 95. For an analysis of Eusebius's position on the question of the destruction and its sources, see Grant, *Eusebius*, 97–113; Walker, *Holy City*, 383–96.

80. Eusebius, *Comm. in Ps.* 87:11–13 (Montfaucon, col. 1064B). Additional examples are enumerated in Walker, *Holy City*, 351 n. 3; Wilken, *The Land*, 79–80. For a detailed list of the passages in which Eusebius makes this move in his commentary on Isaiah, see Hollerich, *Eusebius*, 176–78.

81. Many examples of this have been gathered and are discussed in Cranz, "Kingdom and Polity," 60–64; Walker, *Holy City*, 368–76.

82. Eusebius, *Eclogae propheticae* 2:2 (Gaisford, col. 1093).

83. Eusebius, *Comm. in Isa.* 22:1 (Ziegler, 144), 26:1 (ibid., 166, lines 3–4), 65:8–9 (ibid., 394, lines 13–15).

84. Eusebius, *DE* 6:24:5–7 (Heikel, 293), 7:1:86–87 (ibid., 313). To my surprise, I have found no expression of this idea in his commentary on Psalms, even though the spiritualizing tendency appears there as well (see n. 80). I have no reasonable explanation for this, but see, perhaps, Walker's reasoning; Walker, *Holy City*, 300.

85. Such as Eusebius, *DE* 1:6:40 (Heikel, 29), 1:6:65 (ibid., 33, lines 18–19), 6:9:5 (ibid., 259); *Theoph.* 1:1 (Lee, n.p.), and see Lee's translation, which correctly cites Isaiah 40:12 as the source of Eusebius's image; *LC* 8:6 (Heikel, 217).

86. Optatus, *Adversus Donatianae* 3:2 (Ziwsa, 70, lines 9–10; 71, lines 2, 13–14, 17).

87. Ibid. (Ziwsa, 70, lines 11–12). See Tsafrir, "Byzantine Jerusalem," 139.

88. Eusebius, *DE* 6:13 (Heikel, 262–67). All the references in parentheses in the body of the book here are to the sections in the Heikel edition, and when necessary to its page and line numbers. Walker, *Holy City*, 54–55, understands this text in a different way. In chapter 4, n. 19, I have discussed his proposal at length and presented my arguments against it.

89. He develops this argument throughout his discussion of Eusebius; see, e.g., Walker, *Holy City,* 100–104, 347ff.; already before him Linder had noted this development; see Linder, "Ecclesia and Synagoga," 1032–33.

90. Eusebius, *DE* 7:3:26 (Heikel, 342, lines 9–11); *Comm. in PS.* 67:29 (Montfaucon, col. 713C). I do not take up here the scholarly dispute about the dating of the commentary on Psalms. Rondeau has argued several times that the commentary is not uniform. While parts of it may have been written after Constantine's accession (especially the famous passage on the Martyrion in the Church of the Holy Sepulcher), she claims, there are strata that date to much earlier; see Rondeau and Kirchmeyer, "Eusèbe de Césarée," cols. 1689–90; Rondeau, *Les commentaires patristiques,* 66–75. Irshai's discussions of the same topic support those of Rondeau; see Irshai, "Constantine," 155–57 (Heb.).

91. Eusebius, *DE* 6:18:17ff. (Heikel, 277–79), and esp. paragraph 17, which presents the Mount of Olives as a metaphor for the church; paragraphs 20 and 26 create the confrontation between the mountain and Jerusalem. This has previously been noted by Walker, *Holy City,* 200–201.

92. Eusebius, *DE* 6:18:23 (Heikel, 278, lines 16–23); trans. with slight changes based on Ferrar, II, 29). But compare with Walker, *Holy City,* 200–201 n. 4. Even if he is correct that Eusebius exaggerates a bit, this cannot negate his testimony as a whole.

93. Eusebius, *Theoph.* 4:20 (Lee, n.p.; Gressmann, 31, lines 11–12). Walker has already noted the distinction that Eusebius makes between the two; see Walker, *Holy City,* 384ff., and my argument here is based on his evidence there. As with the commentary on Psalms (see n. 90), it is difficult to determine the precise date for the *Theophany.* The traditional view holds that this work comes from Eusebius's later days—e.g., Wallace-Hadrill, *Eusebius,* 52–55, 58. Others, led by Barnes, *Constantine,* 187–88, criticize that view, dating the text to the period prior to Constantine's victory. Neither side bases its conclusions on absolute evidence. That being the case, the phenomenon revealed here may be added to the considerations that support a later date for the work.

94. See the examples enumerated in n. 79. See further, Eusebius, *Eclogae propheticae* 1:8 (Gaisford, cols. 1044–49), 3:63 (ibid., cols. 1161–65).

95. Walker, *Holy City,* 384–85, notes several examples of this formulation, and any number of others might be added; e.g. Eusebius, *Comm. in Isa.* 2:5–9 (Ziegler, 18, lines 6ff.), 3:4–11 (ibid., 23, lines 15ff.), 6:11–13 (ibid., 42, lines 30ff.), 22:2–3 (ibid., 144, lines 22–29). In all these, Eusebius emphasizes the difference between the city inhabited by Gentiles and the destroyed Temple. On the motif of the destruction in Eusebius, see n. 79. The division of Eusebius's writings into early and late works in accordance with his position on the city and the Temple is not unambiguous; differing attitudes to the city and Temple can also be found in earlier writings, especially in those of doubtful date, such as the *Commentary on Psalms* (e.g., those adduced by Walker, *Holy City,* 384–85 n. 88, and other examples may be added here as well). Nevertheless, and especially if we set aside the commentary on Psalms, the argument here is based principally on the total weight of the references to the city and Temple. In other words, most of the early references to the destruction refer to Jerusalem and the Temple as a single unit, whereas most of the later references allude to them as two separate entities.

96. Eusebius, *Theoph.* 4:3 (Lee, n.p.). He expresses the same idea also at 4:16, distinguishing between the city, which the Romans conquered, and the Temple, which they destroyed. To this can be added the descriptions of the destruction in the *Theophany,* in which the city is not mentioned at all, only the Temple (and the altar); e.g., 3:26; 4:14,

15, 17. Likewise, in Eusebius's treatise "on the Tomb of the Savior" (preserved in chapters 11–18 in *De laudibus Constantini*), the destruction applies to the Temple and "their [the Jews'] royal seat," but Jerusalem is not mentioned by name; see Eusebius, *LC* 17:8 (Heikel, 256, lines 14–15).

97. Eusebius, *VC* 3:33 (Heikel, 93). Many have noted this formulation and have located the roots of this imagery in the New Testament's references to a "New Jerusalem" (especially Rev 21:2).

98. E.g., Eusebius, *VC* 3:36 (Heikel, 93–94), 3:43 (ibid., 96, line 1); regarding the church on the Mount of Olives, see Eusebius, *LC* 9:16 (Heikel, 221).

99. So Schwartz already understood; Schwartz, "The Encaenia," 269.

100. Walker's book (*Holy City*) is devoted to the differences between Eusebius and Cyril. On Jerusalem in Jerome's writings, see Abel, "Saint Jérôme," 131–55, and Newman, "Jerome, 241–53"; both focus on the physical information about the city as reflected in Jerome and do not examine his conceptual framework. The latter still awaits a separate study. See, in the meantime, Hunt, *Holy Land*, 192–93; Kelly, *Jerome*, 195–209.

101. Eusebius's attitude toward ancient Jerusalem is not entirely clear. However, a number of places in his writings suggest that he viewed it positively. For example, in his *Commentary on Psalms* 68:26 (Montfaucon, col. 53C) he states that the city is no longer the city of God, and from this we may conclude that it once indeed was. So Walker, *Holy City*, 375.

102. Cyril of Jerusalem, *Catech.* 14:16 (Touttée and Maran, col. 845), 17:22 (ibid., col. 993), 31 (ibid., col. 1004). And see Walker, *Holy City*, 325–30.

103. Jerome, *Ep.* 46:7–8 (Hilberg, 336–39). And see Wilken, *The Land*, 124. It should be noted that Jerome's attitude toward the city was more complex and that he more than once minimized its value and reviled it—e.g., Jerome, *Ep.* 58:2 (Hilberg, 529–30). Abel had already taken note of this; see Abel, "Saint Jérôme," 132–33.

104. Cyril of Jerusalem, *Catech.* 10:11 (Touttée and Maran, cols. 676–77; trans. NPNF, 2, VII, 60). The same distinction between Old and New Jerusalem appears also in *Catech.* 13:71 (Touttée and Maran, col. 781).

105. Newman, "Jerome," 226–28, has gathered together all the places in which the destruction is mentioned in Jerome's writing. An examination of this list shows that, when Jerome took up the subject of the destruction, he emphasized the destroyed Temple (and Mount Zion) but did not articulate the tension between the city and the Temple that was so notable in the writings of his predecessors. One may suppose that, having arrived in Jerusalem only at the end of the fourth century, Christians already took the city's Christian status for granted, and all that remained was the antagonistic attitude toward the site of the Temple.

106. For a thorough treatment, see Baldovin, *Urban Character*, 45–104.

107. But compare Linder, "Jerusalem," 139 (Heb.), who refers to the Typikon (annual liturgical calendar) of the Church of the Holy Sepulcher, which makes it sound as if some of the Jerusalem processions passed through the Temple plaza. It is, however, hard to trust this text. The Typikon is dated to the tenth century, and the copy before us was made only in the twelfth century. It is difficult, at this stage of research, to determine whether the reference in question reflects the practice in the Byzantine period or whether it is, in fact, a later custom, perhaps even a Crusader practice. The Temple compound's return to the heart of Christian consciousness in the Crusader period requires further study.

108. Many have noted this phenomenon; see, e.g., Baldovin, *Urban Character,* 45–104; Nibley, "Christian," 230–31. The roots of this phenomenon are discussed in Bachmann, *Jerusalem und der Temple,* 332–68.

109. In the language of W. K. L. Clarke, quoted in Nibley, "Christian."

110. Many scholars have discerned this; see, e.g., Baldovin, *Urban Character,* 83–90. On the importance of the "place" in this liturgical system, see J. Smith, *To Take Place,* 86–95. Cyril of Jerusalem, more or less a contemporary of Egeria, exhibits a similar attitude toward the city's sites; see, e.g., the instance cited in n. 104, and also Walker, *Holy City,* 37; Wilken, *The Land,* 113–14. For a somewhat more moderate approach, see Bradshaw, *The Search,* 200–201.

111. Already noted by Wilkinson, *Egeria's,* 38. See *Itinerarium Egeriae* 26 (Franceschini and Weber, 72); and the same in *Armenian Liturgy,* reading for 14b February (Renoux, 229). On this holiday, see K. Stevenson, "The Origins and Development of Candlemas," 316–46.

112. This is the common explanation among the scholars listed in n. 48.

113. Recently in Tsafrir, "Byzantine Jerusalem," 143–44.

114. So ibid. It should be noted that not everyone has interpreted the omission of the Temple Mount from the map as an ideological expression; e.g., Guthe, "Das Stadtbild Jerusalems auf der Mosaikkarte von Madeba," 129. It should further be noted that, in purely imaginary works of art that have no connection with the physical landscape of Jerusalem, artists did not avoid depicting the Temple. A good example of this is the mosaic on the triumphal arch in the Santa Maria Majore Church from the first half of the fifth century. At the margins of the scene of Jesus's presentation in the Temple pictured there, the Temple building appears in its full glory; see Leclercq, "Chandeleur," 3:1, cols. 207–8; Brenk, *Die frühchristlichen Mosaiken,* 19–24 (a photograph of the mosaic—pl. 47).

115. Eusebius, *DE* 2:3:66 (Heikel, 73, lines 2–3).

116. Cyril of Jerusalem, *Catech.* 10:19 (Touttée and Maran, col. 688).

117. On this work, see at length Kühnel, *From the Earthly,* 63–72 (with extensive bibliographical references).

118. Epiphanius, *Haer.* 46:5:4–5 (Holl, II, 209); trans. according to Amidon, *The Panarion,* 167.

119. *Itinerarium Burdigalense* 593:4 (Geyer and Cuntz, 16); *Itinerarium Egeriae* 37:1ff. (Franceschini and Weber, 80–81); *Breviarius de Hierosolyma* 2 (Weber, 109–10); Theodosius, *De situ Terrae sanctae* 7 (Geyer, 117–18). And see Wilkinson, *Jerusalem Pilgrims,* 174–78.

120. In addition to the studies noted in n. 48, see also, with an emphasis on Golgotha, Aptowitzer, "Les éléments juifs," 145–62; Jeremias, "Golgotha und der heilige Felsen," 74–128.

121. Eusebius's words have been preserved in a catena for Genesis; see Françoise Petit, *Catenae graecae in Genesim et in Exodum* (*CCSG* 2; Turnhout: Brepols, 1977), 156 (I am grateful to Edward Kessler for having drawn my attention to this source). On the broad parallel that church fathers drew between Jesus's crucifixion and the binding of Isaac, and on its sources, see Lerch, *Isaaks Opferung* (he does not refer to the previously mentioned passage from Eusebius); Van den Brink, "Abraham's Sacrifice," 140–51; and recently Kessler 2004.

122. *Breviarius de Hierosolyma* 2 (Weber, 109–10); Theodosius, *De situ Terrae sanc-*

tae 7 (Geyer, 117–18); *Itinerarium Antonini Placentini* 19 (Geyer, 138–39); Adomnan, *De locis sanctis* 1:6:2 (Bieler, 191). And see Kretschmar, "Festkalender," 97–99.

123. Theodoret of Cyrrhus, *Eranistes* 3 (Ettlinger, 209, lines 7–8). See also Ousterhout, "The Temple," 47.

124. *Mearath Gazze* (Bezold, 146–48). See Aptowitzer, "Les éléments juifs," 149–51; Kretschmar, "Festkalender," 84–86. Not everyone shared this radical view; Jerome, for example, knew very well that Mount Moriah was the site of the Jewish Temple and was not connected with Golgotha; see Abel, "Saint Jérôme," 150.

125. Concerning Mount Zion, see the summaries cited in chapter 4, n. 2.

126. Cyril of Jerusalem, *Catech.* 10:19 (Touttée and Maran, col. 688); *Ep. Const.* 4 (Bihain, 288); Adomnan, *De locis sanctis* 1:23:13 (Bieler, 201); Strategius, *Expugnationis Hierosolymae* (Arabic version) 13:10 (Garitte, 166). I thank my friend Nimrod Luz for helping me understand the Arabic.

127. E.g., Jerome, *Ep.* 108:12:1 (Hilberg, II, 320); Paulinus of Nola, *Ep.* 31:4 (Hartel, 271). For the roots of these traditions as well as for extensive discussion about the churches on the Mount of Olives and the liturgy that developed there, see Desjardins, "Les vestiges du Seigneur au Mont des Oliviers," 51–72; Walker, *Holy City,* 199ff.; Wilkinson, *Jerusalem,* 166–67.

128. Adomnan, *De locis sanctis* 1:22 (Bieler, 199). It is precisely the parallel from Eucherius, which Wilkinson (*Jerusalem,* 110 n. 35) believes to be a source for Arculf, that demonstrates the opposite, since the Temple, which appears in the former work, is absent in the latter one. There is no doubt that Arculf was also acquainted with the Temple, as he mentions it there in 1:1:14 (Bieler, 186), but here we are discussing the conceptualization of the area and the way it functioned in his consciousness. John of Damascus, a resident of Jerusalem in the early eighth century, reflects a similar image of Jerusalem; see John of Damascus, *Orationes de imaginibus tres* 3:34 (*PG* 94, col. 1353).

s i x : The Temple Mount, the Rabbis, and the Poetics of Memory

1. This chapter is based on a broader study of mine, in which I was able to exhaust more fully the wide range of rabbinic evidence supporting my thesis and to discuss the minute details of its analysis; see Eliav, "The Temple Mount, the Rabbis, and the Poetics of Memory."

2. Among others, Lawrence Schiffman has accentuated this point in numerous studies. See, e.g., Schiffman, "The Qumran Scrolls and Rabbinic Judaism," 552–71.

3. See my comment and references in the introduction.

4. The most influential work on this topic remains Halbwachs's *La mémoire collective.* Already also a classic for Judaic studies is Yerushalmi, *Zakhor.* For a more postmodern take on the same issues, see the variety of studies collected in Bal et al., eds., *Acts of Memory.*

5. For the scientific aspect, a good summary may be found in Conway, *Cognitive Models of Memory.*

6. Hutton, *History as an Art of Memory.*

7. An inclusive summary of the allusions to Jerusalem in rabbinic literature with references to previous collections and scholarly discussions is Gafni, "Jerusalem," 35–59 (Heb.). A few scholarly collections in recent years were also devoted to exploring the

various facets of Jerusalem in ancient Jewish civilization. See, e.g., Poorthuis and Safrai, *The Centrality of Jerusalem;* Levine, *Jerusalem.*

8. For a comprehensive treatment of this aspect, see Ben-Shalom, "Events and Ideology," 1–12 (Heb.).

9. On how the destruction of the Temple affected Judaism and its institutions, see, e.g., Cohen, "Destruction," 18–39; Cohen, "The Temple," 151–74; Bokser, "Rabbinic Responses," 37–61; Aderet, *From Destruction to Restoration,* 2–5 (Heb.).

10. See, e.g., tSotah 15:12–14 (Lieberman, 243–44), and other sources are listed in Lieberman, *Tosefta Kifshutah,* 8:774. For the connections between the synagogue and its prayers, on the one hand, and the Temple and its sacrifices, on the other, see, e.g., Cohen, "The Temple"; and lately Fine, *This Holy Place;* Reif, "Jerusalem in Jewish Liturgy," 424–37.

11. Fine, *This Holy Place,* 95–126.

12. Irshai, "Constantine," 129–78 (Heb.). Contra, e.g., Stemberger, *Jews and Christians* 40–43; Limor, "Christian Sacred Space and the Jew," 60–62.

13. Many of the sources were collected and discussed by S. Safrai, "Pilgrimage," 376–93 (Heb.); Wilken, *The Land,* 105–8.

14. B. Mazar, *Excavations,* 23.

15. Barag, "Glass Pilgrim Vessels from Jerusalem." On the menorah as a Jewish symbol in this period, see Levine, "History and Significance," 131–53; Hachlili, *The Menorah.*

16. B. Mazar, *The Mountain of the Lord,* 257; Ben-Dov, *Shadow,* 218–19.

17. *Itinerarium Burdigalense* 591:4–6 (Geyer and Cuntz, 16). For a more detailed consideration of the act described here, see n. 113.

18. Ibid. 592:6–7 (Geyer and Cuntz, 16).

19. For a thorough discussion of these interpretations, see Taylor, *Christians and the Holy Places,* 207–20.

20. Jerome, *Comm. in Seph.* 1:15–16 (Adriaen, 673).

21. Nau, "Résumé de monographies syriaques," 120.

22. *SifreDeut* 43 (Finkelstein, 95). See my treatment of this passage and its parallels in the introduction.

23. yPes 7:11 (35b). On the 'agof, see Jastrow, *Dictionary,* 13; Levy, *Wörterbuch,* 23.

24. See Gafni, "Jerusalem"; Guttmann, "Jerusalem," 251–75; Golinkin, "Jerusalem in Jewish Law and Customs," 408–23.

25. For a sample of the disparate opinions that have been expressed on this issue in recent years, see Cohen, "The Temple"; Z. Safrai and Safrai, "The Sanctity of Eretz Israel and Jerusalem," 344–71 (Heb.); Henshke, "The Sanctity," 5–28 (Heb.); Hezser, "The (In)Significance of Jerusalem in the Talmud Yerushalmi," 11–49.

26. References to this source are provided in the next note and in my discussion later in the chapter.

27. mMid 1:1–3, 2:1–2. The version of the Mishnah used throughout this chapter is checked against that of the manuscript Kaufman A50 in the Hungarian Academy of Sciences, facsimile edition, Jerusalem 1968. I do not generally use alternative readings unless they are important for the matter at hand. The translations into English are based on Danby, *The Mishnah,* with changes where I feel they do not represent the original Hebrew precisely.

28. mParah 3:3, 6; tParah 3:2–7 (Zuckermandel, 631–32).

29. *mBik* 3:4; *tBik* 2:10 (Lieberman, 292).

30. *mPes.*5:10.

31. *tSot* 7:13 (Lieberman, 195), also cited in *bYoma* 69a.

32. *mSheq* 7:2.

33. The main versions of this halakha, see *Sifra* Qedoshim 7:1 (Weiss, 90d–91a); *mBer* 9:5; *SifreDeut* 258 (Finkelstein, 282); *tBer* 6:19 (Lieberman, 38–39). Amoraic literature also cites these sources. The midrash in *Sifre* is brought in *bYev* 6b; the passage in the Tosefta is cited with slight changes in *yBer* 9 (14c); *EcclR* 4:17; *bBer* 62b. For a detailed discussion of this text, see Eliav, "The Temple Mount."

34. *tSanh* 2:6 (Zuckermandel, 416); *yMSh* 5:6 (53c); *ySanh* 1:2 (18d); *bSanh* 11b.

35. As concluded by many; see, e.g., Herr, "The Calendar," 856–57; Goodblatt, *The Monarchic Principle*, 211–12. But cf. Neusner, *The Rabbinic Traditions*, 1:356–58.

36. *mTaʿan* 3:8. Some of the textual witnesses, including the printed editions, have "went out" instead of "went up." In the Tosefta version of the story, the Temple Mount does not appear at all; see *tTaʿan* 2:13 (Lieberman, 334–35). For a discussion of the various versions, see Lieberman, *Tosefta Kifshutah*, 5:1096–97.

37. *mSuk* 4:4. See, e.g., Kohut, *Aruch Completum*, 1:166–67, s.v.; Krauss, *Griechische*, 2:117–18.

38. Synagogue and academy house: *tSuk* 4:5 (Lieberman, 273). Parallels and discussion of variants in Lieberman, *Tosefta Kifshutah*, 4:888. Academy house and lawcourt: *tSheq* 3:27 (Lieberman, 219); *tHag* 2:9 (Lieberman, 383); *tSanh* 7:1 (Zuckermandel, 425). For a full discussion of these sources with reference to their parallels in the New Testament, which reaches rather different conclusions about the actual situation, see Krauss, *Synagogale Altertümer*, 66–72; Levine, *The Ancient Synagogue*, 52–58.

39. *tShab* 13:2 (Lieberman, 57). Other versions of this tradition are listed by Lieberman. The London manuscript has R. Gamaliel "standing," and in *yShab* 16:1 (15c) the location is said to be "the building on the Temple Mount" instead of the step, presumably to allow "a tier of bricks" for the stashing of the translation.

40. *tKel bava batra* 2:2 (Zuckermandel, 591).

41. *mKel* 1:8, and also *SZ Naso* 5:2 (Horovitz, 228); *tKel bava Qamma* 1:6–7 (Zuckermandel, 569–70).

42. *yPes* 7:11 (35b).

43. *yPes* 7:8 (35a).

44. *yBeṣah* 2:4 (61c); *yHag* 2:3 (78a).

45. *TanB Ḥukat* 40 (Buber, 124). Similarly in the printed edition of the *Tanḥuma* (Ḥukat 17), and *NumR* 19:19, which is known to be nearly identical to the *Tanḥuma* for these biblical portions.

46. *GenR* 61:7 (Theodor and Albeck, 668). For another version of this legend in the Scholion to the Scroll of Fasting (*Megillat taʿanit*) and other parallel texts in Amoraic literature, see Noam, "*Megilat Taʿanit* and the Scholion," 208–12 (Heb.). The designation "Temple Mount" only appears in what Noam calls the "patchwork version" of the Scholion and is thus influenced by Genesis Rabba. Concerning the *empilia*, see Krauss, *Griechische*, 61–62.

47. See Weiss-Halivni, *Midrash*, 22–25.

48. *mBik* 1:8–9 (trans., with minor changes, Danby, *The Mishnah*, 94).

49. *MRS* 23:19 (Epstein and Melamed, 219). See Weiss-Halivni, *Midrash*, 23. Actually, the classical commentators on the Mishnah had already noticed the internal con-

tradition in this halakha. Halivni himself refers the reader to the famous eighteenth-century rabbinic scholar known as the Vilna Gaon, and even before Halivni, Lieberman reviewed other commentators who discussed this issue; see Lieberman, *Tosefta Kifshutah*, 2:828. As they generally do in such cases, traditional scholars take a harmonistic approach toward the sources. Thus, for example, the Vilna Gaon expunged the word "Mount" from the last part of the halakha in *Mishnah Bikkurim*, suggesting that the proper wording is, "and how do we know that he is liable for them until he brings them to the house (Temple)," thus resolving the contradiction. Clearly, however, this correction has no support from any of the known textual witnesses, all of which read "the Temple Mount," and thus misses the historical aspect of halakhic development.

50. Weiss-Halivni, *Midrash*, 23.

51. Halivni's thesis is even more far reaching since he claims, based on this analysis, that the genre of midrash predates the Mishnaic form. My discussion below adds to doubts that were posed in regard to this preposition. On the whole subject, see Kalmin, "Midrash, Mishnah, and Gemara," 78–84 (on Halivni's discussion of the Temple Mount, see p. 82).

52. *SifreDeut* 77 (Finkelstein, 142); *tBik* 1:5 (Lieberman, 287). On the location of this cistern, see *m'Eruv* 1:14; *mMid* 5:4. For discussion of the sources and earlier bibliography, see J. Schwartz, "Be'er ha-Qar, Bôr Heqer and the Seleucid Akra," 14–16 (Heb.).

53. *'Azara* (which I have been translating as "inner Temple court"), at least in the Mishnah, always refers to the area west of the women's courtyard (map 3: B), whether it includes only the so-called court of the Israelites or also the priestly court. Some typical examples of this terminological phenomenon are discussed below (the public reading of the biblical section concerning the king, the slaughter of the Passover sacrifice in three groups, and others). The history of the expression *Beit ha-beḥirah* (the chosen house) was recently discussed by Henshke, "The Sanctity," 10–17 (Heb.), who showed that it originally did not mean "the Temple" but rather the area upon which the Temple was built. The following points are important for the present discussion: Henshke admits that this term was later used only to refer to the Temple; and even if the *Mekhilta of R. Simeon b. Yoḥai* reflects the early use of the term, this may be the source of the halakha that places the limit of liability at the Temple Mount, but it then just corroborates the fact that "the Temple Mount" is a later expression that replaced "the chosen house."

54. I Kgs 8:30; Dan 6:11; 3 Ezra 4:58 (Rahlfs, 884). This is also how the prayer of Sarah facing the window is interpreted: Tob 3:11 (Hanhart, 83). See also Urbach, *The Sages*, 54–63; Ehrlich, *Non-Verbal Language*, 64–96 (Heb.).

55. *tBer* 3:15–16 (Lieberman, 15–16); *SifreDeut* 29 (Finkelstein, 47). Later versions and parallels from Geniza are enumerated in Lieberman's edition. Concerning the major difference in wording between the Tosefta and the *Sifre*, where the former has "they direct their heart" throughout, while the latter (as well as the Mishnah cited in the following note) has "they turn their faces toward . . ." in some of the instances, see Lieberman, *Tosefta Kifshutah*, 1:44; Ehrlich, *Non-Verbal Language*.

56. *mBer* 4:5.

57. *yBer* 4 (8c). The fact that this source speaks about turning one's face, while the source from the Tosefta is about the direction of one's heart, is not relevant for the present study. The parallels in the Tosefta already include turning one's face; the important point is that the hierarchy of places remains the same in the two versions, except for the source in the Palestinian Talmud under discussion here. Another parallel version in

CantR 4:4 has preserved a mixed reading, "Those who stand in prayer in Jerusalem turn their faces toward the Temple. . . . Those who stand on the Temple Mount turn their faces toward the Holy of Holies." This version may well reflect an intermediate stage in the transmission of the tradition, between the early versions and the one in the Palestinian Talmud.

58. E.g., Lieberman, *Tosefta Kifshutah*, 1: 44 (Heb.), who compares the Palestinian Talmud version to other readings but soon concludes, "They are the same"; Ginzberg, *A Commentary*, 3:379 (Heb.); Aderet, *From Destruction*, 103, "During the Second Temple period the Jews had the custom of praying while facing Jerusalem *and the Temple Mount*" (Heb.; emphasis added). This harmonistic approach illustrates the obliviousness toward the developments in meaning and significance of the Temple Mount that occurred over time.

59. Other versions are *CantR* 4:4; *bBer* 30a. Extensively discussed in Ginzberg, *A Commentary*, 3:398–99 (Heb.).

60. *yYoma* 1:1 (38c); *bYoma* 11b. I am not aware of any evidence to support Lieberman's reading (*Tosefta Kifshutah*, 4:719) in the Palestinian Talmud " . . . to the gates of the Temple [*habayit*] and the inner Temple courts." Perhaps it is a typographical error.

61. *SifreDeut* 36 (Finkelstein, 67); *tYoma* (Kippurim) 1:2 (Liberman, 220).

62. *mTaʿan* 2:5. All variants mentioned in the following discussion are taken from Malter, *The Treatise Taʿanit of the Babylonian Talmud*, 55ff. The Mishnah does not state what exactly was enacted by the two Tannaim, and there were differences of opinion on the matter in the Talmud and among the Geonim; see, e.g., Büchler, *Types of Jewish-Palestinian Piety* 222–41.

63. *bRH* 27a; *bTaʿan* 16b.

64. *tHag* 2:11 (Lieberman, 385–86); also in *bBeṣah* 20a.

65. E.g., Neh 2:8, 7:2; *mPes* 7:8; *mZev* 12:5; *mParah* 3:1; *mTam* 1:1; Josephus *JA* 15:403, 409 (Marcus, VIII, 194–96); *BJ* 1:75 (Thackeray, I, 38). For a full discussion of the numerous sources mentioning the term *birah*, and the suggestions made by scholars for its meaning as well as its location, see Mandel, "'Birah,'" 195–217 (Heb.); J. Schwartz, "The Temple," 29–49.

66. Mandel, "Birah,'" 209–10 (Heb.).

67. For a wider apparatus of examples supporting my case, see Eliav, "The Temple Mount."

68. J. Schwartz, "Once More on the Nicanor Gate," 245–83.

69. *Mek* Shirata 9 (Horovitz and Rabin, 148–49).

70. *Mek* Pisḥa 16 (Horovitz and Rabin, 60, line 19).

71. *Ps.-J. Deut* 3:25 (Clarke, 213).

72. *SifreDeut* 28 (Finkelstein, 44).

73. *mHag* 1:1.

74. Only one other rabbinic text supports this assertion. An early rabbinic fragment that was preserved only in the Yemenite medieval text *Midrash ha-Gadol* (from which Epstein and Melammed reconstructed the *Mekhilta of R. Simeon b. Yoḥai*) conveys a similar position: "And when you do not celebrate [the three pilgrimage festivals] properly, I consider it as if you unlawfully used [*meʿilah*] the Temple Mount and the [Temple] inner courts"; see *MHG* Exodus 24:13 (Margulies, 542) = *MRS* 24:13 (Epstein and Melammed, 218).

75. *yHag* 1:1 (76a). See Weiss-Halivni, *Midrash*, 24–25. For more about the statuettes

of pilgrimage and their fulfillment precisely at the Temple, see S. Safrai, "The Duty of Pilgrimage to Jerusalem," 69–72 (Heb.).

76. *tḤag* 1:1 (Lieberman, 374).

77. *Mek* Kaspa 20 (Horovitz and Rabin, 333).

78. In Ḥoni's case, however, there is no decisive evidence about who formulated the story in this way or who introduced the term "Temple Mount" and its precipitous image. One hint that "the Temple Mount" might have been added at a later stage is that other versions of the story, first and foremost that in the Tosefta, do not mention the Temple Mount at all. According to the account in the Tosefta, the people of Jerusalem were sent out of the city to the "cliff of the ʿOphel." Also relevant here is the tradition rendered by the Yerushalmi in connection with the Ḥoni story, according to which the people "went up to the Temple Mount" because it was covered with a roof; see *yTaʿan* 3:10 (66d). This is clearly an exaggeration, or a late product of the imagination, since the sheltered portions of the Temple area included only a relatively narrow strip of surrounding colonnades and the royal basilica to the south of the complex but surely not the entire compound. Also note that the description here is somewhat opposed to that in the Mishnah, where the reason for going up to the Temple Mount was its (imagined) height: when Jerusalem was flooded, its inhabitants climbed up to the highest place. Why would someone change the description of the place from "high" to "covered"? Perhaps this derived from the acquaintance of the Palestinian Amoraim with the area, which showed them that the Temple Mount is not the highest place in Jerusalem. To those who look at Jerusalem from the Mount of Olives, as people in that period often did, this is very clear (see also fig. 1).

79. *mMid* 2:1 (trans. Danby, *The Mishnah*, 591).

80. *mMid* 2:2, 1:1–3.

81. *mKel* 1:8; *SifreNum* 1 (Horovitz, 4, lines 7–9); *tKel* Bava Qamma 1:12 (Zuckermandel, 570). References to later rabbinic compositions that incorporate this excerpt are listed in Horovitz's notes.

82. From among the many studies discussing this issue, listed above in chapter 1, nn. 68, 70, see, e.g., Albeck, *Shishah*, 5:431, who summarizes his discussion as follows: "It may be assumed that the measures in the *Mishnah* are consistent with the real situation" (Heb.); Avi-Yonah, "Beit ha-miqdash ha-sheini," 394, 414–15. Avi-Yonah attributes the measure of 500-by-500 cubits to the days of the high priest known as Simeon the Righteous, at the beginning of the second century BCE (p. 394). In order to give meaning to these figures at the time of Herod, Avi-Yonah outlines a sort of "Temple Mount enclosure" on his map (p. 415), between the Herodian enclosure and the Temple; he also moves the *soreg* (the stone railing) from the place assigned to it by the Mishnah and claims that it "apparently circumscribed the 500 x 500 cubit square" (p. 414). The same proposal is taken up in S. Safrai, "Temple: Second Temple," col. 965; S. Safrai, "The Temple," 865–66. Such a claim totally contradicts *mMid* 2:3, which states that the *soreg* was inside the Temple Mount and not surrounding it. Avi-Yonah himself does not even apply his own interpretation in his map (!), drawing the *soreg* in the customary way, as enclosing only the "rampart" (*ḥeil*). He thus ends up with three areas: from the walls of the enclosure to what he calls the "Temple Mount area," from this area to the *soreg*, and from there to the walls of the Temple inner court. The harmonistic nature of such a reconstruction is obvious. For another fantastic reconstruction, see Kaufman, "The Meaning of the Temple Mount," 7–16 (Heb.; esp. 8–10, where he surveys medieval sages and present-day rabbis who discussed this issue).

See also Ritmeyer, "Locating the Original Temple Mount," 25–45 (esp. 44, where there is a concise survey of the suggestions that have been made for identifying the square in the past century). The very name of his paper reveals the methodological blunder underlying it. Ritmeyer, like many other scholars, simply assumes that there was an ancient Temple Mount, which the Mishnah was referring to in its description of a 500-by-500-cubit square, and he channels his virtuoso architectural talents into locating it (see fig. 3).

83. Ezek 42:20. Even those scholars who noticed this parallel did not give it any weight in their historical reconstructions. See, e.g., Albeck, *Shishah*, 5:431; J. Schwartz, "The Temple," 31 n. 9.

84. For the calculations leading to this conclusion, see Yadin, *Temple Scroll*, 1:242–43.

85. Josephus, *JA* 8:96 (Marcus, V, 622). Scholarly discussions about Josephus's descriptions of the Temple of Solomon are numerous; for a representative summary see Feldman, *Josephus*, 438–44; Yadin, *The Temple*, 192–94.

86. 2 Macc 3:4 (Kappler and Hanhart, 55). For the various suggestions scholars offered regarding the nature of this office and the extent of its authority, see, e.g., Goldstein, *2 Maccabees*, 201–3.

87. Josephus, *BJ* 6:294 (Thackeray, III, 460).

88. Acts 4:1; 5:24.

89. Some scholars identify the office of the "deputy [*Segan*] [high] priest" with the previously mentioned *stratēgos* of Josephus and *Acts*. But it seems to me that the duties of this man, which surface in rabbinic texts time and again, did not include security tasks but lay rather in the realm of worship—particularly because one holder of this title (Ḥanina, or Ḥananiah according to some textual witnesses) belonged to the circle of the Pharisees, and many rabbinic traditions are cited in his name. E.g., *tYoma* (Kippurim) 1:4 (Lieberman, 221); *tParah* 4:6 (Zuckermandel, 633); *yYoma* 3:8 (41a). Contra: Büchler, *Die Priester und der Cultus*, 103–18; Goldstein, *II Maccabees*, 201–3; Schürer, *History*, 2:276–78.

90. *mʿOrlah* 2:12; Nehemiah 7:2. For this identification, see J. Schwartz, "The Temple," 46–47 and n. 45.

91. *Scholion to Megillat Taʿanit* 25 of Sivan (Lichtenstein, 328, line 4).

92. See, e.g., Albeck, *Shishah*, 6:508; Guttmann, "Jerusalem," 269–70; Z Safrai and Safrai, "The Sanctity," 364 (Heb.).

93. Ezek 5:5. The issue at hand is also related to the "navel of the Earth" paradigm, which I discuss later in this chapter. On the biblical conception, see Bettenzoli, *Geist der Heiligkeit*, 105–51; Haran, *Temples and Temple-Service*, 175–88. And in general: J. Smith, *To Take Place*, 47–73; Wilken, *The Land*, 11–14.

94. *Sifre* Deut 145 (Finkelstein, 200); *tMeg* 2:16 (Lieberman, 352).

95. On this set of halakhot and the changes the rabbis introduced to it over time, see my detailed study in Eliav, "The Temple Mount."

96. *MHG* Exodus 24:13 (Margulies, 542) = *MRS* 24:13 (Epstein and Melammed, 218).

97. *TanB* Ḥuqqat 40 (Buber, 124); *NumR* 19:19.

98. *tKil* 5:27 (Lieberman, 226; trans. I. Mandelbaum in Neusner and Sarason, 1:274).

99. *yKil* 9:2 (32a).

100. *GenR* 65:22 (Theodor and Albeck, 741–42; trans. Freedman and Simon, 2:599). An alternative version for this legend in *TanB* Toldot 10 (Buber, 132) reads "Temple" in-

stead of "Temple Mount." But in this case it seems like an erroneous variant. See Buber's comment in n. 68.

101. The entire series of interpretations presented here was preserved in *TanB* Shemot 10 (Buber, 5–6); *ExodR* 2:2 (Shinan, 104–5). See also: *MidrPss* 11:3 (Buber, 98–99). For a detailed discussion of the various opinions about the *Shekhina* and its location that were prevalent in antiquity, see Urbach, *The Sages*, 37–65.

102. The former was preserved in the so-called Rome manuscript. (Cod. Vat. Ebr. 34) of the *Tanhuma*, a copy of which was used by Buber, as well as in Exodus Rabbah. Buber preferred it to the other textual witnesses (which read "mountain"—*har*—instead of "destroyed"/*harev*), asserting, "it is the correct version"; see his comments on the *Tanhuma* (*TanB*, 5–6 n. 48). R. Aha's statement appears in all the previously listed sources (n. 101) as well as in *CantR* 2:9.

103. E.g., Meir Ben-Dov, "From the Temple to the Western Wall," in Ben-Dov et al., *The Western Wall*, 53–54 (Heb.).

104. *mYoma* 5:2.

105. *tYoma* (Qippurim) 2:14 (Lieberman, 238).

106. In addition to the bibliography listed in chapter 1 (where there are also references to the Second Temple sources), see Aptowitzer, "Les éléments juifs," 145–62; Jeremias, "Golgotha und der heilige Felsen," 91–98; Terrien, "The Omphalos Myth and Hebrew Religion," 315–38; Böhl, "Über das Verhältnis," 253–70; Ginzberg, *The Legends*, 5:14–15; Lieberman, *Hellenism in Jewish Palestine*, 175 n. 103; J. Levenson, *Sinai*,117–19; Z. Safrai and Safrai, "The Sanctity," 349 (Heb.). It seems to me that caution should be exercised in attributing this notion to every source that hints at images of centrality. For example, when Hecataeus of Abdera, in a fragment preserved by Josephus, relates that the Temple enclosure was "in the very center of the city" (Josephus, *Ap.* 1:198 [Thackeray, I, 242]), it does not mean that he is expressing the Omphalos idea. A second example for such scholarly misunderstandings involves the previously discussed writings of Melito of Sardis (see chapter 5).

107. Noticed by Ginzberg, *The Legends*, 5:15. Cf. Albeck, *Shishah*, 2:469.

108. Later developments in the image of the stone show that its separation from its original Temple environment allowed it a life of its own, sort of an autonomous character. Some later rabbinic compositions still preserve the memory of its function within the layout of the Temple or as part of ceremonies in the Day of Atonement; other instances, however, completely detach the stone from its past, furnish it with new substance, and link it to new contexts that at times even somewhat contradict the way it was originally perceived. For example: *LevR* 20:4 (Margulies, 453–55) = *PRK* 26:4 (Mandelbaum, 391). The stone obliterated with the destruction of the Temple: *yPes* 4:1 (30d) = *yTaʿan* 1:6 (64c); *TanB* Qedoshim 10 (Buber, 78); *NumR* 12:4; *CanR* 3:10. The reference to the foundation stone as the "navel of the earth" appears only in late rabbinic sources such as the *Tanhuma*, which also bestow this image upon other constituents of their world (such as the city of Tiberias and the institution of the Sanhedrin). As far as I know, this association was first made by the *Tanhuma* (ibid.), and from then on different forms of such amalgamation took root in various sources. See A. Jellinek, *Bet ha-Midrash* (facsimile ed.; Jerusalem, 1967) 5:63; *MidrPss* 91:7 (Buber, 400); *PRE* 35.

109. See Livne-Kafri, "The Moslim Traditions," 165–92; Elad, *Medieval Jerusalem and Islamic Worship*, 51–130.

110. *MHG* Genesis 2:7 (Margulies, 78). Indeed, parallel traditions (which are listed by Margulies) associate these characteristics with the sanctuary itself, specifically mentioning the ashes (written in Hebrew with similar consonants as the word dust—ʿein/ʾaleph-peih-reish) on the altar and the Temple. Concerning midrashim about Adam's having been created from the dust/ashes of the Temple and the cultural context in which they were formulated, see Gafni, "Pre-Histories of Jerusalem," esp. 11. Regarding the Temple as a place of atonement, see Z. Safrai and Safrai, "The Sanctity," 356–57.

111. *LevR* 13:2 (Margulies, 272–73); *PesR* addendum 3 (Friedmann [ʾish-shalom], 198–99). Other versions, which do not include the pericope about the Temple Mount, are listed by Margulies. More traditions of R. Simeon b. Yoḥai about Mount Moriah are listed and discussed in Beer, "Shimʿon," 361–75 (Heb.).

112. E.g., *yBer* 4 (8c) = *CantR* 4:4 (toward the end of the pericope). A large collection of passages on Mount Moriah was collected in M. D. Gross, *ʾOtsar ha-ʾagadah ha-talmudit veha-midrashit* (3 vols.; Jerusalem: Mosad ha-rav Kuk, 1961) 2:633–34. On the binding of Isaac, see Ginzberg, *The Legends,* 5:253. On Ornan's threshing floor: Beer, "Shimʿon," 365–68 (Heb.).

113. Discussed at length in Levine, *The Ancient Synagogue;* Cohen, "The Temple."

114. Scholars have generally tended to bring the traveler's testimony together with that of Jerome, considering the former too to speak of the Ninth of Av mourning. But, as Irshai correctly noted, "this has no real support from the text"; see Irshai, "Constantine," 173–74 (Heb.). Those who held this view are listed there, n. 145. The fact that the traveler describes the rending of clothes and crying cannot be considered evidence since, as the sources discussed here show, Jews were required, at least by rabbinic halakha, to rend their garments whenever they entered Jerusalem. As for the anointing of the stone with oil, Irshai (p. 147) suggests seeing it as an analogy to Jacob's act in Beth-El. See also Cohn, "Second Thoughts about the Perforated Stone on the Haram of Jerusalem," 144–45. Cohn speculates that this was an act forced upon the Jews by the Christian authorities. The thesis of the current study suggests that the ceremony should be connected with the formulations about the foundation stone discussed previously and thus seen as a liturgical application of that image. This, too, however, is only a proposition. Concerning other sacred stones on the Temple Mount, see chapter 2. Donner's position that the stone in the traveler's description must have been outside the Temple Mount altogether because the Jews could not have prayed on the site of the Temple is an obvious anachronism; see Donner, "Der Felsen und der Tempel," 8.

115. The main source for this is the baraita in *yMQ* 3:7 (83b); *bMQ* 26a; *Minor Tractates Semaḥot* 9:19 (Higger, 165–67). For a detailed survey and discussion of all sources pertaining to this issue, see S. Safrai, "Pilgrimage," 382–85 (Heb.). Various scholars have suggested that for some time after the destruction Jews continued to perform various Temple rites, such as offering sacrifices and bringing the second tithe and eating it within Jerusalem. The majority of scholars, however, have correctly rejected these conjectures; see S. Safrai, "Pilgrimage," 376–81 (Heb.).

116. Already understood in this way by S. Safrai, "Pilgrimage," 385 (Heb.).

117. *DeutR* Va-ethannen (Lieberman, 34, 43). A similar passage of the same textual tradition is found in *TanB* Leviticus 8 (Buber, 5–6), and in the printed edition 6, but it would seem that these texts were already adapted to the accepted version throughout rabbinic literature, so that "the Temple Mount" appears there instead of "the Temple."

118. Weiss and Netzer, *Promise and Redemption*, 30–31. All following quotations from their study are from these pages.

119. Mordekhai Margaliot, *Hilkhot Erez Yisrael min ha-Geniza* (Jerusalem: Mosad ha-Rav Kuk, 1973), 139–41. See also Wilken, *The Land*, 105–7; S. Safrai, "Pilgrimage," 381 (Heb.); Reiner, "Pilgrims and Pilgrimage," 163–64 (Heb.). Reiner dates the text to the thirteenth century, whereas Margaliot claims it was two centuries earlier. An interesting parallel to this fragment from a medieval account that was appended to a manuscript of Ecclesiastes Rabbah was published by Hirshman, "The Priest's Gate," 217–27 (Heb.). But the ceremony there, despite its striking similarities to the description given here, as well as to what is related by Barsauma (see n. 20) about the assembly of the Jews on the holiday of Tabernacles, took place outside the Temple Mount and was centered on the Mount of Olives to the east (for more information about the medieval assemblies on the Mount of Olives, see Hirshman's bibliography). This source may reflect the Muslims' occupation of the area, which undoubtedly put an end to the Jews' assemblies there.

120. See Urbach, "Yerushalim," 376–91 (Heb.).

121. No existing rabbinic text was compiled before 70 CE, even though there are some portions that scholars believe were composed and edited before the destruction or just after (e.g., the first few chapters of *Mishnah tractate Yoma*, as well as tractates *Tamid* and *Middot*). See Strack and Stemberger, *Introduction*, 124–33.

122. Rightly pointed out by, Goodblatt, "The Temple Mount," 101 n. 28.

Bibliography

PRIMARY SOURCES

Acts of Justin and Companions [*Acta Martyrum*]—Herbert Musurillo, *The Acts of the Christian Martyrs* (Oxford: Clarendon, 1972), 42–61.

Acts of Thomas (Acta Thomae) [*Acts Thom.*]—Maximilianus Bonnet, *Acta Apostolorum Apocrypha* (II.2; Hildesheim: G. Olms, 1959), 99–291; William Wright, *Apocryphal Acts of the Apostles (Syriac Version)* (London: Williams & Norgate, 1871); Wilhelm Schneemelcher, ed., *New Testament Apocrypha* (trans. Robert M. Wilson; 2 vols.; rev. ed.; Cambridge: James Clarke, 1991–92), 2:322–411.

Adomnan, *De locis sanctis*—L. Bieler, *Adamnani de locis sanctis, CCSL* 175:185–234; John Wilkinson, *Jerusalem Pilgrims before the Crusades* (Warminster: Aris & Phillips, 1977), 95–116.

Alexander Monachos, *Inventio crucis*—J. Gretser, *PG* 87:3, cols. 4015–76.

Ammianus Marcellinus, *Res Gestae*—John C. Rolfe, *Ammianus Marcellinus* (3 vols.; LCL; Cambridge: Harvard, 1935–39).

Apocalypse of Elijah [*Apoc. El.*]—Georg Steindorff, *Die Apokalypse des Elias: Eine unbekannte Apokalypse und Bruchstücke der Sophonias-Apokalypse* (TU 17:3a; Leipzig: J. C. Hinrichs, 1899); James H. Charlesworth, ed., *The Old Testament Pseudepigrapha* (2 vols.; Garden City, N.Y.: Doubleday, 1983), 1:721–53.

(First) Apocalypse of James [*1 Apoc. Jas.*]—Douglas M. Parrott, ed., *Nag Hammadi Codices V, 2–5 and VI, with Papyrus Berolinensis 8502, 1 and 4* (NHS 11; Leiden: Brill, 1979), 65–103.

(Second) Apocalypse of James [*2 Apoc. Jas.*]—Douglas M. Parrott, ed., *Nag Hammadi Codices V, 2–5 and VI, with Papyrus Berolinensis 8502, 1 and 4* (NHS 11; Leiden: Brill, 1979), 105–49.

Apocalypse of Peter [*Apoc. Pet.*]—Dennis D. Buchholz, *Your Eyes Will Be Opened: A Study of the Greek (Ethiopic) Apocalypse of Peter* (SBLDS 97; Atlanta: Scholars Press, 1988).

(Gnostic) Apocalypse of Peter [*Apoc. Pet.*]—*The Facsimile Edition of the Nag Hammadi Codices: Codex VII* (Leiden: Brill, 1972), 76–90; James M. Robinson, ed., *The Nag Hammadi Library in English* (Leiden: Brill, 1977).

Apocryphon of James [*Ap. Jas.*]—Harold W. Attridge, ed., *Nag Hammadi Codex 1 (the Jung Codex)* (NHS 22; Leiden: Brill, 1985), 28–53.

Apocryphon of Jeremiah [*Ap. Jer.*]—Karl H. Kuhn, "A Coptic Jeremiah Apocryphon," *Le Muséon* 83 (1970) 291–326.

Apocryphon of Joseph [*4Q372*]—Eileen Schuller, "4Q372 1: A Text about Joseph," *RQ* 14 (1989–90) 349–76.

Appian, *Historia romana*—Horace White, *Appian's Roman History* (4 vols.; LCL; London: W. Heinemann, 1912–13).

Aristophanes, *Plutus* [*Pl*]—Benjamin B. Rogers, *Aristophanes* (3 vols.; LCL; Cambridge: Harvard University Press, 1968), 3:361–467.

Armenian Liturgy—Athanase Renoux, *Le Codex arménien Jérusalem 121* (*PO* 36:2; Turnhout: Brepols, 1971), 210–373; Frederick C. Conybeare and Arthur J. Maclean, *Rituale Armenorum* (Oxford: Clarendon, 1905).

Avot de Rabbi Nattan [*ARN*]—Salomon Schechter, *Aboth de Rabbi Nathan* (Vienna: Knöpflmacher, 1887; repr., Hildesheim, 1979).

Barsauma, *Vitae*—François Nau, "Résumé de monographies syriaques: Histoire de Barsauma de Nisibe," *ROC* 18 (1913) 270–76, 379–89; 19 (1914) 113–34, 278–89.

Barnabas, *The Epistle of Barnabas* [*Barn.*]—Kirsopp Lake, *The Apostolic Fathers* (2 vols.; LCL; London: W. Heinemann, 1912–13), 1:340–409.

2 Baruch (Syriac) [*2 Bar*]—S. Dedering, *Apocalypse of Baruch* (Vetus Testamentum Syriace 4:3; Leiden: Brill, 1973).

4 Baruch (Paraleipomena Jeremiou) [*4 Bar.*]—Robert A. Kraft and Ann-Elizabeth Purintun, *Paraleipomena Jeremiou* (SBLTT 1; Missoula, Mont.: Society of Biblical Literature, 1972).

Bavli [*b* with name of tractate]—Printed edition (Wilna: Romm, 1880–86); Isidore Epstein, ed., *The Babylonian Talmud: Translated into English with Notes, Glossary and Idices* (35 vols.; London: Soncino, 1935–52).

Ben Sira, Wisdom of Ben Sira [*Sir*]—Joseph Ziegler, *Sapientia Iesu Filii Sirach* (Septuaginta: Vetus Testamentum Graecum 12:2; Göttingen: Vandenhoeck & Ruprecht, 1965).

Breviarius de Hierosolyma—W. Weber, *Breviarius de Hierosolyma*, CCSL 175:106–12; John Wilkinson, *Jerusalem Pilgrims before the Crusades* (Warminster: Aris & Phillips, 1977), 59–61.

Canticles (Song of Songs) Rabbah [*CantR*]—Printed edition (Wilna: Romm, 1887).

Cassius Dio, *Historicus* [*Hist.*]—Earnest Cary, *Dio's Roman History* (9 vols.; LCL; London: W. Heinemann, 1914–27).

Chronicon Adler—Elkan N. Adler and Max Séligsohn, "Une nouvelle chronique samaritaine," *REJ* 44 (1902) 188–222; 45 (1902) 70–98, 160, 223–54; 46 (1903) 123–46.

Chronicon Paschale—Ludwig A. Dindorf, *Chronicon Paschale* (*CSHB*; Bonn: Weber, 1832).

Clement of Rome, *Epistulae* [*Ep.*]—Kirsopp Lake, *The Apostolic Fathers* (2 vols.; LCL; London: W. Heinemann, 1912–13), 1:125–63.

Cyril of Jerusalem, *Catecheses ad illuminandos* [*Catech.*]—A. A. Touttée and P. Maran, *PG* 33, cols. 331–1060; *NPNF* 2, VII, pp. 1–143.

———, *Epistula ad Constantium imperatorem* [*Ep. Const.*]—E. Bihain, "L'épître de Cyrille de Jérusalem à Constance sur la vision de la Croix: Tradition manuscrite et édition critique," *Byzantion* 43 (1973) 264–69; Leo P. McCauley and Anthony A. Stephenson, *The Works of Saint Cyril of Jerusalem* (2 vols.; FC 64; Washington, D.C.: Catholic University of America Press, 1969–70), 2:231–35.

———, *Sermon on the Paralytic (In paralyticum)*—*PG* 33, cols. 1132–53; Leo P. McCauley and Anthony A. Stephenson, *The Works of Saint Cyril of Jerusalem* (2 vols.; FC 64; Washington, D.C.: Catholic University of America Press, 1969–70), 2:209–22.

Damaskius Diadochos, *Vitae Isidori reliquiae*—Clemens Zintzen, *Vitae Isidori reliquiae* (Hildesheim: G. Olms, 1967).

Deuteronomy Rabbah [*DeutR*]—Printed edition (Wilna: Romm, 1887); Saul Lieberman, *Midrash Debarim Rabbah* (Jerusalem: Bamberger and Wahrmann, 1940).

Dialogue of Timothy and Aquila—Frederick C. Conybeare, *The Dialogues of Athanasius and Zacchaeus and of Timothy and Aquila* (Anecdota Oxoniensia I.8; Oxford: Clarendon, 1898); Robert G. Robertson, "The Dialogue of Timothy and Aquila" (Th.D. thesis, Harvard University, 1986).

Didache (XII Apostolorum)—Kirsopp Lake, *The Apostolic Fathers* (2 vols.; LCL; London: W. Heinemann, 1912–13), 1:305–33.

Diodorus Siculus, *Historicus* [DS]—Charles H. Oldfather, *Diodorus of Sicily* (12 vols.; LCL; London: W. Heinemann, 1933–67).

Ecclesiastes (Qohelet) Rabbah [*EcclR*]—Printed edition (Wilna: Romm, 1887).

1 Enoch [*1 En.*]—Michael A. Knibb, *The Ethiopic Book of Enoch* (2 vols.; Oxford: Clarendon, 1978).

Ephrem, *Contra Julianum* [*Hymns against Julian*]—Edmund Beck, *Des heiligen Ephraem des Syres: Contra Julianum* (*CSCO* 174; Louvain: CorpusSCO, 1957), 71–91; Samuel N. C. Lieu, *The Emperor Julian: Panegyric and Polemic* (Liverpool: Liverpool University Press, 1986).

———, *Hymns on Paradise*—Edmund Beck, *Des heiligen Ephraem des Syres: Hymnen de paradiso* (*CSCO* 174; Louvain: CorpusSCO, 1957), 1–70; Sebastian Brock, *Hymns on Paradise* (Crestwood, N.Y.: St. Vladimir's Seminary Press, 1990).

Epiphanius of Salamis, *Panarion (Adversus haereses)* [*Haer.*]—Karl Holl, *Epiphanius: Panarion haer.* (reedited by J. Dummer; GCS 25, 31, 37; Berlin: Akademie-Verlag, 1980); Frank Williams, *The Panarion of Epiphanius of Salamis* (2 vols.; NHS 35–36; Leiden: Brill, 1987); Philip R. Amidon, *The Panarion of St. Epiphanius, Bishop of Salamis* (New York: Oxford University Press, 1990).

Epiphanius the Monk, *De locis sanctis*—Herbert Donner, "Die Palästinabeschreibung des Epiphanius Monachus Hagiopolita," *ZDPV* 87 (1971) 62–82; John Wilkinson, *Jerusalem Pilgrims before the Crusades* (Warminster: Aris & Phillips, 1977), 117–21.

Epistle to Diognetus—Kirsopp Lake, *The Apostolic Fathers* (2 vols.; LCL; London: W. Heinemann, 1912–13), 2:347–79.

Eucherius, *Epistula ad Faustum*—Johannes Fraipont, *Eucherii (quae fertur) de situ Hierosolimae: Epistula ad Faustum presbyterum, CCSL* 175:235–43; John Wilkinson, *Jerusalem Pilgrims before the Crusades* (Warminster: Aris & Phillips, 1977), 53–55.

Eusebius, *Chronicon*—Rudolf Helm, *Eusebius Werke: Die Chronik des Hieronymus* (GCS 47; Berlin: Akademie-Verlag, 1956); Josef Karst, *Eusebius Werke: Die Chronik aus dem armenischen übersetzt* (GCS 20; Leipzig: J. C. Hinrichs, 1911).

———, *Commentarii in Isaiam* [*Comm. in Isa.*]—Joseph Ziegler, *Eusebius Worke: Der Jesajakommentar* (GCS 57; Berlin: Akademie-Verlag, 1975).

———, *Commentarii in Psalmos* [*Comm. in Ps.*]—B. de Montfaucon, *Eusebii Caesariensis commentaria in Psalmos* (*PG* 23, cols. 441–1221).

———, *De laudibus Constantini* [*LC*]—Ivar A. Heikel, *Eusebius Werke: Tricennatsrede an Constantin* (GCS 7; Leipzig: J. C. Hinrichs, 1902), 193–259; Harold A. Drake, *In Praise of Constantine* (Classical Studies 15; Berkeley: University of California Press, 1976).

———, *De martyribus Palestinae*—Eduard Schwartz, *Eusebius Werke: Über die Märtyrer in palästina* (GCS 9.II; Leipzig: J. C. Hinrichs, 1908), 905–50; William Cureton, *History of the Martyrs in Palestine by Eusebius Bishop of Caesarea: Discovered in a Very Ancient Syriac Manuscript* (London: Williams & Norgate, 1861); Hugh J. Lawlor and John E. L. Oulton, *Eusebius Bishop of Caesarea: The Ecclesiastical History and the Martyrs of Palestine* (2 vols.; London: S.P.C.K., 1927–28), 1:327–400.

————, *Demonstratio Evangelica* [*DE*]—Ivar A. Heikel, *Eusebius Werke: Die Demonstratio evangelica* (GCS 23; Leipzig: J. C. Hinrichs, 1913); William J. Ferrar, *The Proof of the Gospel being the Demonstratio Evangelica of Eusebius of Caesarea* (2 vols.; New York: Macmillan, 1920).

————, *Eclogae propheticae*—T. Gaisford, *Eclogae Propheticae* (*PG* 22, cols. 1021–73).

————, *Historia ecclesiastica* [*HE*]—Eduard Schwartz, *Eusebius Werke: Die Kirchengeschichte* (GCS 9:1–2; Leipzig: J. C. Hinrichs, 1903–8); William Wright and Norman McLean, *The Ecclesiastical History of Eusebius in Syriac* (Cambridge: Cambridge University Press, 1898); Kirsopp Lake et al., *Eusebius: The Ecclesiastical History* (2 vols.; LCL; London: W. Heinemann, 1926–32).

————, *Onomasticon* [*Onomast.*]—Erich Klostermann, *Eusebius Werke: Das Onomasticon der biblischen Ortsnamen* (GCS 11:1; Leipzig: J. C. Hinrichs, 1904).

————, *Praeparatio Evangelica* [*PE*]—Karl Mras, *Eusebius Werke: Die Praeparatio evangelica* (GCS 43:1–2; Berlin: Akademie-Verlag, 1954–56); Edwin H. Gifford, *Eusebius: Preparation of the Gospel* (London: H. Frowde, 1903).

————, *Theophania* [*Theoph.*]—Samuel Lee, *Eusebius Bishop of Caesarea on the Theophania: A Syriac Version* (London: Society for the Publication of Oriental Texts, 1842–43); Hugo Gressmann, *Eusebius Werke: Die Theophanie—Die griechischen Bruchstücke und Übersetzung der syrischen Überlieferungen* (GCS 11:2; Leipzig: J. C. Hinrichs, 1904).

————, *Vita Constantini* [*VC*]—Ivar A. Heikel, *Eusebius Werke: Über das Leben Constantins* (GCS 7; Leipzig: J. C. Hinrichs, 1902) 1–148; *NPNF* 2, I, pp. 481–559.

Exodus Rabbah [*ExodR*]—Printed edition (Wilna: Romm, 1887); for the first 14 *parashot*—Avigdor Shinan, *Midrash Shemot Rabbah: Chapters I–XIV* (Jerusalem: Devir, 1984).

3 Ezra (The Apocryphal Ezra)—Alfred Rahlfs, *Septuaginta* (2 vols.; Stuttgart: Privilegierte Württembergische Bibelanstalt, 1935), 1:873–903.

4 Ezra (Apocalypse of Ezra)—Albertus F. J. Klijn, *Der lateinische Text der Apokalypse des Esra* (TU 131; Berlin: Akademie-Verlag, 1983); Michael E. Stone, *Fourth Ezra* (Minneapolis: Fortress, 1990).

Genesis Rabbah [*GenR*]—Printed edition (Wilna: Romm, 1887); Judah Theodor and Chanoch Albeck, *Midrash Bereshit Rabba: Critical Edition with Notes and Commentary* (2nd ed.; Jerusalem: Wahrmann, 1965); Harry Freedman and Maurice Simon, *Midrash Rabbah: Genesis* (2 vols.; 3rd ed.; London: Soncino, 1939).

Gregory of Nazianzus, *Orationes 4–5* (*Contra Iulianum*) [*Or.*]—Jean Bernardi, *Grégoire de Nazianze: Discours 4–5 contre Julien* (*SC* 309; Paris: Cerf, 1983); Charles W. King, *Julian the Emperor* (London: G. Bell, 1888), 1–121.

————, *Orationes 27–31* (*The Five Theological Orations*)—Paul Gallay and M. Jourjon, *Grégoire de Nazianze: Discours 27–31 discours théologiques* (*SC* 250; Paris: Cerf, 1978); *NPNF* 2, VII, pp. 284–328.

Gregory of Tours, *Glory of the Martyrs (De gloria beatorum martyrum)*—Thierry Ruinart, "Sancti Georgii Florentii Gregorii episcopi Turonensis libri miraculum I: De gloria beatorum martyrum," *PL* 71, cols. 705–800; Raymond Van Dam, *Gregory of Tours: Glory of the Martyrs* (Liverpool: Liverpool University Press, 1988).

Hebrew Bible—Masoretic version (by name of book).

Ignatius of Antioch, *Epistulae* [*Ep.*]—Kirsopp Lake, *The Apostolic Fathers* (2 vols.; LCL; London: W. Heinemann, 1912–13), 1:166–277.

Irenaeus, *Adversus haereses* [*Haer.*]—Adelin Rousseau et al., *Irénée de Lyon: Contre les hérésies* (Livre 1; *SC* 264; Paris: Cerf, 1979); (Livre 2; *SC* 294; Paris: Cerf, 1982); (Livre 3; *SC* 211; Paris: Cerf, 1974); (Livre 4; *SC* 100:2; Paris: Cerf, 1965); (Livre 5; *SC* 153; Paris: Cerf, 1969); *ANF* 1:315–567.

————, *Epideixis tou apostolikou kerygmatos* (in Armenian) [*Epideixis*]—Joseph P. Smith, *St. Irenaeus: Proof of the Apostolic Preaching* (ACW 16; Westminster: Newman, 1952).

Itinerarium Antonini Placentini—P. Geyer, *Antonini Placentini Itinerarium, CCSL* 175:129–74; John Wilkinson, *Jerusalem Pilgrims before the Crusades* (Warminster: Aris & Phillips, 1977), 79–89.

Itinerarium Burdigalense—P. Geyer and O. Cuntz, *Itinerarium Burdigalense, CCSL* 175:1–26; John Wilkinson, *Egeria's Travels* (London: Aris & Phillips, 1971), 153–63.

Itinerarium Egeriae—A. Franceschini and R. Weber, *Itinerarium Egeriae, CCSL* 175:37–103; John Wilkinson, *Egeria's Travels* (London: Aris & Phillips, 1971), 91–147.

Jerome, *Commentarii in Isaiam* [*Comm. in Isa.*]—Marcus Adriaen, *Commentariorum in Esaiam, CCSL* 73–73A.

————, *Commentarii in Matthaeum* [*Comm. in Mt.*]—D. Hurst and Marcus Adriaen, *Commentariorum in Matheum, CCSL* 77.

————, *Commentarii in Sophoniam* [*Comm. in Seph.*]—Marcus Adriaen, *Commentariorum in Sophoniam prophetam, CCSL* 76A:655–711.

————*Commentariorum in Danielem*—F. Glorie, *Commentariorum in Danielem, CCSL* 75A.

————, *De viris illustribus*—Ernest C. Richardson, *Hieronymus: Liber de viris inlustribus* (TU 14:1; Leipzig: J. C. Hinrichs, 1896) 1–56; *NPNF* 2, III, pp. 359–84.

————, *Epistulae* [*Ep.*]—Isidorus Hilberg, *Sancti Eusebii Hieronymi epistulae* (2nd ed.; CSEL 54–56; Vienna: Verlag der Österreichischen Akademie der Wissenschaften, 1996); *NPNF* 2, VI, pp. 1–295.

————, *Homiliae*—D. G. Morin, *Tractus sive homiliae in Psalmos, in Marce evangelium aliaque varia argumenta, CCSL* 78; Marie L. Ewald, *The Homilies of Saint Jerome* (FC 48, 57; Washington, D.C.: Catholic University of America Press, 1964–66).

John Chrysostom, *Adversus Iudaeos orationes*—*PG* 48, cols. 843–942; C. M. Maxwell, "Chrysostom's Homilies against the Jews: An English Translation" (Ph.D. diss., University of Chicago, 1966).

————, *Commentarius in Isaiam*—*PG* 56, cols. 11–94; Duane A. Garrett, *An Analysis of the Hermeneutics of John Chrysostom's Commentary on Isaiah 1–8 with an English Translation* (Studies in the Bible and Early Christianity 12; Lewiston, N.Y.: E. Mellen, 1992).

John Lydus, *Liber de mensibus* [*De Mensibus*]—Ricardus Wünsch, *Ioannis Laurentii Lydi: Liber de mensibus* (Leipzig: B. G. Teubner, 1898).

John Malalas, *Chronographia*—Ludwig A. Dindorf, *Ioannis Malalae: Chronographia* (*CSHB;* Bonn: Weber, 1831).

John of Damascus, *Orationes de imaginibus tres*—*PG* 94, cols. 1232–1420; David Anderson, *St. John of Damascus: On the Divine Images* (Crestwood, N.Y.: St. Vladimir's Seminary Press, 1980).

John Rufus, *Peter the Iberian* [*Vita*]—Richard Raabe, *Petrus der Iberer* (Leipzig: J. C. Hinrichs, 1895).

Josephus, *Antiquitates Judaicae* [*JA*]—Henry J. Thackeray, Ralph Marcus, and Louis H.

Feldman, *Josephus: Jewish Antiquities* (LCL; Cambridge: Harvard University Press, 1930–65).

———, *Bellum Judaicum* [*BJ*]—Henry J. Thackeray, *Josephus: The Jewish War* (LCL; Cambridge: Harvard University Press, 1927–28).

———, *Contra Apionem* [*Ap*]—Henry J. Thackeray, *Josephus: Against Apion* (LCL; Cambridge: Harvard University Press, 1926).

———, *Vita* [*Vit.*]—Henry J. Thackeray, *Josephus: The Life* (LCL; Cambridge: Harvard University Press, 1926).

Jubilees [*Jub.*]—James C. VanderKam, *The Book of Jubilees* (*CSCO* 510–11; Leuven: E. Peeters, 1989).

Judith [Jdt]—Robert Hanhart, *Iudith* (Septuaginta: Vetus Testamentum Graecum 8:4; Göttingen: Vandenhoeck & Ruprecht, 1979).

Julian, *Against the Galileans (Contra Galilaeos)* [*Galil.*]—Wilmer C. Wright, *The Works of the Emperor Julian* (3 vols.; LCL; London: W. Heinemann, 1923–53), 3:318–427.

———, *Epistulae* [*Ep.*]—Wilmer C. Wright, *The Works of the Emperor Julian* (3 vols.; LCL; London: W. Heinemann, 1923–53), 3:1–293.

———, *Letter to a Pagan Priest* [*Ep.* 89]—Wilmer C. Wright, *The Works of the Emperor Julian* (3 vols.; LCL; London: W. Heinemann, 1923–53), 2:296–339.

Justin Martyr, *1 Apologia* [*1 Apol.*]—Miroslav Marcovich, *Iustini Martyris: Apologiae pro Christianis* (PTS 38; Berlin: W. de Gruyter, 1994); Thomas B. Falls, *Saint Justin Martyr* (FC 6; New York: Christian Heritage, 1948).

———, *Dialogus cum Tryphone Iudaeo* [*Dial.*]—Georges Archambault, *Justin: Dialogue avec Tryphon* (Paris: A. Picard, 1909); Thomas B. Falls, *Saint Justin Martyr* (FC 6; New York: Christian Heritage, 1948), 139–366.

Lactantius, *Divinarum institutionum*—Pierre Monat, *Lactance: Institutions divines* (SC 204, 205, 326, 327, 377; Paris: Cerf, 1973–1992); Mary F. McDonald, *Lactantius: The Divine Institutes* (FC 49; Washington, D.C.: Catholic University of America Press, 1964).

Lamentations Rabbah [*LamR*]—Solomon Buber, *Midrasch Echa Rabbati* (Wilna: Romm, 1899; repr., Hildesheim: G. Olms, 1967).

Letter Attributed to Cyril of Jerusalem—Sebastian P. Brock, "A Letter Attributed to Cyril of Jerusalem on the Rebuilding of the Temple," *BSOAS* 40 (1977) 267–86.

Letter of Aristeas [*Let. Aris.*]—André Pelletier, *Lettre D'Aristée a Philocrate* (SC 89; Paris: Cerf, 1962); James H. Charlesworth, ed., *The Old Testament Pseudepigrapha* (2 vols.; Garden City, N.Y.: Doubleday, 1983–85), 2:7–34.

Leviticus Rabbah [*LevR*]—Mordecai Margulies, *Midrash Wayyikra Rabbah* (5 vols.; Jerusalem: Ararat, 1953–60).

1 Maccabees [1 Macc]—Werner Kappler, *Maccabaeorum libri I–IV: Maccabaeorum liber I* (Septuaginta: Vetus Testamentum Graecum 9:1; Göttingen: Vandenhoeck & Ruprecht, 1936); Jonathan A. Goldstein, *1 Maccabees: A New Translation with Introduction and Commentary* (Garden City, N.Y.: Doubleday, 1976).

2 Maccabees [2 Macc]—Werner Kappler and Robert Hanhart, *Maccabaeorum libri I–IV: Maccabaeorum liber II* (Septuaginta: Vetus Testamentum Graecum 9:2; Göttingen: Vandenhoeck & Ruprecht, 1976); Jonathan A. Goldstein, *2 Maccabees: A New Translation with Introduction and Commentary* (Garden City, N.Y.: Doubleday, 1983).

3 Maccabees [3 Macc]—Robert Hanhart, *Maccabaeorum libri I-IV: Maccabaeorum liber*

III (Septuaginta: Vetus Testamentum Graecum 9:3; Göttingen: Vandenhoeck & Ruprecht, 1960); James H. Charlesworth, ed., *The Old Testament Pseudepigrapha* (2 vols.; Garden City, N.Y.: Doubleday, 1983), 2:509–29.

4 Maccabees [4 Macc]—Alfred Rahlfs, *Septuaginta* (2 vols.; Stuttgart: Privilegierte Württembergische Bibelanstalt, 1935), 1:1157–84; James H. Charlesworth, ed., *The Old Testament Pseudepigrapha* (2 vols.; Garden City, N.Y.: Doubleday, 1983), 2:531–64.

Martyrdom of Polycarp [*Mart. Pol.*]—Kirsopp Lake, *The Apostolic Fathers* (2 vols.; LCL; London: W. Heinemann, 1912–13), 2:312–49.

Mearath Gazze—Carl Bezold, *Die Schatzhöhle (Mearath Gazze)* (Leipzig: J. C. Hinrichs, 1883–88; repr., Amesterdam: Philo Press, 1981); Ernest A. Wallis-Budge, *The Book of the Cave of the Treasures* (London: Religious Tract Society, 1927).

Mekhilta de-Rabbi Ishmael [*Mek*]—Haim S. Horovitz and Israel A. Rabin, *Mechilta de-Rabbi Ismael: Cum variis lectionibus et adnotationibus* (2nd ed.; Jerusalem: Wahrmann, 1970); Jacob Z. Lauterbach, *Mekhilta de-Rabbi Ishmael* (3 vols.; Philadelphia: Jewish Publication Society of America, 1933).

Mekhilta de-Rabbi Simon [*MRS*]—Jacob N. Epstein and Ezra Z. Melamed, *Mekhilta de-Rabbi Simʿon b. Yoḥai* (Jerusalem: Sumptibus, 1965).

Melito of Sardis, *De Pascha*—Stuart G. Hall, *Melito of Sardis: On Pascha (and Fragments)* (Oxford: Clarendon, 1979).

Midrash ha-Gadol [*MHG*]—For Genesis and Exodus: Mordecai Margulies, *Midrash ha-Gadol on the Pentateuch: Genesis–Exodus* (2 vols.; Jerusalem: Mosad ha-Rav Kook, 1967); for Leviticus: Adin Steinsaltz, *Midrash ha-Gadol on the Pentateuch: Leviticus* (Jerusalem: Mosad ha-Rav Kook, 1976); for Numbers: Z. Meir Rabinowitz, *Midrash ha-Gadol on the Pentateuch: Numbers* (Jerusalem: Mosad ha-Rav Kook, 1967); for Deuteronomy: Solomon Fisch, *Midrash ha-Gadol on the Pentateuch: Deuteronomy* (Jerusalem: Mosad ha-Rav Kook, 1972).

Midrash on Psalms [*MidrPss*]—Solomon Buber, *Midrash Tehillim* (Wilna: Romm, 1892; repr., Jerusalem, 1966).

Minor Tractate: Semaḥot—Michael Higger, *Treatise Semahot* (repr., Jerusalem: Makor, 1970).

Mishnah [*m* with name of tractate]—Based on manuscript Kn, Hungarian Academy of Sciences, manuscript A 50, from the library of David Kaufmann; facsimile edition by George Beer, The Hague, 1929; reprinted in smaller format (Jerusalem: Mekorot, 1968); Herbert Danby, *The Mishnah* (Oxford: Oxford University Press, 1933).

New Jerusalem [*5Q15*]—Jósef T. Milik, "Description de la Jérusalem Nouvelle," *DJD* 3:184–93.

New Testament [by name of individual book]—Kurt Aland et al., eds., *The Greek New Testament* (3rd ed.; New York: United Bible Societies, 1975).

Numbers Rabbah [*NumR*]—Printed edition (Wilna: Romm, 1887).

Optatus, *Adversus Donatianae*—Carolvs Ziwsa, *S. Optati Milevitani libri vii* (*CSEL* 26; Vienna: F. Tempsky, 1893); Oliver R. Vassall-Phillips, *The Work of St. Optatus, Bishop of Milevis, Against the Donatists* (London: Longmans, 1917).

Origen, *Commentarii in Canticum canticorum* [*Comm. in Cant.*]—Willem A. Baehrens, *Origenes Werke: Homilien zu Samuel I, zum Hohelied und zu den Propheten, Kommentar zum Hohelied in Rufins und Hieronymus' Übersetzungen* (GCS 33; Leipzig:

J. C. Hinrichs, 1925), 61–241; Luc Brésard et al., *Origène: Commentaire sur le Can-
tique des Cantiques* (*SC* 376; Paris: Cerf, 1992); Ruth P. Lawson, *Origen: The Song of
Songs Commentary and Homilies* (ACW 26; Westminster: Newman, 1956).

————, *Commentarii in Iohannem* [*Comm. in Jn.*]—Erwin Preuschen, *Origenes Werke:
Der Johanneskommentar* (GCS 10; Leipzig: J. C. Hinrichs, 1903); Ronald E. Heine,
Origen: Commentary on the Gospel According to John Books 1–10 (2 vols.; FC 80, 89;
Washington, D.C.: Catholic University of America Press, 1989–93).

————, *Commentarii in Lucam* [*Comm. in Lc.*]—Max Rauer, *Origenes Werke: Des
Lukas Kommentars* (GCS 49; Berlin: Akademie-Verlag, 1959), 227–336; Joseph T.
Lienhard, *Origen: Fragments on Luke* (FC 94; Washington, D.C.: Catholic University
of America Press, 1996), 165–227.

————, *Commentarii in Matthaeum* [*Comm. in Mt.*]—Erich Klostermann, *Origenes
Werke: Origenes Matthäuserklärung I: Die griechisch erhaltenen Tomoi* (GCS 40;
Leipzig: J. C. Hinrichs, 1935); *ANF* 10:409–512.

————, *Commentarii in Matthaeum (Fragments)*—Erich Klostermann, *Origenes
Werke: Origenes Matthäuserklärung III: Fragmente* (GCS 41:1; Leipzig: J. C. Hinrichs,
1941).

————, *Contra Celsum* [*Cels.*]—Marcel Borret, *Origene: Contre Celse* (*SC* 132, 136, 147,
150; Paris: Cerf, 1967–69); Henry Chadwick, *Origen: Contra Celsum* (Cambridge:
Cambridge University Press, 1980).

————, *De principiis*—Paul Koetschau, *Origenes Werke: De principiis* (GCS 22; Leipzig:
J. C. Hinrichs, 1913); *ANF* 4:223–382.

————, *Epistula ad Iulium Africanum* [*Ep.* 1]—Nicholas de Lange, *Origène: La lettre à
Africanus sur l'histoire de Suzanne* (*SC* 302; Paris: Cerf, 1983), 469–573; *ANF* 4:385–
92.

————, *Fragmenta in Lucam*—Max Rauer, *Origenes Werke: Des Lukas Kommentars*
(GCS 49; Berlin: Akademie-Verlag, 1959), 227–336; Joseph T. Lienhard, *Origen: Fragments on Luke* (FC 94; Washington, D.C.: Catholic University of America Press,
1996), 165–227.

————, *In Exodum homiliae xiii* [*Hom. in Ex.*]—Marcel Borret, *Origène: Homélies sur
l'Exode* (*SC* 321; Paris: Cerf, 1985); Ronald E. Heine, *Origen: Homilies on Genesis and
Exodus* (FC 71; Washington, D.C.: Catholic University of America Press, 1982).

————, *In Jeremiam homiliae*—Pierre Husson and Pierre Nautin, *Homélies sur Jérémie*
(*SC* 232, 238; Paris: Cerf, 1976–77).

————, *In Leviticum homiliae xvi* [*Hom. in Lev.*]—Willem A. Baehrens, *Origenes
Werke: Homilien zum Hexateuch in Rufins Übersetzung* (GCS 29; Leipzig: J. C. Hinrichs, 1920), 280–507; Gary W. Barkley, *Origen: Homilies on Leviticus* (FC 83; Washington, D.C.: Catholic University of America Press, 1990).

————, *In Lucam homiliae xxxix* [*Hom. in Lc.*]—Max Rauer, *Origenes Werke: Die Homilien zu Lukas in der Übersetzung des Hieronymus und die griechischen Reste der Homilien* (GCS 49; Berlin: Akademie-Verlag, 1959), 1–222; Joseph T. Lienhard, *Origen:
Fragments on Luke* (FC 94; Washington, D.C.: Catholic University of America Press,
1996), 3–162.

Orosius, *Historiarum adversum paganos*—Karl F. Zangemeister, *Pauli Orosii: Historiarum adversum paganos* (*CSEL* 5; Leipzig: B. G. Teubner, 1882), 1–600; Roy J. Defer-
rari, *Paulus Orosius: The Seven Books of History against the Pagans* (FC 50; Washington, D.C.: Catholic University of America Press, 1964).

Oxyrhynchus (Papyrus) 840 [Poxy]—Bernard P. Grenfell and Arthur S. Hunt, *Fragment of an Uncanonical Gospel from Oxyrhynchus* (London: Oxford University Press, 1908), 1–10.

Paulinus of Nola, *Epistulae [Ep.]*—Guilelmus de Hartel, *Sancti Pontii Meropii Paulini Nolani: Epistulae* (*CSEL* 29; Vienna: F. Tempsky, 1894); Patrick G. Walsh, *Letters of St. Paulinus of Nola* (ACW 35–36; Westminster: Newmann, 1966–67).

Pesher to Psalms [4Q171]—John M. Allegro, *Qumran Cave 4* (*DJD* 5; Oxford: Clarendon, 1968), 42–50.

Pesiqta Rabbati [PesR]—Meir Friedmann ('Ish Shalom), *Pesikta Rabbati* (Vienna, 1880).

Pesikta de Rav Kahana [PRK]—Bernard Mandelbaum, *Pesikta de Rav Kahana According to an Oxford Manuscript* (2 vols.; New York: Jewish Theological Seminary of America, 1987).

Peter the Deacon, *De locis sanctis*—R. Weber, *CCSL* 175:93–103; John Wilkinson, *Egeria's Travels* (London: Aris & Phillips, 1971), 180–210.

Philo of Alexandria, *De specialibus legibus*—Francis H. Colson, *Philo* (11 vols.; LCL; London: W. Heinemann, 1937–39), 7:97–607, 8:1–155.

———, *In Flaccum*—Francis H. Colson, *Philo* (11 vols.; LCL; London: W. Heinemann, 1941), 9:295–403.

———, *Legatio ad Gaium [Legat.]*—Francis H. Colson, *Philo* (11 vols.; LCL; London: W. Heinemann, 1962), 10:1–187.

Philostorgios, *Historia ecclesiastica [HE]*—Joseph Bidez and Friedhelm Winkelmann, *Philostorgius Kirchengeschichte* (2nd ed.; GCS 21; Berlin: Akademie-Verlag, 1972); Edward Walford, *The Ecclesiastical History of Sozomen* (London: H. G. Bohn, 1855).

Pirke de Rabbi Eliezer [PRE]—Printed Edition with commentary of David Luria (Warsaw: Bomberg, 1852).

Pliny the Elder, *Natusalis Historia [NH]*—Harris Rackham, *Pliny: Natural History* (10 vols.; LCL; Cambridge: Harvard University Press, 1942).

Polyaenus the Macedonian, *Strategematan*—Edvard Wölfflin and Johannes Melber, *Polyaeni strategematon libri viii* (Leipzig: B. G. Teubner, 1887).

Proteuangelium Iacobi [Prot. Jas.]—Émile de Strycker, *La forme la plus ancienne du Protévangile de Jacques* (Subsidia hagiographica 33; Brussels: Société des Bollandistes, 1961); Wilhelm Schneemelcher, ed., *New Testament Apocrypha* (trans. Robert M. Wilson; 2 vols.; rev. ed.; Cambridge: James Clarke, 1991–92), 1:421–39.

Pseudo-Clementine, *Recognitiones [Ps.-Clem.]*—Bernhard Rehm, *Die Pseudoklementinen II: Rekognitionen in Rufins Ubersetzung* (GCS 51; Berlin: Akademie-Verlag, 1965); Wilhelm Frankenberg, *Die syrischen Clementinen mit griechischem Paralleltext* (TU 48:3; Leipzig: J. C. Hinrichs, 1937), 2–237; ANF 8:75–211.

Pseudo-Cyprian, *De montibus Sina et Sion*—Wilhelm A. Hartel, *S. thasci caecili Cypriani opera omnia* (*CSEL* 3:3; Vienna: C. Geroldi, 1871), 104–19.

Pseudo-Jonathan Targum [Ps.-J.]—Ernest G. Clarke, *Targum Pseudo-Jonathan of the Pentateuch* (Hoboken, N.J.: Ktav, 1984).

Quaestiones Bartholomaei—A. Wilmart and E. Tisserant, "Fragments grecs et latins de l'Évangile de Barthélémy," *RB* 10 (1910) 161–90, 321–68; Wilhelm Schneemelcher, ed., *New Testament Apocrypha* (trans. Robert M. Wilson; 2 vols.; rev. ed.; Cambridge: James Clarke, 1991–92), 1:539–53.

Rufinus, *Historia ecclesiastica [HE]*—Theodore Momsen, "Die lateinische Übersetzung des Rufinus," *Eusebius Werke: Die Kirchengeschichte* (ed. Eduard Schwartz; GCS 9:1–2; Leipzig: J. C. Hinrichs, 1903–8).

Scroll of Fasting (*Megillat ta'anit*)—Heinrich Lichtenstein, "Die Fastenrolle: Eine Untersuchung zur jüdisch-hellenistischen Geschichte," *HUCA* 8–9 (1931–32) 257–351.

Septuagint—John W. Wevers et al., eds., *Septuaginta: Vetus Testamentum Graecum* (Göttingen: Vandenhoeck & Ruprecht, 1939–93).

Sibylline Oracles [*Sib. Or.*]—Johannes Geffcken, *Die Oracula Sibyllina* (GCS 8; Leipzig: J. C. Hinrichs, 1902); James H. Charlesworth, ed., *The Old Testament Pseudepigrapha* (2 vols.; Garden City, N.Y.: Doubleday, 1983), 1:317–472.

Sifra—Isaac H. Weiss, *Sifra de-ve Rav hu sefer torat kohanim* (Vienna: Shlosberg, 1862); Jacob Neusner, *Sifra: An Analytical Translation* (2 vols.; BJS 138–40; Atlanta: Scholars, 1988).

Sifre to Deutoronomy [*SifreDeut*]—Louis Finkelstein, *Siphre ad Deuteronomium* (Berlin: Jüdischer Kulturbund in Deutschland, 1939; repr., New York, 1969); Reuven Hammer, *Sifre: A Tannaitic Commentary on the Book of Deuteronomy* (New Haven: Yale University Press, 1986).

Sifre to Numbers [*SifreNum*]—Haim S. Horovitz, *Siphre de-be Rab: Fasciculus primus—Siphre ad Numeros adjecto Siphre Zutta* (Leipzig: Gustav Fock, 1917; repr., Jerusalem, 1966).

Sifre Zuttah [*SZ*]—Haim S. Horovitz, *Siphre de-be Rab: Fasciculus primus—Siphre ad Numeros adjecto Siphre Zutta* (Leipzig: Gustav Fock, 1917; repr., Jerusalem, 1966).

Sirach [Sir]—*see* Ben Sira.

Socrates Scholasticus, *Historia ecclesiastica* [*HE*]—Günther C. Hansen, *Sokrates Kirchengeschichte* (GCS, n.s., 1; Berlin: Akademie-Verlag, 1995); *NPNF* 2, II, pp. 1–178.

Sozomen, *Historia ecclesiastica* [*HE*]—Joseph Bidez and Günter Christen Hansen, *Sozomenus Kirchengeschichte* (GCS 50; Berlin: Akademie-Verlag, 1960); *NPNF* 2, II, pp. 239–427.

Strategius, *Expugnationis Hierosolymae* (Georgian and Arabic versions)—Gérard Garitte, *La prise de Jérusalem par les Perses en 614* (*CSCO* 202–3; Louvain: CorpusSCO, 1960); Gérard Garitte, *Expugnationis Hierosolymae A.D. 614 recensiones Arabicae* (*CSCO* 340, 341, 347; Louvain: CorpusSCO, 1973–74); Frederick C. Conybeare, "Antiochus Strategos' Account of the Sack of Jerusalem in A.D. 614," *EHR* 25 (1910) 502–17.

Sulpicius Severus, *Chronicon*—Carolus Halm, *Sulpicii Severi Opera* (*CSEL* 1; Vienna: C. Geroldi, 1866).

Tacitus, *Historiae*—Clifford H. Moore, *Tacitus: The Histories* (4 vols.; LCL; London: W. Heinemann, 1925–37).

Tanḥuma [*Tan*]—Printed edition (Wilna: Romm, 1831).

Tanḥuma Buber [*TanB*]—Solomon Buber, *Midrasch Tanhuma* (2 vols.; Wilna: Romm, 1885; repr., Jerusalem, 1964).

Temple Scroll [*11Q19*]—Yigael Yadin, *The Temple Scroll* (3 vols.; Jerusalem: Israel Exploration Society, 1983).

Tertullian, *Adversus Marcionem*—Ernest Evans, *Tertullian: Adversus Marcionem* (Oxford: Clarendon, 1972).

Testament of Solomon [*T. Sol.*]—Chester C. McCown, *The Testament of Solomon* (UNT 9; Leipzig: J. C. Hinrichs, 1922); James H. Charlesworth, ed., *The Old Testament Pseudepigrapha* (2 vols.; Garden City, N.Y.: Doubleday, 1983), 1:935–87.

Testament of the Twelve Patriarchs—Marinus de Jonge, *The Testament of the Twelve Patriarchs* (Leiden: Brill, 1978).

Theodoret of Cyrrhus, *Eranistes*—Gérard H. Ettlinger, *Theodoret of Cyrus: Eranistes* (Oxford: Clarendon, 1973); *NPNF* 2, III, pp. 160–244.

———, *Historia ecclesiastica* [*HE*]—Léon Parmentier, *Theodoret Kirchengeschichte* (GCS 19; Leipzig: J. C. Hinrichs, 1911); *NPNF* 2, III, pp. 33–159.

———, *Historia religiosa*—Pierre Canivet and Alice Leroy-Molinghen, *Théodoret de Cyrrhus: Histoire des moines de Syrie* (*SC* 234, 257; Paris: Cerf, 1977–79); Richard M. Price, *A History of the Monks of Syria by Theodoret of Cyrrhus* (Cistercian Studies 88; Kalamazoo, Mich.: Cistercian Publications, 1985).

Theodosius, *De situ Terrae sanctae*—P. Geyer, *Theodosii: De situ Terrae sanctae*, CCSL 175:115–25; John Wilkinson, *Jerusalem Pilgrims before the Crusades* (Warminster: Aris & Phillips, 1977), 63–73.

Tobit [Tob]—Robert Hanhart, *Tobit* (Septuaginta: Vetus Testamentum Graecum 8:5; Göttingen: Vandenhoeck & Ruprecht, 1983).

Tosefta [*t* with name of tractate]—For *Zeraim, Moed, Nashim,* and the 3 *Babot* of *Neziqin:* Saul Lieberman, *The Tosefta* (5 vols.; New York: Jewish Theological Seminary, 1955–88); for all the rest: Moses Zuckermandel, *Tosefta* (2nd ed.; Jerusalem: Wahrmann, 1970); Jacob Neusner and Richard S. Sarason, eds., *The Tosefta: Translated from the Hebrew* (6 vols.; New York: Ktav, 1986).

Wisdom of Solomon (Sapientia Salomonis) [Wis]—Joseph Ziegler, *Sapientia Salomonis* (Septuaginta: Vetus Testamentum Graecum 12:1; Göttingen: Vandenhoeck & Ruprecht, 1962).

Yalkut Makhiri—Albert W. Greenup, *The Yalkut of R. Machir bar Abba Mari of the Twelve Prophets* (4 vols. in 2; London: n.p., 1909–13).

Yerushalmi (Palestinian Talmud) [*y* with name of tractate]—Printed edition (Venice: Bomberg, 1523–24); Jacob Neusner, ed., *The Talmud of the Land of Israel: A Preliminary Translation and Explanation* (35 vols.; Chicago: University of Chicago Press, 1982–94).

SCHOLARLY WORKS

Abel, Félix-Marie, *Histoire de la Palestine* (2 vols.; Paris: Gabalda, 1952).

———, "Saint Jérôme et Jérusalem," *Miscellanea Geronimiana* (ed. Vincenzo Vannutelli; Rome: Tipografia Poliglotta Vaticana, 1920), 131–55.

———, "La sépulture de Saint Jacques le mineur," *RB* 28 (1919) 480–99.

Abel, Félix-Marie, and Jean Starcky, *Les livres des Maccabées* (3rd ed.; Paris: Cerf, 1961).

Abler, Ronald, John S. Adams, and Peter Gould, eds., *Spatial Organization: The Geographer's View of the World* (Englewood Cliffs, N.J.: Prentice-Hall, 1971).

Aderet, Avraham, *From Destruction to Restoration: The Mode of Yavneh in (the) Re-Establishment of the Jewish People* (Jerusalem: Magnes, 1990) (Heb.).

Adler, Michael, "The Emperor Julian and the Jews," *JQR* 5 (1893) 591–651.

Albeck, Chanoch, *Shishah sidrei Mishnah* (6 vols.; Jerusalem: Devir, 1952–59).

Aline, Marie, "La forteresse Antonia à Jérusalem et la question du Prétoire" (Ph.D. diss., Ecole Biblique, 1955).

Aptowitzer, Victor, "Les éléments juifs dans la légende du Golgotha," *REJ* 79 (1924) 145–62.

Aram Veeser, Harold, ed., *The New Historicism* (New York: Routledge, 1989).

Arcelin, Patrice, "Arles protohistorique, centre d'échanges économiques et culturels," *Sur les pas des Grecs en Occident: Hommages à André Nickels* (ed. Patrice Arcelin et al.; Études massaliètes 4; Paris: Errance, 1995), 325–38.

Arndt, William F., and F. Wilbur Gingrich, *A Greek-English Lexicon of the New Testament and Other Early Christian Literature* (2nd ed.; rev. and augm. from Walter Bauer's *Griechisch-deutsches Wörterbuch zu den Schriften des Neuen Testaments und der übrigen urchristlichen Literatur;* Chicago: University of Chicago Press, 1979).

Arnold, Philip P., and Ann Grodzins Gold, eds., *Sacred Landscapes and Cultural Politics* (Burlington, Vt.: Ashgate, 2001).

Arnould, Caroline, *Les arcs romains de Jérusalem: Architecture, décor et urbanisme* (*NTOA* 35; Göttingen: Vandenhoeck & Ruprecht, 1997).

Assaf, Shmuel, and Leon A. Mayer, eds., *Sefer Ha-Yishuv* (Jerusalem: Devir, 1944).

Attridge, Harold W., *The Epistle to the Hebrews* (Philadelphia: Fortress, 1989).

Avalos, Hector, *Illness and Health Care in the Ancient Near East: The Role of the Temple in Greece, Mesopotamia, and Israel* (HSM 54; Atlanta: Scholars Press, 1995).

Avigad, Naḥman, *The Upper City of Jerusalem* (Jerusalem: Shimonah, 1981) (Heb.).

———, *Discovering Jerusalem* (Nashville: Nelson, 1983).

Avi-Yonah, Michael, "Beit ha-miqdash ha-sheini," *Sefer Yerushalaim* (ed. Michael Avi-Yonah; Jerusalem: Mosad Byalik and Devir, 1957), 392–418.

———, *Historical Geography of Palestine: From the End of the Babylonian Exile to the Arab Conquest* (3rd ed.; Jerusalem: Bialik Institute, 1963) (Heb.).

———, "Jerusalem in the Hellenistic and Roman Periods," *The Herodian Period* (ed. Michael Avi-Yonah and Zvi Baras; WHJP 7; Jerusalem: Jewish History Publications, 1975), 212–19.

———, *The Madaba Mosaic Map* (Jerusalem: Israel Exploration Society, 1954).

———, "The Samaritan Revolts against the Byzantine Empire," *Eretz Israel* 4 (1956) 127–32 (Heb.).

Aziza, Claude, "Julien et le Judaïsme," *L'empereur Julien: De l'histoire à la légende, 331–1715* (ed. René Braun and Jean Richer; Paris: Belles Lettres, 1978), 141–58.

Bachmann, Michael, *Jerusalem und der Temple: Die geographisch-theologischen Elemente in der lukanischen Sicht des jüdischen Kultzentrums* (BWANT 109; Berlin: Kohlhammer, 1980).

Bagatti, Bellarmino, *The Church from the Gentiles in Palestine: History and Archaeology* (trans. Eugene Houade; Jerusalem: Franciscan Printing Press, 1971).

———, *Recherches sur le site du Temple de Jérusalem, Ier–VIIe siècle* (Jerusalem: Franciscan Printing Press, 1979).

———, "Resti romani nell' area della Flagellazione in Gerusalemme," *LASBF* 8 (1957–58) 309–52.

———, "Il 'Tempio di Gerusalemme' dal II all' VII secolo," *Bibl* 43 (1962) 1–21.

Bahat, Dan, *The Illustrated Atlas of Jerusalem* (Jerusalem: Carta, 1989).

Bal, Mieke, et al., eds., *Acts of Memory: Cultural Recall in the Present* (Hanover, N.H.: Dartmouth College, University Press of New England, 1999).

Baldovin, John F., *The Urban Character of Christian Worship: The Origins, Development and Meaning of Stational Liturgy* (OCA 228; Rome: Pont. Institutum Studiorum Orientalium, 1987).

Balz, Horst, and Gerhard Schneider, eds., *Exegetical Dictionary of the New Testament* (3 vols.; Grand Rapids, Mich.: Eerdmans, 1990–93).

Bammel, Caroline P., "Law and Temple in Origen," *Templum Amicitiae: Essays on the Second Temple Presented to Ernst Bammel* (ed. William Horbury; JSNTSup 48; Sheffield: JSOT Press, 1991), 464–76.

Bar, Doron, "Aelia Capitolina and the Location of the Camp of the Tenth Legion," *PEQ* 130 (1998) 8–19.

———, "Aelia Capitolina's Main Street Layout: Where Was the Main Cardo of the City?" *New Studies on Jerusalem: Proceedings of the Seventh Conference* (ed. Avraham Faust and Eyal Baruch; Ramat-Gan: Yad Yitshak Ben-Tsevi, 2001), 159–68 (Heb.).

Barag, Dan, "Glass Pilgrim Vessels from Jerusalem," *Journal of Glass Studies* 12 (1970) 35–63; 13 (1971) 45–63.

Baras, Zvi, "The Testimonium Flavianum and the Martyrdom of James," *Josephus, Judaism, and Christianity* (ed. Louis Feldman and Gohei Hata; Detroit: Wayne State University, 1987), 338–48.

Barker, Margaret, "Temple Imagery in Philo: An Indication of the Origin of the Logos," *Templum Amicitiae: Essays on the Second Temple Presented to Ernst Bammel* (ed. William Horbury; JSNTSup 48; Sheffield: JSOT Press, 1991), 70–102.

Barnard, Leslie W., *Justin Martyr: His Life and Thought* (London: Cambridge University Press, 1967).

Barnes, Timothy D., "The Composition of Eusebius' Onomasticon," *JTS*, n.s., 26 (1975) 412–15.

———, "The Composition of Cassius Dio's Roman History," *Phoenix* 38 (1984) 240–55.

———, *Constantine and Eusebius* (Cambridge: Harvard University Press, 1981).

———, *Tertullian: A Historical and Literary Study* (rev. ed.; Oxford: Clarendon, 1985).

Barr, James, "St. Jerome's Appreciation of Hebrew," *BJRL* 49 (1966–67) 281–302.

Barrett, Charles K., "Attitudes to the Temple in the Acts of the Apostles," *Templum Amicitiae: Essays on the Second Temple Presented to Ernst Bammel* (ed. William Horbury; JSNTSup 48; Sheffield: JSOT Press, 1991), 345–67.

Bartlett, John R., *The First and Second Books of the Maccabees* (Cambridge: Cambridge University Press, 1973).

Baruch, Yuval, et al., "The Northern Wall of Jerusalem in the 3rd–6th Centuries CE in Light of New Excavations near the Herod's Gate," *Judea and Samaria Research Studies* 12 (ed. Yaacov Eshel; Kedumim: Ariel, 2003), 175–82 (Heb.).

Bauckham, Richard, "James and the Jerusalem Church," *The Book of Acts in Its Palestinian Setting* (ed. Richard Bauckham; vol. 4 of *The Book of Acts in Its First Century Setting;* Grand Rapids, Mich.: Eerdmans, 1995), 415–80.

Bauer, Walter, *Rechtgläubigkeit und Ketzerei im ältesten Christentum* (BHT 10; Tübingen: Mohr, 1934).

Beasley-Murray, George R., *A Commentary on Mark Thirteen* (London: Macmillan, 1957).

Bechert, Tilmann, and Willem J. H. Willems, *Die römische Reichsgrenze von der Mosel bis zur Nordseeküste* (Stuttgart: Theiss, 1995).

Beer, Mosheh, "Shim'on Bar Yoḥai and Jerusalem," *Jerusalem in the Second Temple Period: Abraham Schalit Memorial Volume* (ed. Aharon Oppenheimer et al.; Jerusalem: Yad Yitshak Ben-Tsevi, 1980), 361–75 (Heb.).

Belayche, Nicole, "Du Mont du Temple au Golgotha: Le Capitole de la colonie d'*Aelia Capitolina*," *RHR* 214 (1997) 387–413.

Ben-Dov, Meir, *In the Shadow of the Temple: The Discovery of Ancient Jerusalem* (trans. Ina Friedman; Jerusalem: Keter, 1985).

Ben-Dov, Meir, et al., eds., *The Western Wall* (trans. Raphael Posner; Tel Aviv: Ministry of Defense, 1983).

Benoit, Pierre, "Découvertes archéologiques autour de la Piscine de Béthesda," *Jerusalem Through the Ages: The Twenty-Fifth Archaeological Convention, October 1967* (Jerusalem: Israel Exploration Society, 1968), 84–75.

———, "L'Antonia d'Hérode le Grand et le forum oriental d'Aelia Capitolina," *HTR* 64 (1971) 135–67.

Ben-Shalom, Israel, "Events and Ideology of the Yavneh Period as Indirect Causes of the Bar-Kokhva Revolt," *The Bar-Kokhva Revolt: A New Approach* (ed. Aharon Oppenheimer and Uriel Rappaport; Jerusalem: Yad Yitshak Ben-Tsevi, 1984) 1–12 (Heb.).

Bernard, John H., *A Critical and Exegetical Commentary on the Gospel according to St. John* (ed. Alan H. McNeile; 2 vols.; Edinburgh: T&T Clark, 1928; repr., New York: C. Scribner, 1929).

Bettenzoli, Giuseppe, *Geist der Heiligkeit: Traditionsgeschichtliche Untersuchung des QDS im Buch Ezechiel* (Florence: Istituto di linguistica e di lingue orientali, 1979).

Beyschlag, Karlmann, "Das Jakobusmartyrium und seine Verwandten in der frühchristlichen Literatur," *ZNW* 56 (1965) 149–78.

Bickermann, Elias J., *Der Gott der Makkabäer Untersuchungen über Sinn und Ursprung der makkabäischen Erhebung* (Berlin: Schocken Verlag, 1937).

Bieberstein, Klaus, and Hanswulf Bloedhorn, *Jerusalem: Grundzüge der Baugeschichte vom Chalkolithikum bis zur Frühzeit der osmanischen Herrschaft* (Wiesbaden: L. Reichert, 1994).

Biguzzi, Giancarlo, *Il tempio di Gerusalemme nel Vangelo di Marco: Studio di analisi della redazione* (Rome: Urbaniana University Press, 1987).

Black, Matthew, *The Book of Enoch, or, 1 Enoch* (*SVTP* 7; Leiden: Brill, 1985).

Blackburn, Simon, *Spreading the Word: Groundings in the Philosophy of Language* (Oxford: Clarendon, 1984).

Blank, Sheldon H., "The Death of Zechariah in Rabbinic Literature," *HUCA* 12–13 (1937–38) 327–46.

Blass, Friedrich, and Albert Debrunner, *A Greek Grammar of the New Testament and Other Early Christian Literature* (trans. and rev. by Ronald W. Funk; Chicago: University of Chicago Press, 1961).

Bloemers, Johan H. F., "Lower Germany: *plura consilio quam vi* Proto-Urban Settlement Developments and the Integration of Native Society," *The Early Roman Empire in the West* (ed. Thomas Blagg and Martin Millett; Oxford: Oxbow Books, 1990), 72–86.

Blomme, Yves, "Faut-il revenir sur la datation de l'arc de l'Ecce Homo," *RB* 86 (1979) 244–71.

Böcher, Otto von, "Die Heilige Stadt im Völkerkrieg: Wandlungen eines apokalyptischen Schemas," *Josephus Studien: Untersuchungen zu Josephus, dem antiken Judentum und dem Neuen Testament* (ed. Otto Betz et al.; Göttingen: Vandenhoeck & Ruprecht, 1974), 55–76.

Boer, Willem den, "Allegory and History," *Romanitas et Christianitas* (ed. Willem den Boer et al.; Amesterdam: North-Holland, 1973), 15–25.

Böhl, Felix, "Über das Verhältnis von Shetija-Stein und Nabel der Welt in der Kosmogonie der Rabbinen," *ZDMG* 124 (1974) 253–70.

Böhlig, Alexander, "Zum Martyrium des Jakobus," *NT* 5 (1962) 206–13.

Boissevain, Ursulus P., *Cassii Dionis Cocceiani: Historiarum Romanarum Quae Supersunt* (5 vols.; Berlin: Weidmannos, 1895–1931).

Bokser, Baruch M., "Rabbinic Responses to Catastrophe: From Continuity to Discontinuity," *PAAJR* 50 (1983) 37–61.

Botterweck, G. Johannes, and Helmer Ringgren, eds., *Theologisches Wörterbuch zum Alten Testament* (Stuttgart: Kohlhammer, 1973).

Bousset, Wilhelm, *Die Religion des Judentums im neutestamentlichen Zeitaler* (Berlin: Reuther & Reichard, 1903).

Bowersock, Glen W., "A Roman Perspective on the Bar Kochba War," *Approaches to Ancient Judaism* (6 vols.; ed. William S. Green; BJS; Missoula, Mont.: Scholars Press, 1980), 2:131–41.

Boyarin, Daniel, *Dying for God: Martyrdom and the Making of Christianity and Judaism* (Stanford: Stanford University Press, 1999).

Bradshaw, Paul F., *The Search for the Origins of Christian Worship* (New York: Oxford University Press, 1992).

Brandon, Samuel G. F., *The Fall of Jerusalem and the Christian Church* (2nd ed.; London: S.P.C.K., 1957).

Branham, Joan R., "Vicarious Sacrality: Temple Space in Ancient Synagogues," *Ancient Synagogues: Historical Analysis and Archaeological Discovery* (ed. Dan Urman and Paul V. M. Flesger; 2 vols.; Leiden: Brill, 1995), 2:319–46.

Bregman, Mark, "Early Sources and Traditions in the Tanhuma-Yelammedenu Midrashim," *Tarbiz* 60 (1991) 269–74 (Heb.).

Brenk, Beat, *Die frühchristlichen Mosaiken in S. Maria Maggiore zu Rom* (Wiesbaden: Steiner, 1975).

Brock, Sebastian P., "A Letter Attributed to Cyril of Jerusalem on the Rebuilding of the Temple," *BSOAS* 40 (1977) 267–86.

———, "The Rebuilding of the Temple under Julian: A New Source," *PEQ* 108 (1976) 103–7.

Broshi, Magen, "Estimating the Population of Ancient Jerusalem," *BARev* 4:2 (1978) 10–15.

Brown, Kent, "Jewish and Gnostic Elements in the Second Apocalypse of James (CG V, 4)," *NT* 17 (1975) 225–37.

Brown, Peter R. L., *The Cult of the Saints: Its Rise and Function in Latin Christianity* (Haskell Lectures on History of Religions, n.s., 2; Chicago: University of Chicago Press, 1981).

———, *The World of Late Antiquity* (London: Thames & Hudson, 1971).

Brown, Raymond E., *The Gospel according to John* (2 vols.; AB 29; Garden City, N.Y.: Doubleday, 1966).

Browning, Iain, *Jerash and the Decapolis* (London: Chatto & Windus, 1982).

Browning, Robert, *The Byzantine Empire* (rev. ed.; Washington, D.C.: Catholic University of America Press, 1992).

Bruce, Frederick F., *Peter, Stephen, James and John: Studies in Early Non-Pauline Christianity* (Grand Rapids, Mich.: Eerdmans, 1979).

Brunt, P. A., "On Historical Fragments and Epitomes," *CQ*, n.s., 30 (1980) 477–94.

Buchholz, Dennis D., *Your Eyes Will Be Opened: A Study of the Greek (Ethiopic) Apocalypse of Peter* (SBLDS 97; Atlanta: Scholars Press, 1988).

Büchler, Adolf, *Die Priester und der Cultus in letzten Jahrzehnt des jerusalemischen Tempels* (Vienna: Alfred Hölder, 1895).

————, *Types of Jewish-Palestinian Piety from 70 B.C.E. to 70 C.E.* (London: Oxford University Press, 1922).

Bull, Robert J., "The Excavation of Tell er-Ras on Mt. Gerizim," *BA* 31 (1968) 58–72.

Bultmann, Rudolf, *Die Geschichte der synoptischen Tradition* (3rd ed.; Göttingen: Vandenhoeck & Ruprecht, 1957).

Busink, Théodore A., *Der Tempel von Jerusalem von Salomo bis Herodes; eine archäologisch-historische Studie unter Berücksichtigung des westsemitischen Tempelbaus* (2 vols.; Leiden: Brill, 1970–80).

Busse, Heribert, and G. Kretschmar, *Jerusalemer Heiligtumstraditionen in altkirchlicher und frühislamischer Zeit* (Wiesbaden: Otto Harrassowitz, 1987).

Carmichael, David L. et al., eds., *Sacred Sites, Sacred Places* (OWA 23; London: Routledge, 1994).

Carrol, Kenneth L., "The Place of James in the Early Church," *BJRL* 44 (1961–62) 49–67.

Carroll, Robert P., "So What Do We Know about the Temple? The Temple in the Prophets," *Second Temple Studies: Temple Community in the Persian Period* (ed. Tamara C. Eskenazi and Kent H. Richards; JSOTSup 175; Sheffield: JSOT Press, 1994), 34–51.

Chadwick, Henry, *The Early Church* (rev. ed.; London: Penguin, 1993).

————, *Origen: Contra Celsum* (rev. ed.; Cambridge: Cambridge University Press, 1980).

Chapman, John, "Zacharias Slain between the Temple and the Altar," *JTS* 13 (1911–12) 398–410.

Chester, Andrew, "The Sibyl and the Temple," *Templum Amicitiae: Essays on the Second Temple Presented to Ernst Bammel* (ed. William Horbury; JSNTSup 48; Sheffield: JSOT Press, 1991), 37–69.

Clements, Ronald E., *God and Temple* (Oxford: Blackwell, 1965).

Clermont-Ganneau, Charles S., *Archaeological Researches in Palestine during the Years 1873–1874* (2 vols.; London: Committee of the Palestine Exploration Fund, 1899).

————, *Recueil d'archéologie orientale* (Paris: Ernest Leroux, 1905).

————, "Une stèle du Temple de Jérusalem," *RA* 13 [= n.s. 28] (1872) 220.

Clifford, Richard J., *The Cosmic Mountain in Canaan and the Old Testament* (HSM 4; Cambridge: Harvard University Press, 1972).

Cohen, Shaye J. D., "The Destruction: From Scripture to Midrash," *Prooftexts* 2 (1982) 18–39.

————, *From the Maccabees to the Mishnah* (Philadelphia: Westminster, 1987).

————, "The Temple and the Synagogue," *The Temple in Antiquity: Ancient Records and Modern Perspectives* (ed. Truman G. Madsen; Religious Studies Monograph Series 9; Provo: Brigham Young University, 1984), 151–74.

Cohn, Erich W., *New Ideas about Jerusalem's Topography* (Jerusalem: Franciscan Printing Press, 1987

————, "Second Thoughts about the Perforated Stone on the Haram of Jerusalem," *PEQ* 114 (1982) 144–45.

Collingwood, Robin G., and Ian Richmond, *The Archaeology of Roman Britain* (rev. ed.; London: Methuen, 1973).

Collins, John J., *Daniel: A Commentary on the Book of Daniel* (Minneapolis: Fortress, 1993).

———, *The Sibylline Oracles of Egyptian Judaism* (SBLDS 13; Missoula, Mont.: Society of Biblical Literature, 1972).

Conway, Martin A., ed., *Cognitive Models of Memory* (Cambridge: Massachusetts Institute of Technology Press, 1997).

Conzelmann, Hans, *Acts of the Apostles* (trans. James Limburg et al.; Philadelphia: Fortress, 1987).

———, *Geschichte des Urchristentums* (GNT 5–6; Göttingen: Vandenhoeck & Ruprecht, 1969).

———, *Die Mitte der Zeit: Studien zur Theologie des Lukas* (BHT 17; Tübingen: Mohr, 1954).

Corbo, Virgilio C., *Il Santo Sepolcro di Gerusalemme: Aspetti arceologici dalle origini al periodo crociato* (3 vols.; Jerusalem: Franciscan Printing Press, 1981–82).

Cotton, Hanna, and Werner Eck, "Ein Ehrenbogen für Septimius Severus und seine Familie in Jerusalem," *Donum Amicitiae: Studies in Ancient History Offered by Friends and Colleagues on the Occasion of the Anniversary of the Foundation of Ancient History in the Jagiellonian University of Kraków* (ed. Edward Dabrowa; Kraków: Jagiellonian University Press, 1998).

Coüasnon, Charles, *The Church of the Holy Sepulchre in Jerusalem* (London: British Academy, 1974).

Couret, Alphonse, *La Palestine sous les empereurs grecs, 326–636* (Grenoble: F. Allier, 1869).

Cranz, F. Edward, "Kingdom and Polity in Eusebius of Caesarea," *HTR* 45 (1952) 47–66.

Crouzel, Henri, "La distinction de la 'typologie' et de 'l'allégorie,'" *BLE* 65 (1964) 161–74.

———, *Origen* (trans. A. S. Worrall; San Francisco: Harper & Row, 1989).

Crown, Alan D., *A Bibliography of the Samaritans* (2nd ed.; ATLA Bibliography Series 32; Metuchen, N.J.: Scarecrow, 1993).

Crum, Walter E., *A Coptic Dictionary* (Oxford: Clarendon, 1939).

Cullmann, Oscar, *Der johanneische Kreis: Sein Platz im Spätjudentum in der Jüngerschaft Jesu und im Urchristentum* (Tübingen: Mohr, 1975).

Daley, Brian E., *The Hope of the Early Church* (Cambridge: Cambridge University Press, 1991).

Daniélou, Jean, *Théologie du Judéo-Christianisme,* (Paris: Desclée, 1958).

Davies, William D., *The Gospel and the Land: Early Christianity and Jewish Territorial Doctrine* (Berkeley: University of California Press, 1974).

Davila, James R., "Moriah," *ABD* 4:905.

De Lange, Nicholas R. M., *Origen and the Jews: Studies in Jewish-Christian Relations in Third Century Palestine* (University of Cambridge Oriental Publications 25; Cambridge: Cambridge University Press, 1976).

de Saulcy, Louis F., *Jérusalem* (Paris: Vve A. Morel et cie, 1882).

De Young, James C., *Jerusalem in the New Testament: The Significance of the City in the History of Redemption and in Eschatology* (Kampen: J. H. Kok, 1960).

Delehaye, Hippolyte, *Les légendes hagiographiques* (2nd ed.; Brussels: Bureaux de la Société des Bollandistes, 1906).

Derenbourg, Joseph, *Essai sur l'histoire et la géographie de la Palestine* (Paris: Imprimerie impériale, 1867).

Derrida, Jacques, *Of Grammatology* (trans. Gayatri C. Spivak; Baltimore: John Hopkins University Press, 1976).

Deselaers, Paul, *Das Buch Tobit: Studien zu seiner Entstehung, Komposition und Theologie* (*OBO* 43; Göttingen: Vandenhoeck & Ruprecht, 1982).

Desjardins, Michel, "Bauer and Beyond: On Recent Scholarly Discussions of *hairesis* in the Early Church," *SecCent* 8 (1991) 65–82.

———, "Les vestiges du Seigneur au Mont des Oliviers," *BLE* 73 (1972) 51–72.

Diamnt, Devora, "4QFlorilegium and the Idea of the Community as Temple," *Hellenica et Judaica* (ed. André Caquot et al.; Leuven: Peeters, 1986), 165–89.

Dodds, Eric R., *Pagan and Christian in an Age of Anxiety* (Cambridge: Cambridge University Press, 1965).

Dommershausen, Werner, *1 Makkabäer, 2 Makkabäer* (Die Neue Echter Bible 12; Würzburg: Echter Verlag, 1985).

Donner, Herbert, "Der Felsen und der Tempel," *ZDPV* 93 (1977) 1–11.

———, *Pilgerfahrt ins Heilige Land: Die ältesten Berichte christlicher Palästinapilger, 4.– 7. Jahrhundert* (Stuttgart: Verlag Katholisches Bibelwerk, 1979).

Drijvers, Hendrik J. W., "The Acts of Thomas," *New Testament Apocrypha* (ed. Wilhelm Schneemelcher and Edgar Hennecke; trans. Robert M. Wilson, 2 vols.; rev. ed.; Cambridge: James Clarke, 1991–92).

———, *Helena Augusta: The Mother of Constantine the Great and the Legend of Her Finding of the True Cross* (Brill's Studies in Intellectual History 27; Leiden: Brill, 1992).

Dubarle, André M., "Le signe du Temple," *RB* 48 (1939) 21–44.

Dubois, Jean-Daniel, "La mort de Zacharie: Mémoire juive et mémoire chrétienne," *REAug* 40 (1994) 23–38.

Duling, Dennis C., "Testament of Solomon," *The Old Testament Pseudepigrapha* (ed. James H. Charlesworth; Garden City, N.Y.: Doubleday, 1983).

Dupont, Jacques, "Il n'en sera pas laissé pierre sur pierre (Marc 13,2; Luc 19,44)," *Bibl* 52 (1971) 301–20.

Duprez, Antoine, *Jésus et les dieux guérisseurs: A propos de Jean V* (CahRB 12; Paris: Gabalda, 1970).

Edelstein, Emma J., and Ludwig Edelstein, *Asclepius: A Collection and Interpretation of the Testimonies* (Baltimore: John Hopkins Press, 1945).

Ehrlich, Uri, *The Non-Verbal Language of Jewish Prayer* (Jerusalem: Magnes, 1999) (Heb.).

Elad, Amikam, *Medieval Jerusalem and Islamic Worship: Holy Places, Ceremonies, Pilgrimage* (Islamic History and Civilization 8; Leiden: Brill, 1995).

Eliade, Mircea, *The Sacred and the Profane: The Nature of Religion* (trans. Willard R. Trask; New York: Harcourt, 1959).

Eliav, Yaron Z., "The Desolating Sacrilege: A Jewish-Christian Discourse on Statuary and Power," *The Sculptural Environment of the Roman Near East: Reflections on Culture, Ideology, and Power* (ed. Yaron Z. Eliav and Elise A. Friedland; forthcoming).

———, "Hadrian's Actions in the Jerusalem Temple Mount According to Cassius Dio and *Xiphilini Manus*," *JSQ* 4 (1997) 125–44.

———, "'Interpretive Citation' in the Epistle of Barnabas and the Early Christian Attitude towards the Temple Mount," *The Interpretation of Scripture in Early Judaism and Christianity* (ed. Craig A. Evans; JSPSup 33; Studies in Scripture in Early Judaism and Christianity 7; Sheffield: Sheffield Academic Press, 2000), 353–62.

———, "'A Mount without a Temple': The Temple Mount from 70 C.E. to the Mid-Fifth Century—Reality and Idea" (Ph.D. diss., Hebrew University, 1998) (Heb.).

———, "Pylè-Puma-Sfat Medinah and a Halakha Concerning Bath-houses," *Sidra* 11 (1995) 5–19 (Heb.).

———, "Realia, Daily Life, and the Transmission of Local Stories during the Talmudic Period," *What Athens Has to Do with Jerusalem: Essays on Classical, Jewish and Early Christian Archaeology in Honor of Gidon Foerster* (ed. Leonard V. Rutgers; Leuven: Peeters, 2002), 235–65.

———, "The Temple Mount, the Rabbis, and the Poetics of Memory," *HUCA* 74 (2005).

———, "The Tomb of James Brother of Jesus as *Locus Memoriae*," *HTR* 97 (2004) 32–59.

———, "The Urban Layout of Aelia Capitolina: A New View from the Perspective of the Temple Mount," *The Bar Kokhba War Reconsidered* (ed. Peter Schäfer; TSAJ 100; Tübingen: Mohr Siebeck, 2003), 241–77.

Evans, Craig A., "Opposition to the Temple: Jesus and the Dead Sea Scrolls," *Jesus and the Dead Sea Scrolls* (ed. James H. Charlesworth; New York: Doubleday, 1992), 235–353.

———, "Predictions of the Destruction of the Herodian Temple in the Pseudepigrapha, Qumran Scrolls, and Related Texts," *JSP* 10 (1992) 89–147.

Fascher, Erich, "Jerusalems Untergang in der urchristlichen und altkirchlichen Überlieferung," *TLZ* 89 (1964) 87–98.

Feldman, Louis H., *Josephus and Modern Scholarship, 1937–1980* (Berlin: De Gruyter, 1984).

Fentress, Elizabeth W. B., *Numidia and the Roman Army: Social, Military and Economic Aspects of the Frontier Zone* (BAR international series 53; Oxford: BAR, 1979).

Ferguson, Everett, et al., eds., *Early Christianity and Judaism* (Studies in Early Christianity 6; New York: Garland, 1993).

Fine, Steven, *This Holy Place: On the Sanctity of the Synagogue during the Greco-Roman Period* (Notre Dame: University of Notre Dame Press, 1997).

Fineman, Joel, "The History of the Anecdote: Fiction and Fiction," *The New Historicism* (ed. Harold Aram Veeser; New York: Routledge, 1989), 49–76.

Finney, Paul C., *The Invisible God: The Earliest Christians on Art* (New York: Oxford University Press, 1994).

Flusin, Bernard, "L'esplanade du Temple à l'arrivée des Arabes d'après deux récits byzantins," *Bayt al-Maqdis: Abd al-Malik's Jerusalem* (ed. Julian Raby and Jeremy Johns; 2 vols.; Oxford Studies in Islamic Art 9; Oxford: University of Oxford, 1992), 1:17–31.

Fox, Robin L., *Pagans and Christians* (London: Viking, 1986).

Fredriksen, Paula, "What You See Is What You Get: Context and Content in Current Research on the Historical Jesus," *Theology Today* 52 (1995) 82–91.

Frend, William H. C., *The Rise of Christianity* (Philadelphia: Fortress, 1984).

Funk, Wolf P., *Die zweite Apokalypse des Jakobus aus Nag-Hammadi-Codex V* (TU 119; Berlin: Akademie-Verlag, 1976).

Gafni, Isaiah M., "Jerusalem in Rabbinic Literature," *The History of Jerusalem: The*

Roman and Byzantine Periods, 70–638 CE (ed. Yoram Tsafrir and Shmuel Safrai; Jerusalem: Yad Yitshak Ben-Tsevi, 1999) 35–59 (Heb.).

———, "Pre-Histories of Jerusalem in Hellenistic, Jewish and Christian Literature," *JSP* 1 (1987) 5–22.

García-Martínez, Florentino, and Donald W. Parry, eds., *A Bibliography of the Finds in the Desert of Judah, 1970–1995* (STDJ 19; Leiden: Brill, 1996).

Gaston, Lloyd, *No Stone on Another: Studies in the Significance of the Fall of Jerusalem in the Synoptic Gospels* (NovTSup 23; Leiden: Brill, 1970).

Germer-Durand, J., "Aelia Capitolina," *RB* 1 (1892) 369–87.

Geva, Hillel, "The Camp of the Tenth Legion in Jerusalem: An Archaeological Reconsideration," *IEJ* 34 (1984) 239–54.

———, "Jerusalem: The Byzantine Period," *NEAEHL* 2:768–85.

———, "Jerusalem: The Roman Period," *NEAEHL* 2:758–67.

———, "Jerusalem: The Second Temple Period," *NEAEHL* 2:717–49.

———, "The Tenth Roman Legion *Did* Camp on the South-West Hill," *Cathedra* 73 (1994) 181–86 (Heb.).

Gil, Moshe, *A History of Palestine, 634–1099* (trans. Ethel Broido; Cambridge: Cambridge University Press, 1992).

Gilat, Yishhak D., *The Teaching of R. Eliezer Ben Hyrcanos* (Tel Aviv: Devir, 1968) (Heb.).

Ginzberg, Louis, *A Commentary on the Palestinian Talmud* (4 vols.; New York: Jewish Theological Seminary of America, 1941–61) (Heb.).

———, *The Legends of the Jews* (2nd ed.; New York: Simon & Schuster, 1953).

Golan, David, "Hadrian's Decision to Supplant 'Jerusalem' by 'Aelia Capitolina,'" *Historia* 35 (1986) 226–39.

Goldstein, Jonathan A., *1 Maccabees: A New Translation with Introduction and Commentary* (Garden City, N.Y.: Doubleday, 1976).

———, *2 Maccabees: A New Translation with Introduction and Commentary* (Garden City, N.Y.: Doubleday, 1983).

Golinkin, David, "Jerusalem in Jewish Law and Customs," *Jerusalem: Its Sanctity and Centrality to Judaism, Christianity, and Islam* (ed. Lee I. Levine; New York: Continuum, 1999), 408–23.

Goodblatt, David, "Ancient Zionism? The Zion Coins of the First Revolt and Their Background," *International Rennert Guest Lecture Series* 8 (2001).

———, *The Monarchic Principle: Studies in Jewish Self-Government in Antiquity* (TSAJ 38; Tübingen: Mohr, 1994).

———, "The Temple Mount: The After Life of a Biblical Phrase," *Le-David Maskil: A Birthday Tribute for David Noel Freedman* (eds. Richard E. Friedman and William H. C. Propp; Winona Lake: Eisenbrauns, 2004), 91–101.

Goodman, Martin, *Mission and Conversion: Proselytizing in the Religious History of the Roman Empire* (Oxford: Clarendon, 1994).

Grabar, André, *Early Christian Art: From the Rise of Christianity to the Death of Theodosius* (trans. Stuart Gilbert and James Emmons; New York: Odyssey, 1969).

———, *Martyrium: Recherches sur le culte des reliques et l'art chrétien antique* (3 vols.; Paris: Collège de France, 1943–46).

Grabar, Oleg, "Jerusalem," *Late Antiquity: A Guide to the Postclassical World* (ed. Glen W. Bowersock et al.; Cambridge: Harvard University Press, 1999), 524–25.

Graetz, Heinrich, *Geschichte der Juden* (Leipzig: Leiner, 1890–1908).

————, "Hagadische Elemente bei den Kirchenvätern," *MGWJ* 3 (1854) 311–19, 352–55, 381–87, 428–31; *MGWJ* 4 (1855) 186–92.

Graf, Fritz, "Heiligtum und Ritual: Das Beispiel der griechisch-römischen Asklepieia," *Le sanctuaire grec* (ed. Olivier Reverdin and Bertrand Grange; Entretiens sur l'Antiquité classique 37; Geneva: Fondation Hardt, 1992), 159–203.

Grant, Robert M., *Eusebius as Church Historian* (Oxford: Clarendon, 1980).

Greenblatt, Stephen J., *Learning to Curse: Essays in Early Modern Culture* (New York: Routledge, 1990).

Gregorovius, Ferdinand, *Der Kaiser Hadrian: Gemälde der römisch-hellenischen Welt zu seiner Zeit* (3rd ed.; Stuttgart: Cotta, 1884).

Grelle, Francesco, *L'autonomia cittadina fra Traiano e Adriano* (Naples: Edizioni scientifiche italiane, 1972).

Grelot, Pierre, "La géographie mythique d'Hénoch et ses sources orientales," *RB* 65 (1958) 33–69.

Griffith, Sidney H., "Ephraem the Syrian's Hymns 'Against Julian': Meditations on History and Imperial Power," *VC* 41 (1987) 238–66.

Groh, Dennis E., "The Onomasticon of Eusebius and the Rise of Christian Palestine," *SP* 18:1 (1989) 23–29.

Gros, Pierre, and Mario Torelli, *Storia dell'urbanistica: Il mondo romano* (Rome: Laterza, 1988).

Gruenwald, Ithamar, "God the 'Stone/Rock': Myth, Idolatry, and Cultic Fetishism in Ancient Israel," *JR* 76 (1996) 428–49.

Gry, Léon, *Le millénarisme dans ses origines et son développement* (Paris: Alphonse Picard, 1904).

Gustafsson, Berndt, "Hegesippus' Sources and His Reliability," *SP* 3 (1961) 227–32 (= TU 78).

Guthe, Hermann, "Das Stadtbild Jerusalems auf der Mosaikkarte von Madeba," *ZDPV* 28 (1905) 120–30.

Guttmann, Alexander, "Jerusalem in Tannaitic Law," *HUCA* 40–41 (1969–70) 251–75.

Hachlili, Rachel, *The Menorah, the Ancient Seven-Armed Candelabrum: Origin, Form and Significance* (Suppl. to JSJ 68; Leiden: Brill, 2001).

Hahn, Johannes, *Zerstörungen des Jerusalemer Tempels* (WUNT 147; Tübingen: Mohr Siebeck, 2002).

Halbwachs, Maurice, *La mémoire collective* (rev. & augm. by Gérhard Namer and Marie Jaisson; Paris: A. Michel, 1997).

Hall, Stuart G., *Doctrine and Practice in the Early Church* (London: S.P.C.K., 1991).

————, *Melito, of Sardis: On Pascha and Fragments* (Oxford: Clarendon, 1979).

Hamilton, Richard W., "Excavations against the North Wall of Jerusalem, 1937–1938," *QDAP* 10 (1944) 1–54.

————, "Jerusalem in the Fourth Century," *PEQ* 84 (1952) 83–90.

Han, Kyu S., *Jerusalem and the Early Jesus Movement: The Q Community's Attitude toward the Temple* (JSNTSup 207; Sheffield: Sheffield Academic Press, 2002).

Hann, Johannes, *Zerstörungen des Jerusalemer Tempels* (WUNT 147; Tübingen: Mohr Siebeck, 2002).

Hanson, Richard P. C., "Biblical Exegesis in the Early Church," *The Cambridge History of the Bible* (ed. Peter R. Ackroyd et al.; 3 vols.; Cambridge: Cambridge University Press, 1963–70), 1:412–53.

Haran, Menachem, *Temples and Temple-Service in Ancient Israel* (Oxford: Clarendon, 1978).

Harnack, Adolf, *Judentum und Judenchristentum in Justins Dialog mit Trypho* (TU 39:1; Leipzig: J. C. Hinrichs, 1913), 47–92.

Harvey, Anthony E., "Melito and Jerusalem," *JTS* 17 (1966) 401–4.

Hatch, Edwin, and Henry A. Redpath, *A Concordance to the Septuagint and the Other Greek Versions of the Old Testament* (2 vols.; Oxford: Clarendon, 1897).

Hayakawa, Samuel I., *Language in Thought and Action* (3rd ed.; New York: Harcourt Brace Jovanovich, 1972).

Hayes, John H., and Carl R. Holladay, *Biblical Exegesis: A Beginner's Handbook* (rev. ed.; Atlanta: John Knox, 1987).

Hayman, Paula, "Some Observations on Sefer Yesira: (2) The Temple at the Centre of the Universe," *JJS* 37 (1986) 176–82.

Hayward, Robert, "The New Jerusalem in the Wisdom of Jesus Ben Sira," *SJOT* 6 (1992) 123–38.

Hazlett, Ian, ed., *Early Christianity: Origins and Evolution to AD 600* (London: S.P.C.K., 1991).

Hefele, Karl J., *A History of the Christian Councils* (trans. William R. Clark; 5 vols.; 2nd ed.; Edinburgh: T&T Clark, 1872–96).

Heinemann, Joseph, *Studies in Jewish Liturgy* (ed. Avigdor Shinan; Jerusalem: Magnes, 1981) (Heb.).

Helfgott, Benjamin W., *The Doctrine of Election in Tannaitic Literature* (New York: King's Crown Press, 1954).

Hen, Yitzhak, "Gregory of Tours and the Holy Land," *OCP* 61 (1995) 47–64.

Henderson, Bernard W., *The Life and Principate of the Emperor Hadrian, A.D. 76–138* (London: Methuen, 1923).

Hengel, Martin, "The Geography of Palestine in Acts," *The Book of Acts in Its Palestinian Setting* (ed. Richard Bauckham; vol. 4 of *The Book of Acts in Its First Century Setting*; Grand Rapids, Mich.: Eerdmans, 1995), 27–78.

———, *Zur urchristlichen Geschichtsschreibung* (Stuttgart: Calwer Verlag, 1975).

Hennessy, John B., "Preliminary Report on Excavations at the Damascus Gate, 1964–1966," *Levant* 2 (1970) 22–27.

Henshke, David, "The Sanctity of Jerusalem: The Sages and Sectarian Halakhah," *Tarbiz* 67 (1997) 5–28 (Heb.).

Herr, Mosheh D., "The Calendar," *The Jewish People in the First Century* (ed. Shmuel Safrai et al.; CRINT I.2; Philadelphia: Fortress, 1974–76), 834–64.

———, "Persecutions and Martyrdom in Hadrian's Days," *Scripta Hierosolymitana* 23 (1972) 85–125.

Hezser, Catherine, "The (In)Significance of Jerusalem in the Talmud Yerushalmi," *The Talmud Yerushalmi and Graeco-Roman Culture* (ed. Peter Schäfer and Catherine Hezser; 3 vols.; TSAJ 79; Tübingen: Mohr Siebeck, 1998–2002), 2:11–49.

Himmelfarb, Martha, *Ascent to Heaven in Jewish and Christian Apocalypses* (New York: Oxford University Press, 1993).

———, "The Temple and the Garden of Eden in Ezekiel, the Book of the Watchers, and the Wisdom of Ben Sira," *Sacred Places and Profane Spaces: Essays in the Geographics of Judaism, Christianity, and Islam* (ed. Jamie Scott and Paul Simpson-Housley; New York: Greenwood, 1991), 63–78.

Hinz, Hermann, "Colonia Ulpia Traiana I: Die Entwicklung eines römischen Zentralortes am Niederrhein," *ANRW* II 4 (1975) 825–69.

Hirshman, Marc G., "The Priest's Gate and Elijah ben Menahem's Pilgrimage," *Tarbiz* 55 (1986) 217–27 (Heb.).

———, *A Rivalry of Genius: Jewish and Christian Biblical Interpretation in Late Antiquity* (trans. Batya Stein; Albany: State University of New York Press, 1996).

Hollander, Harm W., and Marinus de Jonge, *The Testament of the Twelve Patriarchs: A Commentary* (*SVTP* 8; Leiden: Brill, 1985).

Hollerich, Michael J., *Eusebius of Caesarea's Commentary on Isaiah* (Oxford: Clarendon, 1999).

———, "The Godly Polity in the Light of Prophecy: A Study of Eusebius of Caesarea's Commentary of Isaiah" (Ph.D. diss., University of Chicago, 1986).

Holum, Kenneth G., "Hadrian and St. Helena: Imperial Travel and the Origins of Christian Holy Land Pilgrimage," *The Blessings of Pilgrimage* (ed. Robert G. Ousterhout; Illinois Byzantine Studies 1; Urbana: University of Illinois Press, 1990), 66–81.

———, *Theodosian Empresses: Women and Imperial Dominion in Late Antiquity* (Berkeley: University of California Press, 1982).

Holum, Kenneth G., et al., *King Herod's Dream: Caesarea on the Sea* (New York: Norton, 1988).

Honigmann, Ernst, *Le couvent de Barsauma et le patriarcat jacobite d'Antioche et de Syrie* (*CSCO* 146, Subsidia 7; Louvain: L. Durbecq, 1954).

———, "Juvenal of Jerusalem," *DOP* 5 (1956) 211–76.

Horbury, William, "Jewish-Christian Relations in Barnabas and Justin Martyr," *Jews and Christians: The Parting of the Ways, A.D. 70 to 135* (ed. James D. G. Dunn; WUNT 66; Tübingen: Mohr, 1992), 315–45.

———, "Old Testament Interpretation in the Writings of the Church Fathers," *Mikra* (ed. Martin J. Mulder; CRINT II.1; Assen: Van Gorcum, 1998), 727–87.

———, ed., *Templum Amicitiae: Essays on the Second Temple Presented to Ernst Bammel* (JSNTSup 48; Sheffield: JSOT Press, 1991).

Hunt, Edgar D., *Holy Land Pilgrimage in the Later Roman Empire, AD 312–460* (Oxford: Clarendon, 1982).

Hurvitz, Avi, "The Evidence of Language in Dating the Priestly Code," *RB* 81 (1974) 41–43.

Hutton, Patrick H., *History as an Art of Memory* (Hanover, N.H.: University Press of New England, 1993).

Hyldahl, Niels, "Die Versuchung auf der Zinne des Tempels," *StTh* 15 (1961) 113–27.

Irshai, Oded, "Constantine and the Jews: The Prohibition against Entering Jerusalem: History and Historiography," *Zion* 60 (1995) 129–78 (Heb.).

———, "Historical Aspects of the Christian-Jewish Polemic Concerning the Church of Jerusalem in the Fourth Century" (2 vols.; Ph.D. diss., Hebrew University, 1993) (Heb.).

Isaac, Benjamin H., "Cassius Dio on the Revolt of Bar Kokhba," *SCI* 7 (1983–84) 68–76.

———, "Inscriptions from Jerusalem after the first Revolt," *The History of Jerusalem: The Roman and Byzantine Periods, 70–638 CE* (ed. Yoram Tsafrir and Shmuel Safrai; Jerusalem: Yad Yitshak Ben-Tsevi, 1999), 167–79 (Heb.).

———, *The Limits of Empire: The Roman Army in the East* (rev. ed.; Oxford: Clarendon, 1992).

————, "Roman Administration and Urbanization," *Greece and Rome in Eretz Israel: Collected Essays* (ed. A. Kasher et al.; Jerusalem: Yad Yitshak Ben-Tsevi, 1990) 151–59.

————, "Roman Colonies in Judaea: The Foundation of Aelia Capitolina," *Talanta* 12–13 (1980–81) 31–54.

Isaac, Benjamin H., and Aharon Oppenheimer, "The Revolt of Bar Kokhba: Ideology and Modern Scholarship," *JJS* 36 (1985) 33–60.

Japhet, Sara, "From the King's Sanctuary to the Chosen City," *Jerusalem: Its Sanctity and Centrality to Judaism, Christianity and Islam* (ed. Lee I. Levine; New York: Continuum, 1999), 3–15.

Jasper, Ronald C. D., and Geoffrey J. Cuming, *Prayers of the Eucharist: Early and Reformed* (3rd ed.; New York: Pueblo, 1987).

Jastrow, Marcus, *A Dictionary of the Targumim, the Talmud Babli and Yerushalmi and the Midrashic Literature* (2 vols.; London: Luzac, 1903; repr., New York: Pardes, 1950).

Jeremias, Joachim, "Golgotha und der heilige Felsen," *Angelos* 2 (1926) 74–128.

————, *The Rediscovery of Bethesda, John 5:2* (New Testament Archaeology Monograph 1; Louisville, Ky.: Southern Baptist Theological Seminary, 1966).

————, "Wo lag Golgotha und das Heilige Grab?" *Angelos* 1 (1925) 141–73.

————, "Die 'Zinne' des Tempels (Mt. 4,5; Lk 4,9)," *ZDPV* 59 (1936) 195–208.

Jones, F. Stanley, "The Martyrdom of James in Hegesippus, Clement of Alexandria, and Christian Apocrypha, Including Nag Hammadi: A Study of the Textual Relations," *SBLSP* 29 (1990) 322–35.

Juel, Donald H., "The Messiah and the Temple: A Study of Jesus' Trial before the Sanhedrin in the Gospel of Mark" (Ph.D. diss., Yale University, 1973).

Kalmin, Richard, "Midrash, Mishnah, and Gemara: The Jewish Predilection for Justified Law," *Conservative Judaism* 39:4 (1987) 78–84.

Kaufman, Asher S., "The Meaning of the Temple Mount," *Asufot* 2 (1988) 7–16 (Heb).

————, "The Temple Compound Made Rectangular," *Proceedings of the Eleventh World Congress of Jewish Studies* (4 vols. in 9; Jerusalem: World Union of Jewish Studies, 1994), 1:46.

Keil, Carl F., *Commentar über die Bücher der Makkabäer* (Leipzig: Dörffling & Franke, 1875).

Kelly, John N. D., *Early Christian Creeds* (3rd ed.; New York: D. McKay, 1972).

————, *Jerome: His Life, Writings and Controversies* (London: Duckworth, 1975).

Kermode, Frank, *The Genesis of Secrecy: On the Interpretation of Narrative* (Cambridge: Harvard University Press, 1979).

Kessler, Edward, *Bound by the Bible: Jews, Christians and the Sacrifice of Isaac* (Cambridge: Cambridge University Press, 2004).

Kimelman, Reuven, "Rabbi Yohanan and Origen on the Song of Songs: A Third-Century Jewish-Christian Disputation," *HTR* 73 (1980) 567–95.

Kindler, Arie, and Alla Stein, *A Bibliography of the City Coinage of Palestine: From the 2nd Century B.C. to the 3rd Century A.D.* (BAR 374; Oxford: Biblical Archaeology Review, 1987).

Kittel, Gerhard, ed., *Theologisches Wörterbuch zum Neuen Testament* (10 vols.; Stuttgart: Kohlhammer, 1932–79).

Klauck, Hans J., "Die heilige Stadt: Jerusalem bei Philo und Lukas," *Kairos* 28 (1986) 129–51.

Klijn, Albertus F. J., *The Acts of Thomas* (NovTSup 5; Leiden: Brill, 1962).

Kohut, Alexander. *Aruch Completum* (Vienna, 1878).

Konrad, Robert, "Das himmlische und das irdische Jerusalem im mittelalterlichen Denken," *Speculum Historiale* (ed. Clemens Bauer et al.; Munich: Alber, 1965), 523–40.

Kopp, Clemens, *The Holy Places of the Gospels* (New York: Herder & Herder, 1963).

Kraeling, Carl H., *Gerasa: City of the Decapolis* (New Haven: American School of Oriental Research, 1938).

Krauss, Samuel, *Griechische und lateinische Lehnwörter im Talmud, Midrasch und Targum* (Berlin: S. Calvary, 1899; repr., Hildesheim: G. Olms, 1964).

———, "The Jews in the Works of the Church Fathers," *JQR*, o.s., 5 (1893) 122–57; 6 (1894) 82–99, 225–61.

———, *Qadmoniot ha-Talmud* (2 vols. in 4; Berlin and Vienna: Benjamin-Hertz, 1924).

———, *Synagogale Altertümer* (Berlin: Harz, 1922).

Kripke, Saul A., *Naming and Necessity* (Cambridge: Harvard University Press, 1980; repr., Oxford: Blackwell, 1998).

Kühnel, Bianca, *From the Earthly to the Heavenly Jerusalem* (RQ suppl. 42; Rome: Herder, 1987).

Kümmel, Werner G., *The Theology of the New Tesatament According to Its Major Witnesses: Jesus, Paul, John* (trans. John E. Steely; Nashville: Abingdon, 1973).

Lampe, Geoffrey W. H., *A Patristic Greek Lexicon* (Oxford: Clarendon, 1961).

Lang, David M., *The Lives and Legends of the Georgian Saint* (2nd ed.; London: Mowbrays, 1976).

Larsson, Edvin, "Temple-Criticism and the Jewish Heritage: Some Reflections on Acts 6–7," *NTS* 39 (1993) 379–95.

Lauverjat, Marc, "L'autre regard Marc 12:37b–13:2," *ETR* 55 (1980) 416–19.

Lawlor, Hugh J., *Eusebiana* (Oxford: Clarendon, 1912).

Leclercq, Henri, "Chandeleur," *DACL* 3:1, cols. 207–10.

———, "Pélerinages aux lieux saints," *DACL* 14:1, cols. 65–176.

Lerch, David, *Isaaks Opferung christlich gedeutet: Eine auslegungsgeschichtliche Untersuchung* (BHT 12; Tübingen: J. Mohr, 1950).

Levenson, David B., "Julian's Attempt to Rebuild the Temple: An Inventory of Ancient and Medieval Sources," *Of Scribes and Scrolls: Studies on the Hebrew Bible, Intertestamental Judaism, and Christian Origins* (ed. Harold W. Attridge et al.; Lanham, Md.: University Press of America, 1990), 261–79.

———, "A Source and Tradition Critical Study of the Stories of Julian's Attempt to Rebuild the Jerusalem Temple" (Ph.D. diss., Harvard University, 1979).

Levenson, Jon D., *Sinai and Zion: An Entry into the Jewish Bible* (Minneapolis: Winston, 1985; repr., San Francisco: Harper & Row, 1987).

Lévi-Strauss, Claude, *Structural Anthropology* (trans. Claire Jacobson and Brooke G. Schoepf; New York: Basic Books, 1963).

Levick, Barbara, *Roman Colonies in Southern Asia Minor* (Oxford: Clarendon, 1967).

Levine, Lee I., *The Ancient Synagogue: The First Thousand Years* (New Haven: Yale University Press, 2000).

———, "The History and Significance of the Menorah in Antiquity," *From Dura to Sepphoris: Studies in Jewish Art and Society in Late Antiquity* (ed. Lee I. Levine and Zeev Weiss; JRA suppl. 40; Portsmouth, R.I.: International Journal, 2000), 131–53.

———, ed., *Jerusalem: Its Sanctity and Centrality to Judaism, Christianity and Islam* (New York: Continuum, 1999).

Levy, Jacob, *Wörterbuch über die Talmudim und Midraschim* (4 vols.; Berlin: B. Harz, 1924).

Liddell, Henry G., and Robert Scott, *A Greek-English Lexicon* (9th ed.; Oxford: Clarendon, 1948).

Lieberman, Saul, *Hellenism in Jewish Palestine* (New York: Jewish Theological Seminary of America, 1950; repr., 1994).

————, *Tosefta Kifshutah: A Comprehensive Commentary on the Tosefta* (10 vols.; Jerusalem: Bet ha-midrash le-rabanim sheba-Amerikah, 1955–88).

Lifshitz, Baruch, "Jérusalem sous la domination romaine: Histoire de la ville depuis la conquête de Pompée jusqu' à Constantin (63 a.C.–325 p.C.)," *ANRW* II.8 (1977) 444–89.

Lightfoot, Robert H., *Locality and Doctrine in the Gospels* (London: Hodder & Stoughton, 1938).

Limor, Ora, "Christian Sacred Space and the Jew," *From Witness to Witchcraft: Jews and Judaism in Medieval Christian Thought* (ed. Jeremy Cohen; Wolfenbütteler Mittelalter-Studien 11; Wiesbaden: Harrassowitz, 1996), 55–77.

————, "The Origins of a Tradition: King David's Tomb on Mount Zion," *Traditio* 44 (1988) 453–62.

Linder, Amnon, "Ecclesia and Synagoga in the Medieval Myth of Constantine the Great," *RBPH* 54 (1976) 1023–60.

————, "Jerusalem between Judaism and Christianity in the Byzantine Period," *Cathedra* 11 (1979) 109–19 (Heb.).

Linski, Leonard, *Names and Descriptions* (Chicago: University of Chicago Press, 1977).

Littell, Franklin H., *The Macmillan Atlas History of Christianity* (New York: Macmillan, 1976).

Livne-Kafri, Ofer, "Jerusalem 'The Navel of the World' in Islamic Tradition," *Cathedra* 69 (1993) 79–105 (Heb.).

————, "The Moslim Traditions 'In Praise of Jerusalem' ('Fadai'l AL-Quds'): Diversity and Complexity," *AION* 58 (1998) 165–92.

Luttikhuizen, Gerard P., *The Revelation of Elchasai* (TSAJ 8; Tübingen: J. Mohr, 1985).

MacDonald, William L., *The Architecture of the Roman Empire* (2 vols.; New Haven: Yale University Press, 1982–86).

MacMullen, Ramsay, *Paganism in the Roman Empire* (New Haven: Yale University Press, 1981).

Magen, Itzhak, "Gerizim, Mount," *NEAEHL* 2:484–92.

————, "Mount Gerizim and the Samaritans," *Early Christianity in Context: Monuments and Documents* (ed. Frédéric Manns and E. Alliata; SBF 38; Jerusalem: Franciscan Printing Press, 1993), 91–148.

————, "Shechem-Neapolis," *NEAEHL* 4:1354–59.

Magness, Jodi, *Jerusalem Ceramic Chronology Circa, 200–800 CE* (JSOT/ASOR Monograph Series 9; Sheffield: JSOT Press, 1993).

————, "A Mithraeum in Jerusalem?" *One Land, Many Cultures: Archaeological Studies in Honor of S. Loffreda* (ed. G. Claudio Bottini et al.; SBF 41; Jerusalem: Franciscan Printing Press, 2003), 163–71.

————, "The North Wall of Aelia Capitolina," *The Archaeology of Jordan and Beyond: Essays in Honor of James A. Sauer* (ed. Lawrence E. Stager et al.; Winona Lake, Ind.: Eisenbrauns, 2000), 328–39.

Maier, Johann, "The Architectural History of the Temple in Jerusalem in the Light of the Temple Scroll," *Temple Scroll Studies* (ed. George J. Brooke; JSPSup 7; Sheffield: JSOT Press, 1989).

Malter, Henry, *The Treatise Taʿanit of the Babylonian Talmud* (New York: Publications of the American Academy of Jewish Research, 1930).

Mandel, Paul, "'Birah' as an Architectural Term in Rabbinic Literature," *Tarbiz* 61 (1992) 195–217 (Heb.).

Mango, Cyril, "The Temple Mount, AD 614–638," *Bayt al-Maqdis: Abd al-Malik's Jerusalem* (ed. Julian Raby and Jeremy Johns; 2 vols.; Oxford Studies in Islamic Art 9; Oxford: Oxford University Press, 1992–99), 1:1–16.

Mann, Sylvia, *Jerusalem, Judea and Samaria* (Weidenfeld Colour Guides to Israel; London: Weidenfeld, 1973).

Manns, Frédéric, *Bibliographie du Judeo-Chritianisme* (*SBF* 13; Jerusalem: Franciscan Printing Press, 1979).

————, "A Survey of Recent Studies on Early Christianity," *Early Christianity in Context: Monuments and Documents* (ed. Frédéric Manns and E. Alliata; *SBF* 38; Jerusalem: Franciscan Printing Press, 1993), 17–25.

Maraval, Pierre, *Lieux saints et pèlerinages d'Orient: Histoire et géographie des origines à la conquête arabe* (Paris: Cerf, 1985).

Marinatos, Nanno, and Robin Hägg, eds., *Greek Sanctuaries: New Approaches* (London: Routledge, 1993).

Marshall, John W., *Parables of War: Reading John's Jewish Apocalypse* (Études sur le christianisme et le judaïsme 10; Waterloo, Ont.: Corporation canadienne des sciences religieuses, Wilfrid Laurier University Press, 2001).

Mathews, Thomas F., *The Clash of Gods: A Reinterpretation of Early Christian Art* (Princeton: Princeton University Press, 1993).

Mattingly, David J., ed., *Dialogues in Roman Imperialism: Power, Discourse, and Discrepant Experience in the Roman Empire* (JRA suppl. 23; Portsmouth, R.I.: Journal of Roman Archaeology, 1997).

Mauss, C., *La piscine de Béthesda à Jérusalem* (Paris: E. Leroux, 1888).

Mayer, Maximilian, "Temenos," *PWRE* V A, cols. 435–58.

Mazar, Benjamin, *The Excavations in the Old City of Jerusalem near the Temple Mount: Preliminary Report of the Second and Third Seasons, 1969–1970* (Jerusalem: Institute of Archeology, Hebrew University, 1971).

————, *The Mountain of the Lord* (Garden City, N.Y.: Doubleday, 1975).

Mazar, Eilat, "The Camp of the Tenth Roman Legion at the Foot of the South-West Corner of the Temple Mount Enclosure in Jerusalem," *New Studies on Jerusalem: Proceedings of the Fifth Conference* (ed. Avi Faust and Eyal Baruch; Ramat Gan: Ingeborg Rennert Center for Jerusalem Studies and Yad Yitshak Ben-Tsevi, 1999), 52–67 (Heb.).

————, "The Ophel Wall in Jerusalem in the Byzantine Period," *Recent Innovations in the Study of Jerusalem: The First Conference* (ed. Zeev Safrai and Avi Faust; Ramat Gan: Ingeborg Rennert Center for Jerusalem Studies, 1995), 48–63.

————, "The Roman-Byzantine Bathhouse at the Foot of the Western Wall of the Temple Mount," *New Studies on Jerusalem: Proceedings of the Sixth Conference* (ed. Avi Faust and Eyal Baruch; Ramat Gan: Ingeborg Rennert Center for Jerusalem Studies and Yad Yitshak Ben-Tsevi, 2000), 87–102 (Heb.).

McGiffert, Arthur C., *The Church History of Eusebius* (*NPNF* series 2; Grand Rapids, Mich.: Eerdmans, 1986).

McGuckin, John A., "Origen and the Jews," *Christianity and Judaism* (ed. Diana Wood; Studies in Christian History 29; Oxford: Ecclesiastical History Society, 1992), 1–13.

McKelvey, R. J., "Christ the Cornerstone," *NTS* 8 (1961–1962) 352–59.

———, *The New Temple: The Church in the New Testament* (London: Oxford University Press, 1969).

Mendels, Doron, *The Rise and Fall of Jewish Nationalism* (New York: Doubleday, 1992).

Meshorer, Yaakov, *Ancient Jewish Coinage* (2 vols.; Dix Hills, N.Y.: Amphora Books, 1982).

———, *City Coins of Eretz-Israel and the Decapolis in the Roman Period* (Jerusalem: Israel Museum, 1985).

———, *The Coinage of Aelia Capitolina* (Jerusalem: Israel Museum, 1989).

Meyer, Heinrich A. W., *Kritisch exegetischer Kommentar über das Neue Testament*, I:2: *Evangelien des Markus und Lukas* (Göttingen: Vandenhoeck & Ruprecht, 1867).

Milik, Jósef T., "La topographie de Jérusalem vers la fin de l'époque byzantine," *MUSJ* 37 (1960–61) 127–89.

Millar, Fergus, "The Roman *Coloniae* of the Near East: A Study of Cultural Relations," *Roman Eastern Policy and Other Studies in Roman History* (ed. Heikki Solin and Mika Kajava; Commentationes humanarum litterarum 91; Helsinki: Finnish Society of Sciences and Letters, 1990), 7–58.

———, *A Study of Cassius Dio* (Oxford: Clarendon, 1964).

Miller, Timothy S., *The Birth of the Hospital in the Byzantine Empire* (Bulletin of the History of Medicine 10; Baltimore: John Hopkins University Press, 1985).

Mitchell, Stephen, *Anatolia: Land, Men, and Gods in Asia Minor* (2 vols.; Oxford: Clarendon, 1993).

Mommert, Carl, *Der Teich Bethesda zu Jerusalem und das Jerusalem des Pilgers von Bordeaux* (Leipzig: E. Haberland, 1907).

Mommsen, Theodor, "Einleitung zu Rufin," *Eusebius Werke: Die Kirchengeschichte* (ed. Eduard Schwartz; GCS 9:3; Leipzig: J. C. Hinrichs, 1909).

Montgomery, James A., *A Critical and Exegetical Commentary on the Book of Daniel* (ICC; New York: Scribner, 1927).

Moore, Carey A., *Judith: A New Translation with Introduction and Commentary* (Garden City, N.Y.: Doubleday, 1985).

———, *Tobit: A New Translation with Introduction and Commentary* (New York: Doubleday, 1996).

Moore, Stephen D., *Poststructuralism and the New Testament: Derrida and Foucault at the Foot of the Cross* (Minneapolis: Fortress, 1994).

Mor, Menahem, *The Bar-Kochba Revolt: Its Extent and Effect* (Jerusalem: Yad Yitshak Ben-Tsevi, 1991), 179–80 (Heb.).

———, "The Samaritans and the Bar-Kokhbah Revolt," *The Samaritans* (ed. Alan D. Crown; Tübingen: Mohr, 1989), 19–31.

Moulton James H., and Wilbert F. Howard, *A Grammar of New Testament Greek* (2 vols.; Edinburgh: T&T Clark, 1919–29).

Mulder, Martin J., ed., *Mikra* (CRINT II.1; Assen: Van Gorcum, 1990).

Murphy, Francis X., *Rufinus of Aquileia (345–411): His Life and Works* (Washington, D.C.: Catholic University of America Press, 1945).

Murphy-O'Connor, Jerome, "The Location of the Capitol in Aelia Capitolina," *RB* 101 (1994) 407–15.

Nau, François, "Deux épisodes de l'histoire juive sous Théodose II (423 et 438) d'après la vie de Barsauma le Syrien," *REJ* 83 (1927) 184–206.

———, "Résumé de monographies syriaques: Histoire de Barsauma de Nisibe," *ROC* 19 (1914).

Nautin, Pierre, "Épiphane (10)," *DHGE* 15, cols. 617–31.

———, *Origène: Sa vie et son oeuvre* (Paris: Beauchesne, 1977).

Neirynck, F., et al., eds., *The Gospel of Mark: A Cumulative Bibliography, 1950–1990* (Leuven: Peeters, 1992).

Nelson, Raymond J., *Naming and Reference: The Link of Word to Object* (London: Routledge, 1992).

Nestle, Eberhard, "Alttestamentliches aus Eusebius," *ZAW* 29 (1909) 57–62.

Neuhaus, Günter O., *Studien zu den poetischen Stücken im 1. Makkabäerbuch* (Würzburg: Echter Verlag, 1974).

Neusner, Jacob, *The Rabbinic Traditions about the Pharisees before 70* (3 vols.; Leiden: Brill, 1971).

Newman, Hillel I., "Jerome and the Jews" (Ph.D. diss., Hebrew University, 1997) (Heb.).

Nibley, Hugh, "Christian Envy of the Temple," *JQR* 50 (1959) 97–123, 229–40.

Nickelsburg, George W. E., *Jewish Literature between the Bible and the Mishnah* (Philadelphia: Fortress, 1981).

———, "Stories of Biblical and Early Post Biblical Times," *Jewish Writings of the Second Temple Period* (ed. Michael E. Stone; CRINT 2.2; Assen: Van Gorcum, 1984), 33–87.

Nicolet, Claude, *L'inventaire du monde: Géographie et politique aux origins de l'Empire romain* (Paris: Fayard, 1988).

Nikiprowetzky, Valentin, "La spiritualisation des sacrifices et le culte sacrificiel au Temple de Jérusalem chez Philon d'Alexandrie," *Semitica* 17 (1967) 97–116.

Noam, Vered, "Megilat Ta'anit and the Scholion: Their Nature, Period and Sources" (Ph.D. diss., Hebrew University, 1997) (Heb.).

Nora, Pierre, ed., *Les lieux de mémoire* (3 vols. in 7; Paris: Gallimard, 1984–86); repr. as *Realms of Memory* (trans. Arthur Goldhammer; 3 vols.; New York: Columbia University Press, 1996–98).

Ottaway, Patrick, *Book of Roman York* (London: Batsford, 1993).

Ousterhout, Robert G., "The Temple, the Sepulchre, and the *Martyrion* of the Savior," *Gesta* 29 (1990) 44–53.

Pagels, Elaine H., *The Johannine Gospel in Gnostic Exegesis* (SBLMS 17; Nashville: Abingdon, 1973).

———, *The Gnostic Gospels* (New York: Random House, 1979).

Paget, James C., *The Epistle of Barnabas: Outlook and Background* (WUNT 2:64; Tübingen: Mohr, 1994).

Parmentier, Martin, "No Stone upon Another? Reactions of Church Fathers against the Emperor Julian's Attempt to Rebuild the Temple," *The Centrality of Jerusalem: Historical Perspectives* (ed. Marcel Poorthuis and Chana Safrai; Kampen: Kok Pharos, 1996), 143–59.

Parrot, André, *Golgotha and the Church of the Holy Sepulchre* (trans. Edwin Hudson; New York: Philosophical Library, 1957).

Parry, Donald W., "Sinai as Sanctuary and Mountain of God," *By Study and Also by Faith: Essays in Honor of Hugh W. Nibley* (ed. John M. Lundquist and Stephen D. Ricks; 2 vols.; Salt Lake City: Deseret, 1990), 1:482–500.

Payne-Smith, Robert, *Thesaurus Syriacus* (2 vols.; Oxford: Clarendon, 1879–1898).

Peleg, Orit, "Roman Marble Sculpture from the Temple Mount Excavations," *New Studies on Jerusalem: Proceedings of the Seventh Conference* (ed. Avi Faust and Eyal Baruch; Ramat-Gan: Ingeborg Rennert Center for Jerusalem Studies and Yad Yitshak Ben-Tsevi, 2001), 129–49 (Heb.).

Perler, Othmar, *Méliton de Sardes: Sur la Pâque et fragments* (*SC* 123; Paris: Cerf, 1966).

Peters, Francis E., *Jerusalem: The Holy City in the Eyes of Chroniclers, Visitors, Pilgrims, and Prophets from the Days of Abraham to the Beginnings of Modern Times* (Princeton: Princeton University Press, 1985).

Pierotti, Ermete, *Jerusalem Explored* (trans. Thomas G. Bonney; 2 vols.; London: Bell & Daldy, 1865).

Pierre, Marie J., and Jourdain M. Rousée, "Sainte-Marie de la Probatique état et orientation des recherches," *PrOrChr* 31 (1981) 23–42.

Poorthuis, Marcel, and Chana Safrai, eds., *The Centrality of Jerusalem: Historical Perspectives* (Kampen: Kok Pharos, 1996).

Pratscher, Wilhelm, *Der Herrenbruder Jakobus und die Jakobustradition* (FRLANT 139; Göttingen: Vandenhoeck & Ruprecht, 1987).

Purvis, James D., *Jerusalem the Holy City: A Bibliography* (2 vols.; Metuchen, N.J.: Scarecrow, 1988–91).

Qausten, Johannes, *Patrology* (4 vols.; Utrecht: Spectrum, 1950–86).

Rakob, Friedrich, "The Making of Augustan Carthage," *Romanization and the City: Creation, Transformations and Failures* (ed. Elizabeth Fentress; JRA suppl. 38; Portsmouth, R.I.: Journal of Roman Archaeology, 2000), 73–82.

Reich, Roni, "Four Notes on Jerusalem," *IEJ* 37 (1987) 164–67.

Reif, Stefan F., "Jerusalem in Jewish Liturgy," *Jerusalem: Its Sanctity and Centrality to Judaism, Christianity, and Islam* (ed. Lee I. Levine; New York: Continuum, 1999), 424–37.

Reinach, Théodore, *Histoire des Israélites* (4th ed.; Paris: Hachette, 1910).

Reiner, Elchanan, "Pilgrims and Pilgrimage to Eretz Yisrael, 1099–1517" (Ph.D. diss., Hebrew University, 1988) (Heb.).

Remus, Harold, "Justin Martyr's Argument with Judaism," *Anti-Judaism in Early Christianity: Separation and Polemic* (ed. Stephen G. Wilson; Waterloo, Ont.: Wilfrid Laurier University Press, 1986), 59–80.

Rengstorf, Karl H., ed., *A Complete Concordance to Flavius Josephus* (4 vols.; Leiden: Brill, 1973–83).

Rennie, Bryan S., ed., *Changing Religious Worlds: The Meaning and End of Mircea Eliade* (Albany: State University of New York Press, 2001).

Renwick, David A., *Paul, the Temple, and the Presence of God* (BJS 224; Atlanta: Scholars Press, 1991).

Rinaldi, Giancarlo, *Biblia Gentium* (Rome: Libreria Sacre Scritture, 1989).

Ritmeyer, Leen, "The Architectural Development of the Temple Mount in Jerusalem" (Ph.D. diss., University of Manchester, 1992).

———, "Locating the Original Temple Mount," *BARev* 18:2 (1992) 25–45.

———, "Reconstructing Herod's Temple Mount in Jerusalem," *BARev* 15:6 (1989) 23–53.

Robertson, Robert. G., "The Dialogue of Timothy and Aquila: A Critical Text, Introduction to the Manuscript Evidence and an Inquiry into the Sources and Literary Relationships" (Ph.D. diss., Harvard, 1986).

Robinson, Edward, *Biblical Researches in Palestine, Mount Sinai and Arabia Petraea* (3 vols.; Boston: Crocker & Brewster, 1841).

Robinson, Thomas A., *The Bauer Thesis Examined: The Geography of Heresy in the Early Christian Church* (Lewiston, N.Y.: E. Mellon, 1988).

Rokeah, David, *Jews, Pagans and Christians in Conflict* (*StPB* 33; Leiden: Brill, 1982).

Rondeau, Marie-Josèphe, *Les commentaires patristiques du Psautier (IIIe–Ve siècles)* (*OCA* 219; Rome: Pontifical Institutum Studiorum Orientalium, 1982).

Rondeau, Marie-Josèphe, and J. Kirchmeyer, "Eusèbe de Césarée," *DSP* 4:2, cols. 1687–90.

Rondorf, W., "Le sacrifice eucharistique," *ThZ* 25 (1969) 335–53.

Rosenau, Helen, *Vision of the Temple: The Image of the Temple of Jerusalem in Judaism and Christianity* (London: Oresko, 1979).

Rousée, Jourdain M., "L'église Sainte-Marie de la Probatique: Chronologie des sanctuaires à Sainte-Anne de Jérusalem d'après les fouilles récentes," *Atti del VI congresso internazionale di archeologia cristiana* (Studi diantichità cristina 26; Rome: Pontificio Istituto di archeologia cristiana, 1965), 169–76.

Rowland, Christopher C., "The Second Temple: Focus of Ideological Struggle," *Templum Amicitiae: Essays on the Second Temple Presented to Ernst Bammel* (ed. William Horbury; JSNTSup 48; Sheffield: JSOT Press, 1991), 175–98.

Safrai, Shmuel, "The Duty of Pilgrimage to Jerusalem and Its Performance during the Period of the Second Temple," *Zion* 25 (1960) 67–84 (Heb.).

———, "Jerusalem in the Halacha of the Second Temple Period," *The Centrality of Jerusalem: Historical Perspectives* (ed. Marcel Poorthuis and Chana Safrai; Kampen: Kok Pharos, 1996), 94–113.

———, "Pilgrimage to Jerusalem after the Destruction of the Second Temple," *Jerusalem in the Second Temple Period: Abraham Schalit Memorial Volume* (ed. Aharon Oppenheimer et al.; Jerusalem: Yad Yitshak Ben-Tsevi, 1980), 376–93 (Heb.).

———, "The Temple," *The Jewish People in the First Century* (ed. Shmuel Safrai et al.; 2 vols.; CRINT 1.2; Assen: Van Gorcum, 1974–76), 2:865–907.

———, "Temple: Second Temple," *EJ* 15 (1971) col. 965.

Safrai, Zeev, and Chana Safrai, "The Sanctity of Eretz Israel and Jerusalem," *Jews and Judaism in the Second Temple, Mishnah and Talmud Period: Studies in Honor of Shmuel Safrai* (ed. Isaiah Gafni et al.; Jerusalem: Yad Yitshak Ben-Tsevi, 1993), 344–71 (Heb.).

Sanders, Ed P., *Jesus and Judaism* (Philadelphia: Fortress, 1985).

Sariola, Heikki, *Markus und das Gesetz: Eine redaktionskritische Untersuchung* (Annales academiae scientiarum Fennicae dissertationes humanarum litterarum 56; Helsinki: Suomalainen Tiedeakatemia, 1990).

Satran, David, *Biblical Prophets in Byzantine Palestine* (*SVTP* 11; Leiden: Brill, 1995).

Savignac, Raphaël, "Inscription romaine et sépultures au nord de Jérusalem," *RB* 13 (1904) 90–99.

Schäfer, Peter, *Der Bar Kokhba-Aufstand: Studien zum zweiten jüdischen Krieg gegen Rom* (TSAJ 1; Tübingen: Mohr, 1981).

———, "Hadrian's Policy in Judaea and the Bar Kokhba Revolt: A Reassessment," *A*

Tribute to Geza Vermes: Essays on Jewish and Christian Literature and History (ed. Philip R. Davies and Richard T. White; JSOTSup 100; Sheffield: JSOT Press, 1990), 288–89.

Schein, Sylvia, "Between Mount Moriah and the Holy Sepulchre: The Changing Traditions of the Temple Mount in the Central Middle Ages," *Traditio* 40 (1984) 175–95.

Schelkle, Karl H., *Theologie des Neuen Testaments* (4 vols. in 5; Düsseldorf: Patmos-Verlag, 1974).

Schick, Conrad, *Beit el Makdas oder der alte Tempelplatz zu Jerusalem* (Jerusalem: Selbst-verlag des Verfassers, 1887).

———, *Die Stiftshütte der Temple in Jerusalem und der Tempelplatz der Jetztzeit* (Berlin: Weidmannsche buchhandlung, 1896).

Schiffman, Lawrence H., "Architecture and Law: The Temple and Its Courtyards in the Temple Scroll," *From Ancient Israel to Modern Judaism: Essays in Honor of Marvin Fox* (ed. Jacob Neusner et al.; 4 vols.; BJS; Atlanta: Scholars Press, 1989), 1:267–84.

———, "Exclusion from the Sanctuary and the City of the Sanctuary in the Temple Scroll," *HAR* 9 (1985) 301–20.

———, "The Qumran Scrolls and Rabbinic Judaism," *The Dead Sea Scrolls after Fifty Years: A Comprehensive Assessment* (ed. Peter W. Flint and James C. VanderKam; 2 vols.; Leiden: Brill, 1998–99), 2:552–71.

———, *Reclaiming the Dead Sea Scrolls* (Philadelphia: Jewish Publication Society, 1994).

Schlatter, Adolf, *Die Tage Trajans und Hadrians* (BFCT I.3; Gütersloh: Bertelsmann, 1897).

———, *Zur Topographie und Geschichte Palästinas* (Stuttgart: n.p., 1893).

Schlosser, Jacques, "La parole de Jésus sur la fin du Temple," *NTS* 36 (1990) 398–414.

Schmidt, Karl L., "Jerusalem als Urbild und Abbild," *Eranos-Jahrbuch* 18 (1950) 207–48.

Schneemelcher, Wilhelm, ed., *New Testament Apocrypha* (2 vols.; rev. ed.; Cambridge: J. Clarke, 1991–92).

Schneider, Gerhard, *Die Apostelgeschichte* (2 vols.; HTKNT 5; Freiburg: Herder, 1980–82).

Schoedel, William R., "A Gnostic Interpretation of the Fall of Jerusalem: The First Apocalypse of James," *NT* 33 (1991) 152–78.

———, *Ignatius of Antioch: A Commentary on the Letters of Ignatius of Antioch* (ed. Helmut Koester; Philadelphia: Fortress, 1985).

Schoeps, Hans J., *Theologie und Geschichte des Judenchristentums* (Tübingen: Mohr, 1949).

Schürer, Emil, *The History of the Jewish People in the Age of Jesus Christ* (rev. & ed. by Geza Vermes and Ferus Miller; trans. T. A. Burkill et al.; 3 vols.; Edinburgh: T&T Clark, 1973–87); translated from *Geschichte des Jüdischen Volkes im Zeitalter Jesu Christi* (3 vols.; 3rd ed.; Leipzig: J. C. Hinrichs, 1901).

Schwartz, Daniel R., *Studies in the Jewish Background of Christianity* (WUNT 60; Tübingen: Mohr, 1992).

———, "Temple or City: What Did Hellenistic Jews See in Jerusalem?" *The Centrality of Jerusalem: Historical Perspectives* (ed. Marcel Poorthuis and Chana Safrai; Kampen: Kok Pharos, 1996), 114–27.

Schwartz, Joshua, "Be'er ha-Qar, Bôr Heqer and the Seleucid Akra," *Cathedra* 37 (1985) 3–16 (Heb.).

————, "The Encaenia of the Church of the Holy Sepulchre, the Temple of Solomon and the Jews," *ThZ* 43 (1987) 265–81.

————, "Gallus, Julian and Anti-Christian Polemic in Pesikta Rabbati," *ThZ* 46 (1990) 1–19.

————, *Jewish Settlement in Judaea after the Bar Kochba War until the Arab Conquest, 135 C.E.–640 C.E.* (Jerusalem: Magnes, 1986) (Heb.).

————, "Once More on the Nicanor Gate," *HUCA* 62 (1991) 245–83.

————, "The Temple in Jerusalem: Birah and Baris in Archaeology and Literature," *The Centrality of Jerusalem: Historical Perspectives* (ed. Marcel Poorthuis and Chana Safrai; Kampen: Kok Pharos, 1996), 29–49.

Schwier, Helmut, *Tempel und Tempelzerstörung: Untersuchungen zu den theologischen und ideologischen Faktoren im ersten jüdisch-römischen Krieg, 66–74 n. Chr.* (*NTOA* 11; Göttingen: Vandenhoeck & Ruprecht, 1989).

Seeligman, Isaac A., "Jerusalem in Jewish-Hellenistic Thought," *Judah and Jerusalem: The Twelfth Archaeological Convention* (Jerusalem: Israel Exploration Society, 1957) (Heb.).

Segal, Arthur, *From Function to Monument: Urban Landscapes of Roman Palestine, Syria and Provincia Arabia* (Oxbow Monograph 66; Oxford: Oxbow Books, 1997).

Shotwell, Willis A., *The Biblical Exegesis of Justin Martyr* (London: S.P.C.K., 1965).

Shukster, Martin B., and Peter Richardson, "Temple and Beth Ha-Midrash in the Epistle of Barnabas," *Anti-Judaism in Early Christianity: Separation and Polemic* (ed. Stephen G. Wilson; Waterloo, Ont.: Wilfrid Laurier University Press, 1986), 17–31.

Sievers, Joseph, "Jerusalem, the Akra, and Josephus," *Josephus and the History of the Greco-Roman Period: Essays in Memory of Morton Smith* (ed. Fausto Parente and Joseph Sievers; StPB 41; Leiden: Brill, 1994), 195–209.

Simon, Marcel, *St. Stephen and the Hellenists in the Primitive Church* (London: Longmans, 1956).

————, *Verus Israel: Étude sur les relations entre chrétiens et juifs dans l'Empire romain, 135–425* (Paris: E. de Boccard, 1948).

Simons, Jan J., *Jerusalem in the Old Testament* (Leiden: Brill, 1952).

Skarsaune, Oskar, *The Proof from Prophecy: A Study in Justin Martyr's Proof-Text Tradition* (NovTSup 56; Leiden: Brill, 1987).

Smallwood, E. Mary, *The Jews under Roman Rule: From Pompey to Diocletian* (2nd ed.; SJLA 20; Leiden: Brill, 1981).

Smid, Harm R., *Protevangelium Jacobi: A Commentary* (trans. G. E. van Baaren-Pape; Assen: Van Gorcum, 1965).

Smith, Jonathan Z., *Drudgery Divine: On the Comparison of Early Christianities and the Religions of Late Antiquity* (JLCRS 14; London: School of Oriental and African Studies, University of London, 1990).

————, *To Take Place: Toward Theory in Ritual* (Chicago: University of Chicago Press, 1987).

Smith, Stephen H., "The Literary Structure of Mark 11:1–12:40," *NT* 31 (1989) 111.

Sokoloff, Michael., *A Dictionary of Jewish Palestinian Aramaic* (Ramat-Gan: Bar Ilan University Press, 1990).

Sophocles, Evangelinus A., *Greek Lexicon of the Roman and Byzantine Periods* (Cambridge: Harvard University Press, 1914).

Stadelmann, Helge, *Ben Sira als Schriftgelehrter* (WUNT 2:6; Tübingen: J. C. B. Mohr, 1980).

Stambaugh, John E., "The Functions of Roman Temples," *ANRW* II 16.1 (1978) 554–608.

Stemberger, Günter, *Jews and Christians in the Holy Land: Palestine in the Fourth Century* (trans. Ruth Tuschling; Edinburgh: T&T Clark, 2000); translated from *Juden und Christen im Heiligen Land: Palästina unter Konstantin und Theodosius* (Munich: C. H. Beck, 1987).

———, *Der Leib der Auferstehung* (*AnBib* 56; Rome: Biblical Institute Press, 1972).

Stern, Menahem, *The Documents on the History of the Hasmonaean Revolt* (3rd ed.; Jerusalem: Hakibuts ha-meuhad, 1983) (Heb.).

———, *Greek and Latin Authors on Jews and Judaism* (3 vols.; Jerusalem: Israel Academy of Sciences and Humanities, 1974–84).

Stewart, Aubrey, and Charles W. Wilson, *Itinerary from Bordeaux to Jerusalem* (PPTS 1:2; London: Committee of the Palestine Exploration Fund, 1896).

Stevenson, James, *The Catacombs: Rediscovered Monuments of Early Chritianity* (London: Thames & Hudson, 1978).

Stevenson, Kenneth, "The Origins and Development of Candlemas: A Struggle for Identity and Coherence," *EL* 102 (1988) 316–46.

Stinespring, William F., "Temple Research in Jerusalem," *Duke Divinity School Review* 29 (1964) 85–101.

Strack, Hermann L., and Günter Stemberger, *Introduction to the Talmud and Midrash* (ed. and trans. Markus Bockmuehl; rev. ed.; Minneapolis: Fortress, 1996).

Stroumsa, Guy G., "Mystical Jerusalems," *Jerusalem: Its Sanctity and Centrality to Judaism, Christianity and Islam* (ed. Lee I. Levine; New York: Continuum, 1999), 349–70.

———, "Which Jerusalem?" *Cathedra* 11 (1979) 118–24 (Heb.).

Sturtevant, Edgar H., *An Introduction to Linguistic Science* (New Haven: Yale University Press, 1947).

Sweet, John P. M., "A House Not Made with Hands," *Templum Amicitiae: Essays on the Second Temple Presented to Ernst Bammel* (ed. William Horbury; JSNTSup 48; Sheffield: JSOT Press, 1991), 368–90.

Sznol, Shifra, "Compounds with 'Anti' in Hellenistic Jewish Sources," *Filologia Neotestamentaria* 3 (1990) 109–13.

Talmon, Shmaryahu, "TABUR HAAREZ and the Comparative Method," *Tarbiz* 45 (1976) 163–77 (Heb.).

Taylor, Joan E., *Christians and the Holy Places: The Myth of Jewish-Christian Origins* (Oxford: Clarendon, 1993).

Telfer, William, "Constantine's Holy Land Plan," *SP* 1 (1957) 696–700 (= TU 63).

Terrien, Samuel, "The Omphalos Myth and Hebrew Religion," *VT* 20 (1970) 315–38.

Testa, Emmanuele, *The Faith of the Mother Church* (trans. Paul Rotondi; SBF 32; Jerusalem: Franciscan Printing Press, 1992).

Thornton, M. K., "Hadrian and His Reign," *ANRW* II.2 (1975) 432–76.

Thrupp, Joseph F., *Antient Jerusalem: A New Investigation into the History* (Cambridge: Macmillan, 1855).

Torjesen, Karen J., *Hermeneutical Procedure and Theological Method in Origen's Exegesis* (PTS 28; Berlin: De Gruyter, 1985).

Townsend, John T., "The Jerusalem Temple in the First Century," *God and His Temple* (ed. Lawrence E. Frizzell; South Orange, N.J.: Institute of Judaeo-Christian Studies, Seton Hall University, 1980), 48–65.

Trombley, Frank R., *Hellenic Religion and Christianization, c. 370–529* (2 vols.; Religions in the Graeco-Roman World 115; Leiden: Brill, 1993–94).

Tsafrir, Yoram, "Byzantine Jerusalem: The Configuration of a Christian City," *Jerusalem: Its Sanctity and Centrality to Judaism, Christianity and Islam* (ed. Lee I. Levine; New York: Continuum, 1999), 133–50.

———, "The Maps Used by Theodosius: On the Pilgrim Maps of the Holy Land and Jerusalem in the Sixth Century C.E.," *DOP* 40 (1986) 129–45.

———, "Muqaddasi's Gates of Jerusalem: A New Identification Based on Byzantine Sources," *IEJ* 27 (1977) 152–61.

———, "The Topography and Archaeology of Aelia Capitolina," *The History of Jerusalem: The Roman and Byzantine Periods, 70–638 CE* (ed. Yoram Tsafrir and Shmuel Safrai; Jerusalem: Yad Yitshak Ben-Tsevi, 1999), 115–66 (Heb.).

———, "Zion: the South-Western Hill of Jerusalem and Its Place in the Urban Development of the City in the Byzantine Period" (Ph.D. diss., Hebrew University Jerusalem, 1975) (Heb.).

Tsafrir, Yoram, and Shmuel Safrai, eds., *The History of Jerusalem: The Roman and Byzantine Periods, 70–638 CE* (Jerusalem: Yad Yitshak ben-Tsevi, 1999) (Heb.).

Tzarfati, G. Ben-Ami, "The Western Wall," *Leshonenu la-ʿAm* 45 (1992) 53–54 (Heb.).

Urbach, Efraim E., *The Sages: Their Concepts and Beliefs* (trans. Israel Abrahams; Jerusalem: Magnes, 1975).

———, "Yerushalim shel matah ve-yerushalim shel maʿalah," *The World of the Sages: Collected Essays* (Jerusalem: Magnes, 1988), 376–91.

Van Belle, Gilbert, *Johannine Bibliography 1966–1985: A Cumulative Bibliography on the Fourth Gospel* (Louvain: Peeters, 1988).

Van den Brink, Edwin, "Abraham's Sacrifice in Early Jewish and Early Christian Art," *The Sacrifice of Isaac: The Aqedah (Genesis 22) and Its Interpretations* (ed. Ed Noort and Eibert Tigchelaar; Themes in Biblical Narrative 4; Leiden: Brill, 2002), 140–51.

Van der Vliet, N., *"Sainte Marie où elle est née" et la Piscine Probatique* (Jerusalem and Paris: École Biblique, 1938).

Van Voorst, Robert E., *The Ascents of James: History and Theology of a Jewish-Christian Community* (SBLDS 112; Atlanta: Scholars Press, 1989).

Verhelst, Stéphane, "L'Apocalypse de Zacharie, Siméon et Jacques," *RB* 105 (1998) 81–104.

Vincent, Hugues, "Jérusalem d'après la Lettre d'Aristée," *RB* 17 (1908) 520–32; 18 (1909) 555–75.

Vincent, Hugues, and Félix-Marie Abel, *Jérusalem: Recherches de topographie d'archéologie et d'histoire* (2 vols. in 4; Paris: Gabalda, 1912–26).

———, *Jérusalem II: Jérusalem nouvelle* (Paris: Gabalda, 1922).

Vincent, Hugues, and A. M. Steve, *Jérusalem de l'Ancien Testament* (3 vols. in 2; Paris: Gabalda, 1954–56).

Walker, Peter W. L., *Holy City, Holy Places? Christian Attitudes to Jerusalem and the Holy Land in the Fourth Century* (Oxford: Clarendon, 1990).

———, *Jesus and the Holy City: New Testament Perspectives on Jerusalem* (Grand Rapids, Mich.: Eerdmans, 1996).

Wallace-Hadrill, David S., *Eusebius of Caesarea* (London: A. R. Mowbray, 1960).

Waller, Elizabeth P., "The Urban Development of Jerusalem under Christian Rule 325 to 638 C.E." (Ph.D. diss., New York University, 1987).

Walter, Nikolaus, "Tempelzerstörung und synoptiche Apokalypse," *ZNW* 57 (1966) 38–49.

Ward, Roy B., "James of Jerusalem in the First Two Centuries," *ANRW* II 26.1 (1992) 779–812.

Ward-Perkins, John B., "Can the Survival of an Ancient Town-Plan Be Used as Evidence of Dark-Age Urban Life," *Splendida civitas nostra: Studi archeologici in onore de Antonio Frova* (ed. Giuliana Cavalieri Manasse and Elisabetta Roffia; Rome: Quasar, 1995), 223–29.

Warren, Charles, *The Temple or the Tomb* (London: R. Bentley, 1880).

Wartensleben, A. Graf von, *Jerusalem: Gegenwärtiges und Vergangenes* (Berlin: P. Scheller, 1870).

Watzinger, Carl, *Denkmäler Palästinas* (2 vols.; Leipzig: J. C. Hinrichs, 1933–35).

Weiss, Zeev, and Ehud Netzer, *Promise and Redemption: A Synagogue Mosaic from Sepphoris* (Jerusalem: Israel Museum, 1996).

Weiss-Halivni, David, *Midrash, Mishnah, and Gemara: The Jewish Predilection for Justified Law* (Cambridge: Harvard University Press, 1986).

Welles, Charles B., *Royal Correspondence in the Hellenistic Period* (New Haven: Yale University Press, 1934).

Wellhausen, Julius, *Analyse der Offenbarung Johannis* (Abhandlungen der königlichen Gesellschaft der Wissenschaften zu Göttingen, philologisch-historische Klasse, n.f. IX:4; Berlin: Weidmann, 1907).

———, *Skizzen und Vorarbeiten* (6 vols.; Berlin: Georg Reimer, 1899).

Wharton, Annabel J., *Refiguring the Post Classical City: Dura Europos, Jerash, Jerusalem and Ravenna* (Cambridge: Cambridge University Press, 1995).

Whitby, Michael, and Mary Whitby, *Chronicon Paschale, 284–628 AD* (Liverpool: Liverpool University Press, 1989).

Whittaker, C. Richard, "Imperialism and Culture: The Roman Initiative," *Dialogues in Roman Imperialism: Power, Discourse, and Discrepant Experience in the Roman Empire* (ed. David J. Mattingly; JRA suppl. 23; Portsmouth, R.I.; Journal of Roman Archaeology, 1997), 143–63.

Wightman, Gregory J., *The Damascus Gate, Jerusalem: Excavations by C. M. Bennett and J. B. Hennessy at the Damascus Gate, Jerusalem, 1964–1966* (BAR 519; Oxford: BAR, 1989).

———, *The Walls of Jerusalem: From the Canaanites to the Mamluks* (Mediterranean Archaeology Supplement 4; Sydney: Meditarch, 1993).

Wilken, Robert L., "*In novissimuis diebus*: Biblical Promises, Jewish Hopes and Early Christian Exegesis," *JECS* 1 (1993) 1–19.

———, *John Chrysostom and the Jews: Rhetoric and Reality in the Late Fourth Century* (Berkeley: University of California Press, 1983).

———, *The Land Called Holy: Palestine in Christian History and Thought* (New Haven: Yale University Press, 1992).

———, "The Restoration of Israel in Biblical Prophecy: Christian and Jewish Responses in the Early Byzantine Period," *"To see ourselves as other see us": Christians, Jews, "Others" in Late Antiquity* (ed. Jacob Neusner and Ernest S. Freirichs; Chico, Calif.: Scholars Press, 1985), 445–53.

Wilkinson, John, "L'apport de Saint Jérome à la topographie," *RB* 81 (1974) 245–57.

————, "Christian Pilgrims in Jerusalem during the Byzantine Period," *PEQ* 108 (1976) 75–101.

————, *Egeria's Travels to the Holy Land* (2nd ed.; London: Aris & Phillips, 1981).

————, *Jerusalem as Jesus Knew It: Archaeology as Evidence* (London: Thames & Hudson, 1978).

————, *Jerusalem Pilgrims before the Crusades* (Warminster: Aris & Phillips, 1977).

————, "Jewish Holy Places and the Origins of Christian Pilgrimage," *The Blessings of Pilgrimage* (ed. Robert G. Ousterhout; Urbana: University of Illinois Press, 1990), 41–53.

————, "Jewish Influences on the Early Christian rite of Jerusalem," *Muséon* 92 (1979) 347–59.

————, "The Streets of Jerusalem," *Levant* 7 (1975) 118–36.

Wilkinson, John, et al., *Jerusalem Pilgrimage, 1099–1185* (London: Hakluyt Society, 1988).

Williams, George, *The Holy City: Historical, Topographical, and Antiquarian Notices of Jerusalem* (2 vols.; 2nd ed.; London: J. W. Parker, 1849).

Wilson, Charles W., *Golgotha and the Holy Sepulchre* (ed. Charles M. Watson; London: The Committee of the Palestine Exploration Fund, 1906).

Wilson, Stephen G., "Melito and Israel," *Anti-Judaism in Early Christianity: Separation and Polemic* (ed. Stephen G. Wilson; Waterloo, Ont.: Canadian Corporation for Studies in Religion, 1986), 91–96.

Wise, Michael O., *A Critical Study of the Temple Scroll from Qumran Cave 11* (SAOC 49; Chicago: Oriental Institute of the University of Chicago, 1990).

Wiseman, James, "Corinth and Rome I: 228 B.C.–A.D. 267," *ANRW* II 7.1 (1979) 438–548.

Wright, Addison G., "The Widow's Mites: Praise or Lament? A Matter of Context," *CBQ* 44 (1982) 256–65.

Yadin, Yigael, ed., *The Temple Scroll* (3 vols.; Jerusalem: Israel Exploration Society, 1983).

Yarbo-Collins, Adela, "The Apocalyptic Rhetoric of Mark 13 in Historical Context," *BR* 41 (1996) 5–36.

————, "Numerical Symbolism in Jewish and Early Christian Apocalyptic Literature," *ANRW* II 21.2 (1984) 1221–87.

Yarnold, Edward, *Cyril of Jerusalem* (New York: Routledge, 2000).

Yerushalmi, Yosef H., *Zakhor: Jewish History and Jewish Memory* (rev. ed.; New York: Schocken, 1989).

Zakovitch, Yair, "The First Stages of Jerusalem's Sanctification under David: A Literary and Ideological Analysis," *Jerusalem: Its Sanctity and Centrality to Judaism, Christianity and Islam* (ed. Lee I. Levine; New York: Continuum, 1999), 16–35.

Index of Ancient Citations

General Index